T0093018

Enterprise Level Security 2

Enterprise Level Security 2

Advanced Techniques for Information Technology in an Uncertain World

Dr. Kevin E. Foltz
Dr. William R. Simpson
Award-winning security architecture team for high-assurance information technology systems

CRC Press is an imprint of the
Taylor & Francis Group, an informa business

First edition published 2020
by CRC Press
6000 Broken Sound Parkway NW, Suite 300, Boca Raton, FL 33487-2742

and by CRC Press
2 Park Square, Milton Park, Abingdon, Oxon, OX14 4RN

CRC Press is an imprint of Taylor & Francis Group, LLC

ISBN: 9780367531737 (hbk)
ISBN: 9781003080787 (ebk)

Typeset in Times
by Deanta Global Publishing Services, Chennai, India

This book is dedicated to our wives, who have put up with many missed engagements while we labored on the things described in this book, and to our partner Coimbatore Chandersekaran, who coached us through many of the processes described herein. The book is also dedicated to our sponsor Frank Konieczny, who kept us on the practical side during these development processes. We further dedicate this to our division director at the Institute for Defense Analyses, Margaret Myers, who has been fully supportive of all our endeavors.

Contents

ELS Extensions – Mobile Devices

ELS Extensions – Other Techniques

Preface

ABOUT THE BOOK

This is the second book on enterprise level security. The first book covered the basic concepts of enterprise level security and the discoveries made during the first eight years of its development. This book has been derived from 16 years of research, pilots, and operational trials in putting an enterprise system together. These chapters cover specific advanced techniques derived from painful mistakes and numerous revisions of processes. This book is not meant as a replacement for the first book, but as a supplement.

From a philosophical standpoint, there have been a number of realizations over the years that have shaped the security measures described in this book. They roughly fall into a few basic categories:

Complexity – The time has passed for simple models. Complexity may be measured in active processes, lines of code, McCabe's fundamentals, or other metrics, but the complexity of what we cannot control is immense, and there are currently no formal or informal methods that can even verify a majority percentage of the execution possibilities. This complexity means that we are destined to have unforeseen and innumerable flaws and exploits in the future. Security principles, on the other hand, are simple, although the maintenance of security principles may lead to complex systems. It is often the compromise of these security principles for expediency or efficiency that leads to vulnerabilities.

Threats – If you are connected, you cannot prevent threats and exploits – you can only mitigate. Maintaining security principles can go a long way toward identifying the exploits through forensics, minimizing damages, and speeding recovery.

Operation – The design must operate in the presence of threats. Threats when discovered will be removed and the systems will be reinstalled and sanitized, but at any given moment it is assumed that threats are present in the system.

Recovery – The design must be resilient because it will be penetrated and exploited. When exploits are discovered, the damage must be assessed and repaired, the system as a whole must be patched, and the exploit must be further mitigated. After that, one can only wait for the next challenge.

Acknowledgments

Much of the material in this book has been published previously in various forms. These documents include a multitude of conference presentations, as well as many technical reports and analyses whose ideas were reviewed by various members of U.S. Air Force Integrated Process Teams too numerous to list here. Their contribution is gratefully acknowledged. The authors also wish to acknowledge Lynne Russillo and Torrance Gloss for their editing expertise, especially the latter, who expended many hours making certain that this book reflects what the authors intended to convey.

Finally, the authors would like to acknowledge the standards producers. These products are valuable and unappreciated, but they provide the glue that holds everything together.

About the Authors

Kevin E. Foltz has over a decade of experience working to improve security in information systems. He has degrees in Mathematics, Computer Science, Electrical Engineering, and Strategic Security Studies. He has presented and published research on different aspects of enterprise security, security modeling, and high assurance systems.

William R. Simpson has over two decades of experience working to improve systems security. He has degrees in Aeronautical Engineering and Business Administration. He also attended several schools for military and government training. He spent many years as an expert in aeronautics before delving into the field of electronic and system testing, and he has spent the last 20 years on IT-related themes (mostly security, including processes, damage assessments of cyber intrusions, IT security standards, IT security evaluation, and IT architecture).

About the Authors

Figures

Tables

1 The First 16 Years

1.1 THE BEGINNING OF ENTERPRISE LEVEL SECURITY (ELS)

Development of ELS began in 2002. At that time, the threats to system security were a growing menace, and the number of system intrusions was rapidly increasing. It was thought that there must be a better way to organize the security model and prevent many of these vulnerabilities. A large number of standards existed, and it was thought that the proper application of these standards could achieve that goal. Standards for Organization for the Advancement of Structured Information Standards (OASIS) [1], National Institute of Standards and Technology (NIST) [2], International Standards Organization (ISO) Common Criteria [3], Internet Engineering Task Force (IETF) [4], and W3C [5] are referenced in this book, and details can be found in the reference section.

And so it began. The work of eliminating the most common vulnerabilities began by focusing on passwords, which are at the root of many, many vulnerabilities, and account maintenance, as out of date, poorly maintained accounts allow for numerous escalation of privilege exploits. Passwords were eliminated by specifying the use of public key infrastructure (PKI) for all system entities. This provided two factors for identity based on something you know (passcode for unlocking the certificate) and something you have [6] (private key to which only the owner has access). The standards already existed and the Department of Defense (DoD) had a robust certificate authority (CA) program. An end-to-end communication architecture with strong encryption would eliminate many of the vulnerabilities "on the wire." Finally, after considering the various forms for access and privilege, it was decided to use a claims-based system that would require a larger back office but could update automatically once it was established. The system would be built in small stages with experimental verification of the processes before implementation.

Figure 1.1 shows the early evolution of ELS. The figure also includes references to the expanded material regarding early development for each of these elements (all in Book 1) [7].

The most important development in the early stages was the establishment of basic tenets. The original six tenets grew to 13 by the time the first book was completed and now number 16. This provided not only a compass to guide our development, but a direct tie to the security concepts in Section 1.3 and the ability to trace back the effects of decisions as shown in Figure 1.2.

1.2 DESIGN PRINCIPLES

Even though most of the design principles were covered in the first book, they are repeated here due to their importance. The first tenet is an overriding issue and is thus numbered 0. The full list of tenets for the ELS model are as follows:

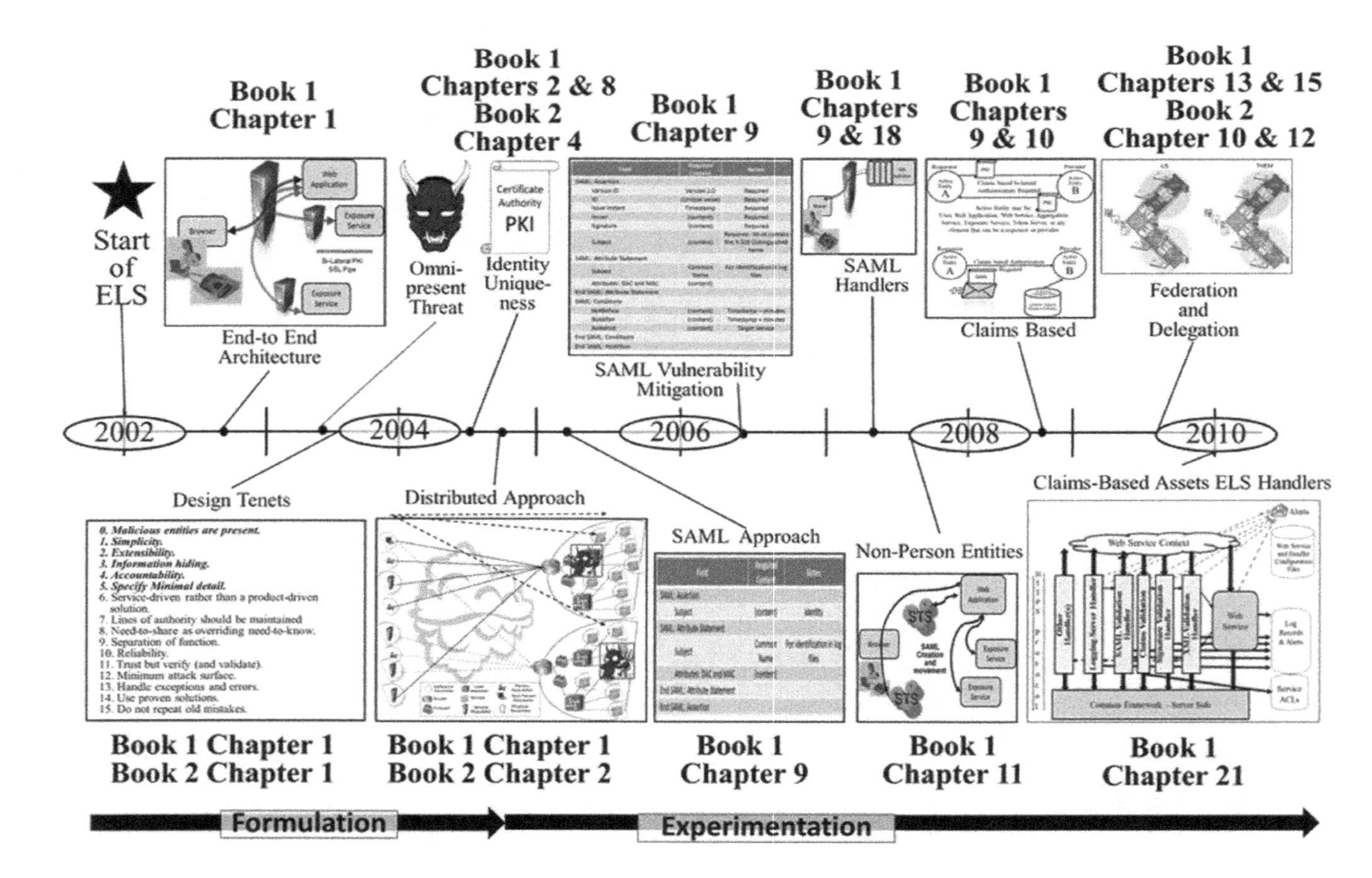

FIGURE 1.1. Early ELS Evolution

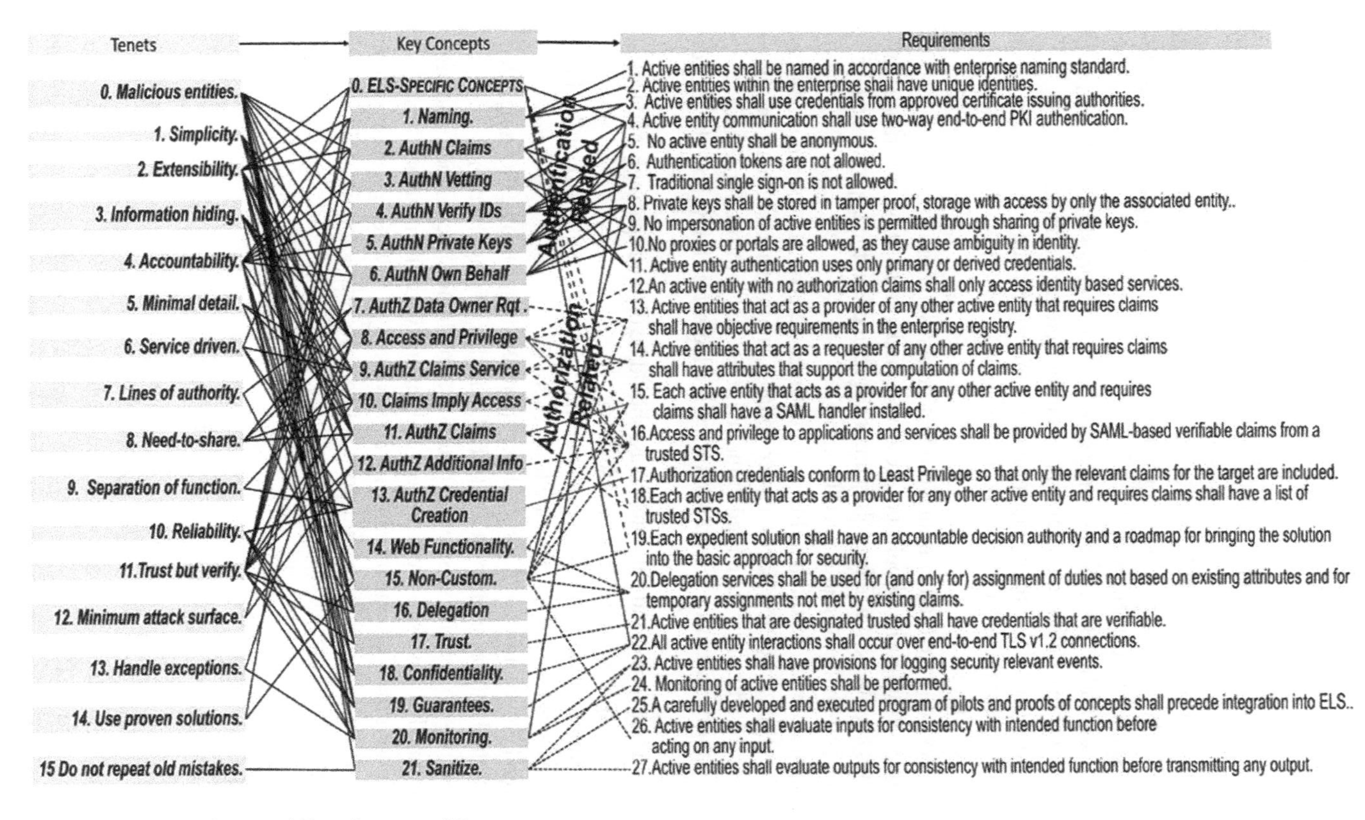

FIGURE 1.2. ELS Fundamental Requirements Map

0. Malicious entities are present, and our systems need to function with these embedded threats rather than rely on filtering them out.
1. Simplicity. Added features come at the cost of greater complexity, less understandability, greater difficulty in administration, higher cost, and/or lower adoption rates that may be unacceptable to the organization.
2. Extensibility. Any construct should be extensible to the domain and the enterprise and, ultimately, across the enterprise and coalition.
3. Information hiding. This involves revealing to the requester and the outside world the minimum set of information needed for making effective, authorized use of a capability.
4. Accountability. This means being able to unambiguously identify and track which active entity in the enterprise performed each operation.
5. Minimal detail. This means providing only the necessary details of the solution for the required level. This preserves flexibility of implementation at lower levels.
6. A service-driven rather than a product-driven solution.
7. Lines of authority should be preserved, and information assurance decisions should be made by policy and/or agreement at the appropriate level.
8. Need-to-share overrides need-to-know.
9. Separation of function. This is sometimes referred to as *atomicity* and allows for fewer interfaces, easier updates, maintenance of least privilege, reduced and easier identified vulnerabilities, and improved forensics.
10. Reliability. Security should work even if adversaries know how the process works.
11. Trust but verify (and validate). Trust should be offered sparingly and trusted outputs still require occasional scrutiny.
12. Minimum attack surface. Fewer interfaces and limited functionality in the interfaces means less exposure to threats.
13. Handle exceptions and errors. Exception handling involves logging, alerting the Enterprise Support Desk (ESD), and notifying the user.
14. Use proven solutions. Select products, technologies, techniques, and algorithms that have sufficient evidence of maturity for their intended use.
15. Do not repeat old mistakes. This means using a flaw remediation system, patching and repairing, and not fielding a software solution with known vulnerabilities and exploits.

1.3 KEY CONCEPTS

The key concepts for ELS are based on these tenets, but they also address specific architectural decisions that relate to the requirements. The concepts form a bridge between the high-level tenets and the technical requirements. The numbers of the tenets that relate to each concept are shown in braces. These relationships can be mapped as shown in Figure 1.2. Further, any relaxation of a fundamental requirement can be traced to the design tenets that are affected.

1. ELS-specific concepts {2, 6, 14}. These are choices based on current technology and are subject to change and expansion as technology changes and the ELS model is developed further. For simplicity, they are considered as a single concept.
   a. PKI credentials are used for active entity credentials [1–4].
   b. Security Assertion Markup Language (SAML) with claims is used for authorization credentials [5].
   c. TLS v1.2 is used for end-to-end confidentiality, integrity, and authentication [6].
   d. A security token server (STS) is the trusted entity for generating authorization credentials.
   e. Exceptions in implementation must have a documented plan and schedule for becoming compliant.
2. A standard naming process is applied to all active entities. {2, 4, 11}
3. Authentication is implemented by a verifiable identity claims-based process. {0, 2, 4, 11}
4. Identity claims are tied to a strong vetting process to establish identity. {0, 4, 11}
5. Active entities verify each other's identity. {0, 4, 11}
6. The verification of identity is by proof of ownership of the private key associated with an identity claim. {4}
7. Active entities act on their own behalf. {0, 1, 12}
8. The claims objective requirement is provided by the data owner. {7, 8}
9. Service providers use identity and authorization credential claims to determine access and privilege. {0, 1, 2, 3, 8, 11, 13}
10. A trusted entity examines the attributes of an entity and determines whether the claims objective requirement is satisfied. {2, 3, 5, 6, 9}
11. A claim in an authorization credential is a statement that an access requirement has been satisfied. {1, 3, 5, 8, 11}
12. The data owner may request additional information about the requesting entity as part of his requirement definition. {1, 2, 11, 12}
13. Authorization credentials are created by a trusted entity for a specific requester, a specific target resource, and a specific level of access. {0, 6, 9, 10}
14. Functionality is to be provided through web services. {6}
15. It is undesirable to work a point solution or custom approach. {1, 2, 5, 14}
16. A formalized delegation policy both within and outside of the enterprise is a requirement. {0, 2, 4, 7, 11}
17. Verification and validation is a requirement for trusted entities. {0, 4, 11}
18. All active entity interactions require confidentiality of data/content exchanged. {0, 3, 10}
19. Guarantee integrity, authenticity, timeliness, and pedigree. {0, 2, 4, 10, 11}
20. Monitoring is a precursor to cybersecurity. {0, 4, 10, 11, 13}
21. Eliminate or mitigate malware. {0, 15}

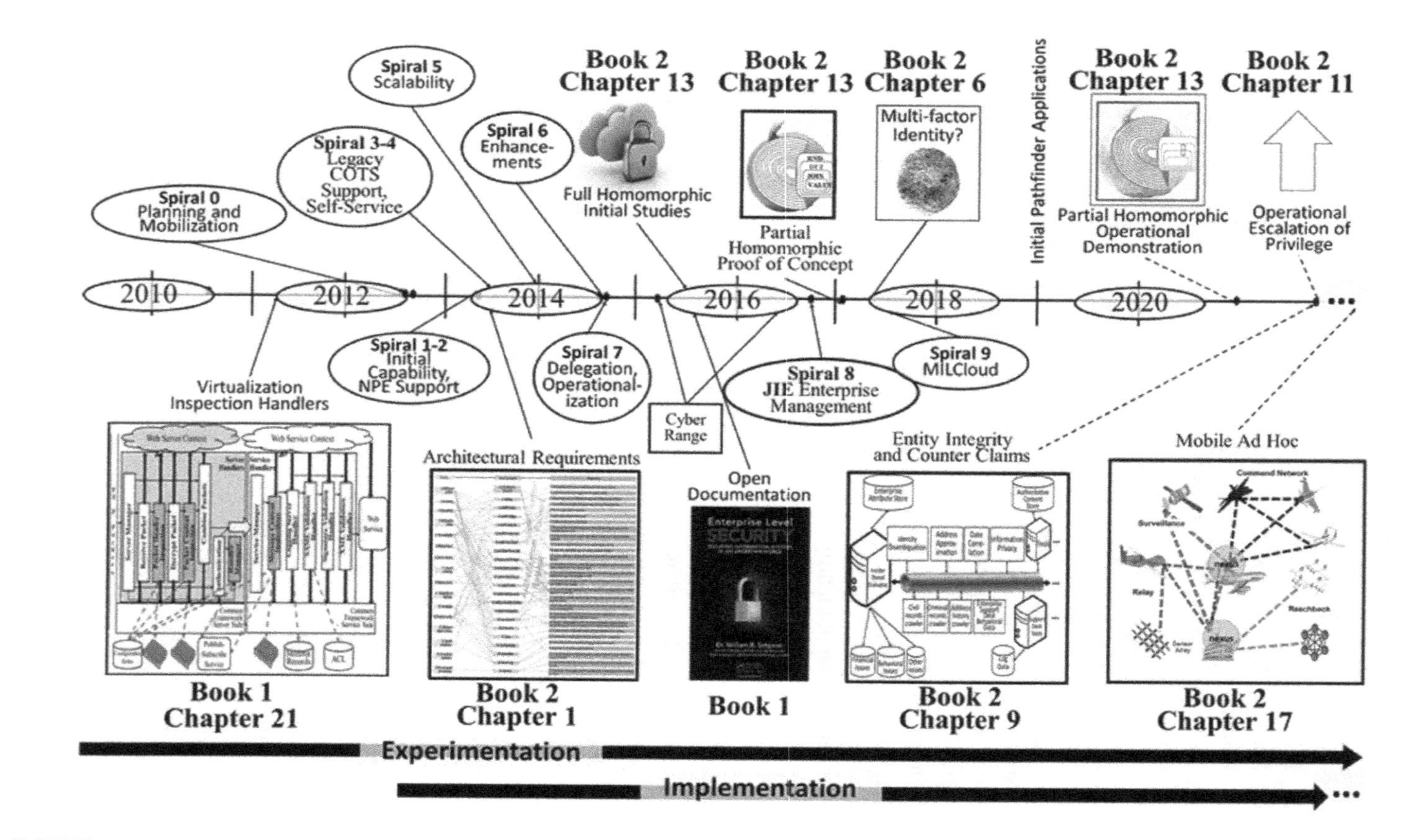

FIGURE 1.3. Implementation Map

1.4 IMPLEMENTATION

The implementation map is shown in Figure 1.3. These topics are covered in this book. The implementation has included a spiral development program and many advanced techniques are yet to be implemented. Note that the architectural mappings described in Section 1.3 were not developed until just before the first book was issued and first published in 2016 [7].

Note also that both the mobile ad hoc described in Chapter 17 and first published in [8] and the partial homomorphic described in Chapter 14 and first published in [9] have yet to be implemented.

There have been many technical reports for the ELS process. The *Consolidated Enterprise Information Technology Baseline* (CEITB) is in its sixth edition, as described in Chapter 23. Open source literature (papers and journal articles) have been written on all topics covered in the two books and are included in the reference section [7–73].

2 A Brief Review of the Initial Book

2.1 SECURITY PRINCIPLES

The material discussed in Chapter 1 led to the establishment of five security principles that must be maintained for computing. These principles provide a foundation for the development process and help to avoid growing complexity in implementation. They also aid with presenting ELS to vendors and potential providers. These principles are:

- Know the Players – enforce bilateral end-to-end authentication;
- Maintain Confidentiality – ensure end-to-end unbroken encryption (no in-transit decryption/payload inspection);
- Separate Access and Privilege from Identity – use an authorization credential;
- Maintain Integrity – know that you received exactly what was sent;
- Require Explicit Accountability – monitor and log transactions.

2.1.1 Know the Players

In ELS, the identity certificate is an X.509 PKI certificate issued by an approved CA [74]. This identity is required for all active entities, both person and non-person (e.g., services, as shown in Figure 2.1). PKI certificates are verified and validated. Ownership is verified by a HOK check. Supplemental authentication factors (in combination with PKI) may be required from certain entities, such as identity confirming information or biometric data as described in Chapter 7. The authentication is bilateral, and it requires both the requester and provider to have PKI certificates. The certificate may reside with the server in the case of the provider, but if the application is a requester of other services, it must also have a PKI certificate.

HOLDER OF KEY (HOK)

This mechanism encrypts a small message with the public key of the receiver. If the receiver can decrypt and respond, then they must have access to the private key, establishing identity.

2.1.2 Maintain Confidentiality

Figure 2.2 shows that ELS establishes end-to-end, transport layer security (TLS) [75] encrypted communication.

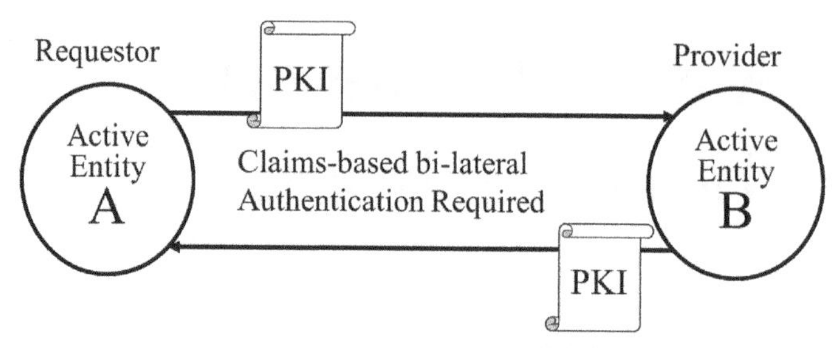

FIGURE 2.1. Bilateral PKI Authentication

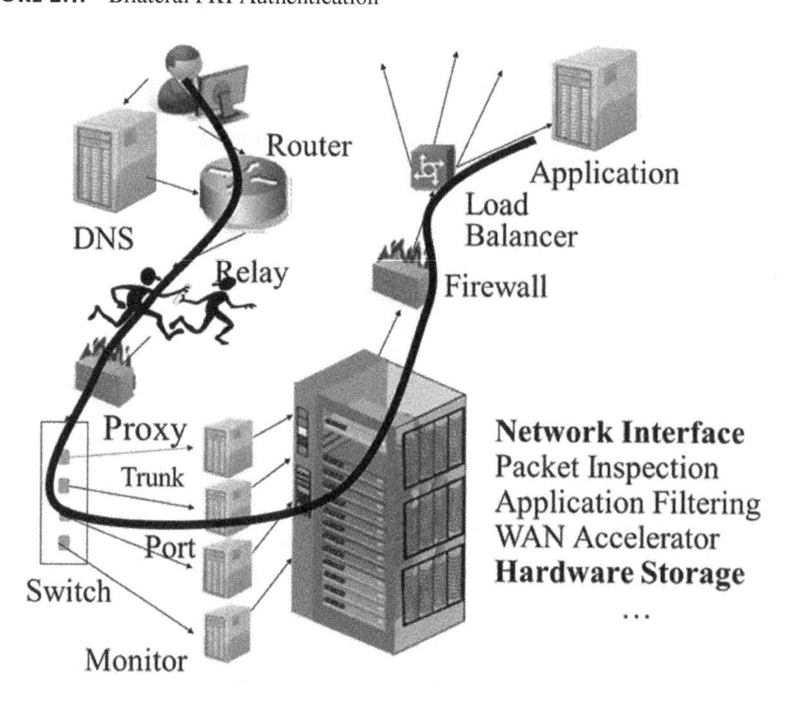

FIGURE 2.2. End-to-End Encrypted Communication

The unique private keys that belong to only the certificate holder are held in hardware storage: PIV type cards with embedded chips, for individuals, and hardware security modules (HSMs) for hardware and software entities.

The private keys are only accessed by the holder, and the keys are never shared with network appliances or other entities. The

> **PERSONAL IDENTITY VERIFICATION (PIV)**
>
> A PIV card is a smart card that contains the necessary data to grant the cardholder access to information systems and assure appropriate levels of security for all applicable applications.

encryption must remain unbroken through service hardware such as routers, firewalls, and load balancers. There are no delegates or proxies that can be used as masquerades.

2.1.3 Separate Access and Privilege from Identity

The separation of identity from access and privilege allows for the breaking of the account paradigm that is the subject of many vulnerabilities. It also allows for the automation of provisioning employees on the move with access and privilege commensurate with their new assignments. ELS can accommodate changes in location, assignment, and other attributes by separating the use of associated attributes from the identity. Whenever changes to attributes occur, claims are recomputed based on new associated attributes, allowing immediate access to required applications.

As shown in Figure 2.3, access control credentials utilize the Security Assertion Markup Language (SAML). SAML was chosen because it has many equivalent properties to the PKI identity certificate. The tokens may be verified (by signature checking) and validated (by checking for trusted issuers). SAML authorization tokens differ from the more commonly used SSO tokens because SAML tokens are not used for authentication in ELS [76].

SAML tokens are created and signed by a security token service (STS). The signatures are verified and validated before acceptance. The credentials of the signers are also verified and validated. The credential for access and privilege is bound to the requester by ensuring a match of the identity used in both authentication and authorization credentials.

SINGLE SIGN-ON (SSO)

A session and user authentication service that permits a user to use one set of login credentials to access multiple applications.

2.1.4 Maintain Integrity

In all cases, integrity in communication means that the message that is received is identical to the message sent (no additions, deletions, or modifications). Integrity is implemented using end-to-end transport layer security (TLS) message authentication codes (MACs), as illustrated in Figure 2.4. These MACs are signed hashes for the material contained in the packet. Chained integrity, where trust is passed on

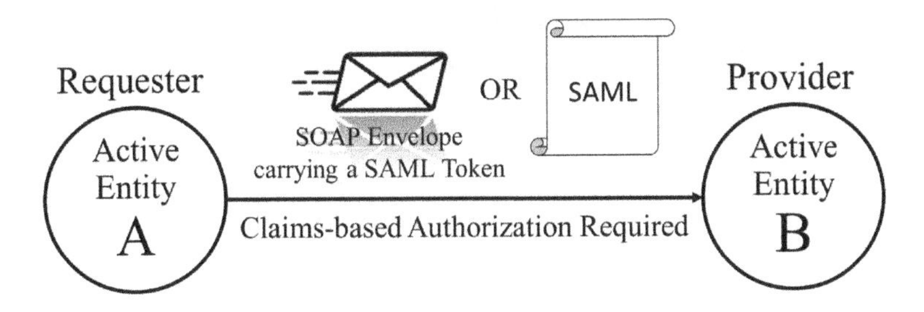

FIGURE 2.3. Claims-Based Authorization

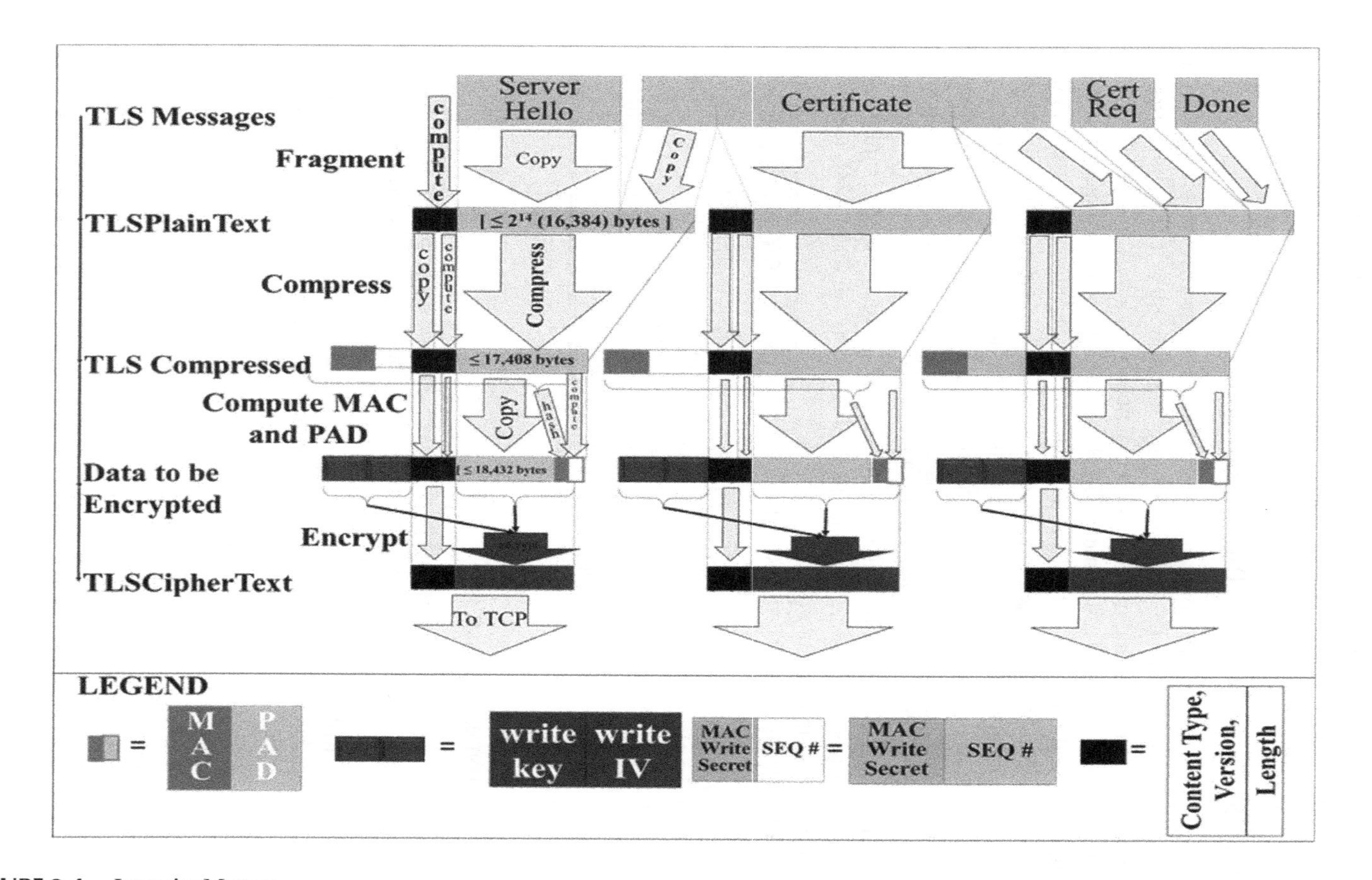

FIGURE 2.4. Integrity Matters

transitively from one entity to another, is not as strong as employing end-to-end integrity. When chained integrity is used through TLS consolidation or other means, each break in the TLS offers an opportunity for exploit. At the application layer, packages (SAML tokens, etc.) are signed, and signatures are verified and validated [77].

2.1.5 Require Explicit Accountability

All active entities with ELS are required to act on their own behalf. No proxies or impersonation is allowed. Accountability is maintained by enforcing the monitoring provisions provided in the first book [7]. For small enterprises, the monitor records must be periodically reviewed for nefarious behavior and archived for forensics when intrusions are suspected or detected.

A repository is recommended for larger enterprises. As shown in Figure 2.5, ELS monitors specified activities for accountability and forensics. The monitor files are formatted in a standard way and stored locally. For enterprise files, a monitor sweep agent reads, translates, cleans, and submits log records to an enterprise store. In this environment, tools may periodically review the records for nefarious behavior. Local files are cleaned periodically to reduce overall storage and to provide a centralized repository for help desk, forensics, and other activities. The details of this activity are provided in [78, 79]. Because this activity is recommended for only large enterprises, it is not recommended in the minimal instantiation of ELS shown in Chapter 3.

2.2 ELS FRAMEWORK

The ELS framework has evolved from a fortress approach, in which the threat is assumed to be stopped at the front door, to a distributed security system that eliminates or mitigates many of the primary vulnerability points inherent with that system, as shown in Figure 2.6. The basic process of identification involves a two-way

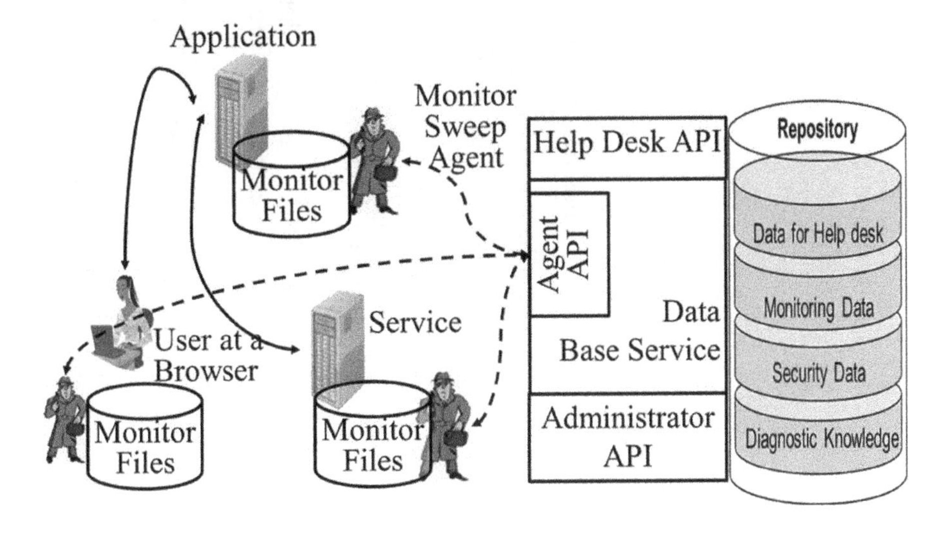

FIGURE 2.5. Accountability through Centralized Monitoring

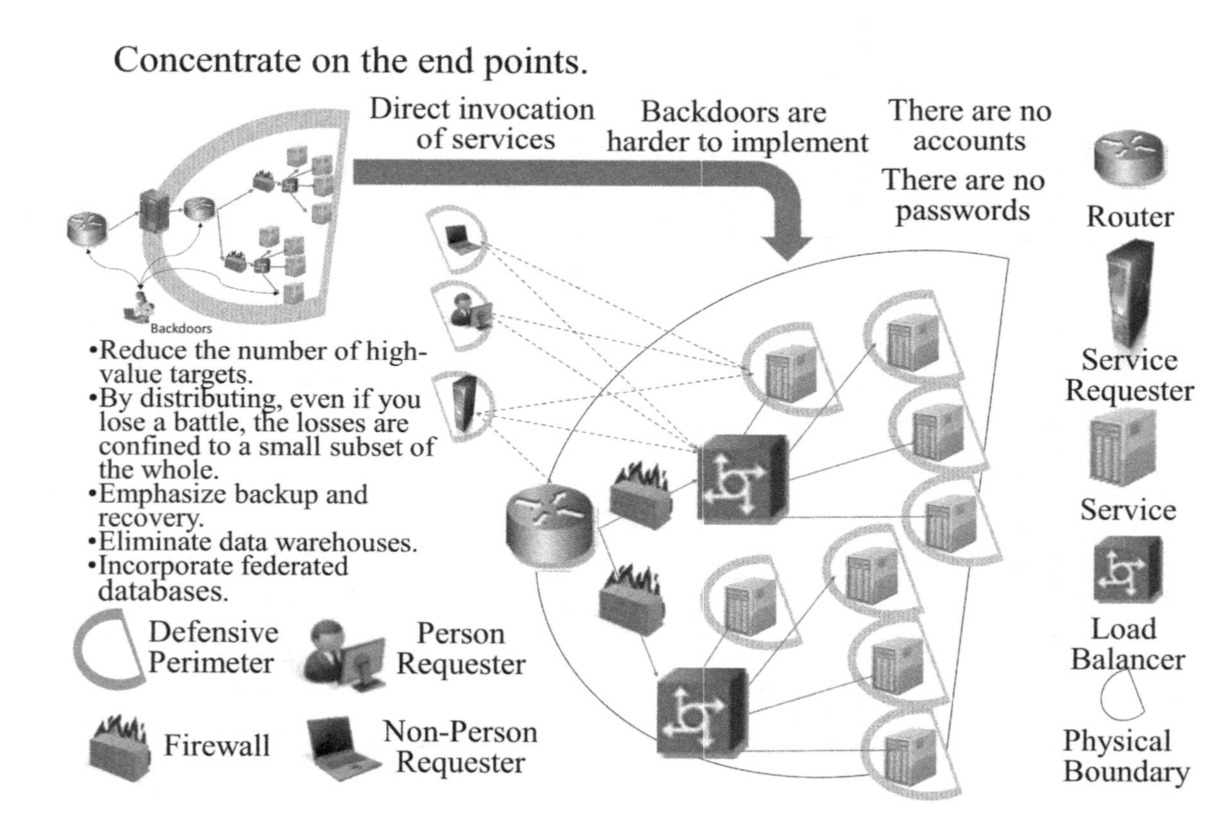
Concentrate on the end points.
Backdoors
Direct invocation of services
Backdoors are harder to implement
There are no accounts
There are no passwords
•Reduce the number of high-value targets.
•By distributing, even if you lose a battle, the losses are confined to a small subset of the whole.
•Emphasize backup and recovery.
•Eliminate data warehouses.
•Incorporate federated databases.
Defensive Perimeter
Person Requester
Firewall
Non-Person Requester
Router
Service Requester
Service
Load Balancer
Physical Boundary

FIGURE 2.6. Distributed Security System

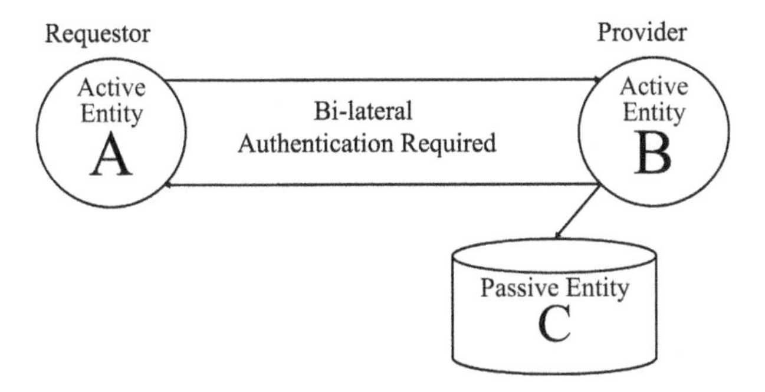

FIGURE 2.7. Communication between Entities

contract between two entities that are initiating a communication. Each entity needs to have some assurance that the party they are engaged with is a known entity and, specifically, the one to whom the communication should be allowed. This is done by the presentation of claims by each party that are verifiable and may be validated. These claims are often in the form of credentials. The basic process is described extensively in Book 1 [7].

Entities may be active or passive. Passive entities include storage elements, routers, wireless access points, some firewalls, and other entities that do not themselves initiate or respond to web service or web application requests. Active entities are those entities that request or provide services according to ELS. Active entities include users, applications, and services. All active entities have PKI certificates (see Chapter 4), and their private keys are stored in tamper-proof, threat-mitigating storage. Communication between active entities requires bilateral, end-to-end authentication using PKI credentials. Authentication is implemented by a verifiable identity claims-based process.

Figure 2.7 illustrates a combination of active and passive entities in a typical request flow. The requester and provider are both active entities using ELS. To complete the request, the provider calls on a passive data store using non-ELS methods. To mitigate the lower security of the provider-to-data-store link, the data store interface is often locked down to communicate with only the provider.

3 Minimal Requirements for the Advanced Techniques

The advanced topics each add a level of complexity to the ELS environment. The topics covered in this book will require an ELS stand-up to implement. But what is a minimal instantiation of ELS? This chapter is designed to answer that question. The minimal instantiation is sparse and you may wish to reinforce some areas. For example, the last security principle of accountability is not implemented in the minimal instantiation. The minimal set of services presented will allow you to have the basic capability in an enterprise security system that requires no passwords and no accounts, and uses no back doors for its operation.

BACK DOOR

A method of bypassing or circumventing normal processes for the sake of expediency, privilege escalation, exploit, or ease of obtaining a functionality. Administrators often use these to batch amend or configure items. ELS administrators and all users use the same processes for access and privilege.

In this chapter, we primarily focus on the infrastructure needed to support the generation of authorization and privilege claims. It is assumed that all communication is conducted through end-to-end TLS with mutual authentication using PKI credentials. This ensures that both sides of the communication know whom they are communicating with, the communication is confidential, and the content maintains end-to-end integrity. The authorization claims process builds on this secure connection to provide access and privilege information for requesters to services [11].

We will cover the core Enterprise Attribute Ecosystem (EAE) functions required to generate authorization claims in an ELS system. Such an instantiation will provide the following:

1. a core capability that meets the ELS security model,
2. a claims-based access and privilege system that is mostly automated and is dynamic, resilient, secure, and extensible, and
3. an ecosystem that can be enhanced for many of the additional capabilities that are part of the overall ELS architecture.

More technical details of ELS, which extend beyond this discussion of the core instantiation, are covered in Book 1 [7].

3.1 NEEDED CAPABILITIES

The following functionalities are required to provide a minimal instantiation of the EAE:

1. an attribute store with sufficient user information for data owners to define access and privilege rules,
2. a registration service for enterprise resources and their access and privilege rules,
3. a service to generate claims and store them when a match between the information available for an individual in the attribute store matches rules for access and privilege, and
4. a set of user convenience services that allow for corrections and adjustments and make the authorization requirements user-friendly.

At the initial establishment of the EAE, all servers and users are provisioned with PKI certificates. The server's private keys are stored in HSMs. All servers are configured to require TLS mutual authentication and strict rules about cipher suites and protocol versions. If the handshake does not match, no communication takes place [13, 14]. Within the EAE, all entities and communication paths are known, so the interfaces, protocols, and authorizations can be strictly controlled.

Figure 3.1 provides a general legend for the objects in the figures that follow. There are three classes of person entities. Users send browser requests to web applications to request data or services. Administrators conduct similar requests, but also

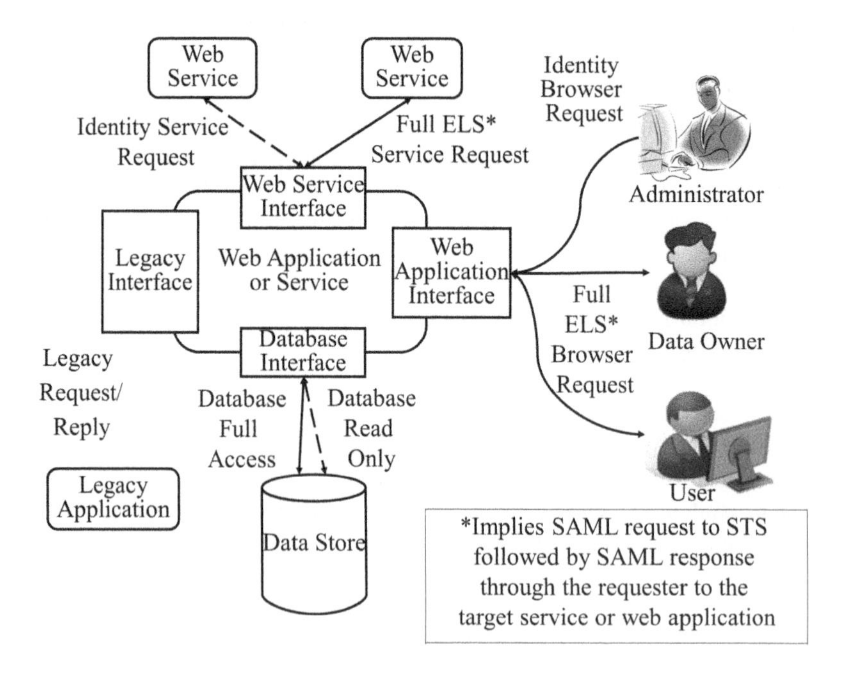

FIGURE 3.1. Enterprise Legend and Nomenclature

perform configuration and receive privileged access. Data owners host web applications and services and set the rules for access for both users and administrators.

There are many types of non-person entities. Web applications and web services provide services and data to requesters, devices that act autonomously, and agents according to the rules set by the data owner. Data stores maintain data pertaining to attributes and access rules.

There are four types of interface, each with one or more communication types. Legacy interfaces use legacy requests and replies and are secured to the extent possible. Database interfaces are used to access data stores, and they may be full access or read-only depending on the sensitivity of the data and the requesting entity. Browser requests typically use SAML authorization, but the identity may be used in cases where security is strict and requesters are known and limited. Web service interfaces are similar to web application interfaces, but they use web service clients instead of browsers. These interfaces are described in detail in Book 1 [7]. For clarity they will not be shown on subsequent graphics.

3.2 CREATING AN ATTRIBUTE STORE

The Enterprise Attribute Store (EAS) consists of a collection of current information about registered enterprise personnel and entities as shown in Figure 3.2. It is a logical construct and may be a single store or a collection of stores. It is independent of the other stores in the EAE and has its own set of access controls.

Many authoritative content stores (ACSs) may be used to populate the EAS. These ACSs may have different access methods and data formats, and all of them have their own associated exposure service that communicates with the ACS and extracts data into a standard format. These data are gathered and placed in an interim store awaiting a periodic update from the EAS Data Import, Aggregation, and Mediation Service.

This service sanitizes input data, tags distinguished names (DNs) for changes, and uploads the data to the EAS. This upload interface is the only write interface to the EAS. The tagging is for use by the claims engine, so it can update the claims for any DN that has changed values. The ACSs may be legacy systems, so the exposure services and sanitization serve to keep the aggregated data in the EAS consistent, clean, and properly correlated. Each service and requester has a small store indicated for monitoring files as required by the security model.

3.3 REGISTERING A SERVICE

The data owner is responsible for registering their enterprise applications and services through an auto registration application as shown in Figure 3.3. This application provides the EAS attribute list, and the data owner defines access control rules (ACRs) as logical combinations of these attributes and other dynamic information, such as time of day. The service and/or application details may be provided as documentation to an administrator for entry into the system.

The Write Attribute List Service is only needed when frequent changes to the schema of the Enterprise Attribute Store occur. They are a convenience for the data

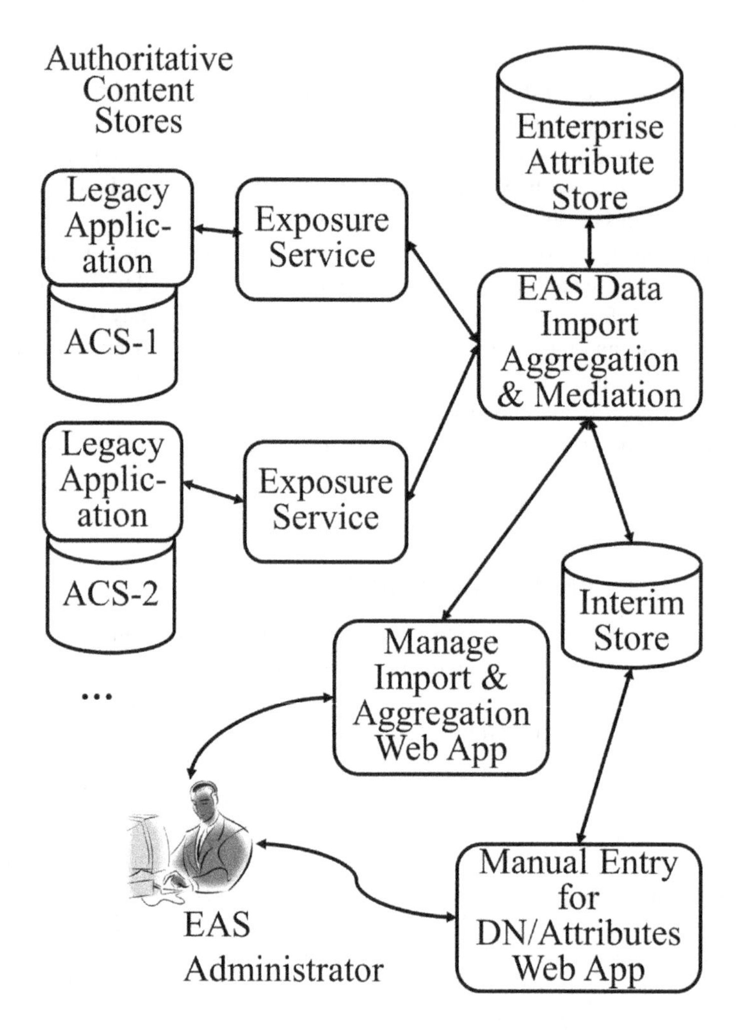

FIGURE 3.2. Creating an Attribute Store

owner to register, and they may be entered manually into the service registry if schema changes are not frequent.

3.4 COMPUTING CLAIMS

With attributes and access rules based on these attributes, there is now enough information in the system to compute access claims [20, 31, 34]. The process is shown in Figure 3.4.

The claims engine is triggered periodically or on demand by the Data Import, Aggregation, and Mediation Service. For each DN that has a change in attributes,

CLAIMS

A shorthand way of stating that a user meets access and privilege requirements for a resource. Claims use labels instead of attributes to avoid personally identifiable information (PII) and provide minimal information to eavesdropping entities.

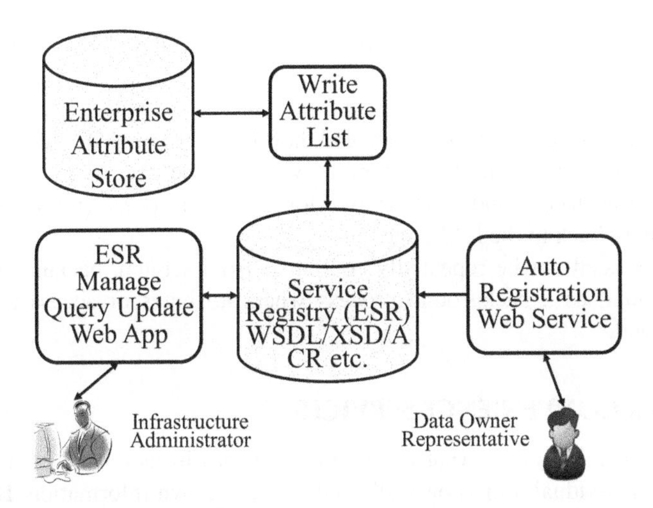

FIGURE 3.3. Registering a Service

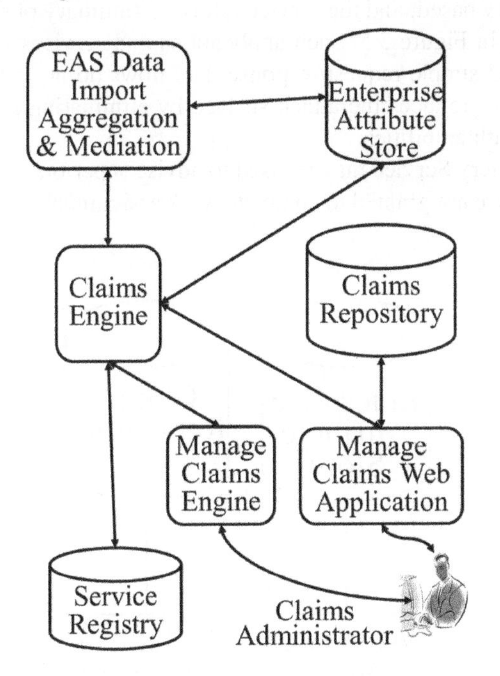

FIGURE 3.4. Computing Claims

the claims are recomputed by reading the ACR for each service and gathering the data to fulfill the ACR from among the stores in the EAE. The new or modified claims are written into the Claims Repository.

The Claims Repository is a precomputed set of access rights for all combinations of requesters and providers. After claims have been computed, the operational system relies on the Claims Repository instead of the EAS. This provides some benefits:

- the EAS has fewer access points and, hence, fewer points of vulnerability,
- a copy of the Claims Repository provides all the needed information to determine access, and it can be used for remote locations with limited connectivity back to the EAE, and
- claims need not be repeatedly computed from scratch, because they are computed as a background process when attributes or access rules are changed.

3.5 USER CONVENIENCE SERVICES

A user may need to know what claims the EAE has in its databases. For privacy reasons, an individual user is only allowed to see his own information. Because all users should be able to access such a service regardless of their attributes, access and privilege is identity based, and the service returns a summary of claims for the individual, as shown in Figure 3.5. Such applications and services with identity-based access control and simple request/response data flows do not establish application layer sessions. This reduces the attack surface by eliminating session cookies and their associated vulnerabilities.

The Claims Query Service may be used to advise superiors or data owners when sufficient claims are not granted to complete work assignments. The data owner may

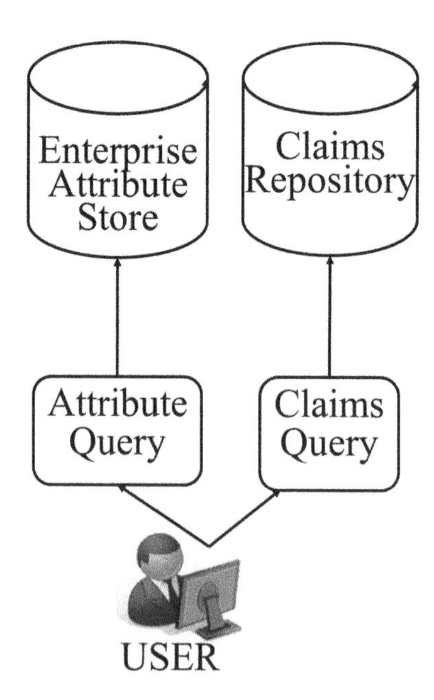

FIGURE 3.5. User Convenience Services

consider revisions. Additionally, the Claims Query Service provides a link to each service that the user has claims to access.

Similarly, the Attribute Query Service returns a summary of attributes with contact information for correcting discrepancies. The user may initiate a request for such a correction, but the owners of the ACSs must actually make the corrections. Such corrections propagate first to the EAS and then to the Claims Repository by the normal update process. Claims can be viewed to troubleshoot application access difficulties, and problems are best discussed with a supervisor to determine whether ACRs should be modified. Such access problems will decrease as the system is refined over time. Note that the enterprise knowledge repository system was not included, but is recommended for large-scale enterprise systems.

3.6 THE ENTERPRISE ATTRIBUTE ECOSYSTEM

Figure 3.6 pulls it all together and shows the back office infrastructure for ELS. The figure includes those applications and services described above, as well as administrative and other functions.

There are multiple ways a user may invoke a web application session. In all cases, the STS will go to the Provide Claims Web Service for claims that the user can assert for the application target. The STS then packages these claims in a SAML token. The invocation methods are as follows:

ECOSYSTEM

All entities in a given environment that interact to achieve a given goal. In this case, all of the data and services that interact to provide ELS functionality.

1. the user sends a request to the STS, indicating the target application, and the STS provides a token and a redirect to the application,
2. the user clicks a link obtained in the Claims Query service, which initiates a request to the STS as above,
3. the user sends a request to the web application, which redirects the user to the STS as above.

SAML handlers need to be integrated into each of the applications. These handlers exist for both .NET and Java applications and may be made available upon request to the authors. The handlers solve many of the Extensible Markup Language (XML) vulnerability issues and are the subject of separate documentation [15].

The third method is the most complicated because the application must detect that no SAML is provided after authentication and redirect to the STS.

The minimal instantiation of the EAE consists of the following 14 information services:

1. Authoritative Content Exposure Service(s). One is required for each ACS, and they depend on the legacy interfaces available. At such time that an authoritative content store becomes ELS compatible and satisfies the ELS integrity requirements, the Content Exposure Service may be dropped and

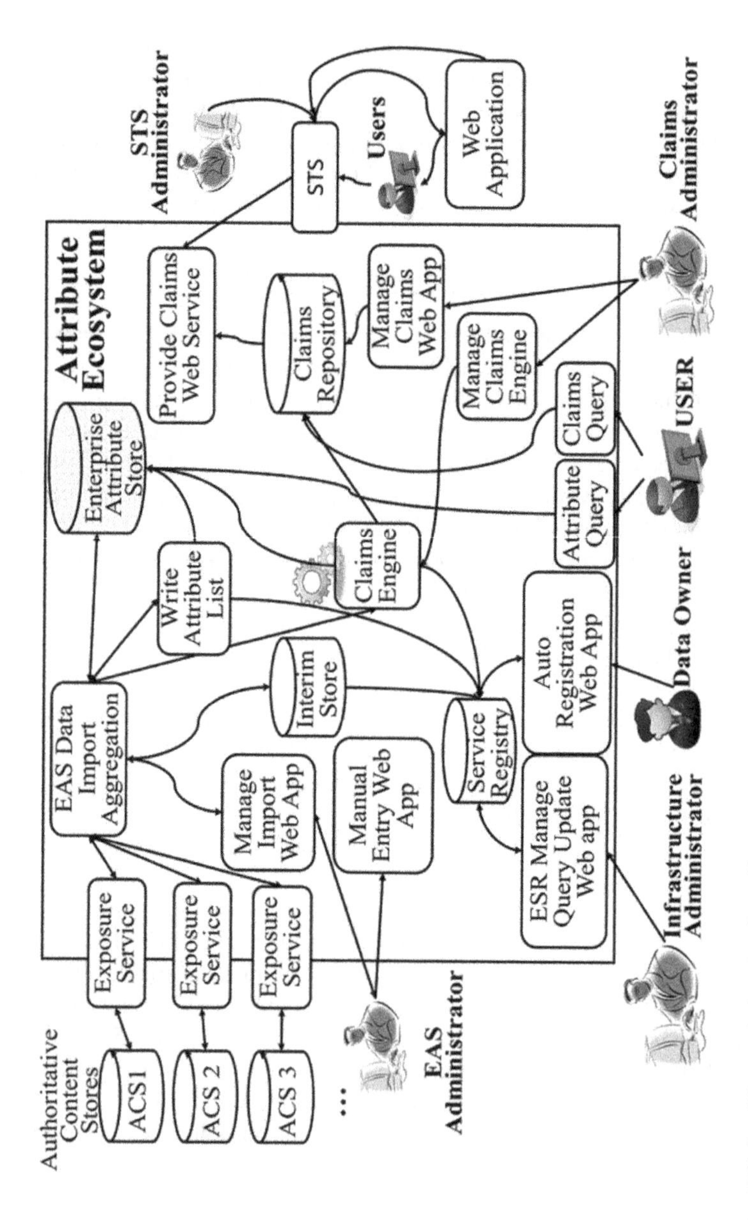

FIGURE 3.6. Minimal Instantiation Attribute Ecosystem

the data may be imported directly by the EAS Data Import, Aggregation, and Mediation Service.

2. EAS Data Import, Aggregation, and Mediation Service. There are three tasks accomplished by this service:
   i. Import: Common sense checks on data (e.g., a receptionist does not normally get promoted to Chief Information Officer (CIO)). This check is needed when the authoritative content store is ELS compatible and meets the ELS integrity requirements.
   ii. Aggregation: Periodic updates to the EAS.
   iii. Mediation: Conversion of different import formats (not needed for ELS compatible ACSs).
3. Manage Import, Aggregation, and Mediation Service. This service configures the service above and may be integrated into the EAS Data Import, Aggregation, and Mediation Service.
4. Manual Entry Web Application for Attributes. This service corrects shortcomings in the automated services. It should be used less and less over time as configurations are improved. This web application may be integrated with the Auto Registration Service or the EAS Data Import, Aggregation, and Mediation Service.
5. Enterprise Service Registry Management Web Application. This service allows configuration and management of the service registry system. This web application may be integrated with the Auto Registration Service.
6. Auto Registration Service. This service permits the data owner to input the ACRs associated with a service. This service will ideally present a user-friendly interface for building logical requirements for individual entity attributes.
7. Claims Engine. This service gathers the data for each individual to make a comparison to the ACR. When a match is found, claims are generated. The new or modified claims are written into the Claims Repository.
8. Manage Claims Engine Service. This service manages the rule sets and configuration of the Claims Engine. This service may be built into the Claims Engine.
9. Manage Claims Web Application. This service corrects shortcomings in the automated services. It should be used less and less over time as configurations are improved.
10. Provide Claims Web Service. This service extracts the claims appropriate to the requester and provides them for use by the STS. This service has a read-only interface with the Claims Repository.
11. Attribute List. This service provides a menu of alternatives to the auto registration service to assist the data owners in formulating ACRs. This service has a read-only interface to the EAS. This service is needed as a check against access and privilege requirements and to assure that values are in the attribute store. This service may be included in the Enterprise Service Registry Management Web Application and/or the Auto Registration Service.

12. Attribute Query Service. This service returns a summary of attributes with contact information for correcting discrepancies. This service has a read-only interface with the EAS. This service may be implemented jointly with the Claims Query Service.
13. Claims Query Service. This service returns a summary of claims for the individual making the request. This service has a read-only interface with the Claims Repository. This service may be implemented jointly with the Attribute Query Service.
14. STS. This provides signed SAML tokens and is a trusted element of the EAE. There are commercial products available to perform this service.

This list may be reduced to as little as eight services if the services are combined, as mentioned earlier. The separation of function and management reduces the attack surface. The STS will likely be purchased as commercial off-the-shelf software, and many other components may also be purchased off-the-shelf. Commercial services usually combine the function with management and configuration. The combining of services is shown graphically in Figure 3.7. The resultant EAE is shown in Figure 3.8.

The minimal instantiation of the EAE consists of five data modules as follows:

1. Interim Store. This holds changed data from ACSs and manual inputs for updating the EAS. It may also include new attributes and identities. This store should be held separately from the EAS for security and integrity reasons.
2. Service Registry. This holds information provided about each web service at registration, such as name, web address, security information, and owner contact information. This store must have a read-only interface for the Claims Engine.
3. EAS. This holds attributes from ACSs and manual inputs for each identity in the enterprise. This store must have read-only interfaces for the Attribute Query Service and the Claims Engine.
4. Claims Repository. This holds computed claims based on web service ACRs and delegated claims for each identity in the enterprise. This store must have a read-only interface for the Provide Claims Web Service.
5. Monitor Records. This holds records in accordance with the ELS requirement for attribution. Each service, application, and requester has such a store with appropriate access and integrity provisions.

3.7 SUMMARY

This initial build is useful for the first adoption of the ELS model and allows for full instantiation of the ELS security model and claims-based access control (CBAC). An intermediate EAE build would include an agent-based architecture, access claim delegation, multi-factor authentication, and endpoint device management. A larger enterprise may require an advanced build, with additional capabilities including a CA for temporary certificates and active entity veracity measures.

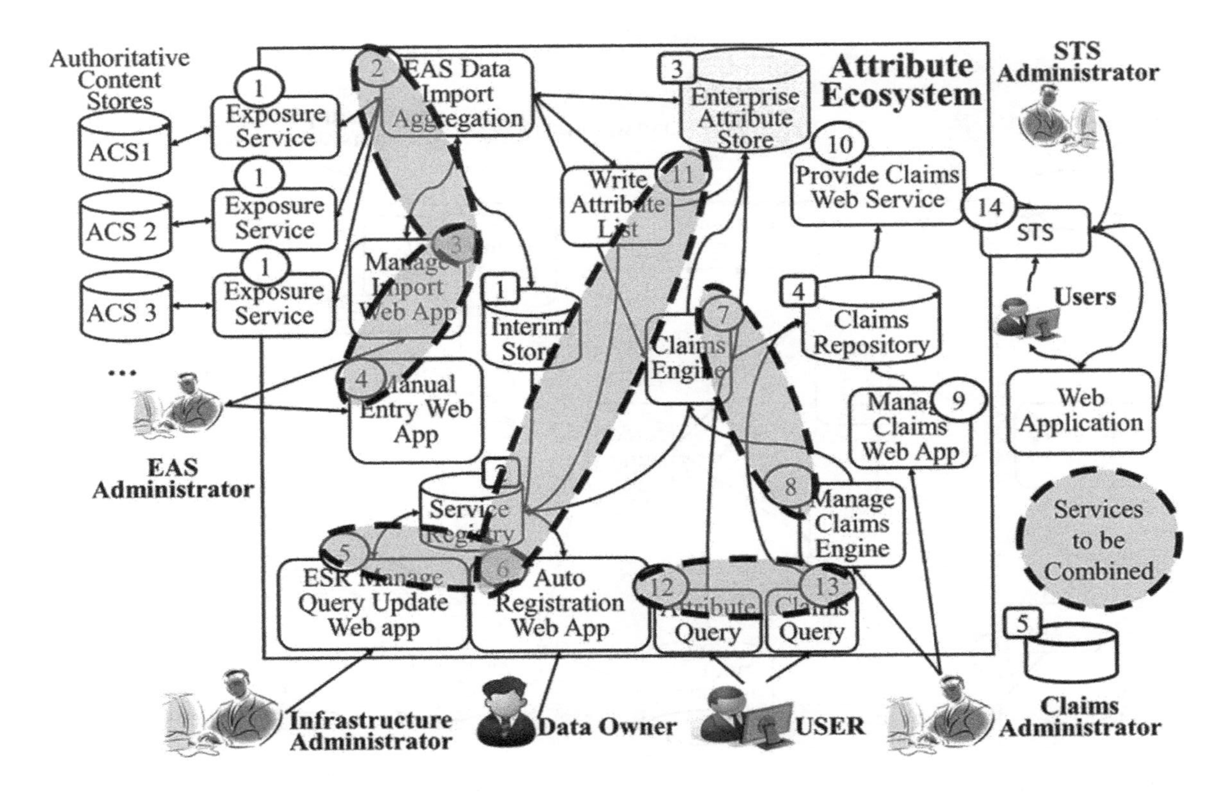

FIGURE 3.7. Minimal Instantiation Combining Services

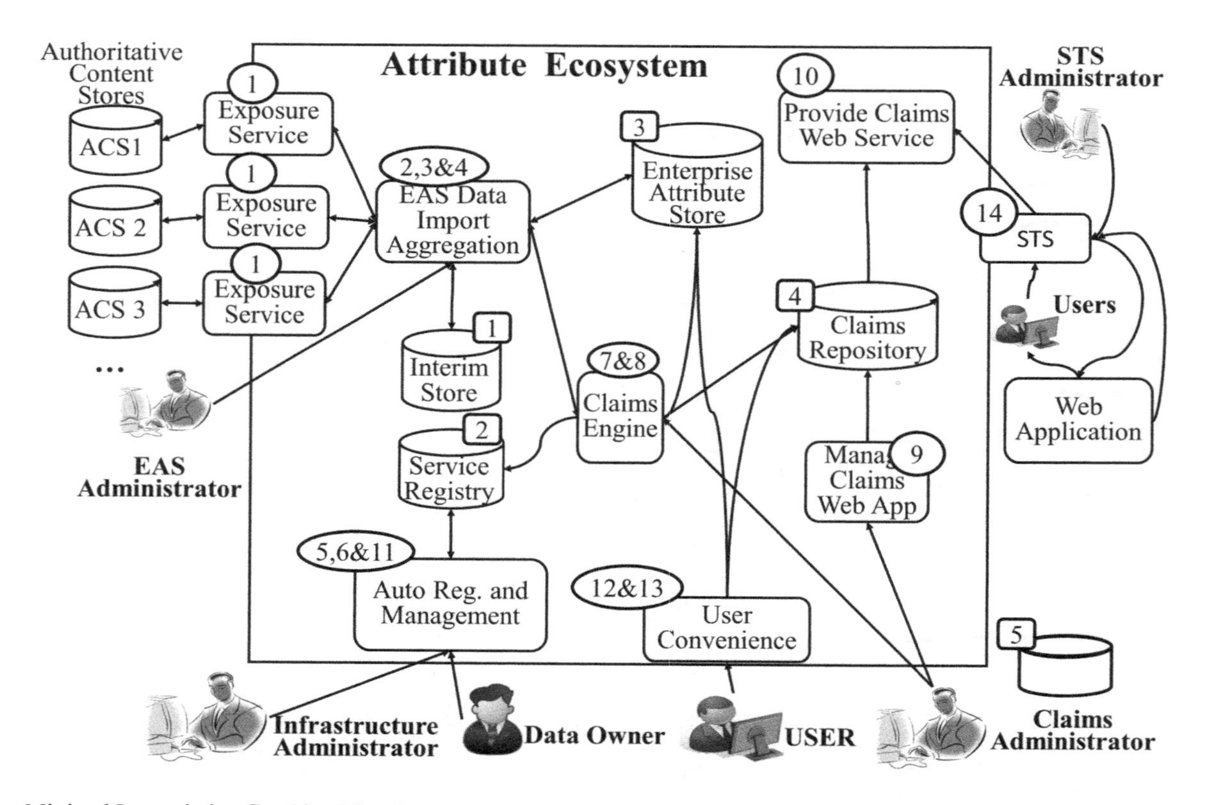

FIGURE 3.8. Minimal Instantiation Combined Services

Identity and Access Advanced Techniques

4 Identity Claims in High Assurance

A key element of ELS is the use of PKI certificates for identity claims. In the end, the public mandate for PKI [80–83], the rich CA that resides within the DoD, and the large number of vulnerabilities and exploits associated with passwords made PKI the clear solution. PKI is also supported by a large number of publically available standards [74].

PKI is an enterprise-wide set of services that supports authentication, digital signatures, encryption, and other public key-based cryptographic functions. These infrastructure services also provide management functions, including the generation of keys and production, distribution, validation, and accounting of public key certificates.

4.1 WHO ARE YOU?

This question was asked and answered in the first text, but it is not without controversy. Identity is complex. If you Google the term, you can come away more confused than when you first started. Identity in popular terms includes a number of attributes that may change over time, like job, feelings, marital status, etc. In information technology (IT), we need to separate the things that are static from the things that are temporal in nature. The simplest definition presented by Merriam-Webster is probably the best place to start: "Identity is who someone is: the name of a person" [84].

For IT purposes, the identity is a label that is recognized and bound to only one entity or object. The binding is achieved by verifying the credentials or claims presented by the entity. This is the static part of identity and can be tied to something you know, something you have, or something you are [6]. Each of these properties is an attempt to bind the name (and associated data and credentials) to the entity.

For purposes of computation, this is the element we rely upon. There are familiar identities (recognized in this domain) and unfamiliar or less familiar identities (not recognized in this domain or not recognized at all). Identity is at the basis of most of our IT security activities. The basic security measures relate directly to identities, and they also deal with a large number of the ELS system tenets (see Section 1.2). For example:

- Malicious Entities – unfamiliar identities.
- Accountability – attributing actions to familiar entities.
- Lines of Authority – an accountability chain.

Many exploits take advantage of confusing identities through masquerade, man-in-the-middle (MITM), and other approaches. In a secure environment, actions that provide access and privilege should always be preceded by a strong identity check. As we know the enemy is present, we must avoid anything that gets between known identities, like proxies and portals. These constructs often confuse the identity issue and lead to vulnerabilities and exploits.

PKI allows entities within an enterprise to validate identities without prior contact with each other. This is done through the exchange of public key certificates, which are digitally signed by a CA. Entities can use the public key to encrypt data to another entity and their private key to decrypt content encrypted to them with their public key. Entities can sign data using their private key and validate other signatures using the signing entity's public key. PKI provides the services necessary to support such operations in a secure and trusted way. These services are described in the following sections.

4.2 ENTITY VETTING

One of the core elements of a PKI is the public key certificate. Each entity is issued a certificate when entering the enterprise. Before such a certificate can be properly issued, the entity to which it is issued must be properly identified, and this identity must be validated through some real-world method. For people, an in-person meeting with proper credentials proving identity as stated by a trusted authority, such as a driver's license, passport, or other government ID, provides the ability to authenticate the person. In addition, paperwork or other proof of the individual's position or role within the organization is needed. Other attributes, such as a fingerprint, photo, or additional attributes may be collected or validated for inclusion in or with the PKI credential. Together, these provide a certification, or vetting, process that establishes the identity of the entity receiving the PKI credential, the validity and accuracy of the information related to that entity, and the authorization of the entity to receive the PKI credential.

Vetting must be done for non-person entities (NPEs) as well. However, the procedure is different from the one used for people, as the NPE is often managed by some people in a particular role and is dependent on these people for proper use of the credential. The vetting for the NPE involves a physical world validation that the software or hardware to be issued a credential is in fact the software or hardware that is identified by the credential. The HSM where the credential and associated keys are to be stored must also be validated for appropriate security measures. This is an additional check that is not performed for people, as people are issued their hardware storage device, such as a smart card, by the PKI issuing authority.

PKI is only as secure as the vetting process, which is the foundation of the trust PKI is based on. If a malicious individual can get a PKI credential through a sub-par vetting procedure, then the security guarantees provided by all other valid PKI credentials are weakened. If the weak vetting is restricted to a particular issuing CA or set of CAs, then the entire PKI is not necessarily affected. The weak CAs can be corrected to improve vetting procedures. In addition, the previously issued certificates should no longer be used. A small number of issued certificates can be revoked. For a larger population of certificates, the issuing CA certificates themselves, if not the parent or root CAs, should be revoked. A new certificate and key pair is then issued to the issuing CAs by their root CA, and new entity certificates are issued under the new vetting procedures and signed with the new CA keys. If the issuing CAs are root CAs, then new trusted root CAs must be established and trust must be removed from the original root CAs.

ROOT CERTIFICATION AUTHORITIES (CAs)

Root CAs are the initial certification authority and identity vetting organization for a governance domain. They may delegate authority to issue certificates to subordinate CAs to share the load of managing many end user certificates, or they may delegate only the minimal necessary authority (in conformance to the best practice principle of least privilege) to issue defined-usage certificates. See Section 4.4, Chapter 7, and Chapter 8 for technical details.

4.3 NAMING

Names must be unique if they are to be of any use. Ambiguity must be eliminated by a method of construction or by registration. The names must be unique across the span that you wish to search and request resources from. Reuse of names may lead to ambiguity, masquerade, or other vulnerabilities, so names must be unique over time and space. This is certainly necessary at the enterprise level, but most likely should extend to federation partners and maybe higher levels. For security reasons, all entities must have PKI certificates and support secure communication protocols including crypto bindings. Names must also be interpretable to the extent possible. This is needed for both human recognition and search and discovery services. The first level of interpretation should be the entity type (person, hardware, software, group, endpoint, enclave, and forest or enterprise name). Names must be reasonably short so as to not cloud human interpretability. The largest name size is arbitrary, but it should encompass enough elements to be usable in search and discovery. Name strings are usually set to a maximum of 256 bytes when encoded. However, we may wish to initially limit this to 40 bytes until additional bytes are needed due to populations. The naming requirements were discussed extensively in Book 1 [7]. The outcome of the naming process is a DN, to be used for all credential generation.

4.4 KEY AND CREDENTIAL GENERATION

After a person or NPE is vetted, the credential generation process begins. This starts with the generation of a public/private key pair. These keys must use a hardware source of sufficient entropy for key generation. The entropy input must be more than the number of bits of security desired. For example, if a random source provides only 4 bits of entropy for each 8 bits of output due to correlation of values or other reasons, and 2,048 bits of entropy are required in the key, then more than 4,096 random bits are required in the key generation process. In addition to using this many random bits, the bits must be processed in a way that maintains maximum output entropy. A cryptographic hash with the desired output bit length is one method of maintaining as much output entropy as possible.

Key pairs must be generated on secure hardware. Software keys are subject to duplication, sharing, and other issues that enable the credentials and keys to lose their association with the vetted entity to which they are issued. Key length is chosen based on the estimated time that an attacker would require to compromise the key using brute force or other cryptanalytic techniques on modern equipment. Although sufficient key length is intended to make such attacks infeasible, future cryptanalytic methods may shorten or eliminate the search time, so end entity certificates expire after a period of time that is long enough to prevent certificate refreshes from interfering with normal business, but short enough to limit exposure to new attacks and cryptanalytic techniques. The generating hardware is also invoked to create a certificate signing request, which includes the generated public key. The CA issues certificates with the public key, the entity's identity in the form of a DN, information relating to other attributes of the entity, allowed usage of the credentials, validity periods, and information about revocation checking.

Information on any issued credential is generally considered non-sensitive and not PII, as the certificates are often exchanged over the Internet in unencrypted form. However, access to a large set of certificates can potentially create problems if the keys are not generated properly, so care should be taken in managing any central certificate repository. This is not a vulnerability in itself, but it helps to reduce the attack surface for related vulnerabilities.

Credential generation for people can be done in person just after vetting. Certificates and keys for hardware are generated by the HSM and stored on the HSM used by the NPE. It is important to validate that the public key included in the certificate was generated by the appropriate HSM. This requires requesting the HSM to decrypt content that was encrypted with the selected public key. Otherwise, an individual could generate their own software key pair, claim that this pair was generated by an HSM, and then proceed to use the software keys with the certificate, again opening up vulnerabilities. The HSM must also be properly validated to ensure that keys cannot be exported in software and that software keys cannot be imported. Only hardware-to-hardware export between trusted HSMs is allowed.

In addition to HSM security properties, the HSM manufacturer must not be able to access private keys stored on any HSM and must not be able to export keys to another HSM that they manufacture.

The credentials for persons provide additional protections. A personal information number (PIN) is used as a second authentication measure. Although a PIN is a weak authentication tool, it is useful when authenticating a single person for a single PIV Card or Common Access Card (CAC), used by the U.S. Department of Defense (DoD) to provide two-factor authentication. Other methods include fingerprints, eye scans, or other biometrics as an additional factor and measure of authenticity. These additional factors could be built into the CAC or PIV device itself, or the pertinent information could be stored on the CAC or PIV, and the device accessing the CAC or

PIV could send live biometric data to the CAC or PIV for comparison. See Chapter 4 for a discussion of how multi-factor authentication is taken into account.

The credential must provide a way to let the user know that it is being used. If PINs or other secondary authentication measures are not cached, the user can be challenged to provide them each time. However, if they are cached for some time period, another method must be used to allow the user to provide positive indication that the private key is to be used. In addition, some means of providing the intended use to the user are beneficial, as malicious actors may request use of the CAC or PIV without identifying the malicious intent, and a user might comply with the request.

These issues relate to the libraries and drivers that run the actual hardware that stores the credentials. This software must be validated and managed through the PKI organization, and it must be provided through a secure channel to those who wish to install it.

Items that must be properly configured include the CAC or PIV itself, so that the CAC or PIV requests the PIN for each private key operation; the operating system, which has its own configuration for PIN caching; any middleware provided, which has a separate set of caching parameters; and any applications, which themselves could take the PIN as input and cache or reuse it. As caching at any one of these layers results in a lack of user confirmation, PKI services must either directly configure and lock down components or set and enforce policies to allow positive user confirmation for all private key operations.

After keys are generated, checks must be done to ensure that no identical or similar keys exist. This should not be an issue, if generation is done properly, but this additional check provides a way to validate that keys are unique and not correlated. For example, Rivest, Shamir, Adleman (RSA) keys use a product of two prime numbers as the basis of the key pair. If the prime numbers are identical for two key pairs, then these identities are able to act as each other. If two key pairs share a single prime number, then it is possible for a third party to use mathematical algorithms to quickly deduce both primes, and hence both private keys. This check must be made against all enterprise-issued credentials, as well as all other credentials or non-credentialed key pairs of similar type that are known to exist. For example, if credentials use RSA 2048 bit keys, then all other known RSA 2048 bit keys must be checked for similar prime factors. In general, these checks take longer as more key pairs are generated, so checking times will continually increase. Changing key types or sizes regularly can alleviate these scalability issues.

4.5 KEY AND CREDENTIAL ACCESS CONTROL

Stored cryptographic keys and credentials must be themselves protected. To avoid a never-ending cycle of requiring crypto-credentials to gain access to crypto-credentials, secondary credentials are used. As described in Section 3.3, the most common human authentication credential factor is a password, passcode, or PIN (something known); the second most common factor is a smart card or mobile device credential store (something owned); the third factor is often biometric (something shown). When two of these are used in combination, it is known as "two factor" authentication. For web-hosted applications and services, these human-specific credentials are securely mapped into cryptographic-key-based credentials such as a PKI X.509 credential, TLS transport header, and ELS session token.

To reduce brute-force attacks on key and credential stores, there are numerous technical requirements for and guidance on "hardened" and "anti-tamper" hardware, as well as "strong" encryption for software key and credential stores.

4.6 KEY AND CREDENTIAL MANAGEMENT

CAs must themselves have a trusted certificate to sign any certificates that they issue. That certificate may be issued by a CA that is higher in the organizational authority hierarchy. This chain of CAs continues up to a trusted root CA for the enterprise, which has a self-signed certificate. Although a secure channel is desired for accessing these trusted certificates, using PKI-enabled TLS such as Hypertext Transfer Protocol Secure (HTTPS) has a chicken and egg problem: it fetches the trusted root CA certificate in order to secure the channel to fetch the trusted root CA certificate.

PKI management must provide an alternative, secure method to distribute valid copies of root CA certificates to all entities within the enterprise. It could be installed from a trusted source when issuing new machines to individuals, included on the CAC, PIV, or HSM at credential generation, or posted in a public place that is widely known and not subject to change by external actors. Note that a public website is not such a public place, as such a site cannot be properly validated.

The PKI services include revoking certificates and checking revocation status of certificates. End entity certificates, such as those issued for applications, services, users, or other requesters, include an Online Certificate Status Protocol (OCSP) Uniform Resource Locator (URL) that is used for validation. Each OCSP endpoint contains revocation status information for certificates issued by a CA and is managed by the PKI service provider. Entities can check revocation status using a query to the OCSP endpoint. The OCSP endpoints must be properly positioned and scaled to handle enterprise-wide access patterns. For disconnected, intermittent, and limited operation, local OCSP servers can be set up using cached CRLs.

Although not part of normal OCSP or certificate revocation list (CRL) operations, lists of certificates and revoked certificate lists are maintained and accessible after certificates expire, as digital signatures or other cryptographic functions may outlive the certificate validity period.

ONLINE CERTIFICATE STATUS PROTOCOL (OCSP)

OCSP is an Internet protocol used to determine the state of an identified certificate. An OCSP client (i.e., browser) will send a status request to an OCSP responder and receive information that provides whether the certificate is valid or revoked.

DISCONNECTED, INTERMITTENT, AND LIMITED BANDWIDTH (DIL)

DIL environments can occur in geographic challenged areas or signal-blocking environments, such as a tunnel or elevator.

Revocation services provide a way to revoke an entity's certificate after it has been lost or otherwise compromised or damaged. Proper verification of the individual requesting revocation must be performed to prevent a denial-of-service (DoS) attack on valid users. However, revocation must not place a high burden on the individual doing the revocation. For most purposes, returning to the location that issued the credential is sufficient, as that location should have enough information about the individual to validate their identity, issue a new credential, and revoke the old credential. In DIL environments, a compromise outside the DIL environment might not matter to the local services, as they are isolated. For example, a compromise of the private key of an individual on a submarine need not affect internal submarine operations by that individual. However, upon returning to the surface, that individual would need a new credential for network-connected services.

OCSP itself must be provided with security guarantees. The CA designates a responder in the certificates it issues. Requesters sign OCSP requests to the responder and send requests through TLS as defined in the U.S. Air Force Consolidated Enterprise IT Baseline Technical Profile (CEITB TP) Provide Cryptographic Services with mutual authentication. Nonces are used to prevent replay attacks. CA keys are stored in hardware. OCSP requesters are configured to treat any response other than "valid" by the OCSP responder, including timeouts, as being "invalid." In the event that OCSP responders are not available, entities may be configured to allow failover to CRLs, but the default is to require OCSP, as CRL updates can introduce additional delays in the availability of revocation status.

NONCE

In cryptography, a nonce is an arbitrary number that is used just once in a cryptographic communication. It is often a random or pseudo-random number issued in an authentication protocol to ensure that old communications cannot be reused in replay attacks.

OCSP responder certificates may be compromised and revoked, so requesters should check their validity as well. This requires a sequence of requests to OCSP responders for CAs, until the root CA is reached. The root CA cannot be validated, as there is no authority that can be trusted to provide such information other than the root itself. Root CAs are often kept offline to minimize the risk of compromise. An online CA, if compromised through its connection, could be used to sign rogue certificates, whereas an offline CA does not allow such an attack.

4.7 KEY AND CREDENTIAL USE

Common uses for PKI credentials include digital signing, key encipherment, data encipherment, key agreement, certificate signing, and CRL signing. Other uses, such as issuing certificates and signing CRLs, are restricted to CAs. The uses and restrictions are encoded into the credential. Finer grained uses can be encoded in the X.509 certificate using "Key Usage" or "Extended Key Usage" fields. Primary uses for ELS include bilateral authentication, setting up key exchanges for TLS usage, digital signatures on SAMLs and Simple Object Access Protocol (SOAP) requests, and encryption of symmetric keys used for bulk encryption.

It is important for entities to validate received PKI credentials. Validation includes the following checks:

- Current time is between validity start and end times.
- Certificate has not been revoked, as confirmed by OCSP response of "valid."
- Identity named in certificate is a valid identity and correctly corresponds to the entity that presented the credential.
- Signature validates with public key of trusted CA certificate, or
  - public key in another potentially untrusted cert that is itself issued by a trusted CA, or
  - public key in a chain of certs that contains a trusted CA certificate.
- Signing CA certificate has "issue certificate" as one of its valid uses.
- Presented certificate lists the intended use as one of its valid uses.
- Use of the "name constraint" extension or other means to prevent trusted external CAs from issuing certificates associated with internal entities.

ENCIPHERMENT

In cryptography, a cipher is an algorithm for performing encryption or decryption – a series of well-defined steps that can be followed as a procedure. An alternative, less common term is *encipherment*. To encipher or encode is to convert information from plaintext into ciphertext or code.

Additional checks include the following:

- Record all certificates seen, and check certificates against prior certificates seen with the same issuer and DN, alternative name, or serial number.

For NPEs, checks are automated and lead to failure if they do not all pass. For people, validation may allow bypassing security failures if the person is notified of all errors and required to positively assert the desire to bypass them. This can be useful for testing or setting up small environments based on the primary PKI without all the required network enterprise services, such as in a DIL environment. For testing and development environments, PKI services can be enabled and disabled as the need arises. Valid credentials should be used for testing prior to fielding systems. A development or test PKI with a separate set of trusted CAs and associated service providers enables a realistic environment that does not contaminate the operational PKI.

The PKI provider sets up policies for use and propagates them through the enterprise with associated training courses. This provides the necessary understanding of what PKI credentials are and how they are to be used, which can stop some social engineering styles of attacks. For example, for ELS, no credentials are allowed to be shared. There are technical components to this, such as preventing private key export from hardware stores, but also personal factors, such as not giving someone your CAC and PIN and instead using delegation services to perform such actions.

Knowledge of the proper use and available services can help maintain the PKI credentials as a trusted source of identity and non-repudiation.

4.8 SOME OTHER CONSIDERATIONS

Identity in the enterprise is a unique representation of an entity. For PKI users, it begins with the CA service that maintains their files. Complexity of PKI is an issue, and there are still a number of vulnerabilities in PKI credentials. The owner of each application ultimately decides what kind of authentication is strong enough through the registration process with EAE.

5 Cloud Key Management

5.1 CLOUDS

Web security has become more important as more aspects of business, government, and everyday life are put online. In parallel to the increased focus on web security is the rise of cloud computing. The cloud computing model offers many cost and efficiency advantages over the on-premise data center model. The cloud model can also offer an advantage in regard to security. A well-run cloud can establish standard security procedures across the entire cloud. An organization hosted in such a cloud benefits by leveraging the work of the full-time, specialized cloud security professionals. Cloud servers are isolated from the internal enterprise network, which may stop server compromises from propagating to more sensitive internal assets.

> **THE CLOUD**
>
> *Cloud computing* is storage of computing resources outside an organization's control. Cloud computing is a type of computing that relies on shared computing resources rather than use of local servers or personal devices to handle applications. This type of computing presents extraordinary security challenges.

The cloud model is not a security panacea. Data can leak between cloud client applications through shared infrastructure [85]. Social engineering can be used against the cloud provider to hijack cloud accounts and associated data and services [86]. Attacks on other unrelated cloud clients can propagate and render cloud assets inaccessible [87]. Cloud employees can be subverted or malicious organizations may infiltrate cloud providers with their own individuals in order to compromise clients from the inside [88]. Key storage hardware can have vulnerabilities [89, 90].

These vulnerabilities are concerning, but they can be addressed. Software and hardware can be updated to block intrusion, leakage, and attack propagation. People can be trained to resist social engineering, or human tasks can be automated. These attacks will never be prevented (only mitigated, at best), but these vulnerabilities are based on mistakes and imperfect implementation more often than on faulty design.

A challenge at the design level is securely managing a web server's private key while utilizing the public cloud. The goal is a server key management design in which keys cannot be duplicated, keys can only be used by authorized individuals, and key operations are timely. At the time of this writing, no known solution has been implemented to attain these goals. This presents a problem for all public cloud-hosted web servers. This chapter presents a review of the security shortcomings of common existing solutions, an analysis of improvements to these solutions, and two proposals for a secure design.

5.2 ELS IN A PRIVATE CLOUD

One important idea in ELS is that all communication and sharing is done with end-to-end integrity and encryption between two endpoints. No other entities are allowed to view or modify such communication. A related idea is that the entities communicating have strong assurance that they are communicating with the intended entity. This relies on strong end-to-end authentication of both entities [13].

Authentication of a server in ELS uses PKI credentials through the TLS protocol. A critical security decision is the method to store and access the private keys associated with server PKI credentials. Any entity that has access to a server's private key can impersonate it, so access to this private key must be restricted to the single server entity to which it is issued. In the ELS model, different instances of a server used for load balancing must have separate individual credentials for attribution purposes. Sharing of private keys, even among otherwise identical server instances, violates ELS basic security principles and is not allowed. Sharing of private keys or other authentication credentials prevents proper attribution and leads to identity confusion, attack forensics ambiguities, and poor security practices. According to ELS rules, servers do not store the private keys in software, because such keys may be copied and exported. A hardware solution is the method of choice for storing and using private keys for high security applications.

Hardware key storage includes smart cards, HSMs, and trusted platform modules (TPMs). Smart cards are used for individuals who move between machines. The smart card allows authentication from any machine that can read the smart card and invoke private key operations. HSMs are used for servers that have fixed locations. A single HSM can be used on a network to support many servers that each has access only to its own key on the HSM through internal security partitioning. TPMs are useful when a user is assigned a specific device, such as a mobile phone, tablet, or laptop that is used exclusively by that user. The single-user model means that the device is under a single person's control, much like a smart card, and a password or smart card logon can be used to secure access to the TPM. Such devices must be managed devices, because loss of a device requires revocation of certificates and remote deletion of associated keys to prevent someone with physical access from extracting or using private keys.

When setting up a server on premise, a trusted individual uses the HSM interface to generate the server's key pair. The public key is exported and included in an identification certificate, which is signed by a trusted CA. The server is configured to connect to the HSM and uses the specified certificate and key. The private key never leaves the HSM, and only the entity identified by the DN of the certificate is allowed to connect to the HSM to use the private key. The connection to the HSM may be established using a hardware token specific to the HSM, so that only hands-on access can be used to set up a connection for a server to use an HSM key. Accountability is tied to the individual doing the key management, who is part of the enterprise and properly vetted. Additionally, the hardware and keys can be monitored using physical security measures, because all access is hands-on. The on-premise security model can also be applied to a private cloud, because the private cloud is also run by trusted enterprise entities.

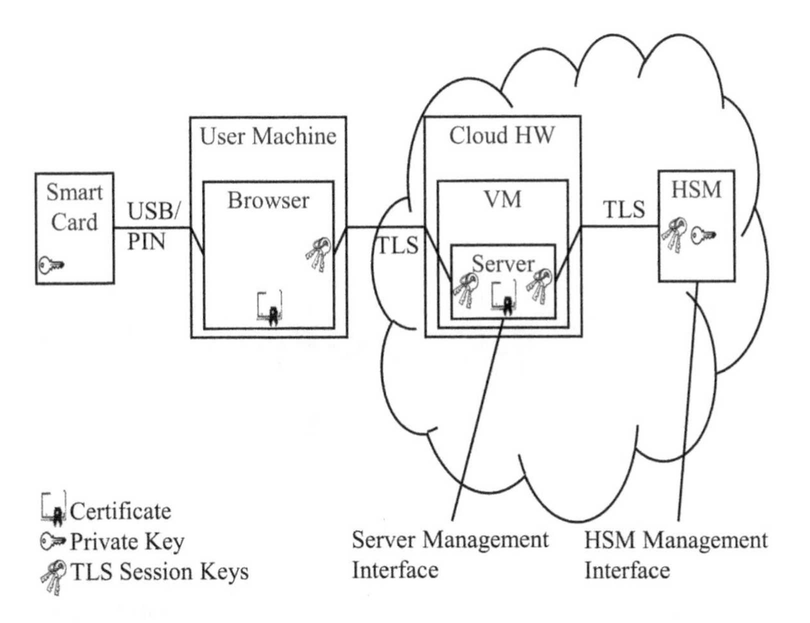

FIGURE 5.1. Normal Web Request Flow

As a first step toward moving to the public cloud, we illustrate the private cloud hosting approach. Figure 5.1 shows a normal request flow from a browser on an enterprise machine to a server hosted in the private cloud on a virtual machine. The browser uses the smart card certificate and private key to authenticate through TLS to the server. The smart card private key is accessed through a Universal Serial Bus (USB) smart card reader, and the smart card is protected by a PIN. The server uses its certificate and HSM key to authenticate to the browser. The connection from the server to the HSM is secured through a separate TLS connection. This HSM connection may be local and long-lived. Session keys are used for the encryption, decryption, and validation of TLS transmitted data.

When there are many requesters and servers, the requester keys are held on different smart cards, but the server keys are often aggregated onto a shared HSM, as shown in Figure 5.2. During the initial TLS connection setup between each server and the HSM, servers are allowed to use only their own private key. This separation relies on proper configuration and internal HSM security mechanisms.

ELS leverages the virtual application data center (VADC) concept [51]. This is a model that focuses on rapid and secure portability of an entire data center across clouds. It enables an enterprise to rapidly respond and transfer assets between cloud providers. The server and key management solution described above does not work for the public cloud, because it relies on access and control of hardware. The solutions must be modified for the public cloud, where such access and control is only available to the cloud provider.

5.3 THE PUBLIC CLOUD CHALLENGE

This section describes server private key management challenges of moving an on-premise or private cloud ELS system to the public cloud.

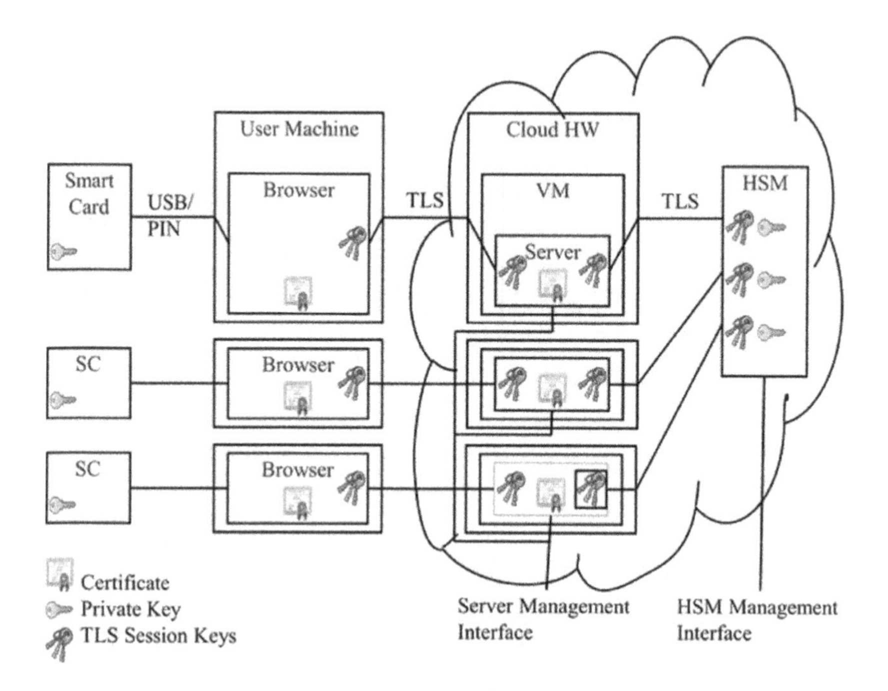

FIGURE 5.2. Request Flows: Multiple Requesters and Servers

5.3.1 Using the Same Design

If the private cloud model were directly applied to the public cloud, the cloud provider would perform the HSM-related actions normally reserved for trusted, vetted individuals within the enterprise. The cloud provider provides an interface to the HSM for key management, and certificate creation can be done offline using the public key.

However, the HSM key management Application Programming Interface (API) is now a cloud-provided software interface that has the potential to act as a MITM between the client and the HSM. As a MITM, it could accept requests for key pair generation on the HSM and then reroute these requests to a software key store, as shown in Figure 5.3. All key operations would be performed by the cloud provider as if on an HSM, though in reality the keys are stored in software. The software key store is controlled by and fully accessible to the untrusted cloud provider. The server connections to the HSM could also be redirected through the HSM MITM to the software key store, which would simply emulate the HSM interface. This example shows that the cloud client has no guarantee that the private keys generated through the cloud HSM API are actually generated or stored in an HSM. For this reason, cloud-provided HSM interfaces do not provide adequate security for ELS.

HARDWARE SECURITY MODULE (HSM)

An HSM is a physical computing device that safeguards and manages digital keys for strong authentication. It also provides cryptoprocessing. These modules traditionally come in the form of a plug-in card or an external device that attaches directly to a computer or network server. Some HSMs can be configured to provide these services to more than one requester (not recommended).

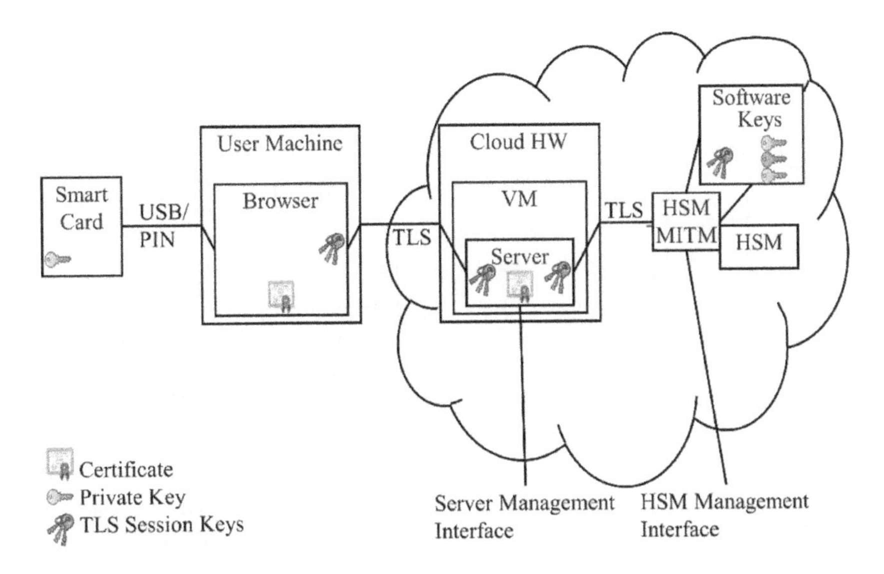

FIGURE 5.3. Rerouting HSM Requests to a Software Key Store

5.3.2 HSM Site Inspection, Virtual Connection to HSM

To ensure HSM key storage, an administrator from the enterprise can visit the cloud provider to generate hardware key pairs on a validated HSM. In this case, the private key is protected by the HSM from a malicious or compromised cloud provider or attacker. The public key can be extracted, and this key can be used to ensure that the cloud provider does not swap private keys. With this method, the hosting enterprise is assured that it is using the correct private key generated in the HSM when the server presents its certificate and the corresponding public key. This is very similar to a client generating keys on their own HSM and then hosting that HSM in the cloud. Either method provides assurance that keys are stored in a known HSM.

If the cloud provider uses a software key management interface, HSM requests are routed through a virtual HSM implemented in software that passes requests to the hardware HSM. Using this approach, an untrusted or compromised cloud provider could allow other requests at the virtual HSM despite locking down the actual HSM, as shown in Figure 5.4. In this case, the single connection to the HSM is shared. Shared access to the HSM may be a less egregious violation of ELS basic principles than exporting a private key, but it is still a fundamental violation because it allows the sharing of a private key with an unauthorized entity. The key itself is adequately protected, but access to the HSM is not.

5.3.3 HSM Site Inspection, Direct Connection to HSM

To mitigate the problems of the software key management interface, the cloud client could require servers to directly connect to the HSM. Under this configuration, there is no ability to share such connections because there is no longer a MITM that the

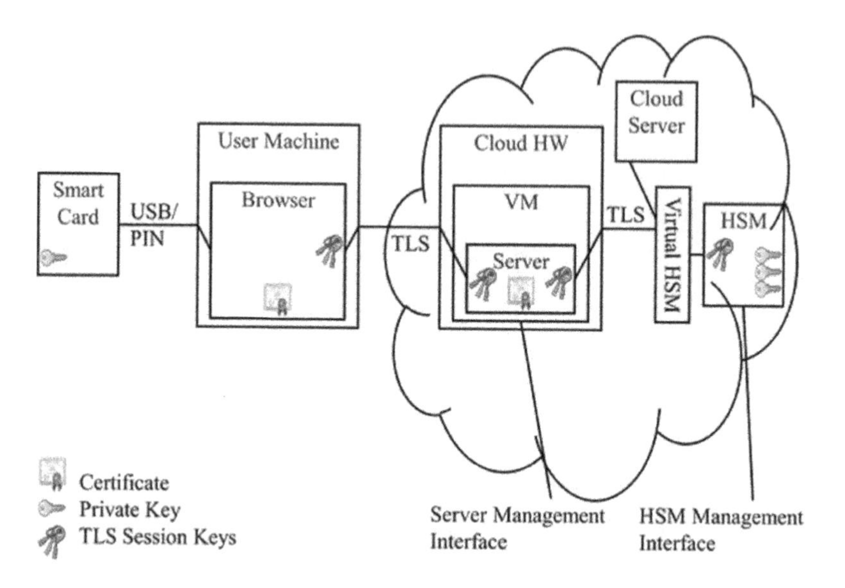

FIGURE 5.4. Virtualizing the HSM Connection

cloud provider controls. Each server must create its own connection to the HSM, and this is done as needed by the cloud provider.

The cloud provider can no longer share an existing connection to the HSM, but it can now create its own new connections in the same way that it sets up a valid connection, as shown in Figure 5.5. This gives the cloud provider the ability to use the private keys in the HSM, which again violates ELS principles.

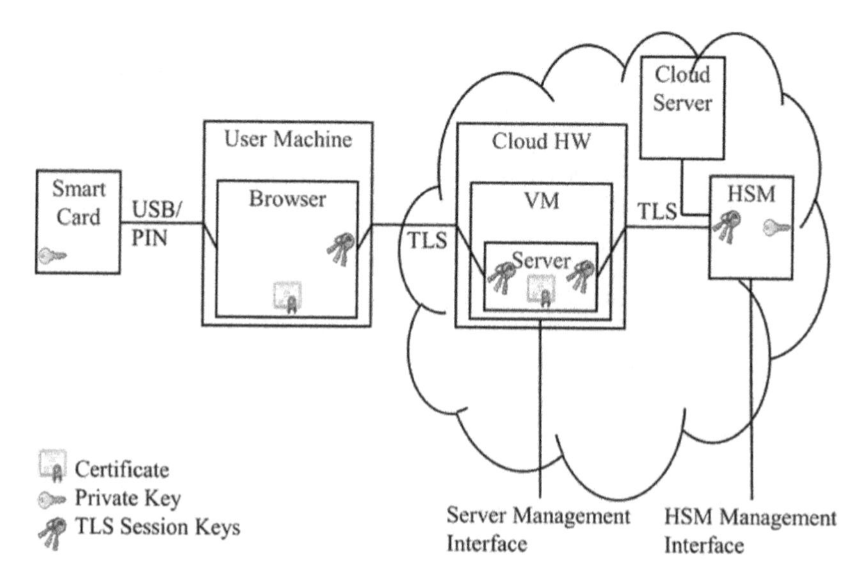

FIGURE 5.5. Adding an Additional Connection to the HSM

5.3.4 HSM Site Inspection, Preconfigured Direct Connections to HSM

In addition to requiring direct connections to the HSM, the hosting enterprise can also create these long-lived TLS connections between the servers and the HSM. Special tokens or keys that are used to create HSM connections are now held by the enterprise and not shared with the cloud provider. This eliminates the cloud provider's ability to create these connections. Now the server private keys are in hardware, and the only connections to the HSM are from the associated servers. This appears to mitigate the previous vulnerabilities due to extra connections to the HSM.

However, the cryptographic keys for the secure HSM connection, along with any other necessary information such as sequence numbers and other internal states, are stored in software on the server as part of the TLS connection state. This sensitive information can be extracted by an untrusted cloud provider by either copying the virtual machine on which the server is running or probing it through hypervisor interfaces. With access to the memory of the machine, methods exist to directly extract TLS keys from an executing application [91]. With these keys and the appropriate state information, the cloud provider can inject new private key usage requests to the HSM by creating the proper messages and updating the elements of the internal state of the server TLS connection, such as sequence numbers, initialization vector (IV) values, and other encryption states, as shown in Figure 5.6.

The failure of this approach is using obscurity for security. Although it may require specialized skills to probe a virtual machine image and manipulate TLS session keys, the cloud provider has the required level of access to perform these actions. Even with dedicated effort to hide the TLS state in the virtual machine, the protection is only obfuscation. The ELS principle, "The system should function even if the attacker knows how it functions," applies to this situation. We must assume the attacker can figure out how our system works and provide security appropriately. The approach above fails to satisfy this ELS security principle.

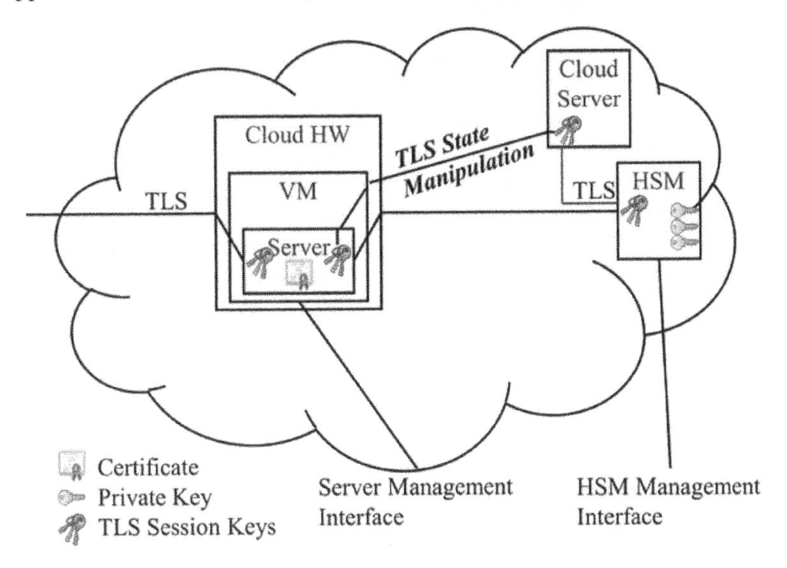

FIGURE 5.6. TLS State Manipulation to Allow HSM Connections

5.4 POTENTIAL HYBRID CLOUD SOLUTIONS

The preceding section has shown examples where the server and HSM are both moved to an untrusted public cloud. This section discusses hybrid cloud solutions that attempt to mitigate some of the problems of the public cloud by splitting assets between the public and private cloud.

5.4.1 HSM in Public Cloud

The first hybrid approach involves splitting the server and HSM so that the HSM is hosted in the public cloud and the server is hosted in the private cloud.

Physical validation of a cloud-hosted HSM stops attacks based on a software-based HSM or MITM, because the HSM that generates and stores the private keys is genuine. The associated public keys can be used to confirm that only the private keys generated on the HSM are being used by the server.

Trusted private cloud operators establish server-to-HSM connections from the private cloud. The public cloud provider sees only encrypted traffic to and from the HSM and has no ability to access the necessary keys to decrypt this traffic or insert new connections.

This approach provides high security, but performance may suffer due to the increased latency from the server to HSM. Every cryptographic operation in the HSM now requires at least one round trip Internet transmission instead of local traffic. It also has the fundamental problem that the benefits of the public cloud model are minimal due to the private hosting of the application. This solution provides security, but it fails to provide performance and other cloud hosting benefits. It effectively becomes a private cloud with a remote, high-latency, and difficult-to-configure HSM.

5.4.2 HSM in Private Cloud

A related option that maintains public cloud benefits is hosting the HSM in a private cloud and the server in the public cloud. However, this option has the server-to-HSM connection problem, because it relies on the cloud vendor to properly set up the server connection and not duplicate, share, or otherwise manipulate it. It also has the performance problem of the long server-to-HSM link.

Despite its problems, this solution does offer some benefits in comparison with a public cloud solution. The local HSM, or a local HSM management interface, can monitor all incoming requests. This provides a record of private key access on the HSM, and this may help to identify unauthorized usage patterns. Each TLS session with the server requires use of the private key, which can be recorded. Host-based security agents deployed to user devices can record client connections to the server. A discrepancy between outgoing user requests and server private key usage requests to the HSM indicates potentially unauthorized private key usage. This monitoring does not prevent unauthorized use of the private keys in the HSM, but it enables detection of potentially malicious activity, and it provides forensic capabilities after such incidents occur.

5.4.3 General Hybrid Challenges

The hybrid cloud encompasses many more options than just splitting assets into a private cloud and a public cloud. There are options for private enclaves in public clouds or public clouds on premise, as well as multi-clouds that span multiple public or private clouds. However, the key feature of all of these options is the idea that different servers are hosted by different entities, and these servers communicate with each other across hosting boundaries. This setup creates an underlying design problem for secure server key management.

When servers communicate across different hosting environments, the requester must authenticate to the provider. The requester private key is used as part of a mutual authentication handshake. However, this private key is vulnerable in a public cloud, so any other services that the public cloud-hosted requester can access using its private key are vulnerable. The public cloud provider can access the requester's private key and use it to form a valid request to a server in another hosting environment. Although the private keys of these servers are not necessarily vulnerable, the data hosted by the servers is.

One implication is that hosting sensitive data on premise or in a private cloud is not adequate protection if entities in a public cloud can access this data. This issue also applies to situations where a user on a secure device accesses data in a private cloud through a public cloud web interface. The public cloud provider can use the authentication private key of the server in the public cloud to access data in the private cloud.

5.5 PROPOSED SECURE SOLUTIONS

The public cloud solutions above are not adequate for the private key management problem. Moving to a hybrid cloud offers some benefits, but it has its own issues. The proposed solutions that follow provide high security designs for server private key management in the public cloud.

5.5.1 Server in HSM

The main problems discussed in this chapter have stemmed from the separation of the server and HSM and the challenge of establishing a secure connection between them. One possible solution is to combine them into a single entity by implementing the entire server and its keys inside the HSM. The HSM server connects with the browser through a TLS connection, as shown in Figure 5.7. The application is preloaded onto the HSM, associated with the proper private keys, and then shipped to the cloud provider. The private key access occurs completely within the HSM, which protects it from the cloud provider. This solves the problem of securely tying the server to its private key by encapsulating them both inside the HSM.

The main hurdle for this approach is that HSMs are expensive, special purpose devices designed specifically for key generation, storage, and use. They are not designed to run arbitrary software, and they typically do not have the storage or

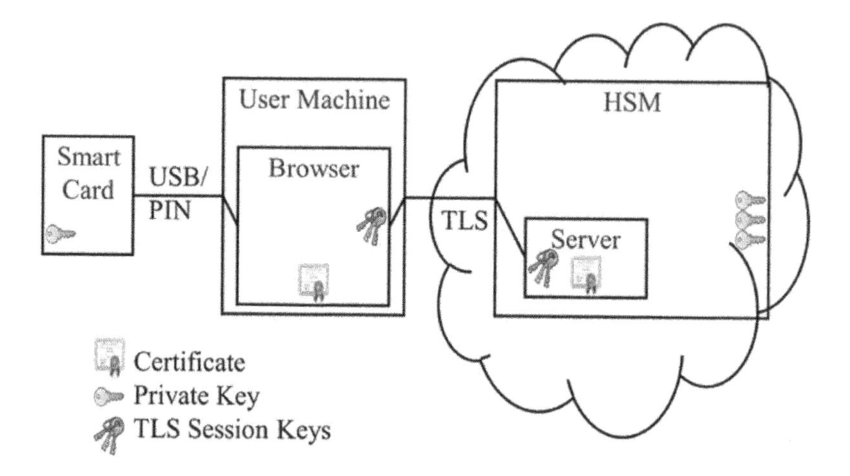

FIGURE 5.7. Proposed Solution with Server in HSM

computation power required to support a full server. These are problems, but they are implementation issues within a fundamentally secure design.

5.5.2 Homomorphic Encryption

Homomorphic encryption allows data to be processed while remaining encrypted [92]. The programs that normally operate on the unencrypted data are transformed to operate on the encrypted data.

In a homomorphic encryption solution, the requester encrypts its requests using homomorphic encryption. These requests are not decrypted at the transformed server. They are used as encrypted inputs to a program that operates on encrypted data. Part of the server processing involves authentication using an HSM. The HSM is also transformed to operate on encrypted data. The server sends encrypted key operation requests to the HSM and uses the encrypted response to authenticate to the requester. Similarly, the server can authenticate as a requester to other servers that accept encrypted requests. The design for the client to server communication is shown in Figure 5.8.

It is possible for an attacker to reverse the transformation on the server and modify the server behavior. This could be used to manipulate the server-to-HSM connection by changing the server's behavior. However, unlike with unencrypted data, the attacker cannot encrypt or decrypt the data that is processed. This keeps the data on this server and on other servers that communicate with it safe. Even without knowing the data, an attacker could create problems by repeating, omitting, or modifying server actions. Techniques in verifiable computing and garbled circuits can be used to mitigate such attacks [93].

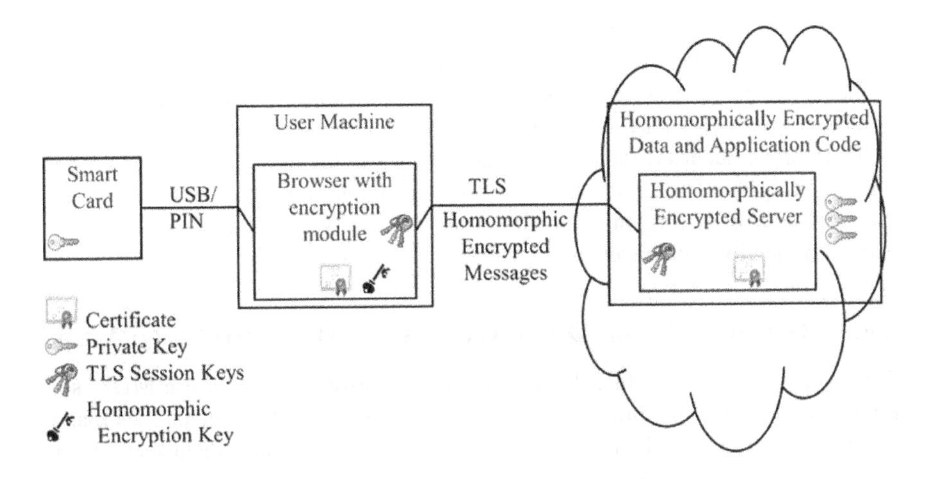

FIGURE 5.8. Proposed Solution Using Homomorphic Encryption

5.6 IMPLEMENTATION

The previous section has discussed designs for server private key security in the public cloud. This section examines implementation issues for these secure designs.

5.6.1 Cloud Vendor Support

The cloud vendor controls the HSM and server and is centrally positioned to provide server private key security. Current cloud providers offer cloud-based key management services backed by HSM key storage. However, they offer virtual HSM interfaces, and controls on key access are set at this virtual interface [94– 96]. The cloud provider allows the enterprise administrator to set permissions on key use, but these permissions apply only to other enterprise users, not to the cloud provider itself. The cloud provider maintains direct control of the HSMs.

One promising approach for server integrity is a method to establish software root of trust unconditionally on hardware [97]. This provides assurance that no malware is present on a machine when it boots. The cloud provider performs this procedure to ensure that no malicious code is hidden on the hardware during the boot process. However, this still relies on the cloud provider to perform the procedure properly. Server private key security must come from outside the cloud provider.

5.6.2 HSM Vendor Support

An HSM can provide the property that a key cannot be duplicated. Major HSM vendors also provide some accommodations to facilitate the move to the cloud [98, 99]. Thales, for example, provides a method to create a key on a local HSM and securely copy it to an HSM in the cloud [100]. This offers a way to remotely generate, update, and remove keys and credentials. It enables the methods in Sections 3.2 or 3.3 to be conducted without physically visiting the cloud HSM. However, this feature does not protect the cloud HSM from the attacks on the server-to-HSM connection. It also explicitly creates a copy of the private key, which is against ELS principles. This capability offers additional convenience but not additional security.

To improve security, the HSM vendor must provide a way to authenticate the server connections. However, the HSM is the key holder for server authentication, so this becomes a bootstrapping problem. Thus, the HSM vendor cannot solve this issue using advanced key management.

5.6.3 Leveraging Mobile Device Management (MDM) for Cloud Assets

Enterprises that issue mobile devices to their employees typically use MDM solutions. These address the problems of unknown networks and hostile entities that are more prevalent outside the protected enterprise network. Management services provide the enterprise access to operating system controls on these devices. These controls can limit device capabilities, applications, sensors, or other functions normally available to the user. In addition, the enterprise has the ability to remotely perform a factory reset, effectively erasing all applications, settings, and data from the device.

Mobile device vendors embed hardware security features to enable secure communication with their devices. For example, the vendor can embed their own PKI root CA public key in the hardware to enable trusted software updates. All updates are signed by a credential that chains to this trusted root CA. Additional hardware protections ensure that only properly signed code is loaded, and irreversible bit flips in hardware indicate malicious or suspicious actions [101, 102].

The MDM services integrate with these hardware protections. The operating system, securely loaded by the hardware after signature validation, provides a set of APIs that can be used to remotely control the operation of the device.

The hardware protections of a mobile device make the device much like an HSM. Recent attempts to extract data from an iPhone proved to be very difficult and costly, even for a well-funded government agency [103]. The ability to remotely manage the phone, and in particular the ability to restrict user functions, makes such a device desirable for cloud hosting environments. In this scenario, the cloud provider acts as the mobile user, and the cloud client acts as the MDM administrator. The client hosts their server on a cloud-provided mobile device and manages it in the potentially hostile cloud environment through the MDM interfaces. This allows the remote client to limit the activities of the hands-on cloud provider instead of the cloud provider limiting the client's activities.

To implement this approach, the cloud provider purchases mobile devices with the appropriate hardware and management capabilities. The client sets up an MDM system and enrolls cloud devices. The cloud provider may perform the initial MDM enrollment, but the client then pushes strict policies to the device to block further actions by the cloud provider. The client, through the MDM interface, would then install appropriate applications, generate private keys in the device's secure hardware, and send corresponding certificates to the device. The device would then operate as a web server on the cloud network. Proper use of TLS would allow the device to securely connect out to requesters or other servers.

During enrollment, it is important to validate the public keys of the devices being enrolled. The vendor must provide a way to identify an authentic device through a registered public key that corresponds to a private key that resides on the device. Otherwise, the vendor could create virtual devices with their own keys that mimic the behavior of authentic devices. The public/private key pair and registration with the vendor allow the client to ensure that the device they are enrolling is an authentic device issued by the correct vendor.

Mobile devices are not as secure as a dedicated HSM for key storage. However, this is an implementation issue – they are designed to provide this capability, just not to the same standards. The concept of a device that is manageable remotely when released into a potentially hostile environment is the right concept for the design of a secure server key management approach in the cloud.

5.6.4 Homomorphic Encryption

The primary issue with the full homomorphic encryption (FHE) approach is performance. Current implementations of FHE, which is required for arbitrary computations, are extremely slow [104]. Somewhat homomorphic encryption (SWHE) and partial homomorphic encryption (PHE) offer some of the capabilities of FHE with better performance, and these may be an option for very simple servers or standard database queries. The use of PHE in standard database queries is an area of ongoing research [105], and initial results for simple database queries have been promising [62]. However, databases are often accessed through web servers, so this is, at best, a partial solution.

Looking forward, active research into homomorphic encryption and its applications promises to improve performance and capabilities [106]. FHE has seen significant performance improvements since its inception, and although it is still far from practical, more theoretical research into algorithms and practical work to build specialized hardware may make it feasible in the near future.

5.7 CLOUD KEY MANAGEMENT SUMMARY

The public cloud offers many desirable benefits in cost, efficiency, and even security, but taking advantage of these while maintaining secure server private key management is a challenge. Problems in the public cloud and hybrid cloud stem from the separation of the server from its authentication key in the HSM. An untrusted cloud provider can exploit this separation to use the private key of the server, and the client cannot prevent this or detect that it is happening in most current designs. The most secure approaches negatively impact performance or forego the benefits of hosting in the public cloud.

The proposed solutions for secure design all encapsulate the server and HSM within a single logical entity. This eliminates the difficult problem of authenticating the server and HSM to each other. Using an HSM as the single logical entity provides a hardware encapsulation that hides the communications between the server and key management within the HSM itself. Using homomorphic encryption creates this single logical entity in software by encrypting the requests and responses and allowing the cloud provider to access and process only this encrypted data.

Current technology appears poised to be able to implement these approaches. Mobile devices include technology that can allow secure remote management and software updates, which is similar to what is required of the "server in HSM" solution. Although current products are not optimized for such use, the goal of providing secure management of a remote device in a hostile environment fits the design goal for a server in a public cloud. The performance of FHE is currently poor, but it is improving, and such improvements are often substantial. Combinations of algorithmic improvements, implementation optimizations, and optimized hardware support are driving performance increases toward a threshold of practicality. Crossing this threshold would provide the critical component needed for the FHE-based design to be implemented.

6 Enhanced Assurance Needs

6.1 ENHANCED IDENTITY ISSUES

Identity in the enterprise is a unique representation of an entity. For users, it begins with the human resources department that maintains their files. The assigned identity is called the *DN*, and it must be unique over space and time. There may be five John Smiths in the enterprise, but only one "John.Smith2534, UID=Finance, HID=Chicago." These and PKI information are normally encoded into a PIV card for network access and provided to the entity for its use. Certain pieces of the information may be tagged as verifiable by DN for identity purposes, such as "mother's middle name."

Because of data sensitivities, enterprise policy, or the shortcomings of PKI, some data owners may not feel comfortable utilizing only PKI certificate possession. On the other hand, a given data owner may feel that a PKI certificate is overkill, and a lesser level of identity assurance is needed. Users that have misplaced or have never had a PIV may use a temporary certificate, which is discussed in the next chapter. We assume they are connected to the enterprise network and a breach would involve not only their application but those of other network participants. For this reason, minimum assurance levels are a requirement. Each application ultimately decides what kind of authentication is strong enough through a registration process with EAE.

The creation of an enhanced identity assurance comprises two separate stages. The first stage is the creation of a *candidate identity* (starting point for identity determination), in which the candidate identity is paired with an enterprise identity, and a DN is determined. This normally begins with presentation of a claim to ownership of a PKI certificate through the use of the PIV. As we will discuss, the process also takes steps to verify that the pairing between the candidate identity and the DN is owned by the individual making the request. The second stage is creation of the *assured identity*. The candidate identity becomes the assured identity when enough correlated information and personal verification about the proposed identity has a sufficient level of pairing with the enterprise identity that it can be trusted with access and privilege to an application using the claims that have been computed for that individual's use.

6.2 SCALE OF IDENTITY ASSURANCE

If you search the literature for multi-factor authentication, you will find many processes using account-based systems and starting with username and password

[107–113]. These systems intertwine the security issues of authentication and authorization. In fact, the popular definition of multi-factor authentication merges the two:

> Multi-factor authentication (MFA) is a method of computer access control in which a user is only granted access after successfully presenting several separate pieces of evidence to an authentication mechanism – typically at least two of the following categories: knowledge (something they know); possession (something they have); and inherence (something they are). [114]

ELS separates the identity and access/privilege security issues. Thus, there are no accounts and no usernames with passwords. Further, ELS uses no proxies and limits access to the EAS, thus reducing the threat surface.

Each data owner will decide what the requirements for access and privilege to their data are, including the level of assurance that is acceptable. ELS represents a strong identity assurance and will be assigned a value of .80. It is assumed that if the data owner wishes strong identity assurance he will specify .70 or .75 as the identity assurance value (from the collection below, the value of .75 requires bio information in the absence of PIV). Identity in the absence of a PIV is discussed in Chapter 7. This will allow all enterprise users with a PIV or a derived credential (discussed in Chapter 8) to actually present access and privilege claims to the application. The lowest level of identity assurance would come from self-assertion; however, we will require several additional factors for this minimum, including a presence in the enterprise catalog, verification by an out-of-band (OOB) method, and of course, for authorization, claims must be available for the individual. This lowest level will be described as user-asserted identity with OOB verification and assigned a value of 0.2. This level of identity assurance is normally provided to the user without a PIV as discussed in Chapter 6.

IDENTITY ASSURANCE

Identity assurance is a measure of the extent to which correlated credentials represent that the individual in question is the enterprise DN.

OUT-OF-BAND (OOB)

OOB represents the use of a second channel for verification. The second channel may be a phone, e-mail, or other non-network asset and is usually presented with a value for verification. The non-network possibilities are derived from the candidate identity values in the EAE and not arbitrary.

It is possible that no assurance of identity is needed. However, for enterprise systems, we assume things like the cafeteria menu and evening social events are on a disconnected network so that the enterprise network is not in danger of compromise by connectivity. For this

HARD TOKEN

A hard token may be a CAC, another PIV, or a credential derived from these. Chapter 8 describes derived credentials.

discussion, we will assume 0.2 for the minimum, which should also be the minimum specified by a data owner. The identity assurance scale will run the full amount of variation to be available for other uses (namely those in Chapter 7).

A total of seven identity cases were developed, as follows, with strengths shown in Table 6.1.

PIV based and below:

1. Bilateral authentication (hard token – PIV) – AUTHN Hard
2. Bilateral authentication (prior-issued soft token) in protected store – AUTHN Soft
3. User-asserted identity with OOB verification – OOB
4. User-asserted identity with OOB verification and with any biometric factor – OOB + Bio
5. User-asserted identity with OOB verification and with any biometric factor and with any non-biometric multi-factor verification – OOB + Bio + 1mf
6. User-asserted identity with OOB verification and with any non-biometric multi-factor verification – OOB + 1mf
7. User-asserted identity with OOB verification and with three non-biometric multi-factor verifications – OOB + 3mf

Enhanced Identity Assurance:

8. Hard token plus one non-biometric multi-factor verification – Hard token + 1mf
9. Hard token plus one biometric authentication – Hard token + 1bio
10. Hard token plus one biometric and one non-biometric multi-factor verification – Hard token + 1bio + 1mf

TABLE 6.1.
Multi-factor Authentication Identity Assurance

Method	Comment – Strength	ID Assurance
1. AUTHN Hard	Standard ELS – Strong	0.80
2. ATHN Soft	Closest to ELS	0.70
3. OOB	A Start – Minimal	0.25
4. OOB + Bio	Solid	0.50
5. OOB + Bio + 1mf	Strong	0.80
6. OOB + 1mf	Moderate	0.60
7. OOB + 3mf	Strong	0.70
Greater than Normal ID Assurance directed by Web Application		
8. Hard token +	Very Strong	0.85
9. Hard token ++	Very Strong	0.90
10. Hard token +++	Highest Value	0.95

6.3 IMPLEMENTING THE IDENTITY ASSURANCE REQUIREMENT

The data owner is responsible for registering their enterprise applications and services through an auto registration application (as shown in Section 3.3). This application provides the EAS attribute list, and the data owner defines ACRs as logical combinations of these attributes and other dynamic information, such as time of day. The ACR elements are checked against the attributes, and unattainable ACRs are rejected. The service and/or application details may be provided as documentation to an administrator for entry into the system. The optional specification of the required identity assurance is available here. The default for identity assurance is 0.80, which corresponds to the user having a PIV with a PKI certificate.

A PIV user may be redirected to the STS when the identity assurance requirement for the web application exceeds 0.80. The post will include the identity assurance value of the user (0.80), the identity assurance value sought, and the audience for the multi-factor authentication. The STS will use the user's PIV to authenticate, and the STS will try to increase the identity assurance to the level sought by the application using the methods shown in Table 6.1. It will return a simple "Accomplished" or "No-Go," which is posted back to the application.

6.4 ADDITIONAL REQUIREMENTS

From an ELS standpoint, accommodation of enhanced assurance adds the following requirements:

a. Data owners must specify the level of assurance on applications when specifying enhanced assurance requirements for access and privilege in the enterprise service registry.
b. The STS must be reconfigured to handle targeted multi-factor authentication and keep track of the identity assurance values.
c. The application must recognize and respond to the STS evaluation of identity assurance.

Additionally:

a. The derived process is not username/password – there are no accounts and no storage of user data.
b. As DN is in EAS, claims are computed for each DN in the enterprise stores as they are for enhanced assurance.
c. All of the ELS software and handlers work without modification.
d. The EAS has same attack surface as before.
e. Only covers person entities (not for NPEs – though an adaptation may be possible).
f. The current identity assurance process treats all biometric identifications the same. For future versions, we may wish to distinguish between the types of biometrics.
g. The current identity assurance process treats all multi-factor queries as the same. For future versions, we may wish to distinguish between the types of multi-factor queries.

6.5 ENHANCED ASSURANCE SUMMARY

We have reviewed the identity issues in a high-assurance security system when security requirements are enhanced. We have also described an approach that relies on high-assurance architectures and the protection elements they provide through PKI while accommodating the requirement for enhanced identity assurance. The basic approach becomes compromised when identity is not verified by a strong credential for unique identification (such as HOK in a PKI). The accommodation of non-PIV users is discussed in the next chapter.

7 Temporary Certificates

There is a need to allow users without PIVs some degree of access based on alternative authentication methods.

7.1 USERS THAT DO NOT HAVE A PIV

PIVs may not be available to all, or a user's device may not be capable of reading and using a PIV. Additional use cases include a lost PIV, waiting for issuance of a PIV, or a user being unable to get a PIV compatible with the ELS CA trust. Additionally, there are federation partners, contractors, and other vetted external individuals with short-term needs. The individual user must be entered into the enterprise system and must have an established DN and attribute data. Claims must be available in the claims store as computed based upon the DN and attributes.

> **PKI CERTIFICATES ARE REQUIRED FOR ELS**
>
> A user without a PIV must first establish identity and then be issued a certificate. The certificate is of short duration to allow the setup of one or two sessions with enterprise applications.

The creation of a non-PIV identity comprises three separate stages. The first stage is creation of a proposed identity. This value is provided by the user or is by assertion of the user. The goal is to correlate this with the enterprise files. It may be an email, a common name, or simply a name. The second stage is creation of a candidate identity (starting point for identity determination), in which the proposed identity is paired with an enterprise identity, and a DN is determined. As we will discuss, the process also takes steps to verify that the pairing between the proposed identity and the DN is owned by the individual making the request. The last stage is creation of the assured identity. The candidate identity becomes the assured identity when enough correlated information and personal verification about the candidate identity has a sufficient level of pairing with the enterprise identity that it can be trusted with access to an application using his/her claims that have been computed for his/her use. If this all sounds familiar, it is. The process for granting a temporary certificate is the same as the process for determining an assured identity for a PIV card holder. The difference between this and the assured identity of Chapter 6 is that the user still does not have a PKI certificate. In order to preserve the ELS paradigm, a temporary soft certificate needs to be provided, and the user claims must be provided with a SAML credential through TLS.

7.2 NON-PIV STS/CA-ISSUED CERTIFICATE

Non-PIV owners go to a special token server with certificate issuance authority (STS/CA) and provide a proposed identity. This may be email or full name, etc. The STS/CA calls a service that scans the EAS and rejects any identity that it cannot find in EAS. The STS/CA then confirms that the requester is not an automated system (via Captcha, etc.). This avoids a number of threat vulnerabilities. The STS/CA then asks questions of the non-PIV user to resolve ambiguity (if present). For example, there are five Jon Smiths in the enterprise, but only one works in Finance. The STS/CA then establishes the DN. To this point, the identity is still a proposed identity. The STS/CA saves the DN attributes in a separate temporary store and sets up a server-side TLS connection. The next step is a requirement: non-PIV users must maintain an OOB contact. One (or more) OOB contact is provided to the human resources for inclusion in the user's enterprise data. The token server resolves OOB (email, phone voice, phone text, etc.) communication methods for DN. We note that OOB means "not on the network," and if the enterprise desk phone is part of the enterprise network, it does not work as OOB. Anyone without at least one OOB contact is rejected.

At this point, the token server sends a one-time token (with a life of 10 minutes or less) to the OOB contact and requests input. No input or improper input will be rejected. A successful exchange results in the identity moving to a candidate identity.

The STS/CA will attempt to identify if the user is using a managed device by looking for bio capability such as face or fingerprints. The STS/CA retrieves the claims from the enterprise claims store for the established DN, presents a choice from among the services the user has claims to, and asks for a selection. This establishes the application for later SAML transmission. The STS/CA chooses the maximum and minimum identity assurance needed for claims. The minimum identity assurance may not be achievable with the device; in this case, a polite rejection is issued.

Otherwise, the token server begins a multi-factor verification, including biological verification, if applicable. Any multi-level failure leads to exit. If the multi-factor maximum achievable authentication for the identity assurance is successful, the identity becomes an assured identity. The STS/CA then creates and issues a temporary certificate in the name of the assured identity DN and separately sends this certificate and the private key to a specially configured application on the user's device for installation. Device Management and installation of approved software are covered in Chapter 18. The temporary certificate contains the identity assurance and has a life of 90 minutes or less. Comments in the temporary certificate specify the assurance level and the method for the application's use as appropriate. The temporary certificate may be reused for the life of the certificate to authenticate to any enterprise application or any STS for claims.

When the user selects an application, the token server posts a SAML through the browser to the application. The SAML is specifically for the audience (selected application). The temporary certificate is used for authentication to the application, and all else works as with normal ELS for an application. The interaction between the STS/CA and the attribute system is shown in Figure 7.1.

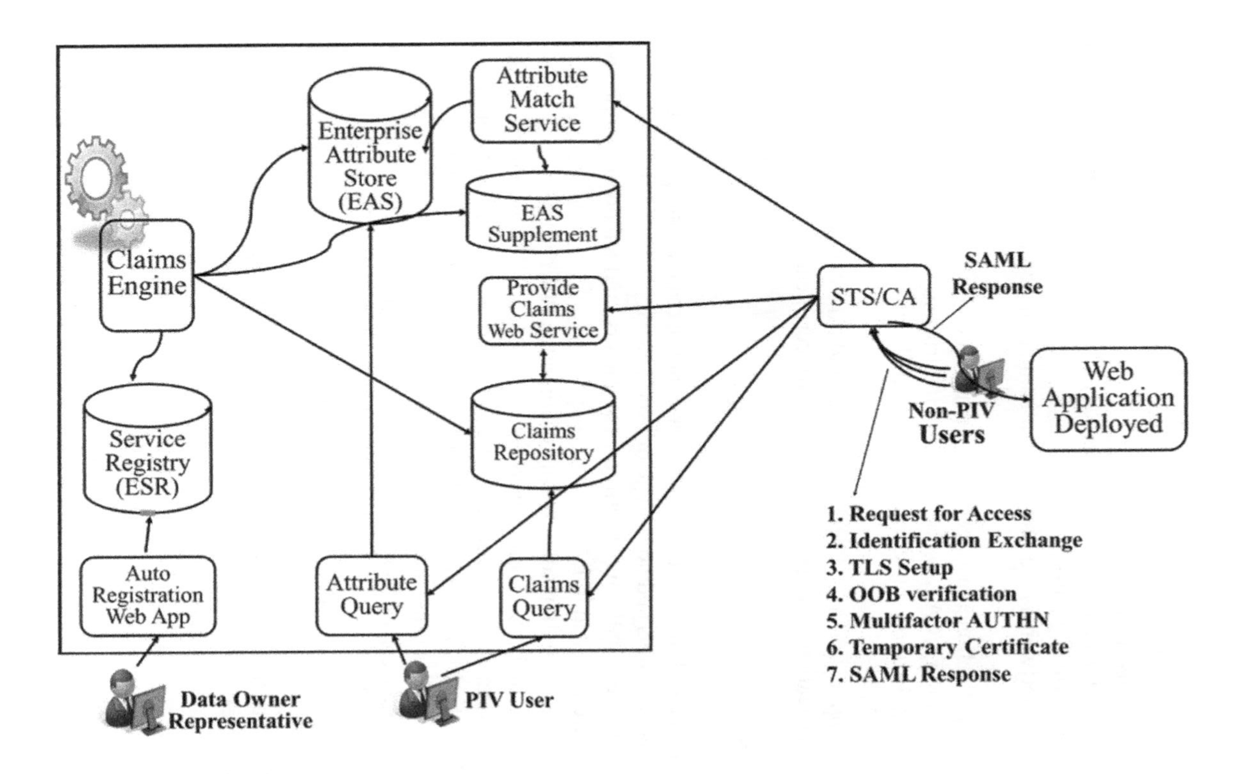

FIGURE 7.1. Partial EAE for Non-PIV Users

7.3 REQUIRED ADDITIONAL ELEMENTS

From an ELS standpoint, accommodation of non-PIV users adds the following requirements:

- STS/CA for non-PIV users must be developed.
- An additional service must be placed in the EAE for comparison of attributes in DN retrieval.
- STS/CA must have full crypto and key management capability (generating asymmetric key pairs).
- Device software is required to install temporary certificates on the end user device.
- The application must recognize temporary certificates generated by the STS/CA (STS/CA must be placed in the trust store).
- The application must recognize SAML certificates provided by the STS/CA.
- The application must check signatures and timestamp, but there is no need for revocation checking of the temporary certificate.

The new additions provide several advantages:

- The derived process in this chapter is not username and password – there are no accounts and no storage of user data.
- The process will handle retirees, contractors, and temporary employees if they are included in EAS.
- The process will handle missing or forgotten PIV cards.
- As DN is in EAS, claims are computed for each DN in the enterprise stores.
- Claims may be from delegation (recommend non-PIV cannot delegate).
- All of the ELS software and handlers work without modification.
- The EAS has same attack surface as before.
- Temporary certificates expire out of system quickly.

However, the following disadvantages are noted:

- Only covers person entities (not for NPEs – though an adaption may be possible).
- New vulnerabilities – software certificates are weaker than hardware certificates (short duration is a mitigation).
- Manipulation of identities is possible (OOB requires the threat to have an OOB device in EAS that is really not part of the network).
- The threat's ability to initiate exchange with STS/CA – because the STS/CA takes on all comers, reconnaissance by threat entities is facilitated.
- Intercept of temporary credentials (transmission in TLS provides some mitigation).
- On-device recovery of temporary credential (short duration provides mitigation).

- Credential forging (signatures and timeouts provide some mitigation).
- The current identity assurance process treats all biometric identifications the same. For future versions, we may wish to distinguish between the types of biometric.
- The current identity assurance process treats all multi-factor queries as the same. For future versions, we may wish to distinguish between the types of multi-factor queries.

7.4 PRECLUDING THE USE OF TEMPORARY CERTIFICATES

ELS is flexible in that it allows the data owner to make most of the authentication, access, and privilege decisions. Although temporary certificates can be a great aid in getting work done, certain applications and data may be sensitive enough to require a hard token (PIV) as part of the identification process. The data owner has two options for precluding the use of temporary certificates:

1. Removal of the STS/CA from the trust store. This will result in a failed authentication. This option may present some difficulty, as the enterprise may have a package of trusted CAs that are distributed to all of the servers and updated occasionally. Removal may create an ongoing maintenance process.
2. Specification of an identity assurance value of .85 or greater. This value is unreachable without a hard token (PIV or derived credential). Table 6.1 in Chapter 6 provides the data for how identity assurance values are computed. This also has the added benefit of invoking multi-factor authentication at the time of authentication. Temporary certificates will not have an identity assurance greater than .80.

7.5 TEMPORARY CERTIFICATE SUMMARY

We have reviewed a particular identity issue in a high-assurance security system when the user fails to meet the PIV requirement. The evaluation and issuance of a credential follows the same basic approach as the enhanced security requirements. We have also described an approach that relies on high-assurance architectures and the protection elements they provide through PKI while accommodating the requirement for some users who do not have PIV. The non-PIV user must be an exception to normal processing. Although it will be compatible with the ELS, it will quickly get bogged down in temporary certificates and accommodations for the user if it is overused. In fact, continual use of this approach may affect the measurement of user veracity as discussed in Chapter 9. The basic approach becomes compromised when identity is not verified by a strong credential for unique identification (such as HOK in a PKI). The accommodation of non-PIV users is discussed in the next chapter.

8 Derived Certificates on Mobile Devices

8.1 DERIVED CREDENTIALS

There are cases where primary credentials are not sufficient for some purpose. A common example is the use of a PIV with a smartphone or other mobile device. Although solutions for this issue exist, they are not practical for a large enterprise and defeat some of the usefulness of the device by requiring additional hardware. A derived credential may be a better option. Mobile devices that contain a PIV card reader will use that solution in lieu of a derived credential. Mobile devices that do not contain a PIV card reader must have derived credentials for each user of the device. Only one user with a derived credential may be logged into the device at a time.

A derived credential is a secondary credential that is issued based on the same vetting procedure as the primary credential. In this sense, the credential's authenticity is derived from the same source as the primary credential's authenticity. The derived credential may take a different form than the primary credential. For example, a derived credential may be a software certificate instead of a PIV. It is important to note that the derived and primary credentials are separate entities, differing in both physical form and logical content.

8.2 AUTHENTICATION WITH THE DERIVED CREDENTIAL

For authentication, the derived credential has the same DN, and it may have the same issuer. It has a different public key and may have a different private key; in addition, if it has the same issuer, it has a different serial number. This allows the authenticating entity to know which credential is being used to authenticate.

8.3 ENCRYPTION WITH THE DERIVED CREDENTIAL

For encryption, the derived credential has the same public key as the primary credential. This is because the public key is used for encryption, so the primary and secondary keys must be the same to allow seamless use of both for the same entity.

One possible exception to this rule is when a primary and all secondary credentials are issued at the same time with different public keys, but some credentials (e.g., the primary one) contain private keys associated with public keys from multiple certificates. This could provide a way to allow a user to decrypt all content if the CAC or PIV is available but only content specifically encrypted to a particular device when using that device. For example, an encrypted email that is particularly sensitive might be encrypted with the CAC or PIV public key to prevent potential disclosure through weaker phone-based security. Less sensitive emails could be encrypted with the phone key and also decrypted using the CAC or PIV on other devices.

8.4 SECURITY CONSIDERATIONS

As a general policy, derived credentials should be at least as secure as primary credentials. For example, a software certificate, which is less secure than a PIV certificate, would require additional protections, such as use on a device with MDM tied to the device's TPM [115] (see Chapter 18). The MDM would require a strong password for the device, isolation of applications, remote wipe capabilities for the private key and certificate, and possibly also location-specific rules, such as restrictions or wiping when outside specified locations. The primary credential is more efficient to use at enterprise scale, and the secondary is used only for specific purposes where the primary is not practical.

TRUSTED PLATFORM MODULE (TPM)

TPM (also known as ISO/IEC 11889 [115]) is an international standard for a secure cryptoprocessor, a dedicated microcontroller designed to secure hardware through integrated cryptographic keys.

8.5 CERTIFICATE MANAGEMENT

The derived certificate is tied to two other certificates, the primary certificate, from which it was derived, and the device certificate, the certificate of the device upon which the derived certificate resides. In certain instances, the devices may host more than one derived certificate. Revocation of a primary or derived credential may or may not require revocation of associated credentials. Primary and derived credentials may be revoked independently if they have different serial numbers and different key pairs. Key pairs should be developed in the HSM, and the public key is used for certificate issuance by the CA. This assures the privacy of the private key.

If a primary credential is revoked to prevent use of a lost credential, such as a lost or missing PIV, then the derived credentials need not be revoked or reissued. The protection provided by the PIV's PIN and physical measures may be enough that the risk of malicious use does not warrant the cost of reissuing all credentials. The same applies for a lost phone with derived credentials. Using a remote wipe capability and password protection on the phone may offer enough protection that the PIV is still acceptable for use.

If a credential is revoked due to problems associated with the owner of the credential or the security of the cryptography or keys, then the primary and derived credentials must be revoked together. A malicious user must be denied access to all credentials. A credential with cryptography or key problems creates a problem for any shared keys across credentials, such as decryption keys, so these must be reissued. As one credential must be reissued, it makes sense to simply reissue all credentials at that time. The device certificate will be revoked if the device has only one temporary credential, but it may be retained if the device has other temporary certificates for other users.

If a device credential is revoked for nefarious behavior or any other reason, the derived certificates on the device must be revoked. This includes any permanent wipe commands issued by the endpoint management service as described in Chapter 18.

Under high security conditions, any security problem with any credential may be deemed sufficient to warrant reissue of all credentials. For DIL environments or other conditions that make reissuing revoked credentials difficult or inordinately time-consuming, revocation may make certain required functionality difficult. A local solution can be arranged until connectivity and credential reissue is possible. This may involve delegation of claims, manual adjustment of the local claims store, or changes to application and service access policies.

9 Veracity and Counter Claims

9.1 THE INSIDER THREAT

> **COUNTER CLAIMS**
>
> A claim that rebuts or diminishes a previous claim. Often, the receiver of the claims and counter claims will adjudicate the result, including, among other things, the denial of access or the limiting of privilege.

Guidance and policies for insider threat are incomplete as of this time. Insiders may be loyal but careless members of the enterprise, or they may have malicious (nefarious) intentions. For the former, training and some limited mechanisms such as white or black listing are useful. Activity monitoring is primarily for forensics. The nefarious insider may know all of the monitoring and avoid it. Veracity (sometimes called reputation) can provide a measure of susceptibility to co-option or conversion. Due to a number of recent malicious insiders such as Edward Snowden [116], Bradley Manning [117], and others [118], each organization must assess its own insider threat situation. An insider threat is:

> a malicious threat to an organization that comes from people within the organization, such as employees, former employees, contractors or business associates, who have inside information concerning the organization's security practices, data and computer systems. [119]

The manifestation of the threat may come from any entity in the environment – person or non-person. The spate of insider activity has led to a U.S. executive order [120] that requires, in part, federal agencies and enterprises to:

> perform self-assessments of compliance with policies and standards issued pursuant to sections 3.3, 5.2, and 6.3 of this order, as well as other applicable policies and standards, the results of which shall be reported annually to the Senior Information Sharing and Safeguarding Steering Committee established in section 3 of this order.

These self-assessments must be included for ELS federal applications [7]. The requirement has led to the development of new products, an overwhelming volume of white papers and other research regarding assessment methods, and a number of patents pending [121–124]. All of this leads to a number of products offering to perform the analysis of entity veracity within the enterprise. A summary of these techniques (through 2011) is provided in [125]. The basic idea is to gather information concerning the trustworthiness of an entity in our system.

9.2 INTEGRITY, REPUTATION, AND VERACITY

Generally, the determination of trustworthiness of an individual is based upon an assessment of the integrity of that individual. One definition of integrity is given below:

> Integrity is the quality of being honest and having strong moral principles; moral uprightness. It is generally a personal choice to hold oneself to consistent moral and ethical standards. In ethics, integrity is regarded by many people as the honesty and truthfulness or accuracy of one's actions. [126]

Social media would define this as *reputation*, which is good because integrity is already overused in the IT literature. However, the literature defines reputation as a soft issue.

> Reputation is the estimation in which a person or thing is held, especially by the community or the public generally. [127]

Microsoft has refined reputation by adding trust:

> Reputation Trust represents a party's expectation that another party will behave as assumed, based upon past experience. Reputation Trust is bidirectional and can be split into Consumer Reputation Trust and Provider Reputation Trust. [128]

But trust is an overloaded term in IT and requires a great deal of context. The dictionary description of *veracity* comes closer to the target, and it is not used in any of the IT contexts associated with ELS:

> Veracity is the quality of being truthful or honest. [129]

From the IT standpoint, we have adopted the concept of veracity and tailored its definition to be more amenable to self-assessment in ELS environments:

> *Entity veracity* is the degree to which an entity is worthy of trust as demonstrated by resistance to or avoidance of factors that denigrate trust or compromise reliability. Positive factors may enhance veracity, and negative ones may reduce veracity. Veracity is based upon recognized accomplishments and failures, along with the associated stress factors or other trust debilitating factors present. A history of actions in difficult circumstances provides strong evidence for or against veracity.

The next step is to determine which of the factors need to be measured.

9.3 MEASURING VERACITY

Figure 9.1 shows the security issues associated with just the computation of an entity's trustworthiness. Integration with sources that are not vetted opens vulnerabilities not tolerated in a high-assurance environment such as ELS. The initial implementation will be done in isolation from the enterprise, and data will be ported

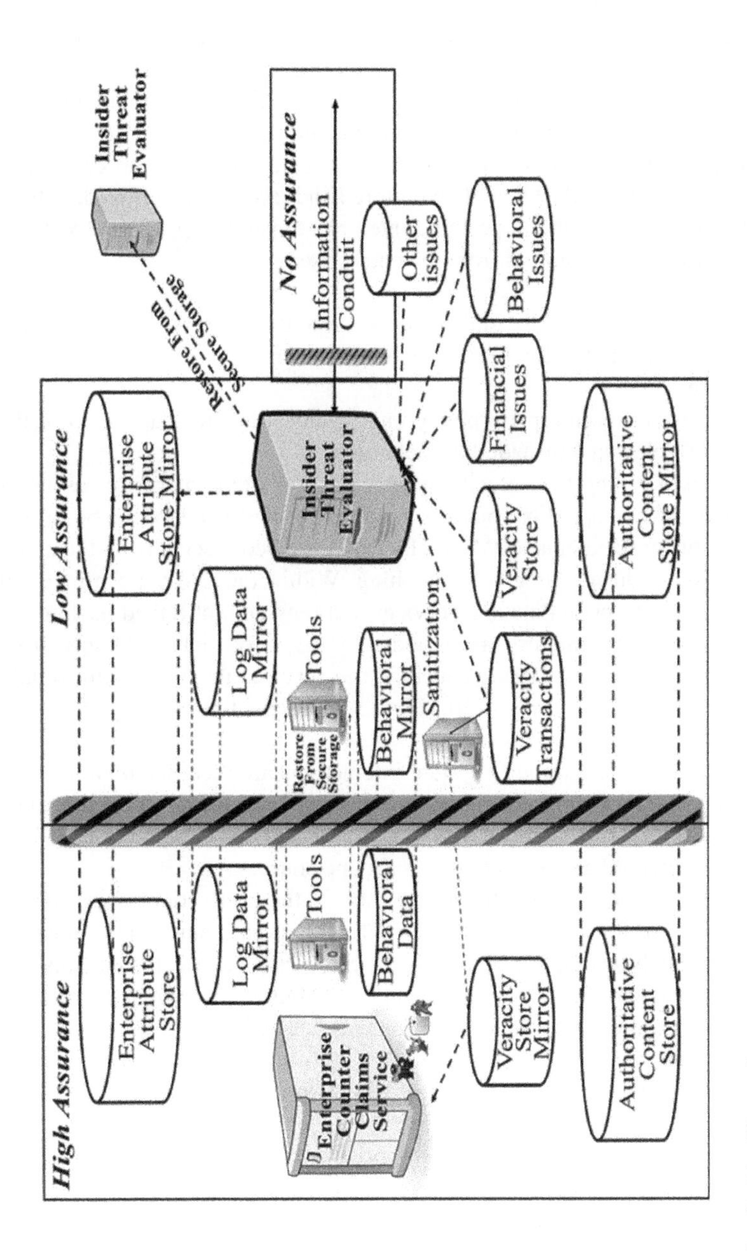

FIGURE 9.1. Insider Threat Setup

to the enterprise. The figure shows the desired ultimate architecture where the computation is isolated, and the enterprise may be provided a read-only interface of the results (which may initially be a mirror of the actual veracity store). Two additional concerns in the figure include a read-only interface from the computation environment to the Enterprise Attribute Store (which may initially be a mirror of the actual Enterprise Attribute Store) and a read-only interface from the computation environment to the enterprise support desk behavioral data (which may initially be a mirror of the actual enterprise support desk behavioral data).

Paranoia is warranted when dealing with unclean data, and the entire insider threat analysis system will be heavily monitored and frequently sanitized, with complete software re-installation at periodic intervals. Several steps should be taken to isolate the veracity computation from the enterprise.

- Openness. Let enterprise stakeholders know the process and effects that they will encounter for the protection of their data and your data and resources.
- Policy. Establish enterprise policy on veracity usage to shape each of the elements below and provide for openness.
- Isolation. Keeping the veracity system isolated from enterprise resources that may be corrupted or abused is paramount. This can be done by setting up a demilitarized zone (DMZ). The DMZ is disconnected from the enterprise except during times of refreshing. Within the DMZ are mirrors of necessary enterprise data and services, but they are not linked back to the enterprise. These mirrors are periodically (e.g., overnight) refreshed from enterprise resources. Less frequently, the services themselves are rebuilt from enterprise resources [130]. Figure 9.1 shows the initial setup of the Veracity System.
- Transactional. The veracity system interactions are recorded on a transactional basis and then executed against the DMZ databases. The online data may have a delay of notionally 24 hours to reflect these transactions [131].
- Analyze. Record and analyze the usage and sources.
- Cleaning and reviewing. During the refresh, the transactions are cleansed and reviewed for nefarious behavior. Those that pass muster are imported into the database that is accessed by the enterprise and executed against the enterprise databases. Those that do not pass muster result in an alert to the security personnel that the transaction was rejected [132].

The figure shows the requirements for the data mirroring:

- Relevant information from the Enterprise Attribute Store that is used for data correlation for each of the unique identities in the enterprise.
- Relevant log data from enterprise activities and veracity computations, which are used for both analysis and later forensics when required.
- Relevant behavioral data from activities within the enterprise to be included in the veracity analyses.
- The veracity store itself for use in the enterprise.

Data mirroring will occur on an exception basis and over a short period, such as every 24 hours, but it should be configurable across a wide range of activity.

Additionally, the analysis tools (including the Insider Threat Evaluator) need to be replicated in the veracity system, because it will be disconnected from the enterprise when computing veracity data. These tools include:

- Identity disambiguation – resolving names and other identity metrics when matches are less than perfect.
- Data correlation between current and old addresses and other confirming data.
- Information privacy elements (such as Social Security numbers, etc.) may be used for correlation, but they need to be marked for special access only and not included in normal reporting.

Software activity is monitored. Suspicious activities will lead to forensics, and the software will be modified to include mitigations and re-generated. However, new and unfamiliar intrusions and nefarious invasions may take some time to sort out.

All software in the veracity system is periodically refreshed from secure memory and reconfigured to avoid as-yet undetected threat activity. The periodicity of this refresh is configurable and may be more frequent during high-threat activity. The second fence (at the information conduit) will be activated during refresh, and the system will be disconnected from the information conduit. The figure also shows the denotation of assurance assigned to each zone. Data from the low assurance zone never leaves that zone with the exception of the sanitized transactional data that is used to update the enterprise veracity store mirror.

Figure 9.2 provides a brief depiction of the information conduit flow. The figure shows how information is imported from a variety of configured sources along the bottom of the conduit. These sources may change from time to time as more reliable or accurate sources are identified.

During normal operation, the system is disconnected from the enterprise and any changes to the veracity database are recorded as transactions. These transactions will be sanitized before updates are accepted on the next refresh cycle. Because the reliability and accuracy of data may be less than satisfactory in many instances, the top half of the information conduit is devoted to tools for correlation of data. In many open sources, correlation by name, residence, and other vital statistics are less than reliable, and veracity metrics must be at least reasonably verified. In many cases, the actions will be discussed, and issues clarified or removed when mistakes are made. Information not deemed unreliable, but not totally verified, will be discounted. This issue is further described under appropriate categories.

Figure 9.3 shows the notional system without the details of mirror and sanitization operations. The flows are only partially complete in that each piece of information obtained from the information sources on the lower side of the conduit must be subjected to the correlation activities on the upper half of the information conduit. Further, any information that makes a change in the veracity store will be recorded as a transaction for later sanitization. The enterprise veracity store will be updated only after sanitization.

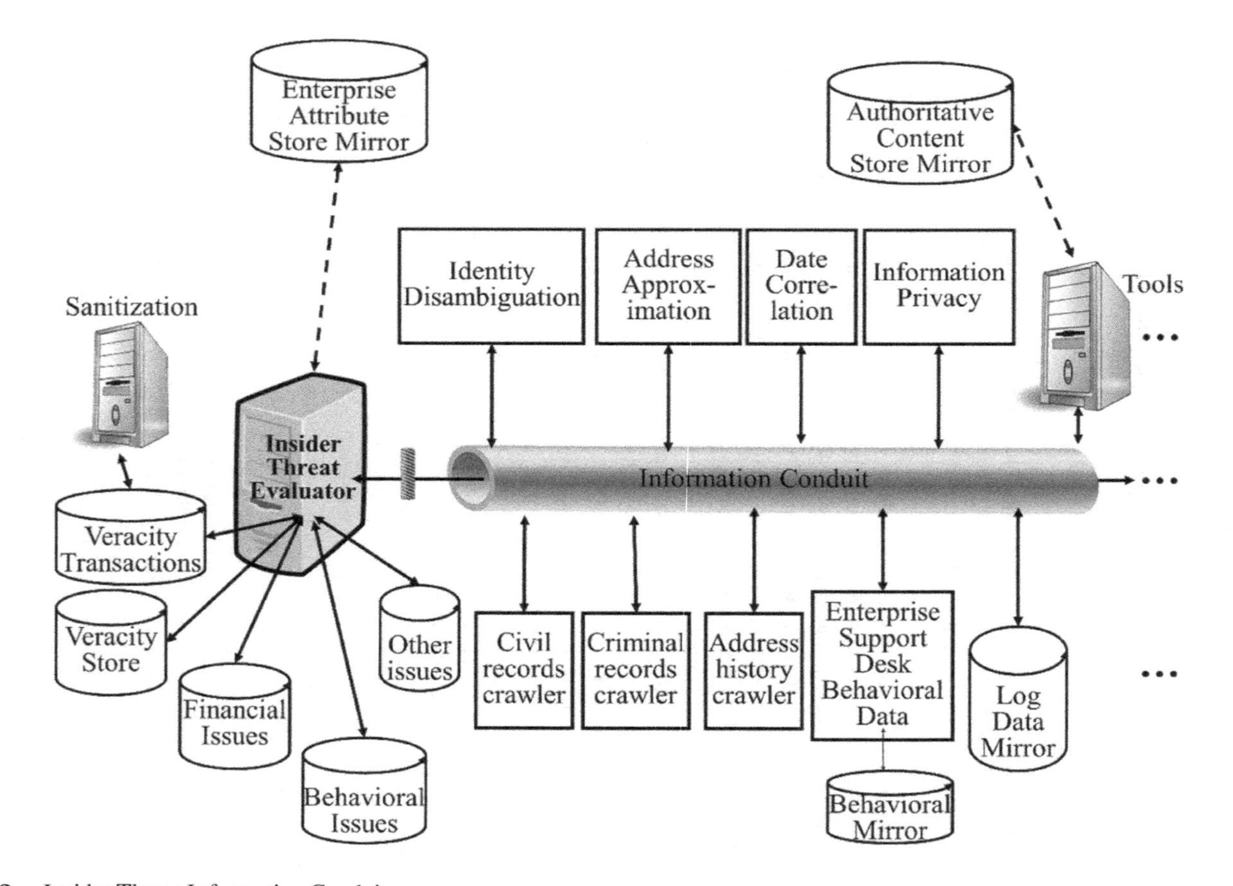

FIGURE 9.2. Insider Threat Information Conduit

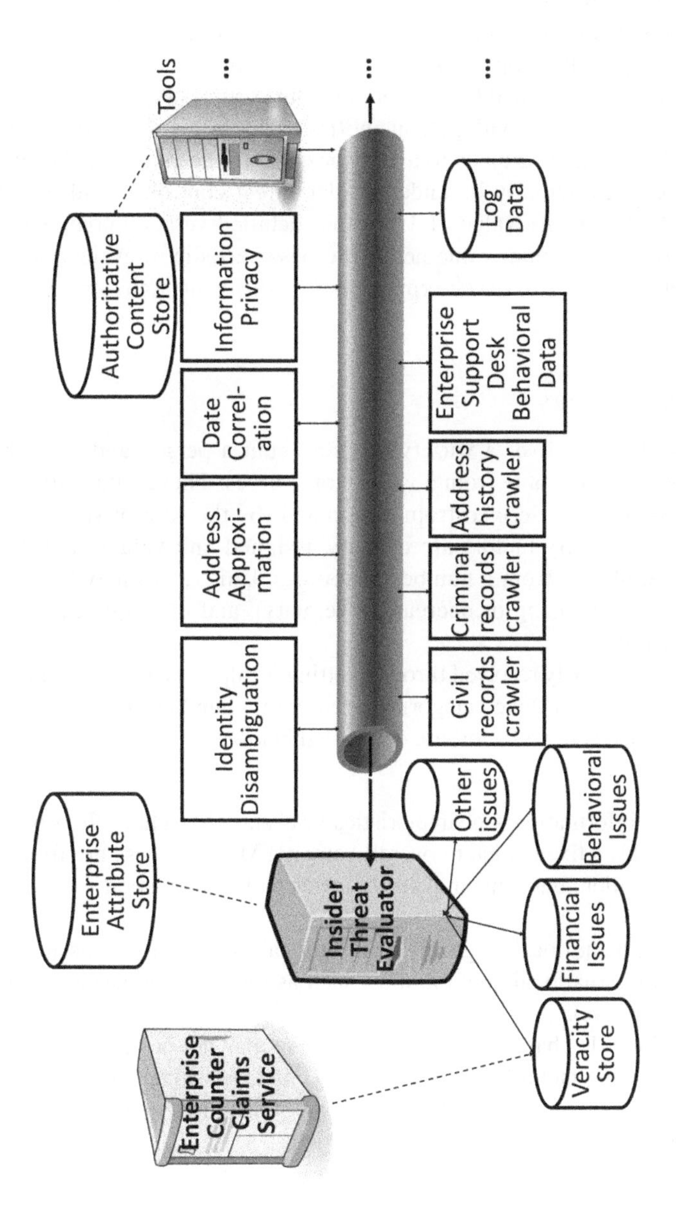

FIGURE 9.3. Insider Threat System

We have presented a form of self-assessment that evaluates veracity from the ELS application security model perspective rather than from the perspective of the product's baseline. This chapter also addresses the issues associated with the self-assessment, and it provides a framework and a process for using veracity information within the ELS application security model. To do this, we examine integrity, reputation, and veracity as they apply to the problem of the insider threat. A list of indicative events may be formulated by category and data sources [133–134].

We start categorization with person entities because this is required in the self-assessment, but veracity extends to all entities within the enterprise because non-person entities may actually be under insider threat control. For all entities, we assume a default veracity value of 1.0 before detailed veracity computations are made. This is the minimum value needed to pass periodic re-evaluations, so it is assumed that all entities in the enterprise possess this value unless veracity factors indicate otherwise.

9.3.1 Person Entities

Person entity factors cover a variety of data about a person and his behaviors, and these factors may come from a variety of sources. These data cannot be considered unless they are derived from designated (by the enterprise) authoritative sources. Entity veracity factors are initially assigned unit values, and these factors may be combined from a number of sources. Unit values may be positive or negative (either increasing or decreasing veracity), and they are later applied to veracity measures.

Any issues previously resolved through vetting or supervisor administrative judgment may be discarded. Five categories, each with a number of subcategories and with each instance being a factor, are delineated below:

Category 1

Community information – characteristics or events that add to the veracity of a person. Each adds a fixed value to overall veracity. Many of these are from sources requiring verification, but some may have sufficient documentation.

a. Ties within the local, regional, and national community. This may also apply to international communities, such as research and academic (positive or negative).
b. Recent job title change. Title changes per se may not be relevant, but they are a verifying factor for some of the other data (positive or negative).
c. Recent relevant awards or job punishments. These data should have records to support the event(s) (positive or negative).
d. Direct support or doubt from notable entities (trust transitivity). An example of this would be a trusted co-worker speaking highly or poorly about an individual. This trust transitivity should be verified wherever possible (positive or negative).

Category 2

Financial information. Degree of debt or other financial burdens since last vetting. These may be age- and source-sensitive, and they may also be attribution-sensitive, as discussed in the next section.

a. Issues with credit cards. Debt and delinquency in credit card accounts may indicate financial problems that would make an individual susceptible to corruption (negative).
b. Large number of credit reports. Usually these indicate shopping for loans even when debt may not reflect these activities (negative).
c. Recent suspicious loan activity. Inaccurate, exaggerated, or fraudulent loan applications (negative).
d. Sudden explained or unexplained wealth. Exceptions may be inheritance or legitimate investment windfalls (negative).
e. Debt exceeds ability to pay. This is a strong indicator of financial problems (negative).

Category 3

Legal issues or other stress factors. These may be age- and source-sensitive, and they may also be attribution-sensitive, as discussed in the next section.

a. Recent death in family. Even expected deaths may cause short-term stress (negative).
b. Poor job performance rating. This is never a good sign and has a direct impact on trust (negative).
c. Divorce. Family disharmony may cause a great deal of stress, dissatisfaction, or depression (negative).
d. DUI (driving under the influence). Issues with drugs and alcohol may be first indicated by a DUI event (negative).
e. Felony or misdemeanor charges. This directly affects the amount of trust one can place in an individual (negative).

Category 4

Discovered secrets. These may be age- and source-sensitive, and they may also be attribution-sensitive, as discussed in the next section.

a. Attempts to hide sexual issues. Sexual issues per se may not be an issue, but hiding these may be a source of blackmail by nefarious people trying to co-opt an individual's assistance (negative).
b. Uncovered alternate identities. Alternate identities are often used for nefarious activities (negative).
c. Residential ambiguity or multiple residences in a locale. These must be confirmed and a rationale established (negative).

Category 5

Unusual behaviors. These will generally be from the Enterprise Support Desk Records and may be considered authoritative.

a. Non-cleared travel. Individuals with clearances are expected to report foreign travel. Lack of this reporting may indicate nefarious activities (negative).
b. Unusual and unexplained IT usage (negative):
   i. Unusual downloads (negative),
   ii. Unusual hours of usage (negative),
   iii. Many applications open at the same time (negative);
   iv. Logging into more than one computer at the same time, or use of multiple accounts on the same computer (negative).
c. Sharing of credentials. This is especially worrisome in the ELS application security model, where unique identification of individuals and full accountability for action are requirements (negative).
d. Frequent use of backup methods. Backups indicate a fear of IT corruption or collapse, or they may just be prudent computing usage (negative).
e. Unusual delegations. This is especially worrisome in the ELS application security model, in which several forms of formal delegation are available to maintain identity and full accountability for action (negative).
f. Extended online absence followed by high activity (not counting the occasional extended vacation or other rationally explained activity) (negative).
g. Unusual hours or time online (different from the pattern recorded for that individual). Each person has developed work habits and, if they are effective, this should not create a problem. However, switching to late hours suddenly may be an indicator (negative).

9.3.2 Non-Person Entities

These factors will generally be from the Enterprise Support Desk Records and may be considered authoritative. All are negative.

9.3.2.1 Non-Person Veracity

Category 6

a. Recent attacks. These are considered unless forensics has found the vulnerability, the data owner has closed the vulnerability, and there has been a complete teardown and rebuild since the attacks.
b. Recognized misuse of privilege. Machine-to-machine privilege is often identity based and not carefully monitored. Moving data to other machines and/or acting as a third-party proxy are examples of privilege abuse. This may be documented through the enterprise support desk analysis of monitoring data.

c. The host server is physically moved outside (or into) a protected area without a change in enterprise registration. All enterprise assets are registered, and the registration must be updated when any changes occur. These situations are difficult to identify and problematic.
d. Call-out to unknown URLs. This is a known sign of exploitation, and unless the device is being used in counter-cybersecurity, it should be considered for a complete teardown and rebuild.
e. Missing log records. This is a clear sign of nefarious activity or sloppy configuration control.
f. Lenient access and privilege requirements. Privileges granted to the device may be greater than needed. This situation may lead to item (b) above.
g. Available software interfaces that are not authorized. One clear step with the ELS application security model is to close all interfaces not being used and remove the software behind those interfaces where possible.
h. Non-uniform identity requirements on interfaces. All interfaces in use should have the same identity assurance requirements or at least the same identity assurance levels.
i. Missing current authorized patches. For example, Industrial Control Systems (ICS) not being patched until they have to be taken offline. This practice can perpetuate vulnerabilities and invite nefarious activity.

9.4 CREATING A MODEL AND COUNTER CLAIMS

A simplified model is developed as a start. While weightings may be applied to the various values of data and information veracity factors, it is best to await some actual experience with the representation before beginning that modification. In the previous section, we delineated five basic categories of veracity for person users and a single category for non-person users for evaluation, subject to data sources and correlation. Accordingly, veracity is described as an *n*-tuple shown below:

9.4.1 For Persons

$$\text{Veracity} = \big(\text{Community} = V_1, \text{Financial} = V_2, \text{Legal} = V_3, \\ \text{Discovered Secrets} = V_4, \text{and Behavior} = V_5\big) \quad \text{(Eq. 1)}$$

9.4.2 For Non-Persons

$$\text{Veracity} = V_6 \quad \text{(Eq. 2)}$$

9.4.3 Computing Veracities

Further, each value, V_i, has a default value of 1.0, which is appreciated by ΔV for each of the unique factors in each category. For example, using category 1:

$$(\Delta V_i)_k = (\pm 0.1) \times \text{source factor 1} \times \text{source factor 2} \quad \text{(Eq. 3)}$$

This applies for every unique occurrence, k, of a factor in paragraph marked category 1.

The default value of 1.0 is reduced by ΔV for each of the unique factors in categories 2–6 where applicable.

$$(\Delta V_i)_k = (\pm 0.1) \times \text{source factor } 1 \times \text{source factor } 2 \quad \text{(Eq. 4)}$$

Where $i = 2\text{–}6$ for every unique occurrence, k, of each subcategory in categories 2–6.

Source factor 1 is 0.5 for publicly derived data and 0.25 for publicly derived data without source citation or date of item. Source factor 1 is 1.0 for authoritative source data. Source factor 2 is 0.5 where attribution is approximate and 1.0 where attribution is certain.

$$V_i = 1.0 + \sum_k (\Delta V_i)_k \quad \text{(Eq. 5)}$$

Counter claims will be provided when requested by the data owner in the registration of his/her service. The counter claims will be given as a vector of values:

$$\text{Counter claim for a person} = (V_1, V_2, V_3, V_4, V_5, \text{none}) \quad \text{(Eq. 6)}$$

$$\text{Counter claim for a non-person} = (\text{none, none, none, none, none}, V_6) \quad \text{(Eq. 7)}$$

Supervisors and data owners will have claims for access to component data from the insider threat server for subordinates (in the case of supervisors) and for application and service users (in the case of data owners). Issues may be marked as resolved at the supervisor's discretion (subject to attribution and logging). For example, the supervisor may mark some issues resolved at periodic vetting.

Actions possible:

1. Threshold for denial of access to resources. (Not recommended.)
2. Threshold for notification to supervisors and data owners. (Recommended.)
3. Reduce privilege. (Not recommended.) This may affect performance reviews and cause the value of veracity to spiral downward.
4. Upon notification, set up a counseling session with the individual or the owner of the asset to review the issues and seek corrections. (Recommended.)
5. After review, the data may be manually reset, if desirable, by providing rationale and obtaining appropriate authority.

In all cases, when requested by the data owner, the counter claim will be passed in the SAML.

9.5 VERACITY AND COUNTER CLAIMS SUMMARY

The formulation of entity veracity provides a method to monitor insider threats. Certain findings are appropriate at this point:

1. For persons, the data associated with information generated prior to the last formal vetting of the person may be marked as resolved at the supervisor's discretion.
2. For persons, automated responses are not warranted at this time.
3. For persons, manual resolutions of unfavorable veracities should be implemented at this time.
4. For non-persons, automated responses may be appropriate.
5. Thresholds and responses should be worked out over time with experience.
6. Self-assessment – data as required by executive order 13587 should be summarized and reported.

The unique security issues are discussed in Section 9.1 of this chapter, and the ethical and legal issues are discussed in Section 9.3. The veracity measures can provide a management view into the insider threat and can be used to satisfy the requirement for self-assessment.

10 Delegation of Access and Privilege

10.1 ACCESS AND PRIVILEGE

Information security systems must strike a balance between simplicity and capability. Simple systems are quick, easy, inexpensive, and understandable. Complexity is the enemy of security, as it often hides vulnerabilities. However, the simplest systems do not allow accurate representations of an organization's security policies. Policies can be complicated, and the security system must embody these complications to enable such rules to be implemented. The result is that security systems capture the majority of common cases and add additional functionality where there is sufficient demand. Organizations reshape their policy to fit within the security system's capabilities and limitations. For a large organization, the limitations are more severe because uncommon situations arise regularly due to the number of people, resources, and services involved, and it is harder to set rules due to the increased complexity of the organization.

Delegation is a solution that allows temporary assignments of access and privilege. It allows the core security rules to be simple and consistent by allowing the complicated, uncommon, and unforeseen situations to be handled locally through delegation authorized by the data owner. This delegation is integrated into the overall security framework to ensure security properties are preserved.

Delegation has been treated as a policy problem [135– 137], an aspect of access control [137, 138], a role definition issue [139–148], a workflow issue [149, 150], and an authorization issue [151, 152]; there are some hybrid approaches that combine these processes [153–156]. We have been unable to find an approach that treats the problem as an identity issue. In this chapter, we treat the problem of delegation as an authorized identity issue. We discuss this in the context of the ELS system and describe methods to enable secure delegation within this framework.

10.2 DELEGATION PRINCIPLES

Before discussing delegation implementation details for ELS, we describe the idea of delegation and the goals that we are trying to accomplish.

Applications and services within an enterprise provide access and privilege to entities based on logical rules that combine user attributes and other external factors. These rules are chosen by the owners of data, applications, and services. In an ideal world, the rules would be set so that all authorized entities receive access and all unauthorized entities receive no access, as shown in Figure 10.1.

However, setting these rules can be difficult, especially when the available attributes do not match the information needed to determine access. Often, the best fit

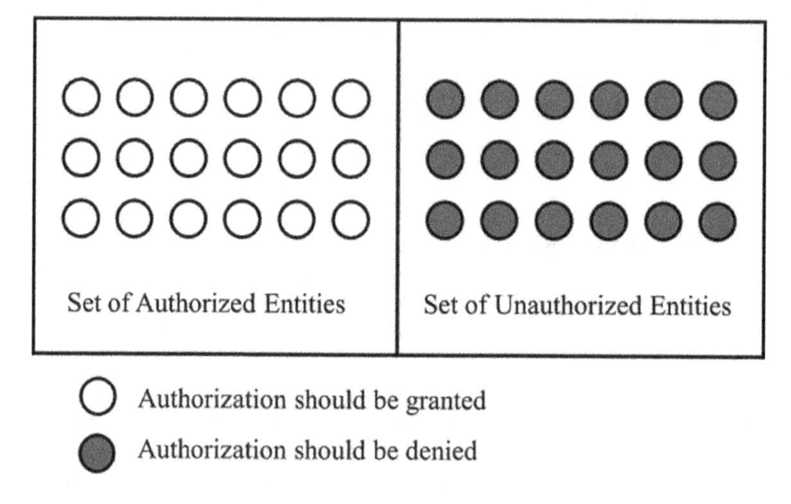

FIGURE 10.1. Ideal Access Control Policy

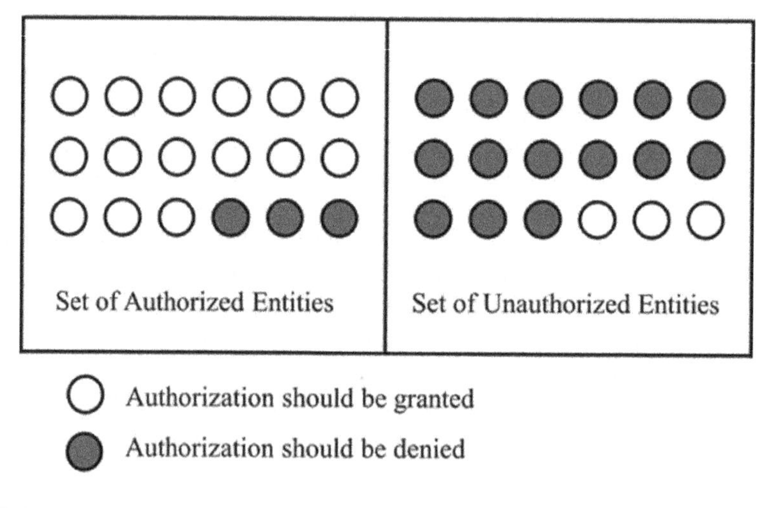

FIGURE 10.2. Best Effort Access Control Policy

allows access to some unauthorized entities and blocks access to some authorized entities, as shown in Figure 10.2.

To provide access to all authorized entities, it is possible to make the access rules more permissive, but this allows even more unauthorized entities to have access, as shown in Figure 10.3.

For high security situations, the opposite approach is more appropriate, in which restrictive access rules block unauthorized entities but also block some authorized entities, as shown in Figure 10.4.

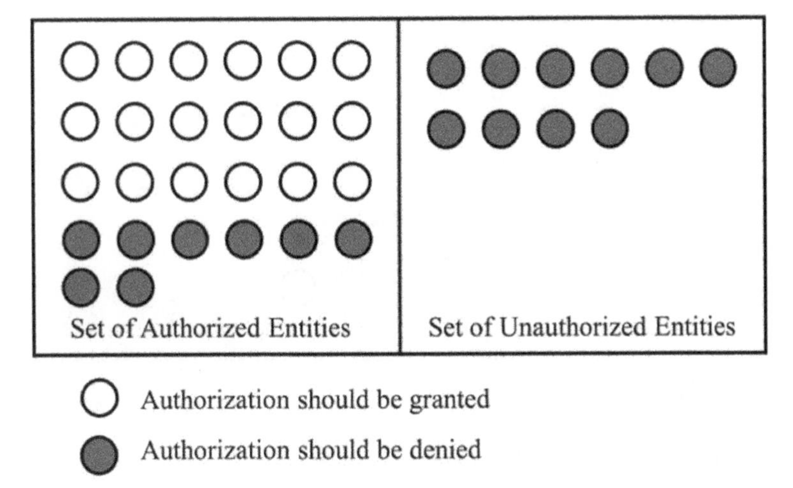

FIGURE 10.3. Permissive Access Control Policy

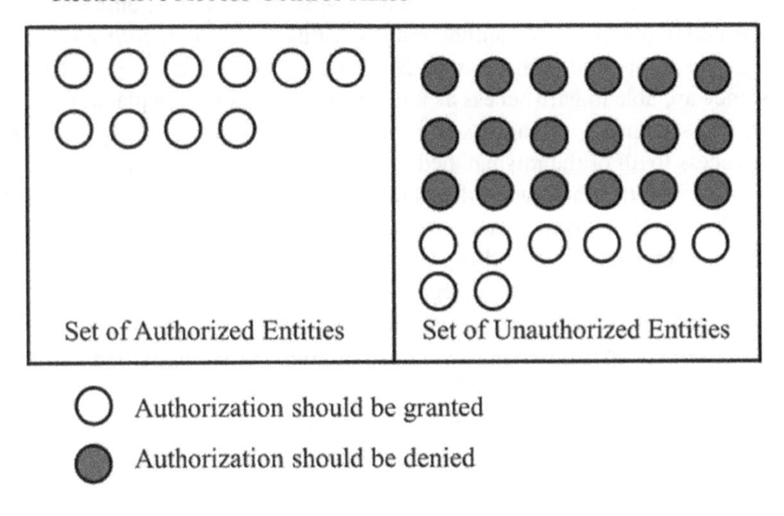

FIGURE 10.4. Restrictive Access Control Policy

The permissive and high-security options are just the endpoints of a spectrum, where a proper balance must be struck between allowing non-authorized entities and blocking authorized entities. However, it is clear that none of the points on this spectrum achieves the desired outcome of allowing all authorized entities and blocking all unauthorized entities. This is where delegation comes in.

With delegation, we can start with the restrictive rules to block all unauthorized entities. Then, we delegate access to any authorized entities that were blocked by the restrictive rules, as shown in Figure 10.5. It is possible for any entity with access to

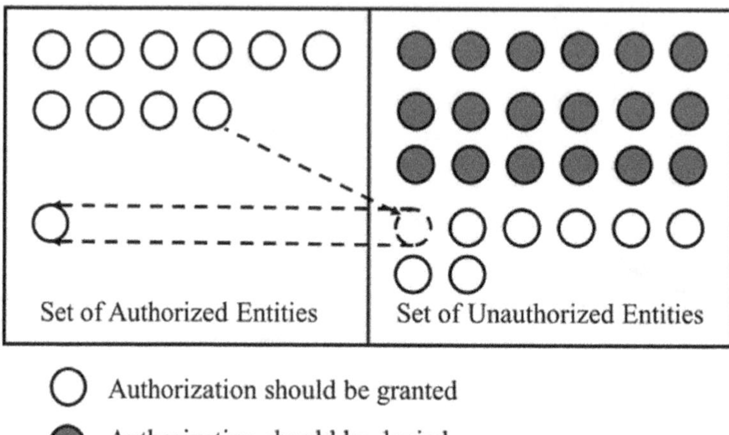

FIGURE 10.5. Restrictive Access Control Policy with Delegation

delegate this access to any entity without access. In this case, one entity with access has delegated that access to an authorized entity that does not otherwise have access. Although the authorized entity in the "No Access" box still does not natively have access, they are able to gain access as long as the delegation is in place. With proper delegation assignments, the access can match the ideal case in Figure 10.1 by delegating access to all of the mismatched individuals.

In some cases, the data owner delegates access and rights. Recognizing that certain people should be given access, the data owner can provide delegated claims to them. In other cases, people working with the data are provided the authority to delegate by the data owner and can delegate to others who they trust to do their duties. Typically, claims are delegated to subordinates by their superiors, but claims can also be delegated to peers in working groups or other temporary collaborations. The core requirement for delegation is that the person doing the delegation has an access claim and permission from the data owner to delegate. No escalation of privilege is allowed through delegation. Only the transfer of existing access claims from one individual to another is allowed.

An individual who has a claim and delegation authority may delegate the claim in accordance with policy. In general, someone who has a claim by virtue of their attributes and delegation authority may delegate that claim. However, someone with a delegated claim may or may not be able to re-delegate that claim. These rules are established by the data owner who defines the access and delegation rules and associated claims.

Another decision by the data owner is whether a person may combine delegated claims with their own claims or combine multiple delegated claims from different sources. The most restrictive solution is to prevent any such combination of claims. However, certain tasks might require a combination of rights. For example, if someone already has a high degree of access and only requires a small additional delegation, the combination would be required, because the small delegation would not allow the full set of operations. However, in other cases, allowing combinations could lead to unanticipated access due to the distributed nature of delegation and access. ELS logs all of these and the Enterprise Support Desk analyzes these logs for nefarious behaviors.

The applications use individual claims or combinations of claims, depending on their internal functions. Some may provide generic services with no refinement, and a single-claim model would work well. Delegating this claim provides access. Other applications may rely on personal or professional information in combination with one or more claims, so simply delegating a claim provides insufficient access and privilege to allow another person to do their assigned tasks. There are also more complex approaches; for example, an application may allow combinations only if both users are from the same group or only if the recipient is subordinate to the delegator. The best approach is the simplest one, which would be a single-claim approach. However, when the application is complicated, it may be necessary to match this complexity with the appropriate rules for combining claims at the application.

One important policy issue to resolve is whether a person should be able to re-delegate a delegated claim. Another is whether a delegator should be able to prevent re-delegation of a claim that they delegate. The question is really how to divide the delegation policy rules among the stakeholders (enterprise, the data owner, the claims owner, and the person with a delegated claim). Each of them has a say in what should and should not be allowed for further delegations. The enterprise needs rules to ensure ELS security properties can be maintained. The data owner must ensure that the proper people receive access. The claims owner and delegated claims owner may have responsibilities and accountability for any further delegation of claims to other individuals.

There is a simple starting point for a solution: anyone with a claim and authorization to delegate may delegate that claim. The delegator sets the rules for further delegation. They may choose to prevent delegation, restrict it to one or more individuals, or restrict further delegation beyond some number of re-delegations. In addition, they may request notification or approval authority for further delegations.

It is possible to assign claims only to people who do not actually use them. The intention is that these people supervise the work associated with these claims and are responsible for determining the people who use them. For example, a manager may be assigned claims, but seldom access the application. Thus, they would delegate their claims to the specialists who actually know how to do the work. The specialists then use their delegated claims to access the application. This use case demonstrates some of the flexibility that delegation allows within an enterprise for assigning access.

An interesting set of questions arises from this, as delegation is itself a service with its own set of claims:

1. Who can access the delegation service?
2. Can access to the delegation service itself be delegated?
3. If so, by whom?

For the first question, the enterprise limits delegation services to entities within the enterprise, even if claims owners wish to allow delegation to individuals outside of the enterprise. The claim owner can bring the individuals into the enterprise or establish a federation agreement to provide them access. Federation agreements are specifically designed to allow non-enterprise partners access to enterprise resources. The details of that access are in the federation agreement [135].

Another important policy issue is how to revoke delegated claims. If Alice delegates claim C to Bob, and then Alice moves offices and loses claim C as a result, what happens to Bob's delegated claim? The desired outcome is that Bob loses the delegated claim, but it is generally a good policy to provide a short, configurable grace period (e.g., seven days) to allow operations to continue unimpeded. This also prevents intermittent losses of Alice's access from revoking the delegation structures in place during the grace period. The delegation would remain in place, but it would be marked as expired or otherwise inactive. Reactivation of Alice's access would restore the active delegation of claim C to Bob and reset the grace period.

Losing a claim due to security problems, such as certificate revocation or forceful removal from the enterprise, requires immediate revocation of all associated identity claims and delegations. This prevents a malicious insider from using delegation to extend access to other identities that they may also control or influence. Normal changes of attributes would allow the grace period. Revocation with security causes or implications would cause immediate revocation of identity certificates, all claims, and all delegated claims, including re-delegations of such claims.

Delegation is not intended to be a permanent solution for enterprise access. Delegation is a way to fix policy issues that the system does not adequately handle while preserving accountability, proper authentication, and authorization. A large number of delegations is a sign that the ACRs or the information they are based on needs refinement. Fixes could include attribute additions to enable more precise access rules or redefinition of ACRs to better capture the intended users.

In some cases, delegation can be used as a more permanent solution even when individual delegations are not permanent, such as assigning roles to subordinates for which position descriptions do not exist within the attribute store. This provides the manager the flexibility to reorganize his subordinates dynamically without having to update the Enterprise Attribute Store. Assuming these changes occur frequently, delegation is a reasonable solution. Assignments for longer-term positions and roles should be included in the attribute store and used directly for access. Delegation is useful when the position itself is temporary, such as with frequent internal reorganizations or temporary working groups.

If delegation is monitored properly, the anticipated usage would be short-term delegations that come and go dynamically. Any delegations that persist for longer periods or are renewed past their expiration repeatedly should be examined to see if a longer-term enterprise solution is available. Delegation, if implemented properly, can offer security levels comparable to normal ELS, because all access and privilege can be monitored with accountability. However, due to the manual processes involved in assigning delegation for short time periods, it is not scalable. For this reason, it is not intended as an enterprise solution, but instead as a local mechanism that preserves the enterprise-wide ELS properties.

10.3 ELS DELEGATION

This section discusses the implementation of delegation within ELS.

10.3.1 Standard ELS Delegation

Standard ELS delegation covers delegation from one member with delegation authority within an ELS enclave to another member within the same ELS enclave. Delegation is an operational solution to poorly defined access and privilege requirements, and it is not meant to replace the more formal definition of access and privilege requirements. Choices are to be made carefully, and it is possible to delegate access and privilege to someone who should not have that access and privilege. Both entities are known and already have the ability to receive a SAML assertion with access claims from an STS. The only change is adding the additional delegated claims to the claims store under the DN of the individual receiving the delegation (the delegatee) for retrieval and insertion into the SAML assertion. Claims have two types: discretionary and mandatory. Discretionary claims include permissions such as access to a service and the ability to copy or modify data, and such claims can be delegated. Mandatory claims belong to the specific DN making a claim. Mandatory claims include clearances, time with the enterprise, non-probationary status, and veracity measures described in Chapter 9. These mandatory claims belong to the delegatee and may not be delegated. Lack of any mandatory claims needed for access could cause a delegation to fail. Other delegation models are derived from this model, and their purpose is to provide delegation options when some of the security services of ELS are not available.

DELEGATION AND ATTRIBUTION

All entities in ELS act on their own behalf. Exercise of a delegated access or privilege is done under the DN of the delegate. Delegation assigns discretionary access and privilege to the delegate if he/she has the mandatory requirements such as rank, clearance, or date of birth. None of the latter can be delegated.

For Alice to delegate claim C to Bob, Alice must be in the EAS, Alice must have claim C, claim C must be delegable, Alice must have delegation authority, and Bob must be listed in the EAS. After accessing the delegation service using her delegation authority, Alice selects claim C from among those available to be delegated. Claims that may not be delegated are either omitted from this list or are included but inactive (e.g., grayed out and not selectable from a list). After selecting claim C, Alice selects Bob as the recipient of the delegated claim. The recipient's DN may be entered manually or selected from a pre-populated list. The list method requires an accurate and current list of all enterprise individuals and a way to effectively search through them for a desired delegation recipient. Such assignments are guaranteed to map to a valid DN, because they are not subject to typing errors. A hybrid approach is also possible, where typing characters in the DN searches and displays matching entities, which may then be selected by clicking.

In general, an individual can delegate to any other individual in the enterprise. The list of claims is in the claims store. The list of entities in the enterprise is in the attribute store. Both are within the EAS. However, there are some detailed issues to consider when using EAS information.

A newly minted identity credential with no associated attributes will not necessarily appear in the EAS internal stores. The EAS is based on identities in attribute stores, and with no attributes for an identity, the identity will not exist in any stores, so the EAS will not know it. A simple solution is to make the list of identities one of the attribute stores, with some token attribute like "enterprise entity" associated with it.

Another question is whether we create an identity list from the EAS or the claims store. Do we store entities without claims in the claims store (e.g., new entities without attributes assigned)? The secure solution is to pull identities from the claims store, because we do not want extra services touching the more sensitive attribute store. In addition to a default "enterprise entity" attribute, we create a default "enterprise entity" claim that is computed for all entities from the "enterprise entity" attribute. This pre-populates both the attribute store and claims store with new identities and allows immediate delegation to these entities. This may be important for new hires, where it is necessary to delegate claims immediately before all the paperwork and official attributes are populated in the attribute stores.

The delegating entity sets certain rules associated with the delegation. These rules are constrained by the delegation rules established at registration of the claim by the resource owner. All claims are also subject to delegation rules established at the enterprise level. Some of the delegation rules pertain to the following:

- Can the entity receiving the delegated claim delegate the claim further? If so, within what limits? How many layers of delegation? How many total delegates are allowed?
- What is the time limit for the delegation?
- Which associated attributes may be passed with the claim to provide privilege in addition to access? In general, attributes are more sensitive than claims, as attributes may contain personal information, whereas claims roll attributes up into a token that only represents satisfaction of an access rule. For this reason, a delegator may wish to restrict which personal attributes can be delegated for fine-grained privileges. Some attributes, such as possession of a security clearance, may not be delegated and must be restricted by the enterprise.
- Can this delegated claim be combined with other native or delegated claims?

All delegations expire within a moderate time period (e.g., 30 days). The enterprise sets an upper bound for delegations, and the data owner may further restrict this time limit. The delegator then sets the delegation period within the data owner's limits. In some circumstances, such as an extended absence due to illness, it may be necessary to set up an extended delegation. Such delegations may be allowed on a case-by-case basis with special approval. Other extended delegations may be set up by superiors to assign responsibilities to their subordinates. Such delegations may be set up for extended periods of time by simply refreshing existing delegations before they expire or reactivating expired delegations during their grace period.

When a delegator's claim goes away, so do all delegations made by that entity. For a normal loss of a claim due to business operations (e.g., position change), there is a grace period (e.g., 7 days) during which otherwise valid claims remain accessible. After this grace period expires, the delegation ends. Upon security-relevant revocation of claims to an entity (e.g., malicious insider detected), all delegations by that user are terminated immediately. Any further delegations are also terminated immediately. Any access that relies in any way on the terminated entity's action is revoked. This prevents potentially malicious actors from having any lasting influence on internal access controls after they leave the enterprise.

Notification is sent to delegators when their delegates re-delegate claims. This is because the original delegator is providing access that is not otherwise allowed and is held accountable for all access delegated to others, directly or indirectly. The original delegator can decide whether they are simply notified or whether they must also approve such further delegations. The notification method can be chosen by the delegator (e.g., email notification or notification upon accessing the delegation service).

Figure 10.6 shows the delegation service location within the EAE. It interacts with the user, the management interface, and the claims exposure and editor service. Normal users have an interface to the delegation service to manage their personal delegations. Delegation administrators have a separate interface that allows them to define enterprise rules for delegation, view enterprise-wide delegation information, and examine logs and other records relating to delegation activity. The delegation service writes new delegated claims to the claims store through the claims exposure and editor service. It also pulls user information from the Claims Repository through this service. Delegation-specific information, such as which claims are delegable, may be included in the Claims Repository as well, so that the delegation service is simply an interface to information in the existing stores. The claims exposure and editor service protects access to the claims store. The delegation service is externally accessible and subject to compromise. The claims exposure and editor service is internal and less subject to compromise, which helps to protect the integrity of the claims store.

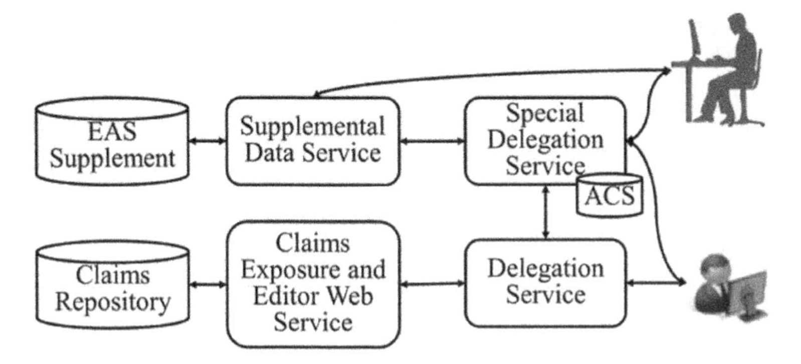

FIGURE 10.6. Delegation Services within the EAE

10.3.2 ID-Based Special Delegation

ID-based special delegation is applicable when only the delegate's ID is available and trusted, and no attributes or other information is available. This is the case for external entities that are not part of the enterprise and do not have authoritative credentials or other information in the EAS attribute stores. For this type of delegation, an ACS is established outside the EAS with the credentials of the external entities. It may also contain appropriate attributes as relevant for delegation. The external nature of the ACS allows simple and immediate revocation for all special delegations, should the need arise. All such ID-based access information must be imported into the ACS prior to delegation.

Because such IDs are not in the EAS, it may be difficult to find non-enterprise identities. The simple but error-prone method of typing a DN into the delegation service is one method. Another solution is to import a list of non-enterprise identities and have the delegation service select from this list (e.g., choose "non-enterprise" and then choose the right DN from the resulting list). One problem with this method is that the list must anticipate everyone and must be updated when new members are added. The best solution is probably a combination of both: provide a searchable list of known external IDs and keep a separate cache of manually entered DNs. This prevents repeated entry of the same DN.

The ability to create a special delegation is not available to all enterprise users as "normal" delegation is. This assignment has inherent risks that normal delegation does not, and the enterprise may restrict this access to help mitigate these risks. Re-delegation of special delegation is disabled by default, but this can be enabled if the data owner and delegator agree it is needed.

As before, there is a question about how to assign the claim for assigning special delegation claims at the enterprise level, and whether the special delegation claim itself can be delegated or special-delegated. These questions are important to answer correctly because they affect the access rules and methods across the enterprise. Such central components require special consideration or explicit ID-based access controls as a bootstrapping method for the rest of the enterprise.

10.4 DELEGATION SUMMARY

Delegation provides a formal, technical means with strong accountability to allow entities to share their access and privileges with others inside or outside of the enterprise. It is a tool to bridge the gap between the desired ACRs and those achievable based on available real-world data. Without such delegation, an enterprise must balance allowing access to unauthorized individuals and denying access to authorized individuals. Delegation allows the enterprise to set more restrictive default rules that block unauthorized access and then provide authorized access as needed to those who are mistakenly excluded by the restrictive rules. Delegation is a temporary fix for inadequate access rules, and the instances of delegation serve to identify areas where more precise user data is required for proper access controls.

11 Escalation of Privilege

11.1 CONTEXT FOR ESCALATION

The ELS framework guarantees strong security within an enterprise. It provides rules for secure, distributable, scalable, and centrally managed authentication and authorization. Entities in the enterprise need only authentication credentials and attributes in data stores, and access is automatically granted to appropriate applications and services throughout the enterprise. This system works for normal operations, but there is often a need for special access or privilege in some contexts or circumstances, which poses a challenge to the ELS framework.

ESCALATION

Escalation of access and privilege may be good or bad. Nefarious entities often use escalation as a means of exploitation. Vetted users may need escalation in dire circumstances. The former is undesirable, and detection mechanisms are put in place to prevent this. Primarily, the latter is foreseen and has a planned implementation.

This chapter discusses options for escalation of access and privilege within the ELS framework. Strict control over access and privilege is necessarily relaxed, but they are supplemented with additional accountability and monitoring to prevent abuse. In addition, this chapter discusses de-escalation, which may be desirable in some situations, such as when the user is captured by enemy forces. The ability to provide access at a minimal level may convince the captor that a detainee is cooperating while protecting critical resources.

The primary factor enabling escalation is knowledge of the context in which a request is made. Context-aware, role-based access control has been studied in a variety of forms. See, for example, [157–161]. Other work focuses more on mobile and pervasive computing paradigms, such as [162, 163]. Others integrate timing and location information, such as [164–168]. There is some work on providing security to such access, such as [169, 170]. Some of the work resembles delegation, which is one person assigning permissions or access to another explicitly, such as [171].

There is also some work in providing methods to escalate in an emergency or other critical situation, such as [172–176]. Some of these talk about human-based systems and methods rather than automated digital methods. Others are digital but provide only weak, if any, attribution. In most cases, the access is managed centrally and not by the owner of the resource being accessed.

Many of the ideas above are already incorporated into the ELS framework, such as access based on environmental conditions and sharing of access with others through delegation. The work presented in this chapter extends these ideas and combines them in a form that provides all of the following:

- Access control based on context, including location, time, and environmental conditions;
- Automated digital access with no requirements for human action or approval at the time of the access;
- The ability to "break glass" and perform approved actions not normally part of duties;
- Strong accountability for such actions;
- Integration with existing security framework of ELS.

The ELS framework is described in Chapter 2, Section 2.2. The following sections discuss escalation and the implementation of escalation within this framework.

11.2 ACCESS AND PRIVILEGE ESCALATION

Access rules for a normal user accessing a service are defined by the data owner and associated with access claims when the service is registered. If a user satisfies an access rule, that user is assigned the corresponding access claim. Claims are computed, stored, and provided to users by the EAE. A user requests a claim at the STS and submits it, packaged in a SAML assertion, to a service. Access is decided by the service based on a comparison of the claim to a local Access Control List (ACL).

This is the default access method for all enterprise services and applications. This is purposely designed to prevent workarounds and back doors. However, there are circumstances in which the chain of command is not available or urgency requires a user to bypass the normal chain of command. This most often occurs in tactical situations and/or battlefield conditions, but it may also occur in business events that move fast.

Escalation is a controlled way to provide entities access to otherwise restricted resources within the proper context. It enables users to increase privilege when a need exists. This access is tightly monitored to ensure that it does not become a recurring pattern, and individuals who use escalation are held accountable for their actions to curb abuse.

Escalation is intended as a last resort for access, to be used only when no other method is available. Redefinition of access rules or reassignment of attributes are the preferred approaches for changing access. These are permanent solutions to providing proper access. They work at the enterprise level to define the user's attributes and the access rules such that the user will be assigned an access claim by the enterprise.

Delegation is the next best option, in which an authorized individual shares access with another individual for a limited period of time. A user with an access claim and delegation privileges for this claim is able to share access with another user by delegating the claim to this user. The delegated claim has an expiration date and is limited to either a fixed maximum time window or the life of the claim for the delegator (whichever ends soonest). Delegation is a medium-term solution to access. It is intended for access that is planned for a limited period of time. It maintains accountability by tracing this access back to the individual who shared it.

A less desirable option is for the data owner to adjust the access by redefining the local ACL. This cuts the enterprise out of the access decision and leaves it entirely up to the data owner. This puts the burden of access security on the data owner and fails to take advantage of the enterprise services for identity and access management. This is intended for very short-term or quick-response access changes. The data owner can instantly allow (or deny) access to an individual without involving enterprise services.

All of these methods require action by someone other than the requester to allow access to the requester. Escalation is reserved for cases in which these individuals are not available, not accessible, or not willing to act. In these cases, the individual desiring access has no other choice but to use escalation to gain access. This is a last resort – it is done entirely by the individual requesting access, and full responsibility and accountability lie with this individual. Escalation is not a license to do whatever the individual wants. The individual must have the privilege of escalation, either as an outright grant from the data owner in the ACR or as a matter of circumstance such as tactical need. Escalation limits are defined in advance by the enterprise and the data owner in order to allow its use when appropriate and prevent widespread use and abuse.

An example of escalation is a situation in which access to satellite links is required but the holder of the privilege has become a casualty in an operation. Non-escalation options require some form of communication with an outside entity who then takes actions that propagate through the system to enable access. If no such communication is available or the time lag is too long, permissible escalation enables people to take actions that are needed in unusual situations.

Access is considered the ability to interact with a service or application. Privilege describes the type of interactions allowed. Simple privileges include read, write, modify, create, delete, position, arm, execute, etc., but privileges can also include arbitrarily complex operations depending on application needs. In some escalation cases, a user without access simply needs access. In other cases, escalation of privilege is required, possibly in combination with access. Escalation of access requires enterprise functionality to provide an escalation claim for the initial communication to start. Privilege escalation is easier because the user is already accessing the service provider with some level of privilege. Escalation of privileges can be built into the application or service, and it would not require any enterprise-level assistance to initiate.

Before discussing escalation in more detail, we highlight the different forms of escalation and identify those we discuss in this work.

- *Aggregation escalation* may be used when a service needs to access a full data set to calculate summary data, such as averages. Escalation occurs upon access to the data needed in the computation when the context allows such extended access. Typically, aggregation escalation is performed by a service that provides summary results to requesters. Although escalation is required for the aggregation, the result masks the individual data items so that requesters do not require escalation or propagate escalated data.
- *Static escalation* is built into the ACR based on attributes in the EAS. This form of escalation is generally available to someone with the appropriate attributes. Such access differs from normal claims-based access because an

explicit decision to use such escalated access is required by the user, and additional rules, monitoring, logging, and alerts may be associated with such use.

- *Dynamic escalation* is built into the claims retrieval process based on contextual information that is retrieved at the time of a claim request. Such escalation cannot be determined in advance, and it is only available to someone when they are in a particular situation for which escalation has been allowed.

This chapter does not discuss aggregation escalation, because this is typically planned in advance and only applicable to automated services. Static escalation and dynamic escalation are applicable to people taking actions in unusual situations and are discussed here. The main difference between static and dynamic escalation is the back-end implementation – the user interface and interaction are likely to be identical in both. As a result, we refer to escalation without specifying static or dynamic when such distinction is not relevant.

Escalation has not yet been developed and tested, and the approach described below is a candidate for implementation. This is a discussion of the elements and approaches for achieving escalation that both extend ELS and provide accountability for actions.

11.3 PLANNING FOR ESCALATION

Escalation must be planned for and allowed by the data owner. This may seem to contradict the nature of escalation, which is an unplanned and unexpected access requirement. However, for consistency with ELS principles, the data owner maintains control over access, which means the data owner defines the normal access rules as well as the rules under which escalation is permitted.

The data owner establishes escalation rules when registering an application or service. Registration includes defining the claims that will be accepted for access and establishing the rules under which these claims are to be issued. In addition to access rules, the data owner is allowed to specify additional rules under which escalation is allowed. The default rules are the enterprise-wide minimum escalation capabilities. This minimum may be "none," but the enterprise may define standard cases for which escalation is always allowed, and data owners are required to observe these minimum standards.

Escalation rules may contain both static and dynamic information. Static portions of the escalation claims are computed like normal claims and stored in the Claims Repository. Dynamic portions of escalation claims are computed at the Provide Claims Service when a user requests a claim. These behaviors are consistent with normal claim requests.

When a user wishes to invoke escalation, the user sends a request for an escalation claim to the STS. This is similar to the request for any other claim, except that the user is prompted for additional confirmation, such as a PIN, to be certain that the user wishes to invoke escalation and not request a normal claim. Because the escalation claims are tied to additional monitoring, alerting, and potential follow-up investigations and oversight, it is important that the escalation claim is distinguished from normal access and that the user is made aware of this difference and forced to take additional action to use such a claim.

An escalation situation is often not a normal situation, and a user may have difficulty establishing identity. Provisions are included within ELS for different forms and levels of authentication. Identity assurance is the process that evaluates the identity-building process in a multi-factor authentication of an individual. The identity assurance requirements for escalation may differ from the normal identity assurance values. These values are set by the data owner for each claim that the data owner defines in the ACR. The additional confirmation for escalation, such as a PIN, can be considered a mandatory part of the identity assurance process, because it confirms not only the intent of the individual but also the identity of the individual.

The data owner may establish different identity assurance values in an escalation situation. In situations in which someone's life may be in danger if service is refused, a lower identity assurance value may be tolerated based on the context. In situations in which the person escalating has the potential to do serious harm to others or to the enterprise, a data owner may require a higher identity assurance value. The data owner decides which identity assurance values to accept within constraints provided at the enterprise level. The identity assurance values for normal and escalated access may be different, but the process of authentication is identical. Identity assurance is discussed in detail in Chapter 6.

The applications and services of a data owner implement authentication rules for escalation to ensure that proper authentication is performed for escalation requests. This authentication is also done at the STS, which provides the SAML assertion with access claims.

ELS systems contain two types of STSs. The first is the normal STS, which uses two-way authentication with client certificates. This STS simply authenticates the user and issues a SAML token. The second is an STS/CA, which uses multi-factor authentication to raise the identity assurance level of the requester to the desired value set by the application and then issues a SAML with claims. If a certificate is not used for authentication, the STS/CA issues to the requester a temporary certificate and public/private key pair, which is installed and used for authentication at the application.

Authentication requirements may depend on the type of claim requested, so the STS and STS/CA pass authentication information about the requester on to the Provide Claims Service. This allows the Provide Claims Service to determine whether minimum identity assurance values have been met for a given claim. The STS already knows which identity assurance level is required for each application and claim, but the check by the Provide Claims Service provides a chance to catch configuration errors or slow updates at the STS. It also allows the STS to modify the identity assurance in escalation events. Another function of the STS is to allow a user to request multiple claims to a particular application, which allows the Provide Claims Service to provide the proper claims to the STS based on the identity assurance level established at the STS for that request. The STS's role is to help the Provide Claims Service by providing the information it needs, and the Provide

Claims Service's role is to issue claims only to properly authenticated and authorized requesters.

To make escalation available in DIL circumstances, the escalation rules, static claims information, and dynamic context information must be available locally. Forward deployment of the claims database makes the claims information available locally, and local servers provide the dynamic information based on the current context. The static portion is generally fixed because the local claims are a static copy of the master Claims Repository from the enterprise, but the dynamic part is recomputed locally and can thus incorporate additional local context as desired by the data owner. This is identical to normal operations, except that local context that is not normally available at the enterprise level may be relevant and available in DIL situations.

11.4 INVOKING ESCALATION

Escalation is a two-step process. First, the invoking entity must authenticate and provide an escalation claim for basic access. Then, within this limited access, the entity takes further action to invoke escalation and receive full access and additional privileges.

If an entity sends only an escalation claim to an application or service, then this entity does not have attributes that satisfy the ACRs associated with any access claim for a particular application or service. This entity may be able to authenticate with a high enough identity assurance value to allow connection to an application, but after establishing the secure connection, this entity can initiate an escalation request only with the target application or service. No other services or privileges are allowed until escalation is invoked. For example, a user may be able to view the home page for an application based upon an escalation claim, but access to detailed information or the ability to make changes is denied unless escalation is invoked from this home page.

An entity that has some subset of the available privileges but not enough to take what they consider needed action is held accountable for an escalation decision. For example, the individual may be able to view detailed information but not access resources such as weapons or satellite links, or that individual may be able to upload data but not view the data of other resources within the mission group. Many of these privileges are specific to the application or service, so a detailed discussion is not as important here as the concept that the user is authorized to do some, but not all, of what they consider necessary. Privilege may be built into the access claim – for example, a claim for viewing data versus a claim for accessing resources. In other applications, these privileges may use the same claim, and user privileges are defined by additional attributes passed with the claim.

This structure of access and privilege is not locked down in ELS, and applications are free to do what serves them best. The presence of an escalation privilege, either by implicit or context-dependent data, will require a routine to deal with escalation and a trigger for invoking escalation. We suggest two triggers: one for normal escalation and one for escalation under duress.

Normal escalation involves the need for information, communication, and or other privileged use of resources beyond normal anticipated usage. A normal user of a service requesting escalation would be afforded the opportunity to view, communicate, or otherwise use resources while extensive logging and alerting are conducted for accountability. It is assumed that the information, communication, and resources extended in escalation will be different from those provided to the normal user of a service. Normal escalation will be triggered by a recognized phrase such as "More Needed." Upon recognition of the key phrase, the user will be challenged immediately with a question and a pre-briefed response. The response may have two values. The first value indicates that the user is aware of the request, has the claim to be able to escalate, and is not under duress. The second response is used to indicate duress as described below.

Under duress, escalation will be triggered by a recognized phrase such as "Open Sesame." Upon recognition of the key phrase, the user will be immediately challenged with a question and a pre-briefed response. The response may have several valid responses, indicating that the user is aware of the request, has the claim to be able to escalate, and the degree of duress (which may affect escalation privileges). Extreme duress would indicate a forced request for escalation by an adversary that may be life threatening, and this would trigger alerts and a misinformation-based mode of communication.

Data owners are ultimately responsible for determining the degree of escalation that is allowed. The enterprise may set basic standards either as a policy or through technical implementations, but the data owner has control within this range. Minimum standards by the enterprise may be the ability to escalate privilege when authentication and access are achieved through standard ELS. This assures someone with access but lacking a needed privilege that they can still access information, communication, and resources necessary to the circumstance if the context is appropriate.

Data owners set escalation capabilities when defining their claims and ACRs at registration or at any time after registration through an update. Part of registration involves setting authentication levels and the forms and combinations of authentication that an application will allow for access. The STS also uses this information to authenticate requesters of SAML assertions for applications and services. An authentication identity assurance value is included in the SAML token in addition to the identity and access claims of the requester.

The STS uses the Provide Claims Service to determine and enforce context for escalation of privilege. The Provide Claims Service compares the current context with the context rules for escalation, and it issues claims when the context rules are met by the current context. The data owner establishes the rules by which these context elements allow escalation.

Escalation will not be necessary for many back-office types of applications or services related to everyday activities. Escalation rules need not be established for these applications and services. Escalation is intended to bring within ELS the unauthorized actions that are already occurring to get work done in dire situations. This makes these actions easier because they are automated, and it also makes them visible to the enterprise. With visibility, corrective actions can be taken, such as expansion of normal or escalation access rules and discipline for abuse of escalation.

11.5 ESCALATION IMPLEMENTATION WITHIN ELS

Five entities are involved in escalation:

- The enterprise, which defines the scope of allowed escalations;
- The data owner, which provides the escalation rules;
- The EAE, which stores the escalation rules with the registration and claims data and enforces these rules through the Provide Claims Service;
- The STS, which uses the data owner rules to determine whether or how to issue claims that may or may not include escalation ability;
- The logging and monitoring infrastructure, which captures information about escalation events, sends alerts, triggers analyses of situational information, and responds to abuses and anomalous behavior.

The first step in setting up escalation in the enterprise is establishing what types of escalation are necessary, desired, and forbidden. Necessary escalation may include either static or dynamic escalation of privilege. The implementation has multiple components. The EAE Registry is where the static escalation rules are stored and used for claims computation, and the Provide Claims Service is where dynamic rules are computed. The data owner still maintains ultimate control over privilege through the use of the internal application logic. The internal logic can refuse escalated privileges when thresholds of identity assurance or context dictate, and the data owner can block even these pre-computed escalation authorities. Due to the nature of escalation, every escalation is a security event that must be logged, alerted, and monitored in more detail than other events. Every escalation has the potential for a security violation, and misuse may be a cause for revocation of privileges or other disciplinary actions.

There are two options for implementing escalation. The enterprise may enforce certain escalation rules by hiding the escalation information from the data owners. This prevents data owners from denying certain enterprise-required escalation capabilities, since the data owners in this option do not know who is escalating and who is using normal access. The other option is to give all the escalation information to the data owners and allow them to make access decisions themselves based on this information. This has the potential drawback of each data owner implementing escalation differently, which would damage cross-enterprise consistency.

The recommendation for the enterprise is to trust the data owners to faithfully implement enterprise policies on escalation. To ensure consistency, periodic testing is performed by the enterprise using dummy accounts. This method of escalation allows the data owners full visibility into which entities are accessing application communication, data, and resources, which enables enterprise security to better respond to escalation through analysis of logging, monitoring, and alerting. This, in turn, may lead to modification of escalation rules for both implicit and context-based escalations. Escalations should be relatively rare, but with millions of transactions being performed in short time periods throughout the enterprise, they will occur often enough for these analyses.

At the other end of the escalation spectrum, the enterprise may have hard limits on how far escalation can go. Allowing high levels of escalation may enable an attacker to rapidly connect, gain access, and perform damaging actions. Even though the escalation process is keyword-protected, challenged, and limited, as well as heavily logged, monitored, alerted, and analyzed, there is concern about opening such an attack surface. Most of the measures related to internal misuse are based on deterrence through attribution and the consequences thereof, but the consequences may be minimal for outside attackers, who often use stolen or forged credentials.

In setting the enterprise scope for escalation, the goal is to provide a minimum level of capability so that requesters are more likely to use access and privilege within ELS than work outside of it. Setting the minimum too low could result in it not being implemented consistently, which results in users working around the system instead of within it. Any problems caused by escalation, such as abuse, must be weighed not against a perfect system but against the alternative of unauthorized bypass of the system, which provides no visibility into the security problems.

The maximum must be set to prevent uncontrolled access to data, communication, and resources. The maximum determined by the enterprise may change over time as policies are refined. A maximum that is too high leads to an easy path in for attackers. A maximum that is too low may prevent people from taking actions that are necessary and lead to the creation of insecure back doors and workarounds.

The recommendation for the enterprise is to err on the side of lower escalation initially. Escalation is initially for life-and-death situations in which no other alternative is available and someone is willing to take full responsibility. For less-immediate challenges, delegation and reassignment of positions allow people access or privilege. Practicing escalation during non-critical situations allows it to be refined for situations in which it is required. Actual experiences under duress can provide guidance for future uses of escalation based on need.

The second step, after the enterprise determines the scope of escalation required and permitted, is for data owners to create the escalation rules for their content. This is done by associating escalation rules with each application, service, and claim. An example of escalation rules is illustrated in Table 11.1. Application #1 generally allows a limited amount of escalation. The user accounts allow a small step up in claims, and full privileges associated with those claims. No requester on the user interface may escalate to Operator because Operators use a separate interface with a separate set of claims. Operators may escalate by one level within the Operator hierarchy and may assume full privileges as well.

The EAE stores the escalation rules along with normal rules for access. Application #1 generally allows a limited amount of escalation. The user accounts allow a small step up in claims, and full privileges associated with that claim. No requester on the user interface may escalate to Operator because Operators use a separate interface with a separate set of claims. Operators may escalate by one level within the Operator hierarchy and may assume full privileges as well.

Application #2 provides more flexibility with escalation. All requests go to a common interface, which allows a higher degree of discrimination in escalation and

TABLE 11.1.
Escalation Rules Example

	Application #1	
Interface	***Claim***	***Authorized Escalation Allowed***
User Interface	None	User claim + limited privileges
	Basic Access claim	Manager + limited privileges
	User claim	Manager + intermediate privileges
	Manager claim	Supervisor + all privileges
	Supervisor claim	All privileges
Administrator/Operator Interface	None	Local Operator + limited privileges
	Local Operator claim	Privileged Operator + all privileges
	Privileged Operator claim	Full Operator + all privileges
	Full Operator claim	All privileges
	Application #2	
Interface	***Claim***	***Escalation allowed***
	None	User claim + limited privileges
	Basic Access claim	User claim + limited privileges
	User claim	User claim + intermediate privileges
	Manager claim	Local Admin + intermediate privileges
	Supervisor claim	Privileged Operator
	Local Operator claim	Full Operator + intermediate privileges
	Privileged Operator claim	Full Operator + all privileges
	Full Operator claim	All privileges

allows normal users with manager or supervisor claims to assume limited Operator roles

The two applications highlight some of the design choices involved in setting up an application. In the first, the user actions and Operator actions are isolated through separate interfaces. This is appropriate for situations in which most people use a service and an Operator occasionally makes changes to how it works. The second is appropriate when a group of people is collaborating with dynamically changing roles.

The first effectively protects the system from rogue users who might escalate and cause damage as Operator, whereas the second enables flexibility in who can take action, which reduces protections but enables the users themselves to organize as they see fit for the situation. The second application also allows more escalation options, as even a requester with no claims can escalate to supervisor.

Table 11.1 is integrated with other information about application access rules. The EAE stores escalation information about both data owner applications and services and enterprise applications and services. The enterprise rules for escalation limits may not apply to all enterprise services. For example, STS administrator escalations may be strictly forbidden because this enables arbitrary assignment of claims through manipulation of trusted root CAs and other critical security rules. Escalation of the delegation service may also be restricted because delegation is an additional form of providing escalation. Combining escalation and delegation may enable unforeseen security vulnerabilities through repeated iteration.

The line between normal applications and services and enterprise applications and services is somewhat blurry. Some normal services may be so central and important that they behave like enterprise services. For example, organizational information may be maintained by different groups, but it may be used for important decisions such as who can delegate to whom, putting it on par with enterprise delegation services in terms of importance and scope. These lines must be drawn on a case-by-case basis by the enterprise. Again, it is best to start with limited escalation until familiarity and normal behavior can be established, leading to a gradual expansion of escalation capabilities. The expansion is accompanied by expanded logging, monitoring, alerting, and analysis capabilities so that accountability remains high for all escalated actions.

The STS has two roles in escalation. First, it may allow requesters with weak authentication (low identity assurance) to present escalation claims. At least one reasonably secure method of establishing identity must be present for any escalation. Multi-factor authentication and other methods already enable flexible authentication that maintains high degrees of certainty about a requester's identity.

The second role for the STS in escalation is through the Provide Claims Service and dynamic escalation claims within the SAML assertion. The requester indicates the target endpoint in the request. Under a normal request, if the user does not have the claims for the endpoint, an error will occur, unless the user has either an implicit or context-determined escalation claim. If the user has an escalation claim but a low identity assurance, the STS also indicates this, in the same way that it indicates authentication assurance levels and methods. This information is provided to the target application with the full details of the identity that the user claims, the level of assurance at which the user has authenticated, and what claims the user was issued. In many cases, this information is pre-populated automatically (e.g., by an application through a redirect to the STS). The user experience involves an affirmation that escalation is required and that such actions are attributed and monitored.

11.6 ACCOUNTABILITY

A critical component of enabling escalation is the additional logging, monitoring, alerting, and analysis that is required to maintain accountability and prevent abuses. Without strong and certain post-escalation review and justification, some users may abuse escalation. With a quick and strong response to escalations, individuals can be trained to seek alternatives, such as delegation, when feasible. Escalation is a last resort, and it must be used that way or it has the potential to undermine the security of ELS. Escalation must be accompanied by a strong program of training and an organizational response that enforces strict disciplinary actions for misuse of escalation. The technical part of escalation covers only the methods to take proper input, allow access, and create logs and alerts.

It is important to educate people about why escalation exists and how it helps them do their jobs while maintaining security in the enterprise. "Education" for some will simply mean learning that escalation exists. Those who are likely to use it will learn how to invoke it properly. Education about escalation should also include the consequences of improper use. Users who know how and when to use escalation, as well as the penalties for misuse, are informed enough to properly use it.

Training must reinforce education through actual use. This might be similar to fire drill training, during which normal rules for high security areas are temporarily reduced to enable people to quickly and safely exit the building. Although actually using escalation regularly as part of training has potential drawbacks, training on stand-alone systems with training data and services would isolate all the logging, monitoring, and alerts from the real-world system and prevent unauthorized access to real data. On real systems, users could simply use escalation claims and view options to escalate without actually invoking them. This would avoid additional accountability actions and potential disciplinary actions while providing a hands-on feel for the real-world escalation capability.

Maintaining accountability requires an organization of geographically distributed people viewing digital records associated with an escalation, interviewing users of escalation to corroborate the context of its use, and applying a system of rules and penalties to deter misuses. If an individual uses escalation, the entire chain of superiors is able to review and question him or her and potentially take action for misuse. Patterns of misuse, which may be discovered by different superiors, are visible through an enterprise system of personal reputation and veracity (see Chapter 9).

11.7 ESCALATION SUMMARY

This chapter has examined escalation within the ELS framework. Escalation is an extension of the normal ELS security controls, intended for infrequent and extraordinary situations in which normal rules are not adequate. Current capabilities within ELS, such as delegation, already allow flexible assignment of access and privilege for non-standard use cases. Escalation is reserved for extreme cases in which an action is absolutely required but prevented through normal ELS. The escalating entity assumes full responsibility for the action. Escalation involves many components of the enterprise, including users, data owners, and enterprise services. Successful implementation requires coordination among these entities to establish not only appropriate digital policies and implementations but also training on usage and responses to abuses. Key words and challenge/response are the mitigating processes that inhibit nefarious use, and escalation may have constraints to limit possible damages. Abuses are treated with loss of privilege and other disciplinary actions.

As an enterprise service, escalation relies heavily on the EAE and its services and data stores. The EAE has an implementation that has experienced analytical evaluation, penetration testing, and many demos. This implementation is a natural testbed for implementing escalation. Further analysis of the EAE will ensure that the EAE implementation of escalation adheres to basic ELS principles. Penetration testing will illuminate areas in which refinement of the security properties is needed, such as the appropriate level of escalation for different enterprise or near-enterprise services.

12 Federation

There is often a requirement to share resources with different enterprises, which poses a challenge to the ELS framework. This chapter discusses options for federation across enterprises in which one enterprise uses ELS [31, 32, , 35, 42]. The partner enterprise may use ELS, another security framework, limited security services, or no security at all. The partner enterprise may be trusted, partially trusted, or untrusted. This chapter provides options for an ELS enterprise to enable federated sharing with other enterprises that have different capabilities and levels of trust. This enables more functionality within the ELS framework and fewer workarounds, which provides stronger and more uniform security measures.

FEDERATION

In this context, federation is the interoperation of two distinct, disconnected networks that may have different internal structures. The federation mediates the identity and access, as well as the other security factors, to allow sharing of information.

Within this chapter, the term "partner" will refer to the other side in a federation agreement. This could be a single individual, an entire enterprise, or anything in between.

12.1 FEDERATION TECHNICAL CONSIDERATIONS

There are several ways to extend the principles of ELS to a federation partner based on the partner's technical capabilities:

- ELS federation,
- ELS-like federation,
- Identity credential federation,
- Weak identity federation,
- Ad hoc federation,
- Person-to-person federation.

The federation options are listed from most to least technologically compatible. Each option on the list implicitly includes the options lower on the list. This section discusses the technical means to accomplish federation for each of the options listed above.

12.1.1 ELS Federation

ELS federation is an agreement to accept identity and access claims from another enterprise. Federation is a long-term substantial agreement that is made at the enterprise level. To resolve federation issues, the federation STS relies on the following information:

- Certificates of Federated STSs for validating signatures in SAML tokens and chain to trusted root CA;
- A set of identity-mapping pairs comprised of Identity1 and Identity2, in which Identity1 in a SAML issued by the federated STS is to be mapped to Identity2 in the local enterprise;
- A set of mapping pairs comprised of Claim A and Claim B, where Claim A in a SAML issued by the federated STS is to be mapped to Claim B in the local enterprise;
- Additional attribute mappings associated with claim mappings.

An example of data captured in federation agreements is shown in Table 12.1. This shows the data for two separate federation agreements.

Each web service in the enterprise has a limited number of trusted root CAs for authentication credentials and trusted STS certificates for SAML signatures stored in its trust store. In ELS federation, a list of trusted partner CAs and STSs is established. Trusted partner CAs for identity credentials are distributed to applications and services. Trusted partner STS credentials are distributed to federation STSs within the enterprise. The federation STS is called by a service when an unknown authorization credential is encountered, and the federation STS checks against known federation partners to validate the credentials, creates a new SAML token with its own signature, and returns this to the application or service for processing.

TABLE 12.1.
Federation Data Requirements

Federation Partner 1 information		
Certificate	Federation Partner 1 certificate and chain to root CA	
Identity Mappings	Identity 1	Identity 2
	Identity A	Identity B
	Identity r	<no change>
	...	...
Claim and Attribute Mappings	Claim A	<null>
	Claim n	Claim z
	Claim y and Attribute q	Claim y and Attribute r
	...	...
Federation Partner 2 information		
Certificate	Federation Partner 2 certificate and chain to root CA	
Identity Mappings	Identity x	Identity y
	Identity Q	Identity R
	...	...
Claim and Attribute Mappings	Claim n	<no change>
	Claim p with Attributes x, y, z	Claim p with Attribute k
	Claim A	<no change>
	...	...

For identity and claim mappings, the special cases of "null" and "no change" are acceptable in addition to explicit values. "Null" removes the claim or identity, while "no change" leaves the original claim or identity. The claims to be mapped must match claims from sources on both sides. Claims in the federation partner SAML must match the federation agreement exactly. Claims in the reissued SAML must match claims for the target application or service. Identity and claim mappings are added to the federation store after an amendment to the federation agreement. Revocation of a federation agreement is accomplished by removing the federation partner from the trusted STS data store.

When a federation STS recognizes and validates a partner authorization credential, it maps the received credential into a new credential – possibly with different identity, claims, and attributes. This new credential is signed by the federation STS and returned to the requesting application or service. The application or service then processes this new SAML token as though it had received it from a valid requester within the enterprise. Failure to validate an incoming SAML token by the federation STS results in an error message response to the application or service, which leads to an authorization failure at the application or service.

12.1.2 ELS-like Federation

If the federation partner is not using ELS but does have a way to provide the security functions that ELS provides, then a more complicated federation agreement may be needed with some translation algorithms. This is similar to ELS federation, but it accounts for different semantics, formats, and data encodings. The mappings may not be exact, in which case there may be some loss of information in the translation. This may hinder automation and scalability, as mismatches in data resolution could lead to denial when access should be allowed or to access when it should be denied. This is generally unavoidable when data is represented in different ways.

These differences also apply to tokens and credentials. Variable strength of credentials in the partner enterprise can weaken the entire authentication process. For example, if the partner provides software authentication credentials for some users instead of hardware credentials for all users, then it is not possible to provide access to hardware-credentialed entities and deny access to software-credentialed entities unless the source of the credential is explicitly provided in the signed portion of the certificate. The secure choice for an enterprise that requires hardware certificates in such a situation is to deny access even though the entities using hardware credentials should be given access.

If the partner uses an authorization credential other than the approved SAML 2.0 format used in ELS, then certain guarantees provided by the SAML format, such as validity windows, signatures, or encryption, may be weaker or nonexistent in the partner authorization token. Even if the token is equally strong, the local STS must be able to understand the partner token format to parse, validate, and translate it into a locally comprehensible SAML for the local applications and services. There are token translators that transform one token format into another, but they address only the format, not the meaning or security properties.

When the partner is "ELS-like," most of the work is already done, and the process of federating is similar to that with an ELS partner. The challenge is working out the small differences and making sure that these small differences do not open up large security holes or prevent large groups of entities from receiving proper access. Shortcuts and workarounds may be necessary to provide a seamless experience to the end users; however, the majority of cases should work with standard translation schemes as long as the protocols, standards, and data formats are commonly used and available.

In the event that formats and data are incompatible, additional work to make needed conversions at the requesting enterprise may solve the problem. For example, many STSs can be configured to issue tokens according to different protocols and formats, so configuring a partner STS to use the proper SAML format could resolve token format differences. Authentication credentials could be addressed by indicating whether a credential is stored in hardware or software so that receiving entities can decide whether to allow access. This could be accomplished by dividing the issuing CAs into those that issue only hardware credentials and those that issue only software credentials. These solutions are intended as quick fixes, and they do not require any new technology. In some cases, these can move an ELS-like partner to an ELS partner, but in most cases they remain ELS-like but with more streamlined operations.

12.1.3 Identity Credential Federation

A federation partner may provide identity credentials but not authorization credentials, such as an account-based system in which the ID is used to log in. Such a system is no longer ELS-like, but the identity credentials can still be used as a starting point for federation.

One solution is to include a mapping from partner identity to local identity that includes associated authorization claims. This would be performed at the STS as part of the federation mappings. This is not the typical use for these mappings, and it requires modifications to Table 12.1 to combine the identity, claim, and attribute mappings. This method works if the identity credential is passed for authentication and the authorization information is exchanged between enterprises and incorporated into the federation agreement. This should generally be used only for small sets of requesters, as these federation mappings are intended to be for claim and attribute equivalences and generic identity transform rules, not explicit per-entity claim and attribute information.

For larger-scale federation, the data owner or some other entity with access to the data can delegate the appropriate claims to the appropriate individuals in the partner enterprise. The delegation framework within ELS is designed to allow such short-term access to specific individuals. In this case, the data owner, not the STS, maintains the mappings through the delegation service. This is a more appropriate place to store this information. However, it still requires manually assigning claims to individuals based on their identities.

The basic structure for federated delegation is shown in Figure 12.1. The dashed lines represent the flow for setting up the delegation. The local delegator uses the

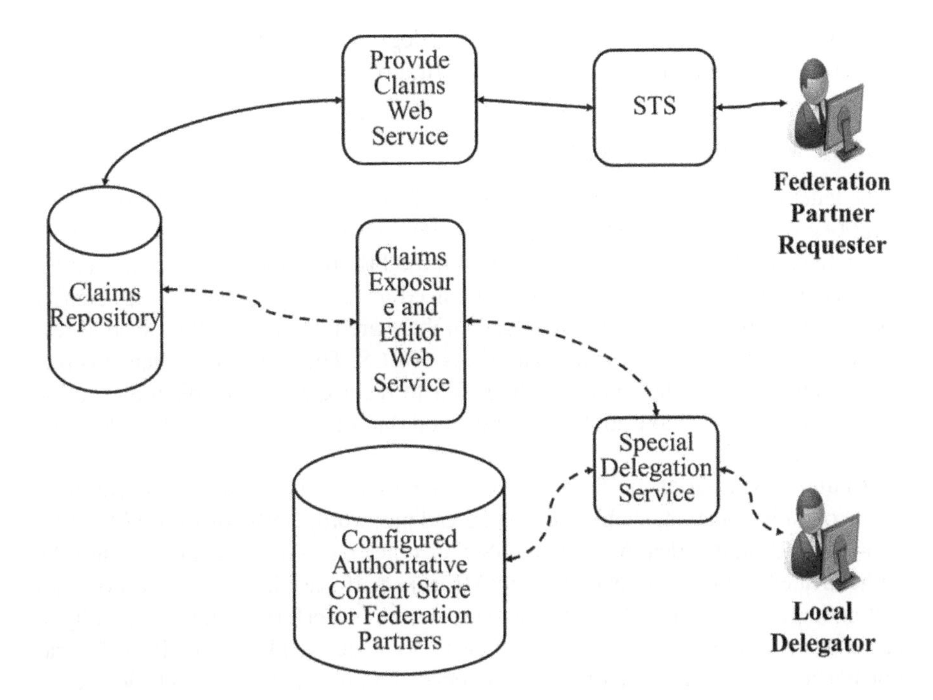

FIGURE 12.1. Identity Credential Federation Using Delegation

Special Delegation Service to assign access claims to the federated partner identity as stored in the authoritative content store for federation partners. The special delegation service is separate from the standard in-enterprise delegation service, and the content store for federation partners is separate from the normal store for in-enterprise entities. This special delegation service uses the claims exposure and editor service to store access claims for the federated identity in the Claims Repository.

The solid lines represent the flow for a federated requester to retrieve a SAML token with delegated claims. The partner interfaces with the STS, just as an in-enterprise user does, and the STS then makes a request, just as for any other requester, to retrieve the claims from the Claims Repository.

A third solution is to use a separate authoritative data store for the partner entities and tie it into the EAS that feeds the SAML creation process. This brings the partner entities into the local enterprise and allows those entities to request local SAML tokens that will work like those from requesters within the enterprise. Maintenance of the authoritative data store could be performed locally within the enterprise or remotely by the partner enterprise. Local maintenance would require detailed manual attention, while remote maintenance would put the responsibility on the partner. This is the best-integrated solution, since the attributes required are brought into the ELS system.

In all cases, a store maintains information about federated identities. For the mapping method, this is the federation agreement at the federation STS, which contains both identity information and claims and attributes used for access. For the delegation method, it is the store used by the special delegation service, which contains only identities and not claims, as these are delegated as needed. With the separate store, this store contains all identities and their attributes.

12.1.4 Weak Identity Federation

If the federation partner does not provide sufficiently strong identity credentials, then identity credential federation is not possible. For example, a username and password authentication system is not compatible with the PKI-based authentication used for ELS. However, if it is determined that the need to federate outweighs the security risks associated with weak credentials, then there are methods to allow such access while preserving many of the security goals of ELS. The primary challenge is that ELS requires PKI authentication to the STS to receive a SAML token and to the application or service to establish a connection, but the federation partner does not have this capability.

To allow creation of the SAML, a separate STS can be set up to receive other forms of authentication, such as username and password, Kerberos over TLS, other non-PKI TLS authentication, tokens, SSO, or other methods. The STS can use the authenticated identity to generate a SAML token. If the identity format does not match the ELS standard DN format, a mapping can be performed algorithmically or based on an enterprise-wide database of identity and derived DN pairs. If the federation partner has an STS that already uses non-PKI authentication, it can be leveraged to create authorization credentials.

Application and service endpoints can rely on alternative authentication methods, map the identity to a derived DN if necessary, and then compare this identity to the identity in the SAML token. In the generated SAML token, the authentication method can be indicated, or federation partners with non-PKI authentication at their STSs can be noted in the federation agreement so that receiving applications and services can enforce access accordingly. For example, standard PKI authentication may provide full access, whereas alternative authentication methods provide limited access that is sufficient for federation purposes. Because there is a clear distinction in authentication method and separate endpoints set up for access, this method provides a way to manage federated access independent of normal access. If a security problem is detected at a federated non-PKI endpoint, that endpoint can be shut down without affecting normal ELS operations.

This process is cumbersome and redundant because it requires new instances of applications and services and potentially a new STS. It may require additional logic to enforce different access based on the authentication method. It also weakens enterprise security by allowing non-ELS access to applications and services that otherwise require ELS. The access can be limited, but it may provide an attacker an easier entrance to ELS-protected data that could be leveraged to gain full access through additional attacks. This should only be attempted for urgent and infrequent federation agreements with the understanding of the risk to all affected applications and services, as well as the risk to the enterprise in general. This is not an ELS-compliant solution, because it fails to satisfy authentication and accountability requirements. However, it is a way that an enterprise can share all or some ELS-protected resources while leveraging existing ELS infrastructure. As a result, this may be a better solution than other options available.

12.1.5 Ad Hoc Federation

If there is no easy way in advance to identify what is to be shared with whom, then an ad hoc approach can address federation requirements. Delegation may be used to explicitly share resources with individuals just as needed. Delegation was mentioned above as an option for the case in which strong identity credentials are available. It is best suited for when the delegation decisions are distributed. A large federation agreement can be implemented by dividing the resources to be shared and the partner entities to be given access into smaller, manageable groups. A large federation agreement is broken into a large number of locally administered smaller agreements. Central control is maintained by the hierarchical structure of the delegations. This may or may not be possible for the structure of the sharing agreement between enterprises.

This approach requires some form of authentication for federated individuals. This is not necessarily a separate solution from those listed above, but instead an option for generating access claims for these methods. This is in contrast to explicitly assigning attributes or claims to these identities or mapping federated identities and claims through a federation STS.

This option is listed after weak identity federation because of the ad hoc and decentralized nature of the sharing. With the previous options, a central source determines who can access which resources. In this case, individuals make these decisions rather than the enterprises forming federation agreements. As a result, from the enterprise perspective, this is less secure, especially as the scope and scale of sharing increase.

12.1.6 Person-to-Person Sharing

If all the solutions above are infeasible (for whatever reason), an individual may make the decision to share information with a federation partner out of band on a person-to-person basis. This type of sharing should be properly authorized, and the person sharing the material should have release authority with guidelines. This could involve emailing documents, placing them on a public website, providing printed copies, or verbally providing the needed information. This goes around ELS by allowing access without any automated enterprise-level checks of identity or access claims. The last two also lack attribution, because the one sharing and the one receiving are the only entities that know about the transaction. In this case, shared information may be fingerprinted or steganographically imprinted for later forensics in case of leaks. Such sharing is difficult to prevent, so small amounts of unauthorized sharing are expected throughout the enterprise and with partners. ELS and the federation options listed above attempt to provide feasible options that are preferable to going completely out of band.

Although this method essentially bypasses most or all ELS security, it is mentioned because it is better than many alternatives that involve giving full electronic access by credential sharing, workarounds, or back doors. This method lacks the formal security of ELS (it may include accountability provisions on the enterprise side), but a human with authority to access and release data ensures that only the necessary information is shared. To help secure this method of sharing information, policies can guide people on which real-world security checks to perform. Person-to-person sharing has a long history prior to electronic sharing, so this accumulated knowledge can be used to shape policy.

12.1.7 Evaluating Options

The options presented above describe a spectrum from full ELS sharing to non-ELS sharing. It is tempting to say that ELS is the most secure and person-to-person is the least secure, but in reality scale matters. The security features are reduced from ELS to person-to-person, but the scale also tends to be reduced. Attacks are easier at the non-ELS end of the spectrum, but their smaller scale is likely to result in smaller incidents. At the full ELS end of the spectrum, the security is high and attacks are difficult, but a successful attack could rapidly escalate to a major incident.

For efficient sharing, ELS provides the most secure solution at scale and should be the preferred choice by the enterprise. Other options provide acceptable security at small scales, but they should not be put to widespread use, because the resulting vulnerabilities quickly escalate as the scale increases. Figure 12.2 shows a notional plot of the vulnerability associated with different federation option as a function of scale. The exact curves vary according to how risk and size are measured, but the key idea is that each federation option will have some maximum scale at which its security is acceptable. At the scale of a few individuals sharing information, the risk remains low for all methods, but as the scale increases, the risk associated with the approaches diverges, with ELS offering the only acceptable solution at full enterprise scale.

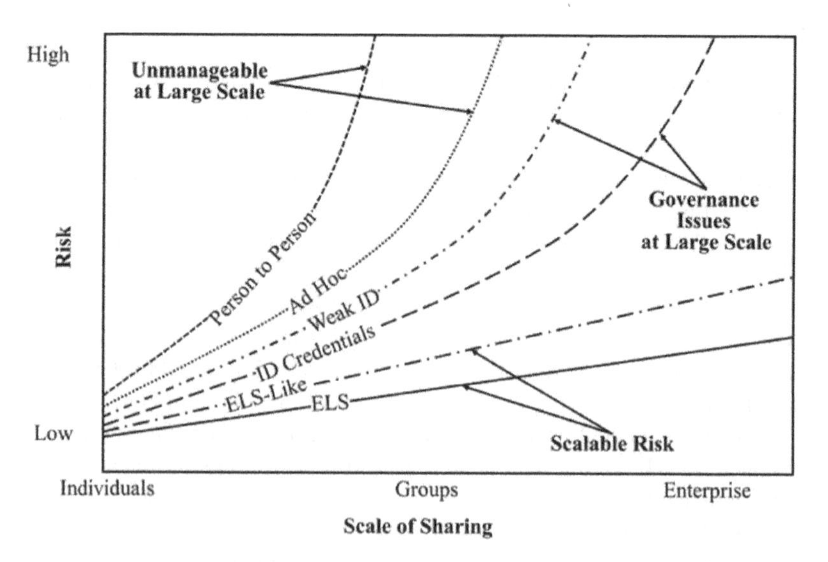

FIGURE 12.2. Notional Comparison of Federation Risk at Scale

Despite the scalability limitations, all approaches can be viable options. For example, "Weak ID" federation, although not desirable compared to ELS, is better than the ad hoc or person-to-person approaches; making all options available provides a smoother continuum of choices based on resources available. A particular enterprise may wish to limit the options to a subset of these or expand to include more. It may be better to adopt a strict "ELS or nothing" policy to motivate partners to adopt ELS, even if it means very limited sharing. For cases in which the focus is on sharing, providing all options helps to provide the best security available for the given situation. To manage overall enterprise risk, it may be necessary to limit the absolute number of federation partners or their constituent members that use each non-ELS type of federation to maintain the overall vulnerability level below a desired threshold.

12.2 FEDERATION TRUST CONSIDERATIONS

The technical considerations are important for federation, but having the technology available does not mean it is a good option. This section takes a different perspective to federation and considers the trade-offs among federation options based on the level of trust that exists with the federation partner. This is usually important to consider when making information or services available to partners and is less important when accessing partner information and services. It is assumed that some sharing is desired, regardless of the level of trust. It is also assumed that sharing should be limited, which is true even within a single enterprise using ELS. The challenge is how to use the available technology to build upon the real-world trust relationships to enable as many valid sharing behaviors as possible while preventing behaviors that are not valid or desired.

In this section, trust is meant to be the degree to which one enterprise believes that the other enterprise will not abuse technical capabilities to violate the agreed-upon terms of the federation agreement. It does not apply to weak security methods such as username/password authentication or weak cryptographic algorithms such as RC4 or MD5.

Trust can be a tricky issue. For example, if one enterprise trusts the root CA of the other enterprise, then PKI authentication can work across the enterprises. Thus, it might be tempting for one enterprise to declare, "Enterprise 1 trusts Enterprise 2's root CA," to make security work. This declaration may sound like, "Enterprise 1 trusts Enterprise 2's root CA, and therefore Enterprise 1 will encode that trust in its system to allow both systems to work together." However, stating trust for the purpose of interoperability is really saying "Enterprise 1 will open up a security vulnerability in its system that Enterprise 2 can exploit and will trust Enterprise 2 not to abuse it." Because such trust opens up vulnerabilities, it is important that statements of trust are truly based on existing or established relationships and not simply put in place for convenience. As trust is usually not an all-or-nothing proposition, any trust relationship must also be accompanied by monitoring and measures to identify and block malicious behavior by a partner, which can be summarized as "trust but verify."

Trusting a partner CA might be a good way to federate with a trusted partner or a partner for whom there is accountability and a long-standing relationship. However, this is risky when an enterprise suspects that the partner may abuse additional privilege, there is no long-standing relationship or accountability, or the damage that can be done is greater than any retribution likely to be enacted. The key is to first decide what to actually trust and then use that as a basis to build the system, not to build a system first and then declare trust where needed to make it work.

This section provides options for what to do with different trust levels. Of course, trust can be increased through external policies and agreements as well, so these options do not exist in isolation from the real world. However, it is often easier to build a system based on existing trust than to establish trust, as changing a technical system to match the real world is often quicker than changing the real world to match a technical system.

12.2.1 Full Trust

If one enterprise fully trusts another enterprise, federation can be accomplished in any number of ways. Examples of this include two divisions within a larger enterprise, a merger between two companies, two parallel systems within a single enterprise, or a hierarchical arrangement in which one group is sharing with another that contains it. In this case, any option will work, and the best choice is usually the one that enables the most integration and sharing, or the one that is simplest to set up. In this case, the degree of ELS compatibility is likely to be the determining factor for choosing a solution.

12.2.2 Infrastructure Trust

If one enterprise trusts the high-level security functions, such as certificate authorities and other enterprise-level functions, then the best option is one that leverages this existing trust and limits access based on these trusted services. For example, if both enterprises use ELS, a federation agreement among STSs is a viable choice, as this leverages trusted root CAs and trusted STSs and attribute stores, which are all high-level security functions.

In some cases, only a part of a partner's ELS infrastructure is trusted or the partner's infrastructure supports most but not all ELS requirements. For example, if the root CA is trusted but the STSs or attribute stores are not trusted, identity-based federation with delegation or a local attribute store for those identities might be a better option. This leverages the existing trust in the identity credentials while providing the claims through the local STS and internally maintained attributes. This provides the function of the untrusted partner STS or attributes in a trusted way. The lack of trust is similar to a lack of technology, as a function that exists but is not trusted is similar to one that is missing.

The complementary situation is when a partner STS is trusted while partner identity credentials are not trusted. This case is not common, because weak authentication to an application often correlates with weak authentication to the STS, which means the SAML token cannot be trusted even if the STS and attribute stores are trusted. The best technical solution when identity services are not trusted may be person-to-person federation, which would limit the scale of sharing to individuals or small groups of known entities.

12.2.3 Individual Trust

In some cases, certain individuals of a partner organization are trusted even though the organization's security functions are not. In this case, identity-based federation may be possible for the specific identities who are trusted. For example, a partner with a smart card credential might be technologically acceptable since the public/private key pair can be recorded and used for authentication without the associated certificate. However, this requires no key escrow or other method be in use by the partner enterprise to duplicate the private key associated with the credential. This method relies explicitly on the strength of the keys associated with the credential and their storage. This fails to achieve the efficiency and scalability of PKI, but it establishes smaller-scale point-to-point trust using specific public/private key pairs. The certificate is replaced by an internal mapping of public keys to identities.

Another option is to provide a local credential to the trusted individual. This brings the individual into the enterprise. This is a well-integrated method, but proper enterprise-level vetting often cannot be completed on such an individual due to the organization he works for. An individual in an enterprise may trust an individual from a partner enterprise, but the enterprise may not trust them sufficiently to issue a credential.

A local attribute store can record attributes for the trusted individual in order to provide proper access credentials through a local STS. This requires the STSs, applications, and services to check not just issuers of certificates, but public keys for specific individual requesters. Revocation checking must also be supported within the enterprise for such individual keys.

A simpler option for leveraging this trust in the individual and associated credential is delegation. This allows resource owners to assign which applications and services a partner can access instead of providing access based on the partner's attributes. Automatic access based on attributes provides more scalability and automation than delegation, because all access must be granted manually for delegation. This might be an acceptable tradeoff when limited data is to be shared with a small number of individuals in a secure way. In this case, the STS operates as usual and only the applications and services are modified to trust individual keys.

12.2.4 No Trust

In some cases, data owners in an enterprise really do not trust a federation individual or his organization not to abuse their access but they still need to provide some access. As they cannot trust individuals, the option of individual trust does not apply. The problem is that any access granted is likely to be abused, such as copying and exfiltrating data or rendering inoperable or untrustworthy any services or devices to which more generous access is granted. In this case, the idea is to limit the individual to only what is needed when it is needed and to heavily monitor activity to detect suspicious behavior where limits cannot be strictly enforced through technology.

Shared information may be fingerprinted or steganographically imprinted for later forensics in case of leaks.

One option is to provide a partner individual with a locked-down device that is preconfigured with a credential that has been delegated appropriate access and to let him use this as his only method of access. In this case, the issuing enterprise tightly controls the hardware, software, credentials, and access. This method limits the information to the display on the locked-down device, which can be remotely monitored. If the device is not returned within the timeframe of the valid access, then it can be remotely disabled through device management policy. Monitoring of the device and the data accessed can also reveal potential exfiltration and initiate disabling of the machine and termination of delegation privileges.

None of the automated technological solutions are viable, because they are designed to facilitate automatic sharing of information. Without trust, no automation is desired. For all trust levels, the idea of "trust but verify" underlies all communication. What changes as trust levels decrease is not just what is shared but the measures taken to prevent, detect, and limit harm from the federation partner.

12.3 FEDERATION CONCLUSIONS

This section examines secure enterprise federation options from the perspectives of both technical capabilities and trust. We review six federation methods:

1. ELS federation,
2. ELS-like federation,
3. Identity credential federation,
4. Weak identity federation,
5. Ad hoc federation,
6. Person-to-person sharing.

All solutions are acceptable at small scale, but only those near the top of the list scale to the organizational or enterprise level while maintaining acceptable security. The best choice is generally the one closest to the top of the above list, but these top-end options require the most infrastructure for proper operation. When less-secure options are chosen, it is important as part of an overall risk management process for the enterprise to monitor and limit the extent of their aggregate use across the enterprise. This limits the scale of the lower options in order to maintain the assurance requirements of the enterprise.

Technological solutions also must be considered in the context of existing trust. A common, but flawed, solution is to choose the best technical solution and simply declare any required trust by formal edict. This masks the underlying trust issues and provides these untrusted partners front-door access to enterprise applications and services. A better approach is to first assess the level of trust in a partner enterprise, its security services, and the individuals involved in the sharing, and then build a federation agreement based on those solid building blocks – and those alone.

ELS Extensions – Content Management

13 Content Object Uniqueness for Forensics

13.1 EXFILTRATION IN COMPLEX SYSTEMS

Transfer of electronic objects through insider activities or penetration and exfiltration is a growing problem. Defense agencies have been losing classified and unclassified documents to insider threats at an increasing rate, and recovery is difficult at best. The first step in pursuing any theft is to identify who might have had access to the stolen item. One can identify suspects based on knowledge of who had access to the controlled access material and on records of anyone who handled it. Attribution is much easier when each instance of an electronic object is unique and a clone can be traced to the individual who accessed the object. If attribution were a given in the theft of electronic objects, deterrence would follow. This chapter describes a twofold mitigation approach. The first form of mitigation is through encryption and tightly controlled access and privilege. The encryption discourages theft or at least makes an adversary work harder to obtain the object. Tight access control ensures a minimum number of individuals in the suspect pool when a theft occurs. The second form of mitigation is through positive attribution of suspects and origins. Knowing that theft will trace back to the individual providing access to the electronic objects should discourage many attempts. This chapter will provide a brief background of a high-assurance security model, content access control and distribution, and a process for providing electronic fingerprints that make electronic objects unique. Finally, we discuss the landscape in terms of electronic objects, instances, and copies.

13.2 PRODUCT IDENTIFIERS

Product identifiers [177] have been with us for a while. A product identifier is a unique label that allows trading partners to easily trace an individual product as it moves through the supply chain. This identifier includes (among other things) the product's lot number, expiration date, product code, and a serial number. The serial number is different for each package or case. This creates a unique identifier – human and machine readable – to enable product tracing throughout the supply chain and enable all trading partners to better detect illegitimate products within the supply chain. Product identifiers are especially important for medicines [178] and food items [179], where theft and counterfeiting are immediate health problems.

If we consider electronic objects as products, then electronic object identifiers may be of some value in determining thefts or counterfeits and may provide some benefits in tracing origins for attribution. Electronic objects are mostly clones of an original with embedded steganographic and license data for ownership claims. In 2014, *The Expendables 3*, a summer action movie with Sylvester Stallone, was stolen from an inadequately protected cloud-based system and leaked to pirates three weeks before its release. It is estimated that the movie has since been downloaded illegally hundreds of thousands of times [180]. The loss in revenue must be staggering.

In addition to lost profits, reputation, corporate stock prices, and national defense can all be damaged by theft and dissemination of controlled electronic objects. The world governments have lost a sizable number of classified and unclassified documents to insider threats. After the losses incurred by a number of malicious insiders, such as Edward Snowden [116], Bradley Manning [117], and others [118], we have no choice but to assess our own insider threat situation.

13.3 HIDDEN MESSAGES

Hidden messages are not new. They are present in advertising, product verification, packaging, and many other items; often not subtle; and designed to be discovered with a little effort. Often watermarks or steganographic messages are placed in files to provide an ownership tag. These are not meant to be found by the casual user, but are extractable if the proper algorithm is known.

13.4 CONTENT MANAGEMENT

Electronic objects are content or information assets that include documents, spreadsheets, diagrams, pictures, videos, web pages, presentations, and other complete or incomplete sets of information. All electronic objects generated within an enterprise are considered authoritative and are under rights management by the enterprise. Rights management is an integral part of the development of these records, but the workings of the rights management system should be transparent to the user. This helps the enterprise with record keeping and document control [47] [60].

13.4.1 Access Control

A primary deterrent to distribution of access-controlled electronic objects is the encryption and access control process. Entities in the environment may be active or passive. Passive entities include information packages, static files, and/or reference data structures. Passive entities are the target of an activity; they do not initiate activities and cannot assume the role of requester or provider. These passive entities are often the target of theft and are a primary yield of penetrated computer systems by the process of exfiltration.

Active entities are those entities that change or modify passive entities, request or provide services, or participate in communication flows. The active entities discussed in this section include the content management system and the content development applications. Each is issued PKI certificates, and private keys of all active entities are stored in tamper proof, threat mitigating storage. Active elements (content development applications) on the user end-devices act in the security context of the user. If the user is on a thin client, the content development applications are web services and have their own certificates and identities. Communication between

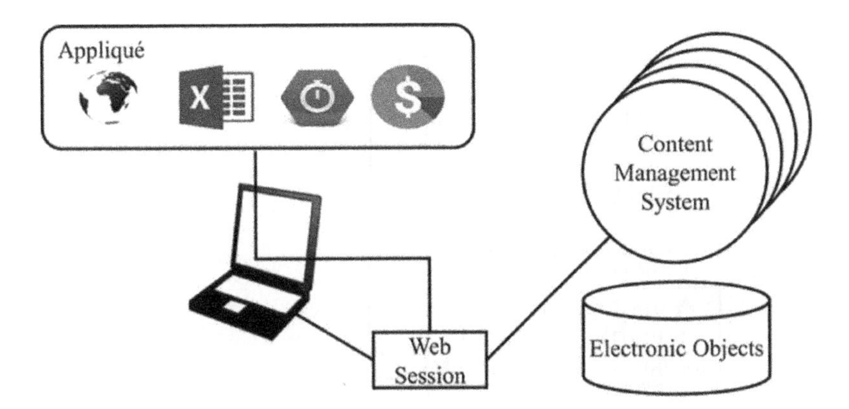

FIGURE 13.1. Communication between Entities

active entities requires full bilateral, PKI-based, end-to-end authentication. This is normally followed by initiation of an encrypted session using some form of TLS.

Authorization in the operational environment is implemented by a verifiable claims-based access control (CBAC) process. Claims are part of an authorization credential issued by a trusted STS and signed by that entity to preserve integrity. A claims-based credential is sent to the provider containing a SAML token that includes issuance time and expiration time.

Figure 13.1 displays a user interacting with the content management system through the content developing application on the user end-device.

13.4.2 Enforcing Access Control

The discretionary access control process enforces both mandatory and discretionary access control. In this process, the electronic object is encrypted. The key to the encryption is contained in the header and is wrapped in the public key of the content manager. The key will only be released when the appliqué confirms that access control is satisfied. Further, the header is encrypted in a key known to the appliqué. The electronic object is provided an extension that directs the request to open the file to the appliqué enforcing access. Authority over the data can be limited by claims, such as those listed here:

1. Claim 1: read, copy, and retain the electronic object.
2. Claim 2: read only on screen, may print the information asset but not cut and paste any parts of the information asset, claimant cannot save to user environment in electronic form.

13.4.3 Components of an Electronic Object

The components of an electronic object stored information asset are provided in Figure 13.2.

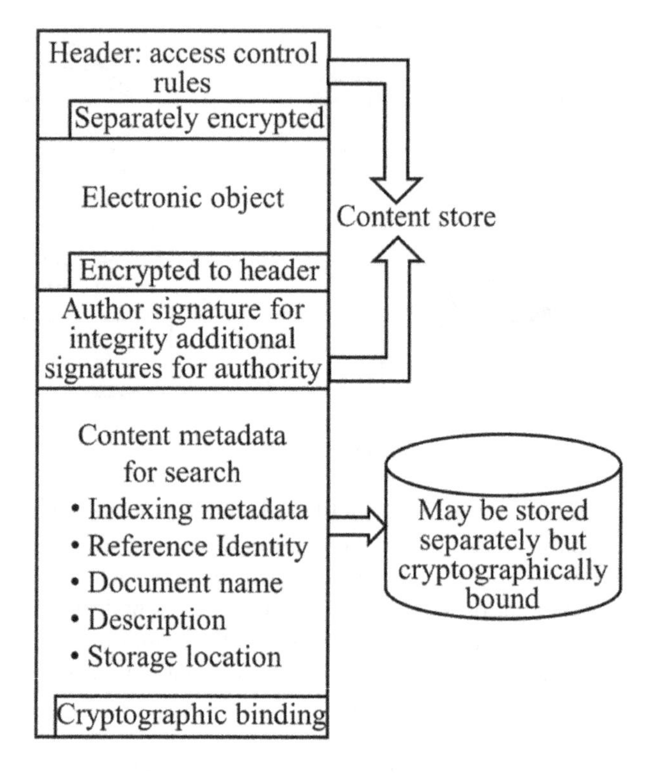

FIGURE 13.2. Authoritative Electronic Object Format

The content is encrypted (except when the electronic object access controls indicate it is uncontrolled with no distribution limitations), with key management being maintained by the content manager and available to the retrieval appliqué software.

Figure 13.3 shows the two cases for content creation and entry into the content management system.

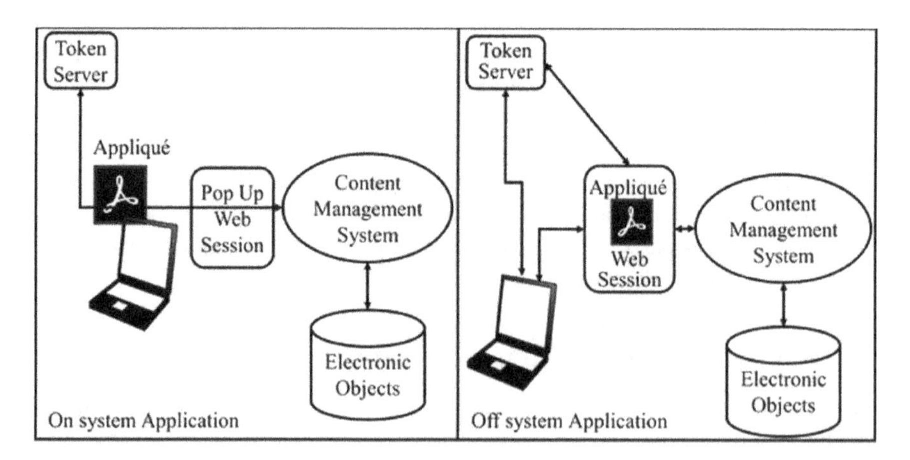

FIGURE 13.3. Content Creation on Save

13.4.4 Responsibilities of the Appliqué

Each application for display of an electronic object contains an appliqué. This appliqué is responsible for a number of items, including:

1. Evaluation of access control requirements and whether or not they are met. Unmet control requirements trigger an alert, monitoring records, and a denial of access.
2. Placing a frame around the display providing distribution and control limitations.
3. Handling the encryption and decryption processes.
4. Adding message fragments to the display for forensics analysis in case the display is photographed for later distribution. The message fragments must be subtle and yet clear enough to appear in a photograph for later recovery. Several such display modifications are shown in Figure 13.4.

Figure 13.4 shows an example of a Visio screen with distributed fragments and other discoverable message information that may be reassembled to provide accountability. The fragments are deliberately non-subtle for illustration purposes. In an actual application, they are more subtle and may be more fractionated; in addition, the message should be repeated throughout the figure. Visible messages may be detected by the threat and scrubbed from the document. However, the additional workload should reduce the volume of material being exfiltrated.

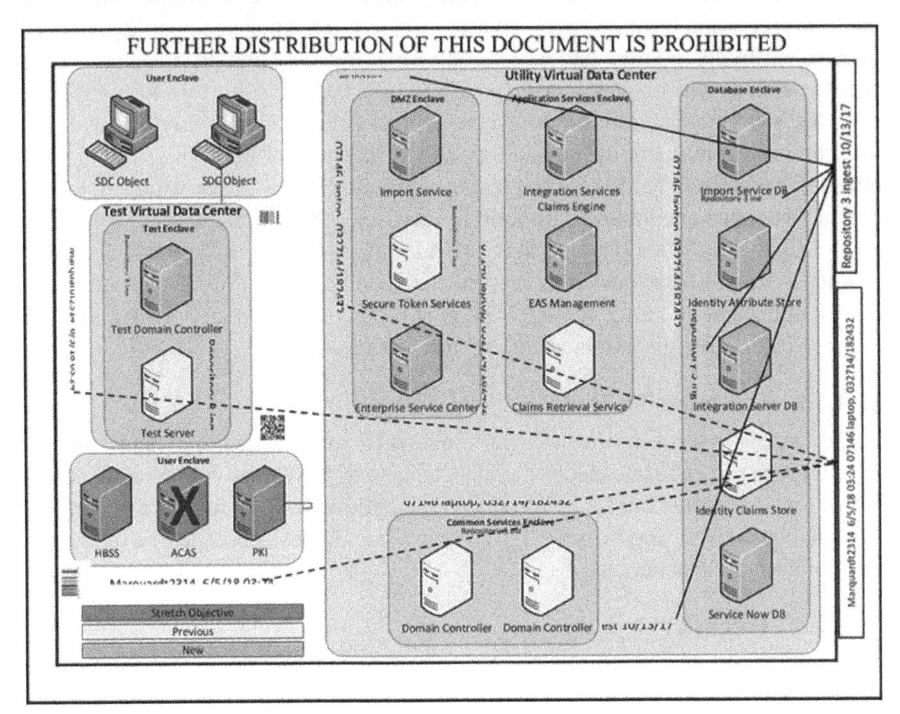

FIGURE 13.4. Display of Electronic Object by Appliqué

A section of text may be used to hide messages by many means. Here the text is used to hide a name through font switching. In this text bold is used but differences between many variants of text may be detectable but not noticeable.

FIGURE 13.5. Text Font Change Example

If the user is authorized to print the document, then similar fragments are added for later forensic analysis. These too must be subtle and survive the printing process for later forensic analysis. Alternative methods exist, including subtle font or formatting changes as shown in Figure 13.5 (can you find "name," "date," and "device"?).

If the user requests a local save, the fragments may not have to be visible for retrieval. Multiple forms of accountability, such as watermarks and non-displayable text in the margins, may be included. If the object is a picture, steganography may be employed. These precautions are taken even though the local save is encrypted and access is matched to the document requester.

13.4.5 Mitigations

Combating insider fraud starts with identifying the types of electronic objects that may be targets and limiting access to those objects. An employee population at risk for insider threats requires increased monitoring of access and privilege, as well as checks on electronic objects that are accessed or used.

Other steps organizations can take to protect against insider threat include the creation or improvement of the auditing and verification of access need for critical objects. Enterprises should also conduct background checks for potential employees, contractors, and subcontractors to look for undisclosed criminal history or any history of financial difficulties that may provide the motive for insider fraud. Access privileges should be reviewed to prevent the accumulation of excess privileges. A thief will expend effort for reward if he is not likely to get caught. Mitigations fall into two categories: discouragement and forensics.

13.4.5.1 Discouraging Theft

Strong access control and encryption make theft more difficult. If and when an intruder seeks to exfiltrate electronic objects, he may have only encrypted files with both strong encryption and access control to fight through. We are aware that intruders aided by insiders may very well overcome some of these obstacles, so the second form of mitigation is pursued.

13.4.5.2 Forensics

The second form of mitigation is in the hidden messages left behind as print, photographic, or electronic embedding. The hidden messages point to the source of a theft so that when a document unexpectedly presents itself on WikiLeaks or elsewhere, the detectives have clues on how that content left the content store. The first effort is to determine whether it is a clone (and a clone of what source) or a copy (and a copy of what source). There are a few terms to define here:

- An *original electronic object* is one that has been ingested into the content management system. This may become automated in the future so that all electronic objects are ingested into the content management system, but until then, all other copies should be destroyed during that process. Ingestion into the management system includes leaving messages behind pointing to the content system on which the object resides. Recall that an electronic object can be documents, spreadsheets, diagrams, pictures, videos, web pages, presentations, and other complete or incomplete sets of information. Some objects may be heavily used and present in more than one management system. The embedded messages should be pertinent to the particular management system.
- An *instance of an electronic object* is a near duplicate of an electronic object. It differs by the embedding of information about who saved the instance and when and where that happened.
- A *clone of an electronic object* is an exact duplicate of an electronic object whether it is an original document or an instance of the document.
- A *copy of an electronic object* is a duplicate that goes through a transition in capturing the contents that may result in a printed or photographed object. The only messages that remain are those that have been inserted into the electronic document and survive the copying process. It is recognized that these messages may be discovered and scrubbed, but this creates a great deal of work for the thief and is hard to do to a large number of objects containing information.

DIGITAL FORENSICS

In this context, forensics is the recovery and investigation of material found in digital devices, often in relation to computer or network exploitation. In this case, the material may be placed in the content.

Forensics on a discovered document can proceed as follows:

Case 1: non-electronic information object.

- The object has no messages at all. There are two possibilities here.
  - Someone on the development team has retained an electronic object that has not been ingested into the content management system, and the development team members should be suspect. Each of their devices should be examined for breach.
  - A copy of an electronic object that is either an original or an instance that has been scrubbed of all messages. The copy should be tested for signs of the scrubbing and, if present, eliminated from this category (in most cases this can be determined even if the object has been re-digitized). In this case, normal forensics must proceed.

Case 2: electronic information object, minimal messaging.

- The object has messages that point to the origin of the object content store and no other messages. This would indicate a breach of that content store.

Case 3: electronic information object, full messaging.

- The object has messages that point to who, what, when, and where the original was accessed. The individual is complicit, careless, or has had their device breached.

13.5 CONTENT OBJECT SUMMARY

We have reviewed the basic approaches to content access control in computing environments. We have also described an approach that relies on high-assurance architectures and the protection elements they provide through PKI. The distribution of private keys is a fundamental violation of a high-assurance model such as ELS. ELS allows us to rely on the PKI elements of the system and greatly reduces the key management requirements normally associated with controlling access to content. ELS also permits the unique encryption of each electronic object, limiting losses to exploits without the growth of key management requirements that normally accompanies such a prolific cryptographic key activity. We have also reviewed at length the embedded message requirements that provide a uniqueness to each instance of an electronic asset. This uniqueness contributes to forensic accountability in the event such losses occur.

14 Homomorphic Encryption

14.1 FULL HOMOMORPHIC ENCRYPTION (FHE)

Most web service providers are partitioned into a front-end web application and back-end stored data. ELS provides secure communication to the web application, and the VADC model extends this to cloud hosting [51]. However, ELS extends only from requester to application, and it does not include the stored data. This data is often the enterprise's most valuable digital asset, and the boundary of ELS between the application and database provides a potential access path that bypasses ELS protections. To maintain ELS security levels in a cloud environment, some means of protecting the data is required.

In addition to the data, the web application may be vulnerable to attacks in a public cloud. Cloud operators may have access to all data in the cloud, and through virtual machine managers, they may also gain visibility into the application code running on the servers.

> **HOMOMORPHISM**
>
> A transformation of one set of information into another set of information that preserves the relations between elements from the original. In this context, the second set disguises the information and relations.c

Homomorphic encryption provides a way to manipulate encrypted data to perform computations without decrypting the data. This is useful for the ELS stored data problem because it allows a web application's stored data to remain encrypted at all times, even during data operations. An attacker at the stored data has no access to plaintext values.

Homomorphic encryption also addresses the web application problem because the web application code can be recompiled to operate on homomorphic-encrypted data. Attackers viewing the web application cannot extract computational process information or unencrypted data from the computation.

When implementing an ELS system in a private data center, there is an implicit safe zone where data and applications can be run. The machines remain under physical control, and the people working on them are part of the enterprise. When moving to the cloud, this safe zone is replaced by a potentially hostile or compromised environment, which threatens to expose sensitive data. Homomorphic encryption offers a way to reclaim this safe zone while maintaining many of the benefits of cloud hosting.

This chapter discusses the methods and issues in using homomorphic encryption within an ELS architecture.

14.1.1 Homomorphic Encryption

Homomorphic encryption refers to methods of encryption that allow operations on the ciphertext to map to corresponding operations on the underlying plaintext. For example, raw, unpadded RSA encryption is performed as follows to compute ciphertext c from plaintext message m:

$$c = ENC(m) = m^e \pmod n \tag{1}$$

The product of two encrypted values

$$c_1 = ENC(m_1) \tag{2}$$

and

$$c_2 = ENC(m_2) \tag{3}$$

is

$$c_1 \cdots c_2 = m_1{}^e \cdots m_2{}^e \pmod n \tag{4}$$

$$= (m_1 \cdots m_2)^e \pmod n \tag{5}$$

$$= ENC(m_1 \cdots m_2) \tag{6}$$

The product of the encrypted values is just the encrypted product of the corresponding plaintext values.

Different homomorphic-encryption schemes have different operations, and the ciphertext and plaintext operations can differ. Paillier encryption, for example, has the property:

$$ENC(m_1 + m_2) = ENC(m_1) \cdots ENC(m_2) \tag{7}$$

In this case, multiplication of ciphertext corresponds to addition of plaintext.

For both RSA and Paillier, only a single operation is possible. In 2009, Gentry published his thesis describing an encryption scheme that allows both addition and multiplication [92]. With these two operations it is possible to compute $1 + (-1) \cdot (a \cdot b)$ for two inputs: a and b. If a and b are binary values, then this is the computation of the NAND function, which can be used to build a logical circuit that can perform any computation. Therefore, such a homomorphic-encryption method allows the computation of any function on encrypted data. This method is called FHE.

Methods such as RSA and Paillier, which allow some computation but not arbitrary functions, are PHE, which is another class of homomorphic encryption that allows the computation of any function on encrypted data (like FHE), but only for a limited number of executions of an operation. For example, it may allow any number of additions, but only up to n multiplications for some number n. These SWHE methods are often related to FHE methods. In particular, Gentry's FHE method builds on SWHE and removes the limit on the number of multiplications through bootstrapping.

Even FHE has its limitations for providing security. Although confidentiality is maintained by keeping data encrypted at all times, integrity requires additional work. An operation on homomorphic data does not leak the value of the data, but the result of such a computation in the cloud has no method of verification. The cloud provider could, for example, replay results of previous computations or encrypt its own chosen results using known public keys.

A solution that provides verifiable computing is presented in [181]. The representation of the circuit that computes the function is garbled in a way that the entity doing the computation does not know what is being computed. This method builds on homomorphic encryption to monitor the integrity of results.

This integrity check is critical to ELS cloud hosting. Because the homomorphic-encryption approach provides confidentiality and integrity, it extends ELS security properties into a hostile cloud environment.

14.1.2 Homomorphic Encryption with ELS

This section discusses the integration of homomorphic encryption into an ELS architecture. However, before examining homomorphic encryption, we first examine the limitations of standard encryption.

14.1.2.1 Non-Homomorphic Encryption

One approach using standard encryption is to host the application locally and store encrypted data in the cloud. The browser and application are outside the cloud in a controlled environment, and the database is inside the cloud. The application encrypts data before sending it to the cloud database and decrypts it after retrieval. The cloud is simply a place to store data. All computation occurs on local, trusted machines. Cryptographic keys are maintained by the local application.

This scenario maintains confidentiality, as only encrypted content is sent to the cloud. However, all processing of data requires the data to be retrieved and decrypted and the computation to be performed locally. If the results of the computation are to be stored, they must be encrypted and sent back to the cloud. Such a model for cloud security works well for all data set sizes, but the size of the data set that is retrieved and sent must be small, and the computation must be quick. In such a case, the main resource requirement is the storage, and the network transmissions and local computation are relatively minor. This could be the case for a forensics archive, in which large amounts of data are stored for potential use but only small portions are actually ever used.

The problem with traditional encryption comes when a computation requires access to all of the data, such as computation of an average or maximum value. In such a case, all of the encrypted data must be retrieved and decrypted, and then the computation can take place on the decrypted values. With limited network bandwidth and potentially limited requester computation resources, the traditional approach has significant overhead. Homomorphic encryption, in contrast, only requires encrypting the request and decrypting the response. The computation is performed on the encrypted values.

The following discussion covers solutions that use homomorphic encryption.

14.1.2.2 FHE with Full Application in Cloud

The most desirable implementation for security is to place the application and data in the cloud, each with homomorphic encryption, and use verifiable computation for the application logic. Figure 14.1 provides the basic concept. This provides confidentiality and integrity of the data and computation results even when hosting in a hostile environment. The requester would need a way to encrypt request data to the application and decrypt encrypted responses from the application.

One approach is to have the requester browser manage this encryption and decryption along with the key generation and management. However, this requires rewriting the browser. A simpler approach is to have a separate module attached to the browser that modifies outgoing and incoming traffic to encrypt and decrypt content, respectively. This enables the browser functionality and cryptography to be modular so that browser updates do not break cryptography and changes in cryptography do not require rewriting browser code.

To the browser, nothing has changed. The cryptographic module handles translation of plaintext requests to homomorphic-encrypted requests. The server code is

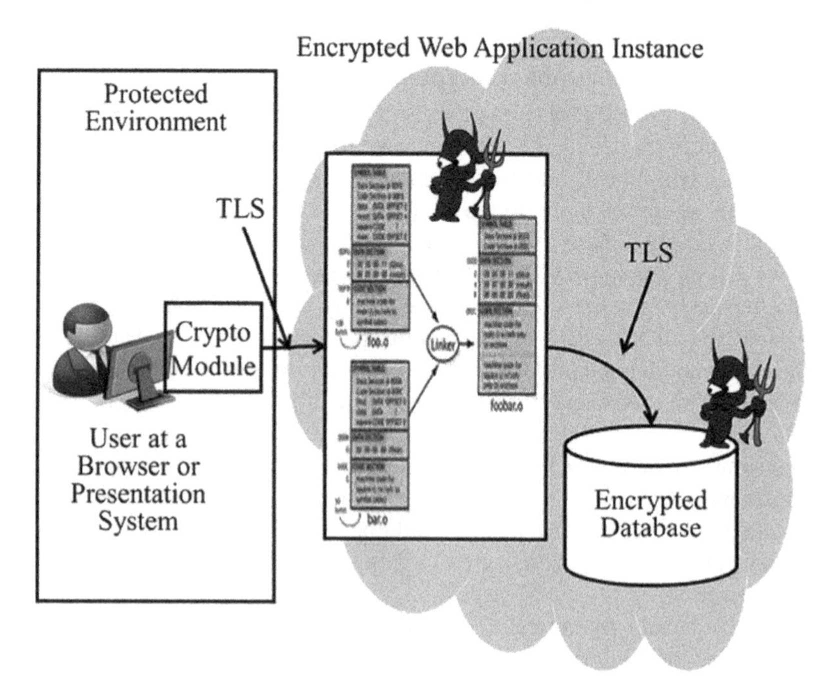

FIGURE 14.1. Full Homomorphic Concept

recompiled to operate on encrypted data with verifiable computing. No homomorphic keys are stored in the cloud, and any server keys for encryption, signatures, or other operations remain encrypted under homomorphic encryption. The browser cryptographic module is responsible for managing and using homomorphic-encryption keys.

14.1.2.3 FHE with Only Data in Cloud

Recompiling applications to operate on homomorphic-encrypted data is not always desirable. In these cases, the application can be hosted locally while the data is hosted in the cloud. The data itself is encrypted for homomorphic operation. This concept is shown in Figure 14.2.

There are two possibilities for how the database is hosted in the cloud: it can be recompiled for homomorphic-encrypted operation, or it can remain as-is and only the data is encrypted. The case in which the database code is recompiled is identical to the case in which the application is recompiled, except that the cryptographic module now attaches to the application calling the database instead of the browser calling the application.

There are some additional considerations for the unmodified database with encrypted data. For homomorphic encryption in which the operations on the plaintext and ciphertext differ, the database commands may need to be rewritten to account for this difference. For example, if addition of plaintext values is accomplished by multiplying ciphertext values, then all database requests to add values must be changed to multiplication requests.

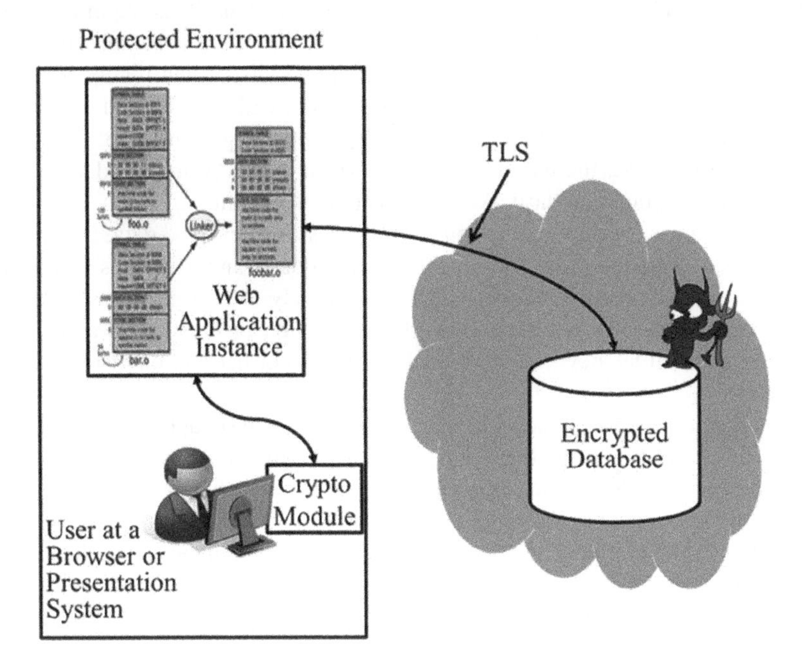

FIGURE 14.2. Protected Application Homomorphic Concept

Even if the operations are the same, the data types and sizes of plaintext and ciphertext may be different. The necessary types and sizes for the ciphertext must be available in the database.

The main advantage of this method over placing the full application data and logic in the cloud is that the application and database code require no changes. The only change is the addition of the cryptographic module to the application to translate database commands into homomorphic-encrypted commands.

14.1.3 Performance Considerations

Homomorphic encryption solves many of the security problems for ELS cloud hosting, but this security comes at a cost. Homomorphic-encryption algorithms are a small subset of possible encryption algorithms, and all of the currently available homomorphic algorithms are slower than traditional encryption algorithms.

However, the comparison is not that simple. Traditional encryption allows only two operations: encryption and decryption. Homomorphic encryption allows those two operations, as well as operations on the data itself. Typically, plaintext operations include addition and multiplication, but the ciphertext operations may be more complicated operations, which can incur performance penalties. To assess the performance of homomorphic encryption, it is important to understand how the fundamental operations of encryption, decryption, addition, and multiplication are used. The performance of these operations must be combined or averaged to provide an overall performance assessment.

There are two generic use cases for homomorphic encryption in the cloud. The first is a bulk load of existing plaintext data and applications. This requires encrypting all the data and applications. This is an infrequent event, but it can be very resource-intensive for large data sets or applications. It is often highly parallelizable, so the main issue is throughput. The time taken will depend on the size of the data set, the available resources, and the computation requirements of encryption. For this first use case, the baseline for comparison is encrypting the data with the Advanced Encryption Standard (AES) encryption algorithm.

The second use case for encryption is user access to encrypted data. If individual users perform the encryption and decryption of requests and responses in a distributed way, the performance of the requests is unlikely to be significantly affected. Unless large data sets are transferred, the encryption or decryption of data will incur only a small latency based on local encryption or decryption of requests and responses.

A central server that manages keys and performs cryptographic operations frees users from key management, but it creates a central bottleneck for performance. The central server must do all encryption and decryption, which may require dedicated computing resources to manage the throughput.

Addition and multiplication are used to manipulate data in the cloud. Such operations do not decrypt or encrypt data, so overall performance depends only on the performance of the ciphertext operations that are used to implement the additions and multiplications on the underlying plaintext.

If the application itself is encrypted, the code will include different additions and multiplications to do computation. This is another area where the specific application will influence performance.

The operational model for an application will be some mix of additions, multiplications, uploads, and downloads. As a result, it is not possible to determine the performance penalty for using homomorphic encryption without knowledge of the application itself. We examine instead the individual operations, which enable further analysis for specific applications.

To track the degradation in performance, a sample database was used with both plaintext and homomorphic searches as a model in [104]. Real-world testing of various homomorphic-encryption methods [182–186] shows that FHE encryption incurs a performance penalty of about 10^{10} compared to the penalty incurred by AES encryption. For example, a 1-ms AES encryption would take about three hours using FHE. This is prohibitively slow, and there is no indication that this will become feasible for real-world applications in the near future.

SWHE methods can be orders of magnitude faster than corresponding FHE methods. Encryption can be roughly $10^{2.5}$ times slower than AES, which is approaching feasibility for specific use cases. However, encryption for operations on data is much slower. Encryption for homomorphic addition is $10^{3.8}$ times slower, and encryption for multiplication is $10^{7.5}$ times slower. These factors make current and near-future adoption unlikely.

An important consideration for real-world performance is the actual time taken, not just the factor above the non-homomorphic operation, as encryption, addition, and multiplication, although all very fast, perform differently. For the current numbers, however, the message is clear that homomorphic encryption retains significant performance penalties and little or no probability that improvements in commodity hardware will be able to reduce these penalties to acceptable levels. The few options available for FHE and SWHE are more like existence proofs than performance-optimized standards. As a result, performance suffers significantly compared to the highly optimized symmetric encryption methods like AES that are in use today.

14.2 PARTIAL HOMOMORPHIC ENCRYPTION (PHE)

FHE allows any computation to be performed on the encrypted data [92]. However, FHE is prohibitively slow for all but the simplest of computations [104]. PHE has higher performance, but it allows only a single type of operation, such as addition or multiplication. An extensive survey of homomorphic-encryption methods is provided in [187].

CRYPTDB

A computer program that keeps track of the encryption keys and structure of a partial homomorphic encryption process and provides encrypt/decrypt services.

The previous section suggests that FHE is not practical, but methods using PHE show promise [9]. Research involving PHE has shown that a Structured Query Language (SQL) database (DB) can be encrypted such that standard SQL queries

> **ERP**
>
> Business process management software that allows the use of a system of integrated applications to manage the business and automate office functions related to technology, services, and often human resources.

can be run against this encrypted database [188]. The encryption is performed by the CryptDB proxy, which is located between the database requester and the database. The CryptDB proxy translates queries on unencrypted data into queries on encrypted data, allowing a user to access the encrypted database as if it were not encrypted. The CryptDB proxy also translates encrypted responses to unencrypted responses [188–192]. The CryptDB architecture is illustrated in Figure 14.3.

This section discusses work to extend CryptDB to operate on an Enterprise Resource Planning (ERP) system. Real systems are not as simple as a single database. A typical ERP system has the following additional complications:

- Proprietary ERP code that cannot be changed,
- Primary and foreign key reference integrity,
- Stored procedures,
- Views, and
- Multiple accounts with different permissions.

The original CryptDB implementation used MySQL and did not account for these complications. We ported CryptDB from MySQL to Oracle's SQL database and addressed the items listed above. This demonstrates that CryptDB can be integrated with existing operational Oracle ERP systems and is not restricted to the research laboratory or custom-built systems.

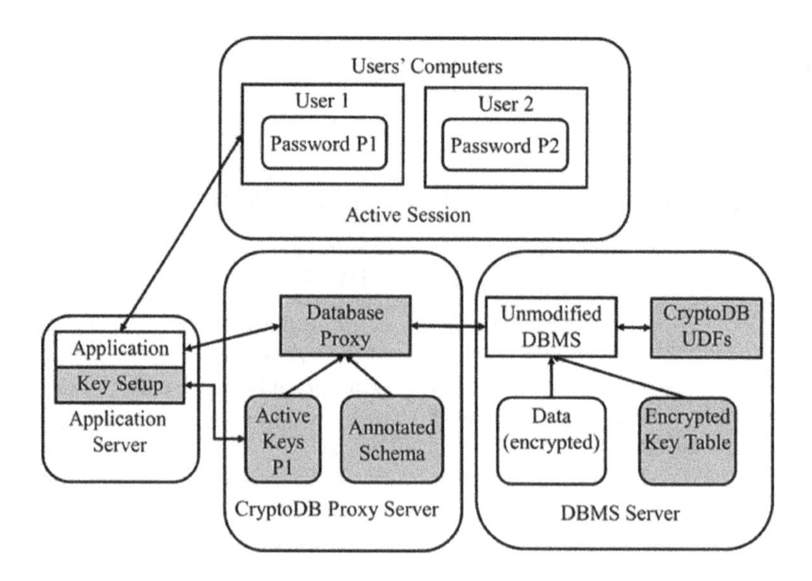

FIGURE 14.3. CryptDB Architecture

14.2.1 Related Work

There are many approaches to securing database information. Monomi, another CryptDB-based approach, allows more complex queries by splitting computation between server and client [193]. The L-EncDB system uses techniques to preserve the data formats and lengths between unencrypted and encrypted data [194].

The BigSecret system secures Not-only SQL (NoSQL) databases using property-preserving encryption on indices of data encrypted with standard techniques [195]. A modular framework for providing varying degrees of privacy and performance for NoSQL databases is provided in [196].

14.2.2 Research Methods

This section presents the experimentation and test process. Maintaining correct functionality was required. Experiments determined relative performance in encrypted searches. This work consists of the following steps:

1. Select database,
2. Determine the selected database schema,
3. Develop PHE schemes,
4. Perform credential mapping,
5. Develop SQL translation schemes,
6. Develop a web application test harness,
7. Establish a set of nominal work queries, and
8. Measure performance.

The implementation was performed in a lab with commodity hardware and software, with the exception of the CryptDB proxy and other code and scripts written specifically for this work.

14.2.3 Human Resources (HR) Database Selection

This work used the Oracle 12c database system and the sample HR database that is provided with it by Oracle. This database was used as the starting point for development and testing. It provided an adequate test system for many of the complexities of a full-scale HR ERP system.

14.2.4 HR Database Schema

The HR database schema consists of seven tables:

- Employees,
- Jobs,
- Job_History,
- Departments,

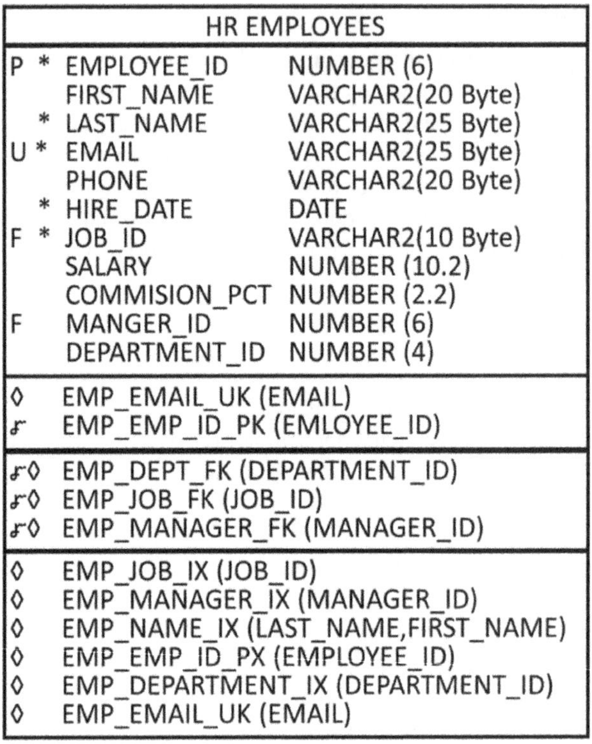

HR EMPLOYEES		
P *	EMPLOYEE_ID	NUMBER (6)
	FIRST_NAME	VARCHAR2(20 Byte)
*	LAST_NAME	VARCHAR2(25 Byte)
U *	EMAIL	VARCHAR2(25 Byte)
	PHONE	VARCHAR2(20 Byte)
*	HIRE_DATE	DATE
F *	JOB_ID	VARCHAR2(10 Byte)
	SALARY	NUMBER (10.2)
	COMMISION_PCT	NUMBER (2.2)
F	MANGER_ID	NUMBER (6)
	DEPARTMENT_ID	NUMBER (4)
◊	EMP_EMAIL_UK (EMAIL)	
	EMP_EMP_ID_PK (EMLOYEE_ID)	
◊	EMP_DEPT_FK (DEPARTMENT_ID)	
◊	EMP_JOB_FK (JOB_ID)	
◊	EMP_MANAGER_FK (MANAGER_ID)	
◊	EMP_JOB_IX (JOB_ID)	
◊	EMP_MANAGER_IX (MANAGER_ID)	
◊	EMP_NAME_IX (LAST_NAME,FIRST_NAME)	
◊	EMP_EMP_ID_PX (EMPLOYEE_ID)	
◊	EMP_DEPARTMENT_IX (DEPARTMENT_ID)	
◊	EMP_EMAIL_UK (EMAIL)	

FIGURE 14.4. HR Schema for Employees Table

- Locations,
- Countries,
- Regions.

The employees table schema is shown in Figure 14.4. The HR schema and the data for the HR database were used for unencrypted operation of the ERP and served as the baseline for performance measurements.

For encrypted operation, the HR database schema had to be modified for encrypted data. This involved modification of data types and sizes to accommodate encrypted data. It also included additional columns for multiple encryption methods where required. The names of tables and columns were encrypted as well. The ERP was not modified for these changes. It communicated through the CryptDB proxy, which mapped requests from the unencrypted schema to the encrypted schema.

14.2.5 Encryption Schemes

Different encryption methods offer different properties that are useful for operations on encrypted data. The proper encryption scheme for data depends on its intended use. The encryption methods and supported SQL operations are shown in Table 14.1.

TABLE 14.1.
Encryption Methods

Type	Encryption Method	SQL Operation
RND	AES in CBC mode	None
HOM	Paillier	Addition
SEARCH	*	Word Search
DET_EQ	AES in CBC mode	Equality
OPE	*	Order
EQ_JOIN	*	Join
OPE_JOIN	*	Range Join

* custom encryption methods.

These encryption methods are listed in approximate order of security protection (from highest to lowest). Security protection decreases as more information is revealed about the data. For example, assuming the cryptographic methods are known, random encryption reveals essentially no information about the plaintext. Deterministic encryption (DET) allows determination of whether two encrypted values have the same plaintext values without revealing what this plaintext is. Order-preserving encryption (OPE) leaks the relative size of the plaintext values without revealing the values themselves.

Generally speaking, the encryption methods reveal the amount of information needed to perform the associated SQL operation. A determination of whether this amount is acceptable must be made at design [189, 191]. We assume it is acceptable for our intended use cases. For cases in which the amount of revealed information is not acceptable, there are methods to reduce it, and these are briefly mentioned as future work.

Because different encryption schemes may reveal different information when the cryptographic methods are known, it is possible to layer them. Plaintext can be encrypted with EQ_JOIN, and this can again be encrypted with DET. We refer to a data element that has undergone this multi-layer encryption as an "onion," with each different encryption method being a layer of the onion. The four encryption onions listed below are used for this work. The Equality (EQ) onion is illustrated in Figure 14.5.

1. Word Search: SEARCH
2. Addition: HOM
3. Equality: RND, DET, EQ_JOIN
4. Order: RND, OPE, OPE_JOIN

The onions-and-layers approach provides increased security by revealing the least secure inner layers only when needed. For simplicity and performance, it is also possible to use only the innermost layer.

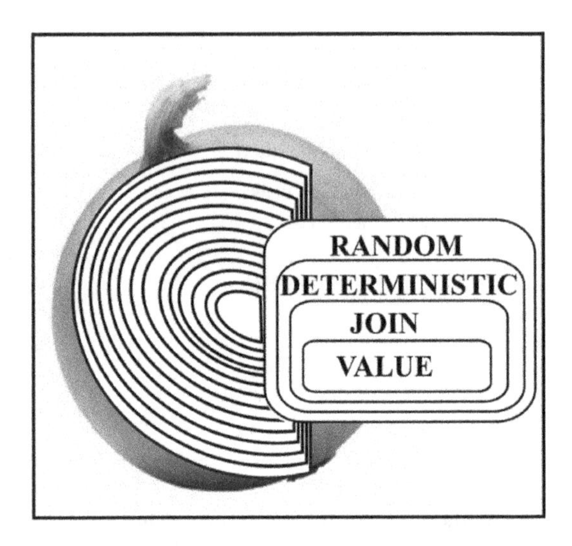

FIGURE 14.5. EQ Onion Layering

14.2.6 Credential Mapping

To provide proper access to different users, different accounts are set up within the ERP and database. The ERP uses its accounts and credentials to make queries to the database. To use these accounts through the CryptDB proxy, separate accounts must be created for the encrypted database. The CryptDB proxy maps the existing accounts for the unencrypted database to accounts for the encrypted database.

In addition to the accounts, there are keys and other information that a user must have to encrypt requests and decrypt responses. These keys are themselves encrypted using information from the user account so that only the appropriate accounts have access to the proper cryptographic keying material. Other accounts may be able to access the database of ERP cryptographic keys, but they will not be able to decrypt and use keys for which they are not authorized.

14.2.7 SQL Translation Schemes

With the encryption methods and accounts set up, we need a way to translate an unencrypted request to an encrypted request. This translation depends on the type of data and the type of encryption. For normal requests, the column names and data are encrypted. For other requests, such as addition, the query itself must be modified. For example, with Paillier encryption, addition of plaintext corresponds to multiplication of ciphertext.

Other translations are similar. Text strings must be converted to binary values for searching. If a numerical value is part of a query, it may need to be encrypted in multiple ways if it is used with data in different columns with different encryption methods or keys.

With multiple users there is no way to know in advance which user will be calling a stored procedure, so encrypted values in stored procedure queries cannot be pre-determined. These values must be inserted at execution by determining the user and updating the query based on the appropriate user-specific information.

14.2.8 Web Application

To test an encrypted database versus an unencrypted database, a web application was implemented to act as a front end for both. This web application ran natively on the unencrypted database, and it could send requests to the CryptDB proxy for operation on the encrypted database. No code changes were needed in the application itself. A configuration change is all that was needed to operate on encrypted data.

In addition to the web application front end, various tools allowed more in-depth testing of the encrypted database. Direct queries of the encrypted database are possible using the sqlplus tool, but due to the encrypted values, it is difficult to create the requests or interpret the results. A script (cryptdb-sqlplus) was developed to make a subset of such queries on the encrypted database. It uses the CryptDB keys and mappings to translate and send user requests to the encrypted DB and translate responses.

14.2.9 Assessments

Assessment of an encrypted database consists of three parts. The first part validates that each implemented capability works as expected. A sequence of requests is made to the unencrypted and encrypted databases, and the results are compared. Identical results confirm that the capabilities are implemented correctly.

The second part consists of performance tests in which the same sequence of queries is sent to the same application, first using the unencrypted database and then using the encrypted database through CryptDB. Latency and throughput of the encrypted database queries are compared to the values for the unencrypted database.

The third part consists of multiple users with simultaneous access to confirm that the multi-user access controls are performing properly and are not negatively affecting performance.

14.2.10 Lab Setup

The development work for the encrypted database was done on a single machine. This allowed functional testing and very limited performance testing. For full performance testing, a dedicated lab was set up with the following equipment:

- Database server laptop;
- Application server laptop;
- Multi-use desktop for application server, loader, and client;
- Additional client laptop; and
- Ethernet switch.

The application server was a Dell Mobile Precision 7710 laptop with four cores at 3 GHz, 64 GB memory, 2 TB SSD, and 1 Gb/s Ethernet running Windows 10.

The database server was nearly identical to the application server, except for two 1 TB PCIe drives in a RAID 0 configuration for storage.

A Dell Precision Tower 7910 served as multi-use desktop. It had dual 20 core processors at 2.2 GHz, 512 GB memory, a 2 TB SSD, and 1 Gb/s Ethernet running Windows 10.

The additional client laptop had two cores at 2.8 GHz, 8 GB memory, and 100 Mb/s Ethernet running Windows 10.

An eight-port gigabit Ethernet switch connected the machines. Software included the following:

- Oracle 12c database – database to store both unencrypted and encrypted data;
- H2 database – database to store the CryptDB keys and other cryptographic and mapping data;
- CryptDB proxy – ported to Oracle from original MySQL implementation;
- WebLogic 12.1.3 – web server for the test application;
- Java JDK 7 update 80 for Windows x64 – platform for various applications;
- JMeter – test tool to execute test scripts and capture performance data;
- Bouncycastle – library for cryptographic operations;
- Cygwin – application that enables Linux-style scripting within a Windows operating system;
- Various scripts and tools developed for automating the setup of the encrypted database and loading the encrypted data into the encrypted database.

14.2.11 PHE Results

This section presents the results for tests of proper functionality of baseline operations and enhancements.

14.2.11.1 Baseline Functionality

The first test examined the port of the MySQL-based CryptDB implementation to an Oracle-based implementation. Direct queries on the encrypted database showed that the tables, columns, and values were properly encrypted. Queries through the CryptDB proxy on the encrypted database provided results that matched those from the unencrypted database. This confirmed the proper functioning of the encrypted database and CryptDB.

14.2.11.2 Enhancements

Next, certain improvements (including referential constraints, views, and stored procedure capabilities) were made to the CryptDB implementation. These features, which are required for an ERP instantiation, were not part of the original MySQL implementation.

Stored procedures in the unencrypted database are converted to stored procedures that perform equivalent operations on the encrypted database. This involves encrypting raw data in the procedures, mapping table and column names, changing operations (such as addition to multiplication for Paillier encryption), and changing commands where appropriate. Stored procedures use the PL/SQL language, and for this work, a core subset of PL/SQL was implemented to enable testing of stored procedures.

Referential constraints are important for primary key and foreign key references. When the primary and foreign keys are encrypted with different keys, the database cannot guarantee integrity across these two columns. CryptDB has been modified to recognize these references and add two additional columns that contain keyed hashes of the primary and foreign keys. The keyed hash of the foreign key is set to reference the keyed hash of the primary key. CryptDB uses the same key to generate the two columns of hashes, which allows the database to maintain referential integrity of the primary and foreign keys through these extra columns.

Views are like tables, but they have some important differences that require special consideration for implementation. For example, a table has one column for random initialization vectors (IVs), but a view must have multiple columns for random IVs because it may be constructed as a join across multiple tables, each with its own IVs. CryptDB must also maintain the mappings from each encrypted column to its IV column.

Like tables, views can operate with different onion layers of encryption. If these layers are unwrapped or rewrapped on the underlying tables, the views must keep track of these changes. A query on a view that requires adjusting onion layers also requires changes to the base tables. As a result, the query translation for views is more complicated, and the resulting query may contain additional queries to change onion layers on the view and associated tables, as well as changes to internal state to keep track of the view-to-table mappings.

Stored procedures are groups of SQL statements and control statements. They offer many benefits, including performance, security, scalability, and maintainability. However, they require extending CryptDB to support creating, dropping, and calling these stored procedures.

Additional complications arise in stored procedures. The same encrypted value in a query may be used across multiple columns and onions. Instead of simply encrypting a value once, it must be encrypted for each possible use. With multiple users, a method for determining which principal is making a request is required to select and use the proper key.

An additional challenge is that a result may be from one or another column, and which column the value comes from is determined at runtime. In this case, CryptDB must keep track of which column, onion, and principal a response came from and use this additional information for proper decryption.

The issues of multi-user stored procedures and dynamic column determination have not been addressed yet, and these present challenges for future work. However, the solution concepts are generally understood, so the challenge is to simply implement them.

14.3 PHE PERFORMANCE EVALUATION

As shown in Figure 14.3, the CryptDB proxy sits between the application and database. It encrypts content going into the database and decrypts content coming out.

It stores encryption keys in encrypted form in the database itself. The user passwords are used to decrypt the appropriate encryption keys. Information about the encrypted schema and which parts of it each user is allowed to access are stored in the annotated schema. CryptDB user-defined functions (UDFs) are stored in the database to help the proxy manipulate the database cryptographic state.

The previous section examined the feasibility of such a setup [62]. It extended the original implementation of CryptDB [197] to include stored procedures, views, and referential integrity of primary/foreign key pairs. There has been some work to test performance of both homomorphic and partial homomorphic encryption. [198] describes a framework for homomorphic-encryption performance testing, and [199] tests the raw cryptographic operations for FHE and PHE methods. This chapter looks at the considerations needed to test a homomorphically encrypted database and the results of testing the ERP system with the extended CryptDB implementation that was described in the previous section.

14.3.1 Evaluation Areas

Performance evaluation covers two main areas: bulk encryption of an existing database and queries against the encrypted database.

14.3.1.1 Bulk Encryption

Bulk encryption is the process of converting an existing unencrypted database to an encrypted database. This process performs multiple encryptions of each data element according to the operations that will be performed on the data and the associated encryption types that support these operations. Evaluation of bulk encryption includes assessment of the amount of time and computation resources required for a baseline data set and an evaluation of scalability to larger data sets.

The time and computation resources are important for determining the practical impact of bulk encryption. A bulk encryption is often performed offline. For operational systems, this requires shutting the system down while the encryption takes place to ensure data is not modified during the bulk encryption process. The bulk encryption time should not exceed a reasonable downtime for the system that uses the data.

Scalability is important for predicting performance with larger data sets. With a fixed set of computation resources, the total computation, and hence the total time, should scale nearly linearly with database size. However, the allowed downtime is often fixed, so another important area of scalability is parallelizability. If this also scales nearly linearly with data size, it means the bulk encryption can be divided up and completed in parallel in the same amount of time regardless of the data size.

14.3.1.2 Encrypted Queries

Query evaluation involves sending different types of queries to the encrypted database to determine performance characteristics. The primary performance measures are latency and throughput.

Latency includes both absolute and relative latency. *Absolute latency* is the amount of time a standard query takes to complete. This is important because longer delays from the encrypted queries can negatively impact the user experience. *Relative latency* is the percent increase in latency compared to unencrypted queries. A user might not notice an increase in latency from 10 ms to 20 ms for an individual query, but composite operations that aggregate many such queries would see significant latency increases.

Throughput is an issue as a system scales up. Even if latency is low for nominal request rates, decreased throughput will create scaling problems that eventually cause latency problems. Contention for critical central resources, such as cryptographic functions that are not parallelizable, throttles throughput as request rates increase. Synchronization causes delays when distributed resources are available but must be locked to maintain data integrity and consistency. The computation resources available provide a limit on overall throughput.

Homomorphic-encryption methods that rely on shared internal state information face potential problems with critical central resources and synchronization. Increased resource requirements for performing complex encryption operations reduce the throughput for a fixed set of resources. Increasing the available resources would alleviate this problem, but it would increase costs.

14.3.2 Setup Considerations

The following are important considerations in setting up homomorphic-encryption performance evaluation:

- Different queries invoke different cryptography with different performance characteristics,
- Combinations of queries with different cryptography are not linear, and
- Initial and steady-state behavior of cryptography can vary significantly.

Standard database testing looks at the database queries and other properties of the database. Homomorphic encryption adds another layer of consideration. It is now also necessary to invoke queries that stress particular types of encryption. Just as certain types of database queries are optimized for performance, the encryption can be optimized for performance based on how different data sets are used. Stressing particular types of encryption can identify these tradeoffs so that appropriate measures can be taken operationally.

Due to the different ways the different types of encryption operate, some are more compute-intensive, and others are more disk- or memory-intensive. Some rely on the proxy to do most of the work, and others push the majority of the work to the database. As a result, stressing a single type of encryption is not sufficient to evaluate overall system performance under a diverse request set. Queries that use encryption types that stress the same resources may combine linearly, such that the total achievable request rate for a combination of requests is just an average of the achievable request rates for the individual requests.

However, if requests use different resources or distribute the resource requirements to different components, it is possible for the requests to receive more responses than the simple average would indicate. This assumes the throughput is bounded primarily by resources. With contention and synchronization, highly non-linear behavior is possible. Thus, to determine the performance for a system, it is important to test not just individual queries, but various combinations of queries.

Testing different queries and combinations of queries results in a large number of test runs. Because the system state can become corrupted, inconsistent, or unknown after a test run, it may be necessary to reset the system state between runs. However, some of the homomorphic-encryption implementations use shared state information that is generated as needed during encryption and decryption. This state information is cached and reused for future queries. This state information is not the data itself, but the supporting cryptographic structures that are used for computing encryptions and decryptions. These optimizations play an important role in making homomorphic encryption feasible, but we must consider the start-up performance separately from the steady-state performance.

In a real system, it is likely that the steady-state performance is most important. For performance evaluation, it is easy to test start-up performance by issuing a small number of queries. Over time, the performance will converge to a steady-state value of latency and throughput. The challenge for testing is to determine the point at which steady-state performance is achieved. Averaging performance across the start-up and steady state provides unreliable numbers. The simple solution is to monitor performance until performance remains steady and then record data starting after that point in time. If the performance remains stable for a time period comparable to the initial transient performance, it is likely that it will remain stable. Accounting for longer-term performance issues is a separate problem. Garbage collection and other infrequent but performance affecting events should be tested as well, but a longer-term test would be necessary.

A method to generate requests and record results is needed to run these tests. One approach for generating requests is a simple web application that takes requests from a browser, translates them into database queries, and returns results in Hypertext Markup Language (HTML) pages. The application approach mimics a full ERP by translating user requests to database queries. A full ERP would have more complicated queries and sequences of queries where the relative performance is more important due to the additional latency of queries. To test such performance, queries can be issued repeatedly to generate higher system utilization that resembles that of an operational ERP.

Although requests are initiated by a browser, it is possible to use a tool to generate many such requests that appear to come from multiple browsers. This approach emulates the aggregated requests from many individual web browsers to the application. With the tool, it is possible to prepare collections of requests that test different types of queries and cryptography. Requests are assigned different weights to form an overall request profile, where each request is repeated at a rate proportional to its weight.

14.3.3 Evaluation Method

Performance evaluation consists of sending requests to the database through the application, waiting for responses, and recording timing information of the requests and responses in order to generate latency, throughput, and other metrics. Because many requests can be handled in parallel by the database, it is necessary to run multiple requester threads in parallel to stress the system and determine maximum performance. With a multi-core desktop, it is possible to achieve true parallelism up to the number of physical cores and virtual parallelism far beyond this limit.

One challenge is that the ramp-up period for multiple users can have a significant effect on performance. If all users start at the same time, they tend to cluster their requests together so that the system receives a group of one type of request, then a group of another type of request, and so on. This degrades performance by focusing the resource utilization rather than spreading it out. To address this, ramp-up times must be chosen so that the different threads are spread across the request sequence. Sudden spikes and drops in central processing unit (CPU) utilization, disk access, and network traffic indicated a failure to adequately space threads. Although such thrashing of resources is a good worst-case test, it is not likely to represent real-world behavior, where requests are made by independent requesters.

For throughput testing, the goal is to see how many requests the system can sustainably complete over a period of time. There are two approaches for this: adaptive and non-adaptive loads. For an adaptive load, a number of threads repeatedly send queries. New requests are only issued after previous requests within the same thread are completed. This keeps the number of parallel requests constant, but the request rate varies with the server's ability to send responses. As the number of threads rises, the throughput initially goes up as more parallelism is achieved. However, when the system is at maximum capacity, the extra threads queue up and wait, and the throughput stagnates while the latency rises. By incrementally increasing the thread count, a performance curve is generated for latency versus throughput; the "knee" in the curve indicates where maximum sustainable capacity is reached. Before the knee, throughput is still increasing with more users; after the knee, latency rises rapidly with little or no corresponding increase in throughput. With this adaptive load, the request rate is determined by the server's response rate. As the server completes more requests, it allows users to send more requests to the server. This is useful for simulating a situation where a few users are making long sequences of requests.

The non-adaptive load is comparable to a large pool of users making short requests. In this case, the request rate is fixed without regard to the server's ability to complete them. The queue length in this case can grow very large, unlike the adaptive load where the number of users, and hence the maximal queue length, is fixed. Non-adaptive loads better test system stability. The non-adaptive load will continue to send requests even as the old ones queue up, and sometimes a large queue of incoming requests can cause additional problems at the server. Thus, a temporary slow-down at the server, such as garbage collection, can cascade into a complete failure as queues form and then grow. Adaptive loads would simply wait until the server responds and hide such problems behind a lower throughput, but non-adaptive loads will maintain request rates and make such problems apparent.

For latency testing, timing information is collected and average latency values for each type of request are computed. It is helpful to first identify the range of achievable throughputs. Latency values are most meaningful when the system is not overloaded. The latency-throughput performance curves can be useful to determine whether a latency measurement is due to real system latency or just queuing of requests due to throughput saturation.

To minimize the warm-up time, queries using the same cryptographic methods are grouped together, and tests are run sequentially on the warmed-up machine. This requires that the state of the system remains clean between tests. Some tests cause the server to fail, and this requires a clean restart and a new warm-up period before resuming tests.

To compute an average performance for a collection of requests, the individual queries are tested first. This shows the extreme cases where particular parts of the system are stressed. Then, combinations of queries show which queries combine well or poorly.

14.3.4 Test Results

This section presents selected results of the above evaluation approach applied to a CryptDB-based system.

14.3.4.1 Bulk Encryption Test Results

Testing of bulk encryption was performed on different data sets to assess scalability. The database was based on the Oracle human resources database provided with Oracle 12c. The employees table contained information about employees (one employee per row). To test different sizes of data sets, the number of employees in this table was varied: the smallest data set contained 10,000 employees, the next largest contained 100,000 employees, and the largest contained 1 million employees. Additional employees were generated randomly. Employee IDs were assigned sequentially. Salaries and other data were assigned randomly within ranges. Managers, locations, and other data that links to other tables were assigned randomly from available options. This provides a set of databases of different sizes that are functional and consistent.

Performance testing of bulk encryption computes the time to do the conversion from the original files to the encrypted files. The loading itself is generally much quicker than the encryption, so the encryption dominates the overall loading time for the encrypted data. In our test using dual 20-core processors in a Dell Precision desktop, the total encryption time for the database with 1 million employees was just under one hour. We deemed this to be feasible for our intended use case, but for other ERPs, a determination would depend on the hardware available, the data set size, and the desired execution time of the encryption.

For scalability, the three data sets were run, and the time for each increased roughly by a factor of 10 as the size increased. This shows that the times scale linearly with the data set size. For parallelization scalability, the tests were repeated on a desktop with 40 cores and a laptop with 4 cores. The speeds of the processors were comparable. The times for the laptop were roughly 10 times longer than those for the desktop, again showing linear scalability.

The combination of these results shows that the workload scales linearly with the size of the database, and the rate of work scales with the number of processors.

14.3.4.2 Single Queries

For query testing, a number of queries were used. Queries Q1 through Q6 returned large data sets, and performance depended primarily on highly variable network speeds, so these are not included. The remaining queries returned smaller result sets, and include the following:

Q7: search for employees with particular department name, job ID, and manager ID values.
Q8: search for employees with particular job ID and manager ID values, and salary between two values.
Q9: search for employees with particular city, job ID, and manager ID values.
Q10: search for employees with particular job ID and department name values, and salary between two values.
Q11: search for employees with particular department name, job ID, and manager ID values.
Q12: search for employees with particular job ID and manager ID values, and salary between two values.
Q13: search for employees with particular first name and job ID values, and phone number that contains a particular substring.
Q14: search for employees with particular last name and department name values, and phone number that contains a particular substring.
Q15: return salary information plus a raise value for employees with particular job ID and manager ID values, and salary between two values.
Q16: Insert an employee.
Q17: Update an employee.
Q18: Delete an employee.

For the queries under test, measurements of latency and throughput were made for different adaptive user loads, and requests were generated by the test tool JMeter. Sample results are shown in Figures 14.6 and 14.7.

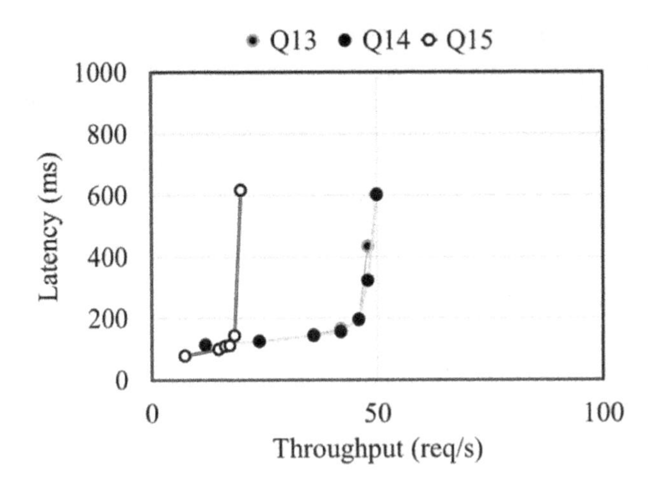

FIGURE 14.6. Latency vs. Throughput for Data Retrieval

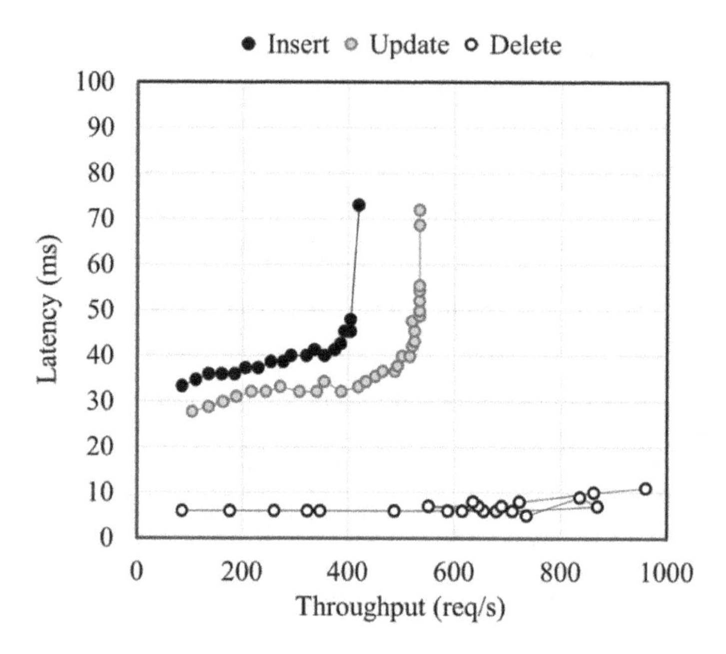

FIGURE 14.7. Latency vs. Throughput for Data Modification

Several key features are visible. First, as the load initially increases, the throughput increases with little effect on latency. Then, at a critical point, the latency rapidly increases while the throughput remains nearly unchanged. This was observed to be the saturation point, where the system resources are consumed and additional requests simply queue up and wait longer. Performance for individual queries is shown in Table 14.2. The throughput measurements are the values at the "knee" in the curve, which is the maximum sustainable throughput. Based on the initial adaptive load results, non-adaptive loads were generated around the knee value to find the highest stable request rate achievable.

14.3.4.3 Combining Two Queries

To test multiple queries, we first examined combinations of two queries. With baseline numbers for individual queries, it is possible to predict the aggregate throughput of combinations of requests. If the throughputs of queries A and B are T_A and T_B, then the resource requirements for a request of type A or B is $1/T_A$ or $1/T_B$, respectively. So, n of A and m of B would require resources $R = n/T_A + m/T_B$. Thus, this

TABLE 14.2.
Individual Query Throughput

Q7	Q8	Q9	Q10	Q11	Q12	Q13	Q14	Q15
600 req/s	308	587	172	592	663	43	45	18

TABLE 14.3.
Query Throughput (Requests per Second)

	Q7	Q8	Q9	Q10	Q11	Q12	Q13	Q14	Q15
Q7	600	407	593	267	596	629	80	83	35
Q8	407	308	404	220	405	420	75	78	34
Q9	593	404	587	266	589	622	80	83	35
Q10	267	220	266	172	266	273	68	71	33
Q11	596	405	589	266	592	625	80	83	35
Q12	629	420	622	273	625	663	80	84	36
Q13	80	75	80	68	80	80	43	44	25
Q14	83	78	83	71	83	84	44	45	26
Q15	35	34	35	33	35	36	25	26	18

sequence would be repeated $1/R$ times per second, with total throughput of $n + m$ requests per iteration, which is $(n + m) / R = (n + m) / (n/T_A + m/T_B)$.

We computed these expected values and compared them to the actual numbers to determine which queries mesh well together. It is expected that actual performance will always improve in comparison with the predicted performance, because similar queries stress the system in the same way and different queries have the potential to stress it in different ways, which improves internal parallelization and aggregate performance.

The expected performance is shown in Table 14.3. The baseline numbers occur along the diagonal. The values in the table are computed as above with $n = m = 1$, indicating an equal number of each query.

The actual performance of each combination of two queries was very close to the predicted values in most cases.

Table 14.4 lists the percent improvement in throughput of the actual above the predicted values, which helps identify areas of significant deviation.

TABLE 14.4.
Deviation from Expected Throughput (Percent Deviation)

	Q7	Q8	Q9	Q10	Q11	Q12	Q13	Q14	Q15
Q7		−1%	−2%	5%	−2%	3%	6%	5%	6%
Q8	−1%		−1%	16%	−2%	26%	11%	7%	9%
Q9	−2%	−1%		5%	−2%	2%	6%	5%	6%
Q10	5%	16%	5%		6%	4%	3%	0%	14%
Q11	−2%	−2%	−2%	6%		4%	7%	5%	6%
Q12	3%	26%	2%	4%	4%		5%	1%	8%
Q13	6%	11%	6%	3%	7%	5%		2%	51%
Q14	5%	7%	5%	0%	5%	1%	2%		45%
Q15	6%	9%	6%	14%	6%	8%	51%	45%	

The largest improvements are seen when Q15 is combined with Q13 or Q14. This indicates that Q15 has very different resource requirements than Q13 and Q14. Upon closer examination, it was observed that Q15 created a very high computational load on the CryptDB proxy due to the complicated encryption and decryption associated with additions, whereas Q13 and Q14 produced a higher load on the database server due to the invocation of a UDF to perform searches of character strings.

14.3.4.4 Combining Many Queries

In normal operations, the system will process queries of many types. To get a broad sense of overall performance, the average latency and throughput of all requests is measured. The results using Queries 7 through 15 are shown in Figure 14.8. The results for encrypted operation are compared to the results for unencrypted operation.

The average latency for the encrypted system is close to double the average latency for the unencrypted system. For short interactive queries, such an increase might not be noticeable, but this could present a significant overhead for large data sets.

The highest achievable throughput on the encrypted system is only one quarter the throughput achieved on the unencrypted system. This is a larger factor, which suggests it will have more impact on operations. However, throughput can be addressed by adding additional resources, offering more flexibility between performance and cost. For a given system, the measurements above will vary based on the mix of query types and their relative weighting and clustering.

14.3.4.5 Initialization and Randomization

Due to the test tool (JMeter) and its ease of use with static requests, all testing was done with the same sequence of queries that had the same values for all queries. This raised the question of whether the query and response values were being cached in

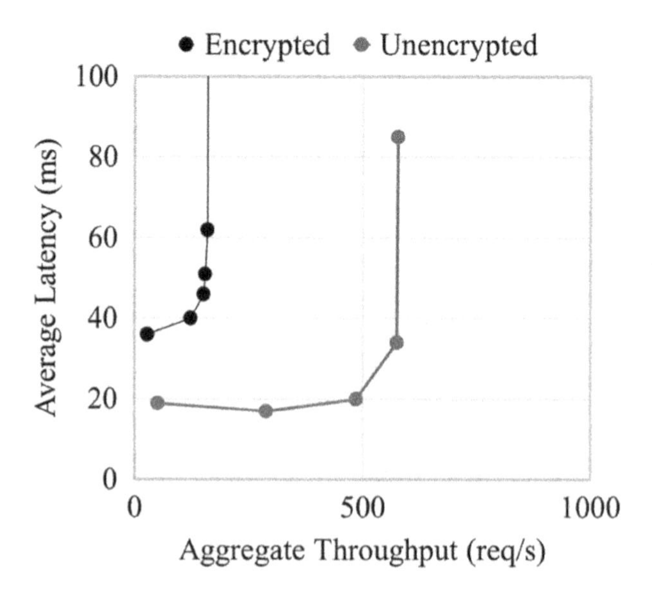

FIGURE 14.8. Performance Summary: Queries 7–15

the database. To test this, a variation of Q10 that used random values for the salary range (called Q10R) was implemented.

The random values created 1 million possible queries. The test was run first sequentially, where 300 iterations of Q10 were followed by 1,300 iterations of Q10R. Results showed slightly higher latency for the random queries, suggesting some internal caching of results. Then, queries alternated between Q10 and Q10R for 1,600 queries. The same overall performance improvement was observed, with a quick drop from a high latency to around 150 ms, followed by a second drop to around 50 ms. These were observed to be synchronous for the alternating queries, showing that the cryptographic state is the largest component of the performance improvement, and the improvement for deterministic over random values is persistent but small.

The first 10 points represent individual values. Points between 10 and 100 represent the average of 10 trials; points at 100 and more represent the average of 100 trials. Iteration numbers represent the average of the trials (e.g., trials 201–300 are plotted at 250.5).

As shown in Figures 14.9 and 14.10, the latency for Q10R is about 23% higher. However, even on unencrypted data, the latency is about 9% higher for random values. This means randomization causes only a 13% (1.23/1.09–1) penalty due to CryptDB for random data versus deterministic data. This is not negligible, but small enough to conclude that deterministic queries are an adequate representation of random queries. The situation for any real-world system is likely to lie somewhere between these values depending on the type of application and the degree of user influence on the values in the database queries from the application.

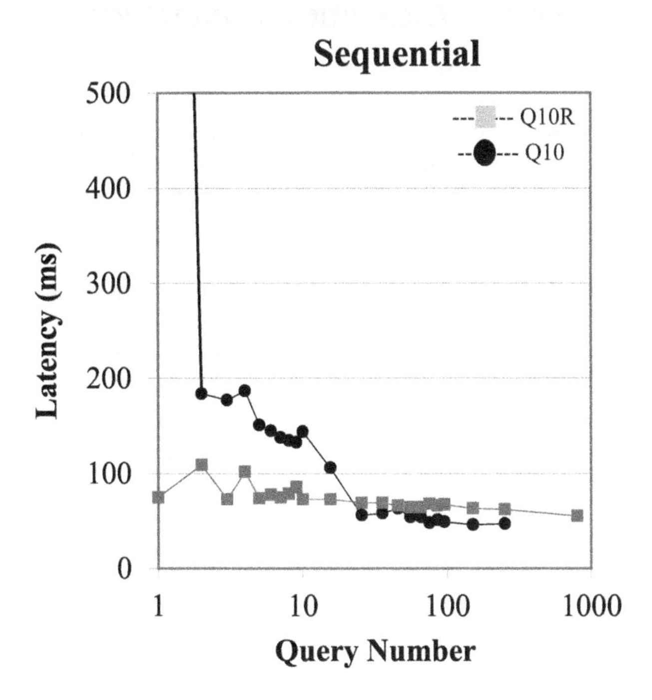

FIGURE 14.9. Initial Latencies: Sequential

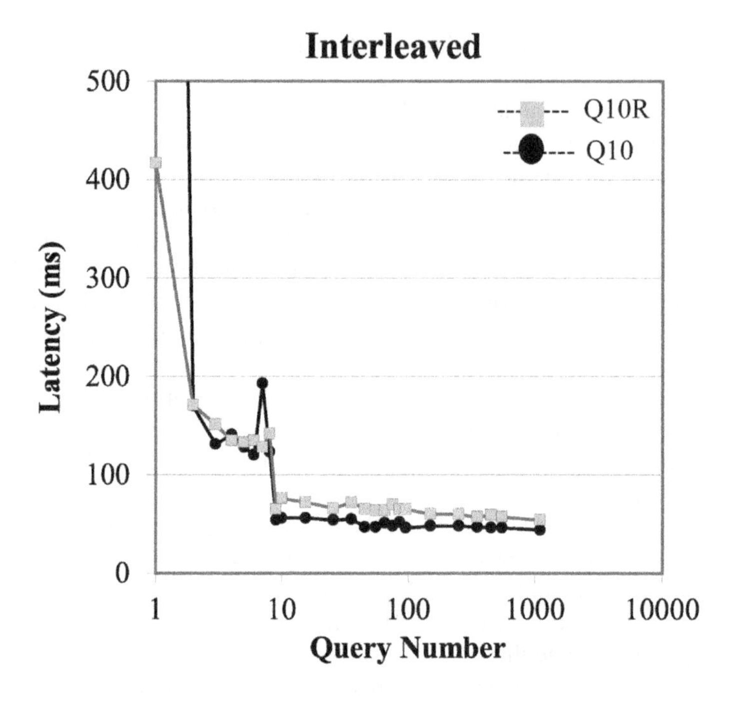

FIGURE 14.10. Initial Latencies: Interleaved

14.4 HOMOMORPHIC ENCRYPTION CONCLUSIONS

With the increasing concern over privacy of data and the concurrent increase in public cloud computing, homomorphic encryption is a potentially useful tool for building a solution that protects data while leveraging the power of the cloud model. FHE provides the ability to protect data in both the application and its database. However, it is prohibitively slow. SWHE and PHE offer more hope for practical solutions to more limited applications.

The CryptDB system was examined and ported to Oracle DB to test PHE as part of an overall method to protect database contents. Additional features and functions were added to support an ERP system, and these additional features were shown to function properly, thus showing the feasibility of hosting an encrypted database in the cloud using PHE.

An accurate assessment of performance is an important step in implementing such a solution. The final section of this chapter examines potential challenges when evaluating performance of a homomorphically encrypted database as part of an ERP. It describes evaluation approaches for providing accurate and reliable results, applies these approaches to an implementation of CryptDB, and presents the performance results. Although encryption results in degradation of latency and throughput, the factors are small integers that would be acceptable for many applications.

ELS Extensions – Data Aggregation

15 Access and Privilege in Big Data Analysis

This chapter describes techniques to provide data mining services to individual entities based on the level of access they have to the data. This allows a wider use of data mining services across the enterprise by allowing more open access to the data mining tools while providing automated access controls at the data sources themselves. This also allows data mining of highly sensitive data sets where no one entity is allowed full access or where data mining across the full data set is prohibited.

15.1 BIG DATA ACCESS

> **BIG DATA**
>
> A field that details methods for computationally analyzing data sets that are too large for traditional data-processing application software to reveal patterns, associations, and trends.

Web services and content access tagging are the primary methods of using ELS to provide access to data. The ultimate goal is to provide standardized interfaces to the data itself, but current database systems are not yet prepared to provide this level of access. The problem of standardized schemas and taxonomies for big data was recently addressed [200], but it only addressed privacy concerns while not addressing security and access restrictions. With ELS, the database interfaces are locked down to a single, highly restricted interface for a single web service. All access is provided through this web service. The ELS model is used at the web service to provide end-to-end authentication and claims-based authorization through a standard set of enterprise-approved protocols and enterprise-provided claims validation and verification code.

Data mining services are provided with a web application front end that provides the same controls on access to all enterprise users. The data mining services rely on the requesters to gain access to data. The data mining application does not itself have access to any data sources. This is in contrast to many systems for which the intermediary has full access and limits access to data based on user accounts, roles, or other internal controls. The web service fronting the database requires authentication and claims from the data mining service, as well as verifiable claims proving that the requester is requesting access to the data. This is done through a combination of authorization credentials by an STS with trust relationships in the enterprise.

Federation allows data to be shared across enterprises. This presents special challenges for data mining, as enterprise trust agreements must be extended in limited ways to federation partners. This chapter discusses some of these challenges and outlines potential solutions that maintain the ELS model.

15.2 BIG DATA RELATED WORK

Big data work has exploded, partly due to an increase in the amount of data available for analysis, and partly due to its own popularity. *Big data* is a broad term for data sets so large or complex that traditional data-processing applications are inadequate [201]. Challenges include analysis, capture, data curation, search, sharing, storage, transfer, visualization, and information privacy [202]. Big data is a moving target based on available technology. We must develop new analyses that assume an abundance of data rather than rely on old methods that attempt to be precise or make use of all of the data but involve extensive time and resources to do such detailed work. Instead of replacing the old methods, big data methods are often a feeder or supplement to them.

Big data analysis can focus on a big picture view of the data to inform further, deeper analysis. Big data analysis can be used to determine what data is available so as to choose the best method for further analysis. It can provide a roadmap of the data, which allows drilling down to key subsets. It can provide a rough estimate of a global parameter that can be adjusted locally. Or, it can be used just to show what is in the data, such as a literary analysis of a large collection of unknown texts.

A lot of the work in data mining focuses on how to use big data sets to do new things. Much of the work uses data that is either publicly available or generated in house. In either case, ACRs are uniform across the data. Public data is available to anyone. In-house data is available to those owning the data. As a result, the problems focus on data quality, data heterogeneity, new applications for the data, combining different data sets, or other issues with the complete data sets.

If data is not available publicly or in-house data is supplemented with restricted data from other sources, access and use rules come into play. For example, advances in personalized medicine may be possible through the use of extensive medical records and genome sequencing. However, medical records and genome sequences may each have their own separate access rules that prevent a general-purpose big data analysis across a population. Some solutions involve creation of "cleansed" data sets for use in analysis, which preserve the basic properties of interest in the data while removing identifying attributes. Others involve an all-powerful entity that is given blanket access to all records with strict controls on what this entity can release, such that end-to-end access rules are preserved while allowing aggregation at the powerful intermediary.

Using cleansed data requires the initial effort to create the cleansed data set, as well as ongoing effort to maintain this data set. This can be a significant effort, and even cleansed data can inadvertently leak sensitive information. Releasing data to a powerful intermediary may not be desirable for sensitive information, as it provides a central point of attack.

This chapter proposes the ELS architecture as a way to manage access for big data analysis across an enterprise. This does not solve the problem of inaccessible data, but does make it easy to set enterprise rules for access so that all data that should be accessible for analysis purposes is accessible.

15.3 BIG DATA WITH ELS

This section describes how to merge big data analysis and ELS. This includes some changes to the way big data analysis is performed to accommodate strict ELS security controls. It also describes how to shape an ELS instantiation to better prepare it for big data analysis.

15.3.1 Basic ELS Preparations

The first step in a secure environment is to issue strong identity credentials. Without these, nothing else works, as verification of identity is at the heart of all ELS security. The recommended approach is PKI using X.509 certificates, but any sufficiently strong authentication for the purposes of the enterprise will suffice.

Next, an attribute store must be established. It must either import or natively manage entity attributes, where entities include users, machines, services, and applications. A central access control registry describes the available enterprise services and their ACRs, as specified by the data owners associated with each service. A claims engine applies entity attributes to the ACRs to generate claims, which are tokens proving an entity is allowed to access a service or application. The claims engine places generated claims into a Claims Repository, which has an associated "Provide Claims" service.

An STS, or collection of STSs, is used by requestors to generate authorization credentials. The requester authenticates to the STS and the STS passes this identity to the "Provide Claims" service to retrieve associated access claims. These are packaged into a SAML token and provided back to the requester, which is signed by the STS for integrity. The requester forwards this to the desired service or application endpoint, which performs security checks on the SAML and authenticated requester identity.

The key to providing analysis services across the secure enterprise is consistency across the enterprise. All data providers must provide a web service interface for their data and possibly a web application if direct user interactions are desired. The web service/application interface, combined with universal strong authentication and SAML-based authorization from trusted STSs, provides the basis to control access to all data across the enterprise.

15.3.2 Big Data Analysis with ELS

After the basic components are in place, big data relies on providing appropriate controls at the data repositories. Data owners can set their own policies depending on the type of data they own, its sensitivity, and any organizational or legal restrictions in place. The EAS can be configured to contain attributes relevant to big data analysis, as these are applicable across an enterprise and apply to many data sets.

The actual big data analysis can be conducted in different ways:

- Local analysis,
- Enterprise level services for data analysis,

- Data-owner-provided tailored analysis services,
- Federated services for multiple data sources.

For local analysis, the individual simply downloads all applicable data to a local system and then performs the analysis. This may stress networks and local computational resources if the data sets are especially large, but it provides a straightforward way to do the analysis using the ELS infrastructure for access controls.

For enterprise level data analysis, tools are made available as enterprise services. In this case, access to these services is open to all, but the access to data is based on the requester of the service. Different entities with different levels of access receive different results from the same query, as they have access to different underlying data. This provides a more scalable solution, as anyone can perform analyses without requiring a dedicated infrastructure. However, personal data sets (i.e., data that is attached to an individual and can only be accessed by that person) would be difficult to perform analysis on, and these are often interesting data sources for broad analyses.

For data-owner-provided services, the data owners provide tailored big data services that involve elevated privileges for certain functions, such as averages, totals, or regional statistics. In this case, the data owner can provide internal mechanisms for broad analysis of data sets while preventing sensitive data from leaking. As the data owner can manage access to the data, the data owner's services can be provided specific privileges that are denied to any other entities. This allows escalation without risking an outside entity's abusing this escalation, as the data owner maintains control of the external access endpoints.

For federated services, groups of data owners create analysis services that have full access to all data sets. The services only provide aggregated statistics from these data sets. This is similar to a single data owner providing such services, except this can scale to the full enterprise and allow analyses across larger data sets.

Local analysis requires the fewest changes to existing data stores, but offers the least scalability and functionality. Use of enterprise services provides more scalability by sharing computation resources and algorithms but lacks aggregation services over full data sets. Data owner services provide greater aggregation across a single data set and, with proper enterprise planning, may offer enterprise-wide scalability. Only federated service models provide full scalability and full aggregation capabilities, but these can introduce security vulnerabilities as a single all-powerful entity that can access many data sources. The best solution for an enterprise depends on the goals, resources, and data protection requirements of the enterprise.

15.3.3 Data-Driven Access Controls

Today, databases have access controls based on user accounts [203, 204]. These limit access to particular rows, columns, views, and actions. However, in an enterprise in which data is shared by many different owners, coordinating the database schemas, accounts, views, and other information is prohibitively costly. In ELS enterprises, the approach is to create views dynamically based on claims. Instead of user accounts or roles, which are managed by the database management system, the data owner maps claims into dynamic views of the data. Each view contains the data that the individual with the associated claim is allowed to access.

The main challenge associated with this approach is coordination of claims and views. A static set of views with associated claims may be sufficient for a static set of access privileges. However, in many cases, the content is generated dynamically. In this case, claims must describe the set of data a requester is allowed to access and may refer to internal schemas to allow proper creation of dynamic views. Coordination of enterprise-wide claims with local database schemas requires careful attention to maintain proper mappings.

As an example of this approach, we consider an enterprise financial database. This database has many predefined roles. These are determined by the data owner and placed in the format of an ACR for storage in the enterprise service registry. The roles may be arbitrarily complex, as the claims engine will compute whether or not they are satisfied and provide any variables or restrictions requested. The result is shown in Figure 15.1.

One issue with this approach is that the claims, which are generally assigned and managed by the data owners within the enterprise, must be used within the database for access controls associated with views [205, 206]. Changes in the EAS may affect low-level access policies of many databases within the enterprise. Database schemas and data elements must be provided with standard definitions to facilitate the analyses, but even under those circumstances, the data may not be equivalent, making joins and other queries that coordinate across databases difficult.

View Template for Financial Analyst

Security Context of Financial Analyst

Project	Total Value	Entry Date	Expense Entry Date	Project Lead	Project lead e-mail	Current Expense	Project Location	Rows eliminated based upon Requester's restrictions Comments
123400r	5.5M	12/11/2013	02/04/2014	George Henry	Ghenry345@ent.org	3.45M	Chicago	Initial contracts provided on 02/04/2014
137800q	Restricted by Project #??????q							
567400r	4.5M	09/10/2013	12/06/2013	Rita Jones	Rjones345@ent.org	3M45M	Chicago	Initial contracts provided on 12/06/2013
713200q	Restricted by Project #??????q							
456200r	4.5M	12/11/2013	02/04/2014	George Henry	Ghenry222@rb.com	2.45M	Chicago	Initial contracts provided on 02/04/2014
Restricted by New York							New York	
778800r	4.5M	09/10/2013	12/06/2013	Harry Ga	Hga778@chi.com	3.45M	Chicago	Initial contracts provided on 12/06/2013
657800s	3.0M	08/02/2012	02/04/2014	Jim Rich	Jrich657@fnl.net	2.45M	Chicago	Initial contracts provided on 10/01/2012 **Awaiting final deliverable sign off on 02/04/2014**
...								

FIGURE 15.1. Access Tailored Data View

15.3.4 Escalation of Privilege

For a complete analysis, the requester may have to use some form of escalation of privilege. Such escalation can be for aggregation or exposure.

Aggregated data is often made available to requesters even though the underlying raw data is not. This occurs when access to aggregated data does not violate the least privilege concept. Examples include statistical values such as the mean, median, and sum; summary geographic distribution data such as value ranges and geographic coincidence; and type sequence summaries for included data. One way data owners could provide this access is by allowing privilege to aggregated data through their access and privilege requirement documentation in the EAE registry. Specific rules determine which aggregations are permitted and who can receive them. In this case, the data owner provides and enforces the access rules. Another option is to escalate privilege in the analysis software in order to view and aggregate the data for restricted users. In this case, the aggregation service has access control responsibilities. The first method is preferable because it gives the data owner control over the data that requesters receive, but the second can be layered on existing data stores.

Escalation for exposure of data provides special access privileges to an individual to perform a specific analysis task. This is a sensitive process, as any mechanism that creates such an escalation may be misused by nefarious entities. Escalation of privilege is a prominent part of many attack vectors. For ELS systems, it is recommended that individuals assigned to the analysis tasks be pre-screened for least restriction. However, the most talented individual or most available individuals may not meet these requirements. In these cases, analysts should be provided delegated claims. In the delegation process, temporary claims are created for individuals by those who have the claims and are willing to be accountable for that delegation. A multi-party delegation by all data owners could allow a trusted entity to perform an analysis across all data sets with restrictions and access expirations that are agreeable to all data owners. In contrast to aggregation escalation, which is often permanent and based on attributes, exposure escalation is temporary and based on exactly the claims required for the task. This limits direct access to the data. Also, unlike aggregation escalation, in which the aggregator is called by many other entities, the exposure escalation is limited to a single entity, reducing the attack surface.

15.3.5 Big Data Analysis Using Federation Data

Big data analysis can be challenging when sharing information across enterprise boundaries. Within an enterprise, organizational boundaries can be addressed using the single common EAS. Such mechanisms do not exist across enterprises. Solutions involving ELS include the following:

- Incorporate outside entities into the EAS,
- Provide separate credentials to vetted outsiders,
- Delegate claims to credentialed outsiders,
- Require a basic ELS setup within the partner organization.

When incorporating foreign entities into the EAS, their existing authentication credentials are trusted. This essentially brings the outsiders into the enterprise. This creates the obvious problem that these entities are not part of the enterprise but are treated as if they were. In some cases, this might be an acceptable solution; in general, it is not.

Vetted outsiders with enterprise-provided credentials are more like enterprise members, as they have received similar vetting. Credentials can reflect that they are not full members if this distinction is important. However, this can be costly and difficult to implement, and it again brings outsiders inside the system.

Delegation allows outsiders to have existing authentication credentials. Claims are delegated directly based on these credentials instead of assigning native attributes from which these claims are computed. In this case, all access and privilege is granted explicitly through a delegation assignment by an authorized individual within the organization. Delegation rules can limit who is allowed, and under what circumstances they are allowed, to delegate.

With a partner ELS setup, identity can be established through PKI or a similar method, and claims can be shared through SAMLs issued internally and validated in the partner organization using federation agreements. These federation agreements translate partner identities, claims, and attributes to local identities, claims, and attributes, such that the two partners need not change their internal security infrastructure. They need only establish a new federation agreement.

Federated ELS provides the cleanest and most secure access, but it requires the most work to set up. Other solutions offer trade-offs between security and ease of setup.

15.3.6 Data Leakage

Data leakage may occur in an ELS environment based on differing access levels. For example, if a certain data element is sensitive, averages would be provided only for a sample size of at least N values in order to help mask the individual data values. If two active entities have access to nearly identical data, there could be information leaks. If both entities compute and compare averages, they can compute the average of the difference, which is a small sample size with less than N items.

For ELS, the same person can often have different roles that allow different levels of access. A single person logging in with different roles can perform analyses and compute statistics that may reveal sensitive information. This is a potential security vulnerability associated with providing very broad access to data analysis. The finer the access controls are, the more potential for data leakage. The enterprise must decide where the proper balance is between accessibility and confidentiality and determine access controls and data analysis functions accordingly.

This is an interesting challenge, because fine-grained access controls generally provide higher security, but in this case, they can hurt it. Fine-grained access controls make the most data available to all entities that are allowed to access it, which is generally an improvement in the trade-off between availability and confidentiality. However, if these controls are fine enough, individual data elements can be extracted through comparison of aggregated results. One solution is to reduce the fidelity of results so that exact values are harder to compute accurately. Another is to restrict the analyses that can be performed. These solutions can address the security problem, but they reduce functionality.

In some cases, the access problems may be more fundamental, involving an inherent conflict between making some data available while hiding other data across a large population with different access rights. In this case, the ELS and big data analysis combination can serve to bring these inconsistencies to the surface so they can be addressed directly. Addressing these issues moves enterprise security from unknown and ad hoc access rules to calculated and conscious choices about data access.

15.4 BIG DATA SUMMARY

ELS enables big data analyses across different data sets with different security restrictions. Non-ELS systems require choosing between security and functionality. Data sets must be public or made available through special agreements despite rules governing use. The restrictions on public data or special agreements are too restrictive for a general purpose method of analysis. With ELS, data owners maintain control over their assets by using enterprise services to determine access based on data-owner-defined rules and trusted Enterprise Attribute Stores. This can be the difference between running a big data analysis of sensitive data and not running it. The flexibility of ELS allows trade-offs to match the security requirements of the data owners and the enterprise.

Federated sharing poses additional challenges as there may be no common language for access rules, no common trusted identity issuer, and no common trusted attribute stores. Without these bases for common security policies, agreements must be put in place to either trust other partners' security infrastructure or integrate their users into an existing ELS infrastructure. Different options exist according to the partner's existing infrastructure and willingness to share and trust security information and functions.

Analysis by different users can result in different results as the data-driven model of ELS provides access based on the requester's credentials. There may be no complete picture of the data if access policies prevent full data access by any individual. However, the whole picture is not achievable in these cases without special security considerations, so ELS provides what is available to each user, which improves availability while maintaining confidentiality. One area of concern specific to ELS and big data analysis is the idea that some data may be leaked by different users using comparative analysis. Although the data sets analyzed may all be big enough to hide individual data values, differences may be small enough to extract details about parts of the overall data sets. Care must be used in coordinating ELS access policies and big data analysis parameters.

For ELS to work, some low-level details must be configured properly. Distributed databases must use standard schemas, standard views, and standard approaches to escalation of privilege where appropriate. This may require internal changes to existing data stores. Within the ELS architecture, other options, such as aggregation services, can provide a quick fix with minimal changes to existing systems.

16 Data Mediation

16.1 MAINTAINING SECURITY WITH DATA MEDIATION

One challenge in sharing information is that the source and recipient of the information may use different units, protocols, data formats, or tools to process information. As a result, a transformation of the data is needed before the recipient can use the information. These conversions introduce potential security weaknesses into an ELS system, so an approach for enterprise-wide mediation is required. Methods commonly used today, such as a MITM translation and an online mediation service, do not preserve the basic ELS tenets and concepts. This chapter examines these existing approaches and compares them with two approaches designed to preserve ELS security. It looks at the complete picture of security, performance, and ease of implementation, offering a framework for choosing the best mediation approach based on the data-sharing context.

DATA MEDIATION

Transformation of data structure, protocols, security features, integrity, and data content to establish an equivalent representation for use in applications, services, and security while maintaining the meaning, integrity, and context of the content.

16.2 THE MEDIATION ISSUE

This chapter describes a way to provide mediation services within an ELS framework. Mediation services present a unique challenge and a tempting target for embedded malicious entities because mediation takes place where data is changed and the normal end-to-end integrity verification methods are not feasible. A malicious entity that compromises a mediation service could selectively feed malicious content to an unsuspecting entity. Detection would be difficult because most entities only understand either the input format or the output format of data and cannot validate the translation. There is no perfect mediation approach, and this chapter discusses various approaches and their trade-offs.

Data mediation is the process of transforming data from one format to another while preserving the original meaning. This is a common problem in large enterprises in which different groups use different methods to represent data. When the data is shared between groups, it is not useful in its native form and must be converted to a new format. Examples include the following conversions:

- Miles to kilometers,
- Address to latitude and longitude,
- Word processing document to Portable Document Format (PDF) file,
- SQL database to XML database.

In general, these conversions may be arbitrarily complex or domain-specific. This chapter addresses the enterprise-wide challenge of doing these conversions in a way that is consistent with ELS. It does not address the development or implementation of the conversion algorithms. It assumes a conversion method exists and addresses the challenge of distributing its use securely across the enterprise.

As part of ELS, certain important properties must be preserved. ELS does not allow any intermediaries to intercept or modify communication between two communicating entities. In the case of mediation, this means that mediation computation is not allowed to take place between the sender and receiver on unencrypted data. For example, using an online translation site to browse foreign language websites does not fit the ELS model, as the translation site is acting as a MITM between the sender and receiver.

ELS requires end-to-end integrity of data. The receiver must know that the received data is what the sender actually sent. Again, the MITM translation does not work because the connection is only with the MITM, who can attest to the integrity of the MITM-to-receiver connection but not the sender-to-receiver connection. ELS requires end-to-end integrity, not piecemeal integrity.

ELS attempts to minimize the number of external entities that must be trusted. The more trust that is required for a solution to work, the fewer options for deployment there are, and those options have more built-in vulnerabilities, as each required trust relationship is a potential point of failure. In any communication, there must be trust between sender and receiver. ELS provides an end-to-end bilateral authenticated TLS connection from trusted sender to trusted receiver, which includes confidentiality and integrity through its encryption and MAC.

Mediation requires a third entity in addition to the two communicating entities. This mediation entity is trusted to accurately transform the sender's information to the receiver's information. It may be a local tool used by the sender or receiver, or it may be a third party that performs the mediation. A sender or receiver can do the mediation but the other entity must trust that the mediation will be performed accurately. When third-party software is used for mediation at an endpoint, the third-party software, and hence the third party providing the software, must be trusted because the endpoint simply executes this code without understanding what it does. In each case, there is a change in the data, and the entity determining this change must be trusted to do it correctly, because neither endpoint can independently verify that the input and output of the conversion correspond to each other.

In some cases, it may be possible to partially verify a conversion, such as converting a Portable Network Graphics (PNG) image to a Joint Photographic Experts Group (JPG) image, because it is possible to look at the result and compare it to the original. But this is only a superficial check. A receiver still needs to trust that the conversion process has not inserted additional information or malicious code. Most endpoints that require mediation services do not have an intimate knowledge of the formats or their potential exploits and vulnerabilities. They simply want to process data in a particular format.

16.3 APPROACHES

Different approaches to mediation are presented below and compared against the requirements for ELS.

16.3.1 MITM Mediation

The first potential solution is a MITM mediation service, shown in Figure 16.1. The requester connects to the mediation service and requests data from a provider. The mediation service then retrieves the desired data, transforms it as necessary for the requester, and provides it to the requester.

This mediation approach does not provide a connection between requester and provider with confidentiality because the mediation service can view all traffic between the requester and provider. It also does not provide a connection with integrity. Although each of the connections with the mediation service has integrity, this is not the same as integrity from requester to provider, because changes to the request and response by the mediation service cannot be identified by the requester or provider. Because the connections lack confidentiality and integrity, the data the requester receives lacks confidentiality and integrity guarantees. Both the requester and provider must trust the mediation service for this solution to work.

The data that must be transmitted in this solution is the data between source and mediation service in its original format and the data between mediation service and requester in its new format, so this method requires two data transmissions. The mediation computation is performed at the mediation service.

16.3.2 Mediation Service

The second potential solution, shown in Figure 16.2, is a mediation service that the requester calls to do mediation. The components of this solution are similar to the MITM solution, but instead of acting as a MITM for the connection between the requester and provider, the mediation service is explicitly called by the requester to mediate the received data.

In this case, there are two connections, both of which meet ELS confidentiality and integrity requirements. However, the mediation service still must be trusted to handle the data, so the confidentiality and integrity of the received data cannot be guaranteed. This solution is slightly better than the MITM solution because the requester does receive the original data with integrity from the provider. Although

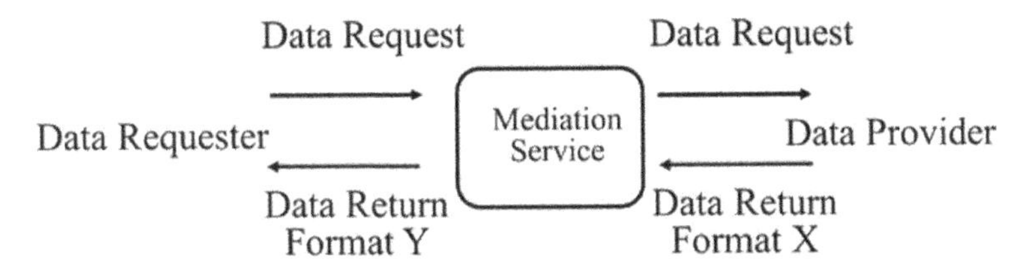

FIGURE 16.1. Man-in-the-Middle Mediation

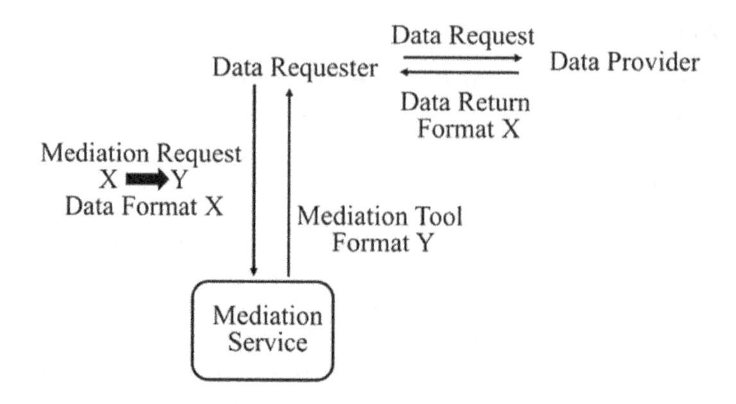

FIGURE 16.2. The Mediation Service

mediation is required before using this data, in many cases, a sanity check can be performed on this data or on a small sample of this data prior to mediation. If independent mediation services are available, it may be possible to provide stronger guarantees on integrity by comparing the output of all such mediation services. However, this is available only at the cost of further reduced confidentiality. Only the requester needs to trust the mediation service for this model to work. The provider implicitly must trust the mediation service because it is possible that any requester will call the mediation service. However, this is rolled into the existing trust of the data requester to properly handle data.

The data to be transmitted in this solution is the data from provider to requester in its original form, this same data from requester to mediation service, and the data from mediation service to requester in the desired form. This approach requires three data transmissions, an increase of one data transmission over the MITM model. Computation is again performed entirely at the mediation service.

16.3.3 Mediation Tool Service

A third potential solution is a mediation service, shown in Figure 16.3, that does not convert data but instead provides a conversion tool in the form of code that runs on

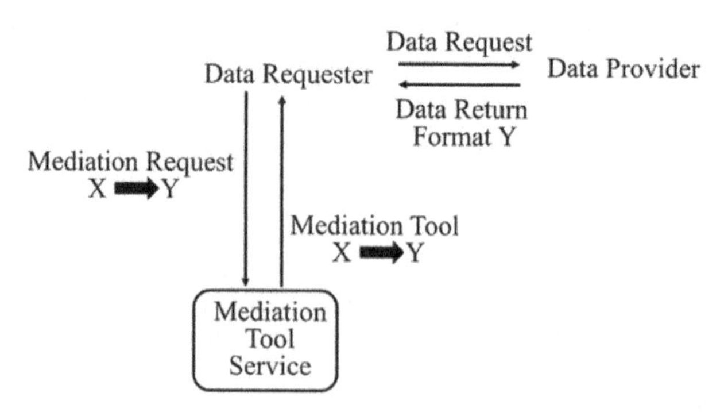

FIGURE 16.3. Mediation Tool Service

the requester's machine. The requester requests and receives the original data from the provider. It then requests a mediation tool from the mediation tool server and performs the conversion using the tool.

Again, there are two connections, both of which meet ELS confidentiality and integrity requirements. In addition, because no data is transmitted to the mediation service, the confidentiality of the data is preserved. The integrity still suffers from the problem of traceability through the conversion process. However, because the algorithm is run locally, this provides higher assurance than relying on the mediation service to both provide and run the conversion. Now the requester must only trust that the conversion tool is correct. Again, comparison of results with other tools can provide some assurance that the data is converted properly. Also, comparison of a hash of the tool can provide assurance that the tool received matches with a known good tool as certified by the enterprise. These still do not provide full data integrity, but this is marginally better than what is possible with the mediation service approach. The solution requires the requester's trust of the mediation tool service.

The data transmissions required involve only the single transmission of the original data from provider to requester. However, a new transmission is now required of the mediation tool from the mediation tool service to the requester. Depending on the size of the tool and the data set, this may require more or fewer transmissions than the MITM solution (two) or the mediation service solution (three). Computation has now shifted from the mediation service to the requester.

A possible performance optimization for computation, especially for mobile or other computationally limited devices, would be to use third-party resources, such as cloud servers, for the computation. However, this introduces an additional trust relationship and additional data transmissions. To preserve security and minimize trust relationships, it is best to keep the computation on the requester's device, despite possible performance issues.

16.3.4 Homomorphic-Encryption MITM

A fourth solution uses homomorphic encryption, in which data is encrypted in such a way that it can be manipulated so as to perform meaningful computations on the data. In this approach, the sender uses homomorphic encryption on the transmitted data, and the mediation service mediates the encrypted data. The mediation service can either be a MITM or called directly by the receiver. In either case, it does not know the original decrypted data – it just needs to perform the homomorphically translated mediation function on the homomorphically encrypted data. This allows more flexibility in how the mediation service is implemented and preserves ELS properties.

For homomorphic encryption, we examine both the MITM and mediation service architectures. The MITM version is shown in Figure 16.4.

With a MITM mediation service, there are two connections. These have the same properties at the connection level as the standard MITM mediation setup. However, the mediation service can no longer view unencrypted content because it operates only on encrypted data. For this reason, confidentiality of the data is preserved

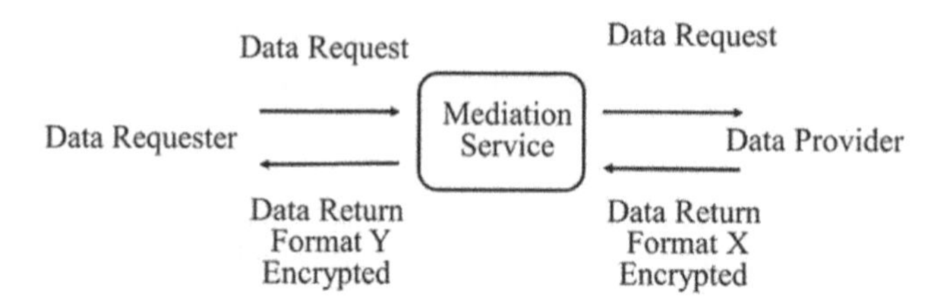

FIGURE 16.4. Homomorphic Encryption

between requester and provider. Integrity, however, is not preserved because the mediation service modifies the content. This invalidates integrity protection on the original data, and any new integrity measures are only from the MITM, not the original source of the data. Like the normal MITM mediation approach, both requester and provider still must trust the mediation service to properly transform the data.

With a separate mediation service using homomorphic encryption, confidentiality is preserved and integrity is similar to that of the normal mediation service approach.

One new security issue with homomorphic encryption is that some data may leak through the homomorphic-encryption schemes, as they must preserve certain properties like sums, products, or ordering of values. An evaluation must be done to determine whether the security properties of the homomorphic encryption are sufficient for protecting the data to be encrypted.

The data transmissions involved are the same as those for normal MITM mediation and mediation service approaches. For the MITM, the data must be transmitted from provider to mediation service and from mediation service to requester. For the mediation service, the data must be transmitted from provider to requester and from requester to mediation service, and then the mediated data must be sent back from the mediation service to the requester.

The computation requirements get more complicated. The mediation computations are done at the mediation service. However, these are now homomorphic-encrypted computations, which are more expensive than normal computation. This imposes an additional burden on the mediation service to perform the mediation computation. The encryption of requests and decryption of received results also impose a potentially large burden on the requester. A possible alternative is the use of PHE, which allows limited operations to be performed on data but is potentially much faster. This is a potential solution to the performance problems of FHE. However, although PHE holds promise for many standard database operations, it is not possible on more complicated transformations like arbitrary mathematical or logical expressions [104].

16.3.5 Comparison of Solutions

Table 16.1 shows a comparison of the different approaches. Confidentiality and integrity generally increase going down the list of methods. In particular, the last three options provide end-to-end data confidentiality, whereas the first two options do not. No solution provides end-to-end data integrity, mainly because the conversion algorithm is treated as a black box, which does not allow traceability of integrity

TABLE 16.1.
Comparison of Mediation Methods

Mediation Method	Connection Confidentiality	Connection Integrity	Data End-to-End Confidentiality	Data E2E Integrity	Needed Trust Relationships*	Data Transfers	Algorithm Transfers	Computation at Mediation Svc	Computation at Endpoint
MITM Mediation	N	N	N	N	2	2	0	1	0
Mediation Service	Y	Y	N	N	1	3	0	1	0
Mediation Tool Service	Y	Y	Y	N	1	1	1	0	1
Homomorphic Encryption (MITM)	Y	Y	Y	N	2	2	0	>1	>0
Homomorphic Encryption (service)	Y	Y	Y	N	1	3	0	>1	>0

*A trust relationship means that the sender or receiver needs to trust someone else with the transmitted data in order for this method to work.

through the conversion process. The mediation tool service allows the possibility of limited integrity checks by examining the actual mediation tool code, but in general, it is difficult to analyze code in this way.

The two MITM-based solutions require both requester and provider to explicitly trust the mediation service, whereas the mediation service and mediation tool service approaches require only the requester to trust the mediation service. This makes the non-MITM solutions easier to adopt, as only the entity requesting the data must trust the mediation service.

For performance, the different approaches use from one to three data transmissions. The mediation tool service approach has the distinction of requiring the least data transmissions, an additional algorithm transfer, and computation on the requester endpoint instead of the mediation service.

16.4 CHOOSING A SOLUTION

Based on the analysis above, the mediation tool service and homomorphic-encryption approaches are superior for security because they preserve end-to-end data confidentiality, whereas the MITM and mediation service approaches do not. These approaches may require additional compute or network resources, but the exact resource implications depend on the data and transformation to be performed.

For large data sets with simple transformation algorithms, the mediation tool service approach is well suited because the algorithm transfer will be fast and the number of data transfers is minimized. The relatively simple transforms can also be easily handled by the endpoint itself. For smaller data sets or more complicated transformations, the first two approaches offer potentially improved performance because the mediation service can perform the computationally intense transformations, and the extra data transfers incur only a small increase in network utilization due to the small data set size. However, this must be balanced with the security risks of lost confidentiality and lost integrity.

For ELS systems, only the mediation tool service and homomorphic-encryption approaches are viable for the general end-to-end mediation problem. However, under certain circumstances, the data may be sufficiently generic that its release is not a problem, or the mediation service may be a trusted party in the transaction. In these cases, the MITM mediation and mediation service approaches conform to ELS because the mediation service is part of the transaction and not just an external party in a two-entity communication.

Ease of implementation of these approaches is an important consideration when building a system. The MITM and mediation service approaches are simple to set up and use. The MITM simply acts as a source for data sets, where the requester indicates the data and format desired. This is the online translation approach. The requester indicates the data to be translated and the source and destination languages, and the translate tool retrieves the data and presents the translation to the requester. The mediation service is similar – the user uploads the data and requests a transformation. Many online base 64 converters use this approach, as do many other file format conversion sites. The requester uploads the data to the site and receives the transformation as a response.

In the MITM approach, the sites often contain public data because the MITM must be able to access it for the transformation, so there is no security concern. For the mediation service, the data sent to the service may be sensitive, so caution is needed in using such sites. In an enterprise, policy may enable a mediation service to access all data in the enterprise, which would expand the scope of a MITM approach but also require access management at the MITM mediation service, which could be used as a back door to access restricted data if not properly secured.

For the mediation tool service approach, the mediation service must choose a representation of the algorithm in code. A simple JavaScript implementation might be appropriate for simpler transformations, whereas an executable might be better for more complicated file conversions. For security, the mediation tool service should sign all executables so that their integrity and source can be verified. These trusted executables can then be installed and used in the future. Changes and updates can be indicated by a changed hash as provided by the mediation tool service. It is important to choose a tool that is compatible with different types of requesters. For example, an executable that runs on a desktop may not work on a mobile device. However, compatibility may require the use of inefficient languages like JavaScript in a browser, so a tradeoff between performance and portability is an important consideration, and multiple tools could be offered to address different requesters' needs.

Homomorphic-encryption implementation is currently very slow, so this is not a viable implementation option for most transformations. However, PHE might be viable for simpler transformations, and as technology develops in both homomorphic encryption and PHE, they may become more mainstream and optimized for performance. The homomorphic-encryption option also requires distributing encryption and decryption keys and metadata to requesters and the mediation service to perform operations and recover the encrypted data. This is an additional security function that the implementation must address.

16.5 MEDIATION SUMMARY

Sharing data among different entities in an enterprise often requires mediation. However, these translations are not always available to those who need them, so this raises the issue of how to implement mediation for the enterprise in a secure way. Simple implementation approaches in common use today do not preserve security properties of the ELS architecture such as end-to-end confidentiality. Approaches that preserve ELS properties offer improved security, but they have different implications for performance and ease of implementation.

ELS Extensions – Mobile Devices

17 Mobile Ad Hoc

17.1 MOBILE AD HOC IMPLEMENTATIONS

Mobile ad hoc networking allows entities to dynamically connect and reconfigure connections to make use of available networking resources in a changing environment. These networks range from tiny sensors setting up communications based on a random or unknown configuration to aircraft communicating with each other, the ground, and satellites. Scenarios have differing requirements in terms of setup, reconfiguration, power, speed, and range. Mobile ad hoc implementations are a derivative of normal network approaches. Additionally, they are required to meet the basic security architecture. Each of these will be reviewed before discussing mobile ad hoc services.

17.1.1 Network Overview

This chapter presents an adaptation of the ELS principles to the mobile ad hoc scenario. The network consists of many different technologies that are split into different layers. One conceptual model for this layering is the Open Systems Interconnection (OSI) [207], a seven-layer model shown in Figure 17.1.

The network layer must be considered to allow upper level layers (including transport, session, and application layers) to conform to the ELS model. This layer provides addresses that are unique within a network, allowing communication through Internet protocol (IP) routers to any other node that is connected to the same network. The use of bridges and network address translation (NAT) allows different networks with overlapping IP addresses to communicate with each other. However, this often relies on the use of TCP port numbers to distinguish endpoints when traversing network boundaries. The IP layer can use IPv4 or IPv6. Each includes a version of IP security (IPSec) that allows authenticated and encrypted communication between devices.

Below the network layer is the data link layer, which connects one device to another. This layer has two sub-layers: the logical link control (LLC) and media access control (MAC). The LLC is the higher sub-layer, focusing on multiplexing, whereas the MAC layer handles addressing and channel access control.

The MAC address is unique to different hardware instances on a subnetwork, allowing unambiguous point-to-point local communication. This can be wired (Ethernet) or wireless (Wi-Fi). It can be point-to-point using a wire from one machine to another, or it can be broadcast using Ethernet or Wi-Fi. Wi-Fi provides security through various protocols, such as Wired Equivalent Privacy (WEP) or Wi-Fi Protected Access (WPA) [208].

Ethernet and Wi-Fi include not just data link layer protocols, but also specifications for the underlying physical properties of the waveforms and the structure

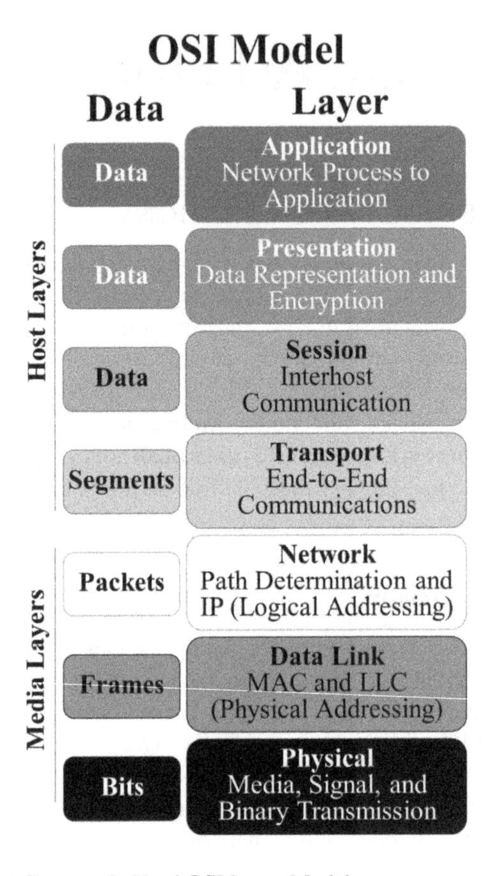

FIGURE 17.1. Most Commonly Used OSI Layer Model

of signals. These can provide some security through frequency-hopping patterns, beamforming, or other physical layer techniques.

In some cases, such as Link 16 [209], multiple layers are integrated into a single protocol. This facilitates communication between layers. It reduces modularity and portability, but it can allow functions like basing higher-layer coding rates and transmission windows on physical layer signal-to-noise ratios. This could distinguish network congestion from jamming and initiate appropriate responses.

17.1.2 Mobile Ad Hoc Networking

Mobile ad hoc networking includes a broad range of possible implementations. These implementations range from unstructured networks like specific mobile ad hoc networks (MANETs) [210], where there is no existing infrastructure and nodes must dynamically configure themselves into a functioning network, to situations in which a mobile node connects to existing infrastructure. This chapter focuses on situations in which nodes come in and out of communication range of fixed infrastructure and situations in which nodes dynamically connect and disconnect to each other and different networks.

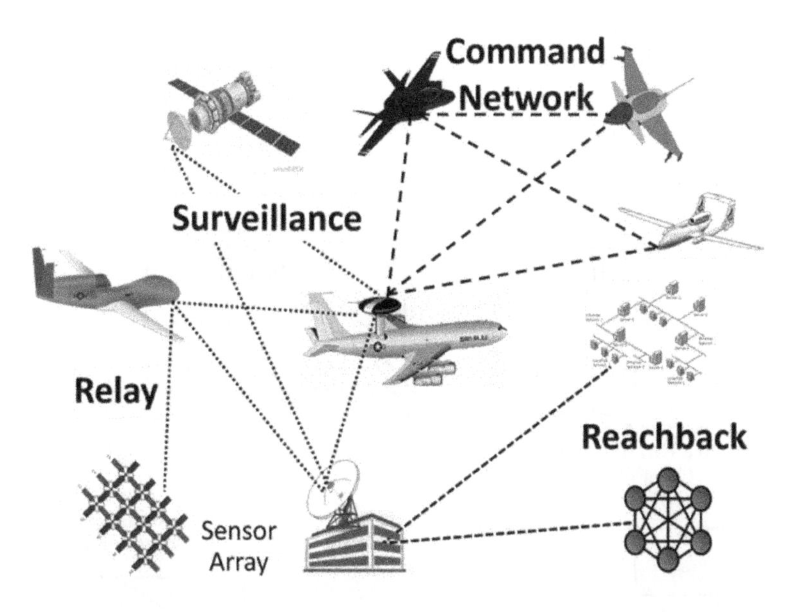

FIGURE 17.2. Ad Hoc Networking Model

These situations allow many of the higher-layer functional and security protocols to function properly. The following sections describe different aspects of the networking infrastructure that together support the concept of ad hoc connections and mobility. Figure 17.2 illustrates those network types.

17.1.3 Mobile Ad Hoc Network Services

The services described in this section are shown in Figure 17.3. These services are automated and seek only operator confirmations when and if required. They reside on each element participating in the networks. Each element in Figure 17.3 must participate in a handshake with the nexus (see Section 17.1.4) that identifies compatible protocols, waveforms, and drivers to establish a connection. These services act as the initial endpoints for connection management. The connection is followed by a bilateral authentication and secure channel to the endpoint device manager service [63].

The endpoint device manager service is the entry point for the requester to access domain services. This must be followed by bilateral authentication at the device level. Basic services are shown on the left (Figure 17.3), building from basic hardware capabilities to supported protocols. Mobile ad hoc network services are on the right, building from hardware and software management to the "Send Data" service that takes data and a destination as an input and sets up appropriate connections and initiates the communication using the supplied data. Arrows indicate dependencies, where arrows point from the service that is used to the service that uses it.

17.1.4 Nexus Elements in the Ad Hoc Network

Certain members of the networks are designated as a nexus. Nexus points may be located throughout the operational area. To qualify as a nexus, the member must

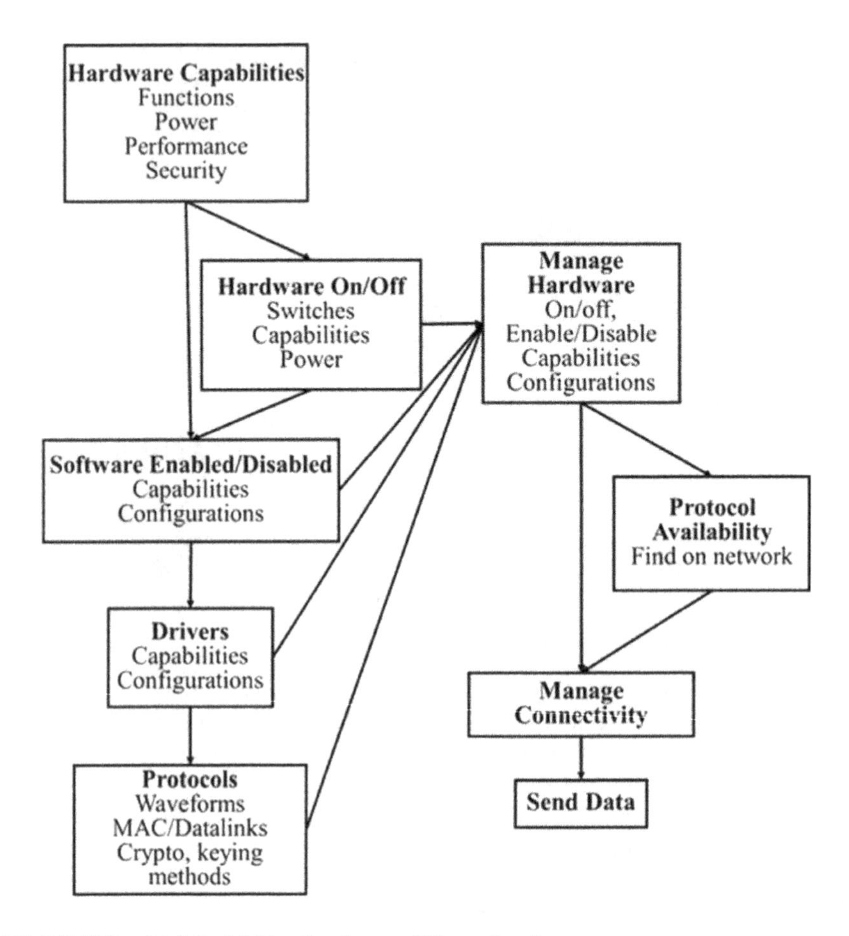

FIGURE 17.3. Mobile Ad Hoc Services and Dependencies

either have reachback to the enterprise, or in the case of DIL, the nexus must be provisioned with all of the elements required to do enterprise business, including but not limited to:

- a fully functional STS,
- a proper subset of the EAS,
- a Claims Repository that matches the elements of the EAS subset,
- a device management service capability.

Nexus elements seek out and provide a handshake to any other nexus points within range. The chaining of nexus points allows reachback from the local network to the enterprise when one or more of the nexus in the chain can reach a network node.

The member must have full system capability and be the manager of ad hoc sub networks. An endpoint device manager service [63] must reside on a nexus, and a nexus must be part of each network and be the entry point for the requester to access domain capabilities. Designated nexus points are shown in Figure 17.4.

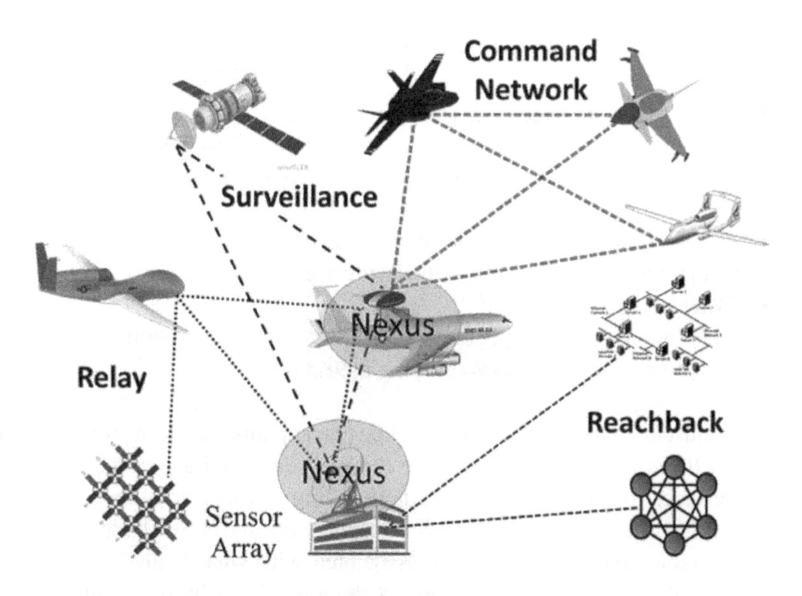

FIGURE 17.4. Designated Nexus Elements

17.2 NETWORK SERVICE DESCRIPTIONS

Network service descriptions are provided in the following sections.

17.2.1 Detection of Hardware Capabilities

This section describes the basic services that provide information about the available hardware and the software that directly controls it. These are typically duplicated for each piece of communication hardware in a device, so higher-layer services have direct and independent control over each hardware interface. The interfaces to the hardware may be specific to the hardware, so higher-layer services provide and use mediation services to interface with these lower-level services.

A node can only join a mobile or ad hoc network if it knows that the network exists. This can be done by continuously polling for available connections or looking for connections when a request is made to connect. Polling involves more ongoing work and power but provides continuous feedback, whereas on-demand connection uses fewer resources but requires explicit instruction and incurs a delay. To bridge these two methods, a local service can be invoked that periodically polls for connections and provides the latest data to higher-layer services. This provides a configurable method to tradeoff between power and responsiveness across all possible connection types.

Connections at the lowest layer involve the signal generation and transmission hardware. This hardware is controlled by drivers or other software that provide an interface to the operating system and local applications and services. The following information is of interest to a nexus point:

- Hardware capabilities that exist for a given device:
  - Capabilities that are supported,
  - Power and other performance that is supported;

- Hardware that is enabled or disabled by physical switches or other hardware mechanisms;
- Hardware that is enabled or disabled by software:
  - Capabilities that are enabled or disabled in the software;
- Hardware that has the appropriate software drivers and other code in place for use:
  - Capabilities that are supported by the drivers or software;
- Protocols that are supported for the hardware:
  - Waveforms,
  - Mandatory Access Control/data link protocols and versions,
  - Crypto protocols, versions, keying methods.

All of these must be exchanged between ad hoc participants and the nexus points. The nexus acts as the controller for subnetwork communications. Each of these translates into local services for mobile and ad hoc networking. The services described in this section provide basic information about what networking is available, what could be made available, and the capabilities associated with what is and what could be available. In addition, some configuration of the lower-layer hardware and software is made available through these services to other services.

The capabilities list for a device describes what hardware is available. This may take different forms. For some devices, it could provide a list of standard hardware regardless of what is currently available, such as standard-issue mass-produced units. Such a service would rely on outside or fixed data sets and not the system itself. Other services describe the hardware interfaces associated with the device. For example, a description of whether USB 3.0 or 2.0 is supported would be useful when deciding which hardware device to attach through a USB port. Such services could be offline, static, or based on querying the actual device to determine what is available. Other services describe what hardware is actually connected. Unlike some of the services described above that rely on fixed or external information sources, this service actually queries the system to determine what is connected. For hardware that is found, additional information can sometimes be provided, such as the capabilities of the hardware in terms of speed, power, or supported frequencies.

In some cases, hardware is available but switched off. This service provides information about the current state of such hardware. In some cases, hardware that is switched off is indistinguishable from hardware that is not present, but a distinction is made when possible. This allows a service to inform a user that a physical action must be taken to enable communication.

In addition to hardware switches, there are ways to enable and disable communication hardware through the use of software. This can be through an application, the operating system, registry items, or device driver settings. A service is provided to describe the current state of the communication hardware and allow changing this state as permitted through software. In addition to a simple on/off switch, software can provide detailed capability and configuration information, such as frequencies, versions, protocols, security settings, and many others.

To use the communication hardware, appropriate drivers and other software must be available and correctly functioning. This service checks hardware for proper operation and reports the status of the hardware and its drivers. This service may simply examine the driver and perform what amounts to static analysis of the system, or it may actually attempt to use the system and check that it responds appropriately. This service provides information about the system and about how it is currently operating. This includes whether the device is functioning, as well as which of its capabilities are working, such as transmission speeds, error rates, or power consumption, and potentially how well those capabilities are working.

This service provides information about particular protocols that run over different communication hardware. The protocols of interest are the protocols specific to the communication hardware. For example, a Wi-Fi protocol service would provide information about the Wi-Fi protocol, not IP or TCP. This service provides information about which protocols are supported by the hardware and which versions of each of these supported protocols are available. Additional information includes which frequencies, waveforms, data link, or MAC layer protocols are supported, and what type of cryptography or other cryptographic protections are available.

17.2.2 Detection of Network Opportunities

This service provides the ability to test enabled hardware for its protocol support at the network layer. This goes beyond the protocol-based services discussed in the previous section, which apply to the hardware protocols. It looks, for example, for Dynamic Host Configuration Protocol (DHCP) servers, network gateways, Domain Name Service (DNS) servers, and other services that would be available in the presence of a network. These are the services that will be used for web service and web application requests. It is important to know whether these services are available and to what extent they are provided. Knowledge about whether the connection is local or connected to other networks provides important information about the type of connection that can be used by other services.

This service includes tests for proxies, gateways, and other forms of network intermediaries. For example, proxies can be detected by accessing known sites and checking the certificate provided through HTTPS. If it does not match the known good certificate, then a proxy is in the middle. This informs decisions about which network to use, as networks with proxies make ELS communication impossible by preventing end-to-end authentication through TLS, but they would be acceptable for low-security traffic.

17.2.3 Selection of Waveforms and Protocols

This service is used to turn hardware on and off in order to use a specific set of communication hardware. In some cases, this capability can function fully in software using the software interfaces described in the previous section. In cases in which physical action is required, a notification to a human or other interface, such as a machine or robot, is required to initiate the hardware action. In either case, the goal is to have the appropriate hardware on and enabled while everything else is off or disabled. This can be for power conservation, stealth, or just a general security practice to reduce unneeded interfaces.

In addition to just turning hardware on and off, this service allows configuration of the hardware, including selection of frequencies, protocol versions, waveforms, and other hardware-level information. This service acts somewhat like a mediation service that provides a standard interface for higher-level protocols to manage the underlying hardware. It translates the hardware and low-level software controls into standard interfaces for the higher layers. This enables a consistent treatment of communication channels and reuse of higher-layer services across the enterprise and different devices within it. This service dynamically maintains a set of connections that provide an optimal allocation of resources to available potential connections based on provided performance metrics. For example, if high-speed connectivity to a particular IP address is desired, the service may continuously poll for available connections and choose the fastest one that has connectivity to the desired endpoint. Other parameters can be weighed against each other as well, such as power consumption, cost, and combinations such as power per bit or power per bit/sec. Additional inputs would be required for this service to operate effectively, including power consumption models, pricing models, and latency and throughput measurements and models.

This service uses the Manage Hardware service to actually make changes to the system and its connectivity. It uses a set of defined metrics, measured and provided information about the available networks and connections, and optimization logic to determine how to invoke Manage Hardware to best provide what is desired.

This service determines which protocols are available, as described above, and it also performs handshakes and information exchanges to establish IP addresses, secure connections, and other functions that actually initiate protocols for connectivity. Examples include DHCP requests, DNS queries, and other protocols that are common first steps toward data transfer after initial basic connectivity is established. Any ongoing "ping"-type communication is handled by this service as well to establish and update what protocols are available.

17.2.4 Service Discovery

Lower-level service discovery is addressed by the Protocol Availability service, but a separate method must be used for ELS web services. In a connected network, the claims query service is used to determine a list of all applications and services to which an ELS requester entity has claims or access through identity. In a DIL mobile ad hoc environment, this service may not be accessible, but a local copy may be available. If so, this can be used for service discovery. This local copy must be hosted in a canonical place that is accessible to anyone on the network for use as an initial access point to any other ELS services and applications available in the local environment. Although the claims query service is part of the ELS suite of services rather than the mobile ad hoc services, it is mentioned here for context. For all communication, the Send Data service is used to choose the hardware, protocol, and associated settings to provide the data transmission and receiving of any associated responses.

This service provides network communication based on any request and uses available connections to send and receive data. Software on a device calls this service to perform any network-based communication, and this service handles all network requests, sets up appropriate connections if available, and takes care of sending the requests and receiving the responses. It notifies the end entity of the status of the current connections. It uses the metrics and parameters for performance, cost, and power as input and passes these on to the Manage Connectivity service to allow it to maintain a set of appropriate connections for communication. However, the Send Data service can override these settings based on current requests. For example, if cost and power are a primary concern, most communications will be disabled by Manage Connectivity. However, when a short high-priority message must be sent on a hardware module that is disabled, Send Data can override the default settings and make performance for that communication a priority for the duration of the communication.

17.2.5 Query/Response Capabilities

Like the service discovery described above, query and response capabilities are based on ELS. After mobile ad hoc services are used to establish connectivity, ELS queries can proceed. If network connectivity provides access to the EAS and other network resources, then a standard ELS query can follow. If the local network is isolated and has its own EAS instance, then the local instance can be used to provide ELS-based access to local resources. If the local network is isolated and does not host its own instance of EAS, then access is limited to the non-ELS services provided on the local network. For intermittent connectivity, asynchronous messaging may be offered as a service, as such communication can be queued until connectivity returns. As with service discovery, the Send Data service handles the sending and receiving of data over the appropriate connections. The following sections describe the steps in setting up a connection. It is expected that this service will handle all of these either directly or indirectly using the previously mentioned services.

17.2.6 Network Broadcast

The first step for a mobile or ad hoc connection is for the network to identify itself to the mobile node. This is typically done through some sort of network broadcast that identifies the transmitter, the network it represents, its address, the protocols supported, the security offered and required, and other relevant information. For Wi-Fi, for example, a beacon message with this type of information is sent 10 times per second. In some cases, this function is disabled or limited.

For Wi-Fi, the Service Set Identifier (SSID) can be hidden so that only nodes that explicitly request the proper ID are allowed to connect. The beacons can be disabled entirely so that the mobile node must know of the network's existence in advance to connect. Other techniques exist to either hide connections or make detection and connection more difficult for unauthorized entities. These are more difficult to implement on wireless networks because the communications are broadcast to an entity in the vicinity, making replay attacks possible. In general, security protocols, such as WPA for Wi-Fi and IPSec for IP-based network layer communications, are a more robust method of limiting access than simple message-content, formatting, or timing-based methods.

For wired networks, security is often minimal, allowing anyone with physical access and connectivity to use available network services. An Ethernet connection usually is initiated automatically when a wire is plugged in to an Ethernet port. Higher-layer services may require further actions for access, but the lower-level connectivity provides little, if any, security.

17.2.7 System Discovery

After the network identifies itself, if it chooses to do so, the mobile node must discover what is available and how to connect [211–213]. With current systems, many possible network connections are available, such as satellite, Wi-Fi, Military Link Systems, broadband, and others. The networks provide information about different connections, and the node must make sense of this and discover which networks are accessible, which protocols and options are supported, which security is supported and sufficient to meet policy requirements, and which connections support higher-layer applications. ELS requires bilateral authentication, but it may be based on identity for access.

17.2.8 Joining a Network

The mobile node, though some internal logic, determines which network to join and initiates a "request to join" handshake [214, 215]. This may involve the exchange of identification information, it may include security parameter negotiation, and it may include protocol negotiation. Wi-Fi often includes security information. Link systems use device profiles to set the message formats and protocols. In any case, this is where the connection from the mobile node to the network node is established, along with any required parameters.

As part of the request to join, physical layer attributes may be collected, such as signal strength, noise level, signal quality, multipath parameters, location information, and supported waveforms and formats. Wi-Fi 802.11n and 802.11ai support beamforming, allowing the multiple antennas at the transmitter and receiver to be used to determine the direction of transmission and can boost the signal in the vicinity of the communicating entities while reducing it elsewhere. This allows reduced power, slightly increased security, and potentially better use of available network resources by reducing interference with other transmissions.

Other more advanced techniques may allow the use of multipath and complicated urban obstacles to be used to enhance channel security, quality, power efficiency, and data rates. The transmitter sends a test signal to the receiver, which then relays the received signal properties back to the transmitter. The transmitter can then reshape the transmission to "invert" the environmental distortion and allow positive reconstruction of signals at the receiver. Listeners at other physical locations will not be able to properly reconstruct the signal. This allows lower power transmission, better signal to noise, and potentially better privacy against eavesdroppers.

17.3 OTHER CONSIDERATIONS

There are several other processes that need to be considered as discussed below.

17.3.1 Exchange of Certificates

One important part of the request to join the network includes the exchange of certificates. The certificates are assigned to devices and allow authentication based on a trusted CA. For ELS, certificates are stored in hardware, such as an HSM or PIV Card [216]. For lower-layer exchanges, the device TPM [217] is the preferred location. Each device is equipped with a TPM or TPM-like hardware certificate and key store, which is used to authenticate to the network or to the mobile node when required.

For mobile devices without hardware stores, a derived credential may be used for the certificate exchange. This derived credential is issued by a trusted registration authority (RA) in the enterprise. The derived credential uses the same original certification as the primary credential. If the primary credential is revoked for reasons relating to certification, the derived credential is also revoked, as its certification is no longer secure. If the primary credential is revoked due to issues specific to the credential instance, then the derived credential may remain valid independently. Depending on the reasons, revocation of the derived credential may or may not lead to revocation of the primary credential.

17.3.2 Device Requirements

Devices allowed to join enterprise networks are registered and managed by the enterprise use restrictions. All devices have a PKI certificate (CA-issued PKI or derived) in hardware storage (preferably in a TPM). The device and the domain controller perform bilateral, PKI-based mutual authentication before establishment of the channel to the endpoint device manager service. The device may also contain one or more individual user certificates (CA-issued PKI or derived) that are activated when the user signs on to the device. The device may be required to register with the enterprise domain and report attestation from the TPM and other data such as location (where appropriate).

After joining the network and properly authenticating, it may be desirable to set up an endpoint device manager service connection to a remote network. This provides an IP-layer secure tunnel through which higher-layer data can be sent. The initial network connection only applies to the link layer or device-to-device connection.

The endpoint device manager connection uses machine certificates to authenticate the mobile node to the endpoint device manager server and the endpoint device manager server to the mobile node. The endpoint device manager server then makes internal network services available to the mobile node. Particular attention must be paid to which nodes are allowed to connect to the endpoint device manager server. The devices must have controls through MDM or through some other verifiable machine hardware and software integrity checks that ensure the device is protected from compromise to a level comparable to that of the internal nodes on the network.

17.3.3 Discovery of Services

After connecting through the endpoint device manager or just to the local network, service discovery can begin. This starts the use of higher-layer protocols, which talk using various protocols over TCP, UDP, or other transport layer protocols. All active entities must have a credential to initiate a request (derived credentials for entities residing on mobile platforms are permitted). For example, the requester may use a known URL, such as the EAS Claims Query service to retrieve a list of available services. These services are provided based on the requesting entity's identity, as provided in a CAC, PIV card, NPE certificate, derived credential, HSM, or other certificate or key store.

Service discovery [211–214] can be initiated locally for DIL environments with a local cache of the Claims Repository and EAS Claims Query service. The claims query service may be modified to provide identity-based, access-only claims. For mobile devices that are provided network connectivity to the primary EAS instance, no cache is required and a normal request is sent. Discovery may be accomplished initially using a Claims Query service. The initial handshake is bilateral, PKI mutual authentication. This service is identity-based and returns links to claims for service that the requester has. The requester must know the local URL for that service.

17.3.4 Request for Service

When access to the EAS is established, the request for service can be sent to the desired application or service or a link in the Claims Query Service return page may be executed. The EAS-provided link redirects to an STS, which provides authorization information in a SAML and then redirects back to the service. The service's ELS handler processes the request and allows access.

Mobile and ad hoc networking requires some level of performance to support higher-layer protocols and applications [218]. In some cases, poor wireless links or intermittent connectivity prevent the networking protocols from functioning well enough to support the higher-layer protocols. In other cases, the implementation of the protocols is inefficient, uses improper configuration, or adds extra components that reduce performance, such as monitoring or filtering. Those factors under the control of the implementer must combine with those not under control to provide a level of service that supports higher-level protocols and applications appropriate for the network and network participants.

17.4 MOBILE AD HOC SUMMARY

We have reviewed the mobile ad hoc issues in a high-assurance security system. We have also described an approach that relies on high-assurance architectures and the protective elements they provide through PKI. The basic approach becomes compromised when identity is not verified by a strong credential for unique identification (such as HOK in a PKI or a credential derived from that credential). The PKI usage is so fundamental to this approach that we have provided non-certificated users a way to obtain a temporary PKI certificate based on their enterprise need and the level of identity assurance needed to provide access and privilege to applications [55]. The process is fully compatible with ELS and works as a complement to existing infrastructure. This chapter has raised a number of issues while also identifying primary capabilities, such as the number and types of hardware and protocols that will be supported. Work has begun on the Layer 7 services necessary to implement an ad hoc networking capability while maintaining the high level of security in ELS.

18 Endpoint Device Management

18.1 ENDPOINT DEVICE CHOICES

When mobile devices began to proliferate in unanticipated forms, it became apparent that a separate management system was needed to secure the multitude of devices that were not under control of the computing center. Within the computing center, a legion of administrators maintained servers and kept them updated, patched, and in proper configuration, but the mobile devices were not always on or connected and were often nowhere near the administrators of the computing system. Several designs for MDM were provided [219–221], and many of these included provisions for devices provided by the enterprise members, collectively known as Bring Your Own Device (BYOD) [222].

> **ENDPOINT DEVICES**
>
> An endpoint device is a destination or a source in a computing communication. Examples of endpoints include:
>
> - Servers
> - Desktops
> - Laptops
> - Mobile devices ...

This chapter discusses device options within ELS as an endpoint management problem. Devices and endpoints within the computer center (on premises) may be managed separately from mobile devices or by the same processes used for mobile devices, reducing the need for administrator actions.

This includes mobile and non-mobile devices, as well as any device that can be an endpoint within enterprise. The ELS design is based on a set of high-level tenets that are the overarching guidance for every decision made from protocol selection to product configuration and use [223]. From there, a set of enterprise-level requirements is formulated that conforms to the tenets and any high-level guidance, policies, and requirements.

18.1.1 Devices to Be Considered

Within the enterprise there are many devices, falling into two categories.

The first category consists of the enterprise infrastructure devices. For the most part, these devices are on premises and maintained by competent professionals. They may be in the cloud through Infrastructure as a Service (IaaS). Administrators maintain servers and HSMs for infrastructure services, keeping them updated, patched, credentialed, and in proper configuration. In the cloud, we may rely on others to do this work, but the enterprise will specify how and when these activities take place. However, many other devices within the enterprise need to be considered:

stand-alone work stations, firewalls, load balancers, routers, and network information devices. All of these may be on premises or in the cloud [224–227].

The second category consists of the mobile devices used for accessing enterprise services. Almost any device can be mobile, including laptops, smartphones, and tablets. This category also includes secondary services that are not on premises or in the cloud. These may be hosted by enterprise individuals or contract parties.

18.1.2 Options for Device Choices

From the standpoint of the enterprise, there are four major choices for devices:

- Enterprise-purchased devices – Hardware and software are configured by the enterprise, and required updates and configuration control are mandated.
- Enterprise-leased devices as part of a cloud operation – Hardware and software are configured by the enterprise, and required updates and configuration control are specified in the cloud contracts.
- BYOD – Purchased by the individual user of the device. Hardware and software are primarily default at time of purchase. Additional software may be controlled by that user, and basic guidelines may be provided by the enterprise, but they are not easily enforced because of the range of devices and capabilities.
- Hybrid approaches – Many are possible: subsidized BYOD when the device meets certain requirements, registration and configuration of BYOD by the enterprise, and others.

18.1.3 The Issue

Current approaches use a fortified gateway to keep unwanted traffic out of the enterprise. This approach is typified by a series of devices screening incoming traffic. These devices include advanced firewalls, intrusion detection devices, packet inspection devices, application filtering devices, and others.

The fortress model – hard on the outside, soft on the inside – assumes that the boundary can prevent all types of penetration [228], but this assumption has been proven wrong by a multitude of reported network-related incidents. Network attacks are pervasive, and nefarious code is present even in the face of system sweeps to discover and clean readily apparent malware.

ELS is a distributed capability designed to counter adversarial threats by protecting applications and data with a dynamic CBAC solution. Many of today's enterprise solutions involve a combination of devices that are located within the computing center or elsewhere, which somewhat blurs the distinction of mobile devices. An aircraft may have several servers running onboard inflight, and a command post set up for a temporary period may also have such an array of capabilities. Users may access these from an office, at home, in a partner's facility, or on the road. ELS helps provide a distributed high-assurance environment in which information can be generated, exchanged, processed, and used.

18.1.4 Device Evaluation Factors

Device management within ELS is viewed as an endpoint management problem. Devices and endpoints within the computer center are managed by the same processes used for mobile devices, reducing the need for administrator actions and allowing for greater automation. The enterprise considered does not include customer interfaces or point-of-sale (POS) capabilities [229, 230]. Inclusion of these activities involves protecting the enterprise from those types of interfaces.

From there, we formulate a set of enterprise-level requirements that conforms to the tenets and any high-level guidance, policies, and requirements. It is in this context that we evaluate device characteristics and determine where the devices may be used. Many of the factors for evaluation do not have a numeric value, so we use a stoplight evaluation approach in which green represents a good value, yellow represents an acceptable but flawed value, and red represents an unacceptable value.

The evaluation of devices will be based on 10 factors:

- Cost – This is an overarching requirement in many enterprises, and a return on investment analysis must be made. For this analysis, a low cost will evaluate as green and a high cost will evaluate as red. This element is the highest weighted factor in many enterprises. The BYOD costs were initially evaluated as green, but subsequently changed to yellow because of the costs associated with mitigations as discussed in Section 18.1.7.
- Monitoring – Enforcement of activity and forensics. The ability to understand the use of a device is a requirement for insider threat evaluation. An ability to monitor any and all activity will be green. Deficiencies will result in a yellow value, and inability or uncertainty will be red.
- Control – Includes everything from enforcement of policies to updates to software and preventing unwise usage. An ability to enforce all of the above will be green. Deficiencies will result in a yellow value, and inability or uncertainty will be red.
- Access Control – The ability to control access and privilege over space and time and context. A high assurance of no unauthorized access or privilege results in a green value. Some uncertainty results in a yellow value, and a great deal of uncertainty results in a red value.
- Policy Enforcement – A specific control that is given emphasis by this factor. Policy often protects the security of the enterprise. Ability to enforce policy at all times is a green evaluation. Inability to enforce policy at times results in a yellow value, and inability to enforce at all or uncertainty about that ability will result in red.
- Confidentiality – Encryption of data in transit and at rest, as well as in display. The ability to provide confidentiality for all of these is evaluated as green and is probably only complete on premises or in some versions of cloud. Deficiencies will result in a yellow value, and inability or uncertainty will be red.
- Integrity – On a transactional basis, messages received are verifiable as the messages sent; data are unaltered by any entity before an enterprise

individual or entity can process that data. The ability to maintain these factors in all communications results in a green value. Some uncertainty results in a yellow value, whereas a great deal of uncertainty results in a red value.

- Availability – Device availability to the user and the enterprise. Mobile devices have no availability to either the user or the enterprise when they are not connected, and they have reduced availability when in a low bandwidth or a weak connection state. A value of green will mean connectivity within a service level agreement (SLA) that may be specified by the enterprise. Yellow will be assigned when some lack of connectivity may prevent either the user or the enterprise from conducting enterprise business. Red implies that availability is poor or unknown.
- Data Security – The ability to prevent data leakage (encrypted or not). No data leakage would be green, and an inability to protect the data would be red. Some leakage from screens may be inevitable for mobile devices and is evaluated as yellow.
- Overall Security – For ELS, this overrides other factors and is the second highest weighted factor. It is a conglomerate of each of the other elements with the exception of cost and availability. The ability to maintain ELS security properties results in a green value. Some loss in ELS security properties results in a yellow value. Inability to provide ELS security properties results in a red value.

18.1.5 Enterprise Device Requirements

Some devices inside the enterprise are directly within physical boundaries that are controlled by enterprise personnel, such as devices that host servers for web applications and web services, utility devices to host network monitoring, load balancers, routers, and domain name service resolvers. These devices are fully in the control of the enterprise. The hardware, software, and networking are all enterprise-owned and registered.

With increasing computation power in smaller devices, many of the functions traditionally implemented on fixed-location devices are now hosted on mobile devices. For simplicity and consistency, all active entities use enterprise-registered devices to access or provide secure services within the enterprise. This includes servers, desktops, laptops, tablets, phones, watches, network appliances, and any other computation device capable of web interactions within the enterprise. These types of devices are enterprise-registered regardless of whether or not they are mobile. It is impossible to determine whether an endpoint is mobile based on its function, so all functions and devices are assumed to be mobile unless registered as fixed enterprise assets confined to an enterprise computing center, such as the devices hosting back-office services, and managed accordingly.

The primary requirement for enterprise-registered devices is to be enterprise-approved hardware containing a tamper-proof method (preferably hardware) for secure key storage and use (SKSU) with attestation. One such standard for this function is the TPM [231]. SKSU is the starting point of trust for enterprise-registered devices. The SKSU manages a public/private key pair in which the latter cannot be removed or copied from the SKSU. The public key is recorded in the device registry when the device is issued to a user. All future communications with the device are tied back to this key pair. The device proves ownership of the private key in order to provide validated information about the device and its properties, such as installed or connected hardware, installed operating system, installed software, and configuration settings. The SKSU is integrated into the operating system to properly account for application and configuration changes. The SKSU is implemented at a sufficiently low level to prevent software attempts to subvert it. This is necessary in particular to prevent leakage of the private key. The SKSU on a mobile device has provisions for storage of PKI certificates for authorized users and temporary certificates for guests [232].

To properly use the SKSU for management functions, a software agent is installed on the device to communicate with enterprise services, establish secure connections, and provide proof that the device is in compliance with enterprise security rules and settings. Without communication from the agent, the claims-based process is interrupted, and access to enterprise services is denied. The agent itself does not provide security functions, and it is not a trusted endpoint, so it could be compromised without harm to the enterprise. It is installed initially by the enterprise, and it is considered an untrusted agent that provides potentially trusted information (i.e., a passive entity). It is simply a functional unit to provide SKSU information and other verifiable information from the device to the enterprise services using the proper formats and protocols. The agent itself can be validated by sending an SKSU-signed attestation of the software on the device. The agent thus asserts its validity through the SKSU.

Registered devices are enterprise working devices and allowed for restricted personal use. Download of applications is restricted by the enterprise to approved applications, and enterprise-related software is maintained by the enterprise. A special browser is provided for communication with the enterprise, and it is white-list controlled. The endpoint device can be disabled by the endpoint device manager for any number of reasons including suspicious history, corruption of the software set, or improper use.

18.1.6 Evaluation Matrix

Figure 18.1 shows the 10 evaluation elements described in Section 18.1.5 mapped to the following four basic device characteristics:

- BYOD – Bring your own device. The enterprise has no say in the device characteristics, usage, or software configuration. The enterprise may make recommendations but has little in the way of enforcement capability.
- Issued for on-premises use – The enterprise purchases, configures, and maintains the devices for life and controls them in a computing center or through contract with an IaaS provider.
- Issued for off-premises use – The enterprise purchases, configures, and maintains the devices for life but allows them to be used outside of a computing center under the control of a trusted enterprise individual.
- Hybrid approach – Described in Section 18.1.5 as approved hardware that is certificated, configured, and registered with the enterprise.

Element	All Devices			
	BYOD*	Issued for on premises use	Issued for off premises use	Hybrid**
Cost	medium	high	high	medium
Monitoring	low	high	high	high
Control (overall)	low	high	high	high
- Access Control	low	high	medium	medium
- Policy Enforcement	low	high	high	medium
Confidentiality	low	high	high	medium
Integrity	low	high	medium	medium
Availability	medium	high	medium	medium
Data Security	low	high	medium	medium
Overall Security	low	high	medium	medium
Evaluation	unacceptable	preferred	acceptable	acceptable
Recommended	Customer Interface or POS*** Nowhere else	Infrastructure And Primary Services	Key Players and Secondary Services	Mobile and Cloud

Highest Weighted Elements (Cost through Overall Security)

* Bring Your Own Device ** Approve, Configure, and Register *** Point of Sale

FIGURE 18.1. BYOD vs. Issued vs. Hybrid Approach

From the data provided in Figure 18.1, it is apparent that none of the options meet the ELS and other requirements with a totally green evaluation. The most ELS-compatible set of device characteristics belongs to those issued for on-premises use (purchased by the enterprise, configured, and maintained by the enterprise). The cost here is prohibitive, and it eliminates the use of mobile devices completely. The least desirable is the BYOD, which essentially has only low cost in its favor. However, the use of BYOD is absolutely necessary in some enterprises. The burden here shifts from protecting the enterprise from the generic threat to protecting the enterprise from the BYOD threat discussed in the next section.

The following recommendations are made for each of the categories of Figure 18.1.

- BYOD – Not recommended for any enterprise application except where line-of-business and/or monetization is required. Under these circumstances, BYOD is recommended for use in customer interface or POS operations and nowhere else, with specific precautions as described in the next section.
- Issued for on-premises use – Recommended for use in infrastructure and primary services to include back-office operations for identity and access control, device management, monitoring devices, and maintenance of the enterprise knowledge base, as well as other key enterprise functionality.
- Issued for off-premises use – Recommended for use by key players and secondary services where on-premises only is too restrictive and where it will be maintained by trusted enterprise individuals.
- Hybrid – Recommended for use in mobile and cloud developments.

18.1.7 Protecting the Enterprise from BYOD

The low security values of Figure 18.1 present a difficult choice for most enterprises. The low security and increased vulnerabilities embodied within a BYOD may pose a significant risk to the enterprise itself. Mitigations should be undertaken when BYOD is authorized. Recommendations include the following:

- Openness. Let your customers know the process and effects that they will encounter for the protection of both their data and your data and resources [233].
- Policy. Establish enterprise policy on BYOD usage to shape each of the bullet points below and provide for the bullet points above [234].
- Configuration. Not all devices may be configured. Those that can may be configured to enterprise security, helping to mitigate some vulnerability [233].
- Isolation. Keeping the user isolated from enterprise resources that may be corrupted or abused is paramount. This can be done by setting up a DMZ. The DMZ is disconnected from the enterprise except during times of refreshing. The DMZ will contain mirrors of enterprise data and services that are not linked back to the enterprise. These mirrors are periodically (overnight or more or less frequently depending on the business model) refreshed from enterprise resources. Less frequently, the services themselves are rebuilt from enterprise resources [130].
- Separation. Parse data into personal and enterprise transactional data. Discard personal data after the session is complete [235].
- Transaction. The customer interactions are recorded on a transactional basis and then executed against the DMZ databases. The user is warned that there may be a delay (notionally 24 hours) before the statements (online or otherwise) reflect these transactions [131].
- Analysis. Record and analyze the users, usage, devices, etc. to refine the elements of this list [233].
- Refreshing the Security State. The system is placed offline, and applications are re-installed and reconfigured. During the refresh, the transactions are cleansed and reviewed for nefarious behavior. Those that pass muster are imported into the enterprise and executed against the enterprise databases. Those that do not pass muster trigger an alert to the customer (if known) that indicates that the transaction was rejected (you can use corrupted data as an excuse) and that the transaction must be re-entered to take effect [132].
- Point of Sale. Use a provider and record the sale and POS provider confirmation as transactions. This avoids liabilities for maintaining credit and other personal information while allowing a swift monetization [236, 237].
- Incident Response. Establish an incident response team, and practice its scenarios from time to time. Incidents are likely with BYOD, but incident response is required whether or not BYOD is a factor [238, 239].

- Insurance. If you use BYOD, the probability of being compromised is high. Insurance can help in the recovery. Insurance should be considered whether or not BYOD is a factor [240, 241].

Based on the analysis of these defensive measures for BYOD, the stoplight value for cost changed from green to yellow.

18.1.8 Device Choice Summary

Deployment of endpoint devices with varying characteristics may be required for operational and other considerations. Security and efficiency are key elements in deciding where and how to deploy such devices. In a high-assurance environment, maintaining tight control of both devices and users is mandatory. Although BYOD may be unavoidable in certain enterprises, the enterprise must not be placed in a vulnerable situation. For enterprise devices, a hybrid approach between BYOD and tightly controlled, issued devices is utilized. In the hybrid approach, certain devices owned by the user may be approved if they meet enterprise requirements and are enterprise configured and registered.

18.2 ENDPOINT DEVICE MANAGEMENT

This part of the chapter discusses device management within ELS as an endpoint management problem. Devices and endpoints within the computer center are managed by the same processes used for mobile devices, reducing the need for administrator actions. This includes mobile and non-mobile devices, as well as any device that can be an endpoint within the enterprise. All devices must comply with requirements as stated in Section 18.1.5.

18.2.1 Device Registry

The enterprise device endpoint registry consists of a database including information on devices, serial numbers, properties, machine certificates/keys, locations, attestation reports, who (persons and/or organizations) the device was issued to, who (persons and/or organizations) the notifications are sent to and how, whether the device is PIV card-enabled for registered users for the device (for mobile, this includes those that have derived credentials recorded with the SKSU) and whether or not a guest logon is allowed, software update status, and incident report reference for the device (if any), as well as other pertinent data. This database is used by the data registration service, the software update service, and other services within the enterprise. Registration and configuration of server endpoints, including endpoint agents, are done through the data owner and the endpoint device registrar. The endpoint registrar is an approved and trained individual who is assigned to a registration unit (similar to PIV issuance stations). Mobile devices will be registered and configured by enterprise support, including the loading of the current containers, endpoint agents, and other software for the particular device, as well as creation and loading of the derived credentials necessary into the SKSU. The standard configurations are available to the registrar in a database. This database is part of or linked to the endpoint authorized software and updates.

Registration and configuration will be redone on a periodic basis, as will derived credentials; coordinating these renewals will minimize administrative time. All other devices will be configured and registered by the administrator assigned to the device in communication with the device registrar. This will minimize updates needed during usage.

The elements of registration are provided in Figure 18.2. The device registration service captures input from the device and the device registrar. The latter includes any information about the device that requires manual entry. The device registrar authorizes the standard software for the device. This may be in a separate store or as part of the software updates store. If this is a renewal, the software will be updated to the latest configured and approved software states. The device registrar also creates and stores derived credentials based on the PIV issued by the authorized CA for the device. The registration service stores these data in the device endpoint registry. The registration service communicates with the device endpoint agent in order to confirm that the attestation report from the agent satisfies what is stored in the device endpoint registry. The device endpoint registry stores the latest valid attestation report for each device, as well as a history of such reports that shows changes over time as appropriate. Any unauthorized change in attestation reports signals a security alert for that device and possible remediation actions.

The device endpoint agent establishes communication with the enterprise endpoint service when connectivity is available to the device. Thereafter, the agent provides a heartbeat [242] at a configurable interval, which begins at device connection and periodically sends the IP address, device ID, attestation, attestation state, location, and other information. Information unchanged since the last heartbeat is omitted. When the user signs in, the user DN and credential type are added. The periodic reporting by an agent was first described by Hong et al. in 2001 [243]. As described in [243], most modern network devices are equipped with management agents,

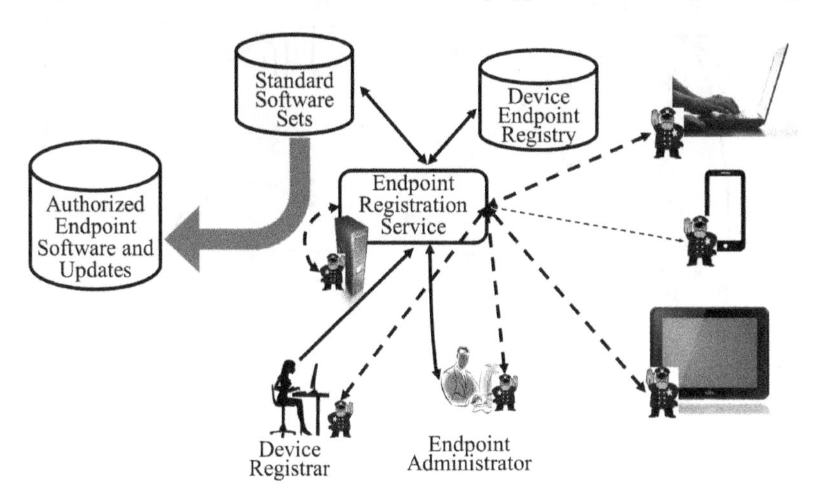

FIGURE 18.2. Elements of Registration

typically a Simple Network Management Protocol (SNMP) agent [244] for computer network devices and a Common Management Information Protocol (CMIP) agent [245] for telecommunication network devices.

What makes this management approach different is the use of on-device attestation. These data are placed in the endpoint/user dynamic binding store. A configurable number of missed heartbeat cycles, for whatever reason, result in the entry being dropped from the endpoint/user dynamic binding. The heartbeat is re-established after connectivity is restored. The agent also provides mandatory log files of activity for the Mobile Device Mandatory Log Files Store, which is periodically swept by the monitor sweep agents. Heartbeats may be of configurable durations. Servers in fixed locations that are expected to be active may have a less frequent heartbeat than mobile devices that are subject to more dynamic data.

The device endpoint agent establishes communication with the enterprise endpoint service (shown in Figure 18.3) when a user logs on to an endpoint device. The purpose is to provide a dynamic binding between the user and the device (including such other information as location) for use by other enterprise services and particularly the Provide Claims Service, which could have restrictions for devices, locations, and other uses of designated enterprise services. Device data is periodically renewed through the heartbeat mechanism described above. When a user logs off of the device, the name is deleted from the dynamic binding store, and logs are provided to the mobile device activity log stores. The heartbeat continues until connectivity with the endpoint service is lost.

The enterprise endpoint service communicates with the endpoint update manager, which stores enterprise-approved software and updates in the authorized endpoint

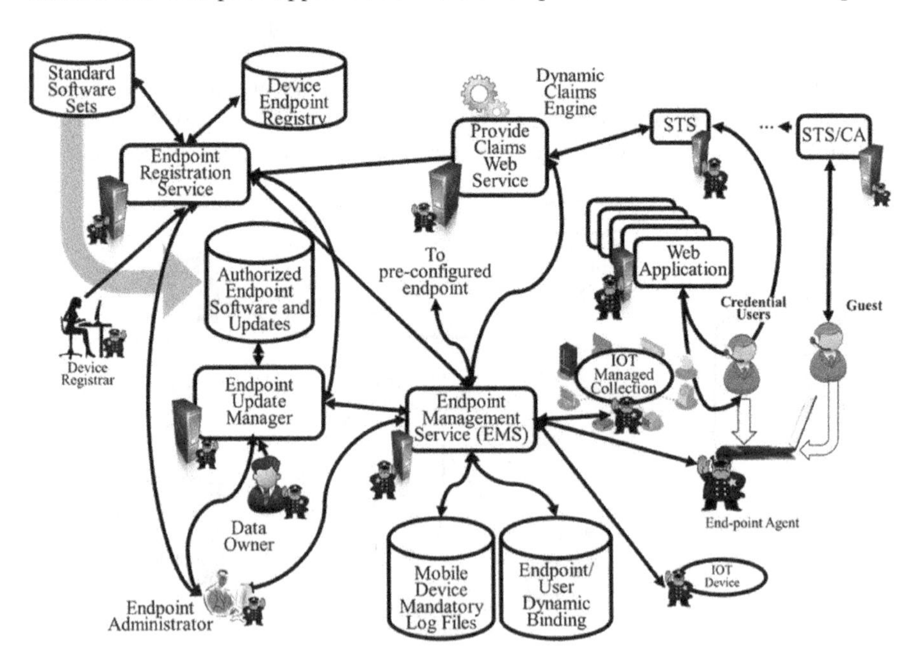

FIGURE 18.3. Endpoint Device Management Process

software and updates store. When an update is available for enterprise endpoint devices, the endpoint administrator provides the update to the endpoint update manger, which places the update in the endpoint software, updates the store, and scans the registration service for candidates for the update, annotating the device endpoint registry as appropriate. The software update has a completion required date, and notice is provided to the recorded notifying individuals.

Those individuals log onto the endpoint device and pull the update from the enterprise endpoint service through the endpoint agent. If this is not accomplished by the required date, the endpoint update manager notifies the relevant individuals and pushes the update to the device when it is logged onto the system.

The enterprise endpoint service:

1. Manages the endpoint/user dynamic binding store. The enterprise endpoint service verifies endpoint presence in the device endpoint registry and the equivalence of the SKSU registry information (and refuses connection when these fail), stores data provided by the endpoint agents when checks are successful, and answers queries from the provide claims web service.
2. Stores the mobile device mandatory log files when these are provided by the endpoint agents.
3. Relays endpoint agent instructions for notification and/or updates as provided by the endpoint updates manager (described in the next section).
4. Issues reboot, shut down, credential revocation, and other termination activities when its own analysis indicates the need or when directed to do so by an authorized entity.
5. Receives and distributes Internet of Things (IoT) data as configured.

Software patches are initially made available to the devices by notification to the registered device users, who initiate an update through the device endpoint agent or other designated means. Patches that have not been updated in a reasonable time or whose updating is urgently required are pushed to the device. In both cases, the device registration is updated through the device endpoint agent, which provides a revised attestation report to the registration service.

Changes in applications are registered and approved. New attestations of approved updates are reregistered in the central store. The endpoint update service contains a schedule for updates that includes availability dates, notification dates, and required completion or push dates. The notifications are provided for the relative endpoint, based upon the software installed in the device endpoint registry to the individual(s) of record in the device endpoint registry by the method(s) indicated in the device registry.

The calendar is used for notifications of scheduled and unscheduled outages as provided by the data owner. The notifications are provided for the relative endpoint, based upon the software installed in the device endpoint registry to the individual(s) of record in the endpoint registry by the method(s) indicated in the device registry.

An endpoint is terminated when a serious deviation from policy is detected, attestation has not been maintained, or when the device is suspected to be compromised or has been involved in nefarious behavior. This is accomplished by sending a "brick" command [246] to the endpoint agent, removing the device from the device endpoint registry, suspending or revoking PKI certificates (PIV and/or derived credentials) of users, disabling Wi-Fi, and disabling email and other functionality.

Disenfranchised devices are wiped [247] selectively or in full (back to the factory default settings). If ownership of the device is in question, the enterprise endpoint manager exercises all of the above. At the discretion of the administrator, a termination notification is sent to the individual(s) of record in the device endpoint registry by the method(s) indicated in the device endpoint registry. All actions are logged, and termination or disenfranchisement triggers alerts.

A user activates a device with PIV readers installed by using the PIV and passcode. For devices without PIV readers installed, a user authenticates himself to the device, thus binding derived credentials to the user. The device endpoint agent provides the user binding to the enterprise. Devices without PIV readers are provisioned with one or more derived credentials for one or more assigned device users. Authentication and binding of mobile devices typically requires a two-factor authentication, as there is no separate hardware device for storage of private keys and the devices are generally physically accessible to non-vetted personnel. The second factor configured for the device is typically biometric (out-of-band is associated with the mobile device) with the biometric determined by device capabilities, such as face recognition, voice recognition, or fingerprint. The call for second-factor authentication comes from the STS upon recognizing the use of a derived credential. Claims are sent to the STS only if the user is coupled to a registered device and the device does not compromise the rules established by the data owner (such as geo-location). Any device that does not have a user/endpoint association in the endpoint/user dynamic binding store trips an error return (and associated logs and alerts) from the provide claims web service.

Certain devices are configured with multiple derived credentials. This allows multiple users to use a single device. The device endpoint agent provides a binding to the user currently logged into the device. Additionally, certain devices provide for device authentication without a certificate. When this occurs, the only option for the user is to proceed to the STS/CA for the issuance of a temporary certificate through multi-factor authentication. This certificate's private key is installed in the temporary memory of the SKSU for this user on this device. The private key should be encrypted using the public key of the SKSU to ensure that only the SKSU can use this software-based private key. The temporary certificate has a short life (currently 90 minutes). This process is described in detail in [55].

18.2.2 IoT Devices

IoT refers to a class of small special application devices that measure environments and/or control specific hardware or both. There are special security considerations for these devices, which are increasingly becoming the target of attacks from Mirai to WannaCry [248]. The IoT is about functionality and has not matured yet in the security domain. Only IoT devices deemed essential for the enterprise should be allowed. All IoT devices deemed essential will be fronted with a device endpoint agent (Section 18.2.3) and physical protection. The device endpoint agent is software on enterprise-approved devices that interacts with central services. It is a functional element that applies requests from the enterprise endpoint service to the local device data from the local device for the enterprise endpoint service. For ELS purposes, IoT devices are of three types:

1. Individual full system devices with a single capability and an enterprise management system, as shown in Figure 18.4. This IoT is an enterprise-registered device and it is configured with a secure key store and an endpoint agent and registered in the endpoint registry as described below. The enterprise endpoint service(s) are configured to check this device for registry and attestation and distribute the information to a designated endpoint.
2. Sensors, aggregations of capabilities, and other collections of devices that are part of a network of devices reporting to a single manager of the IoT collection, as shown in Figure 18.5. The individual elements of the collection are not considered registered devices, but the managers of the IoT collection are enterprise-registered devices and are configured with a tamper-proof secure key store and an endpoint agent, and registered in the endpoint registry as described below. The enterprise endpoint service is configured to check this device for registry and attestation and distribute the information to a designated endpoint.
3. Individual devices with a single capability but less than full system capability that are unable to act as an ELS compliant device, as shown in Figure 18.6. These devices may be employed only when they are hardwired

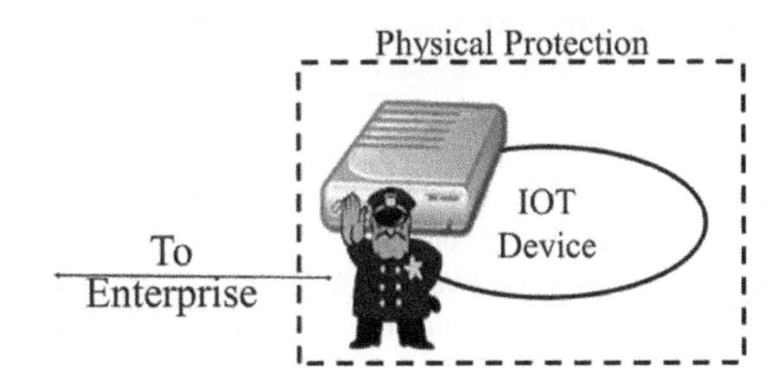

FIGURE 18.4. Full System IoT Device

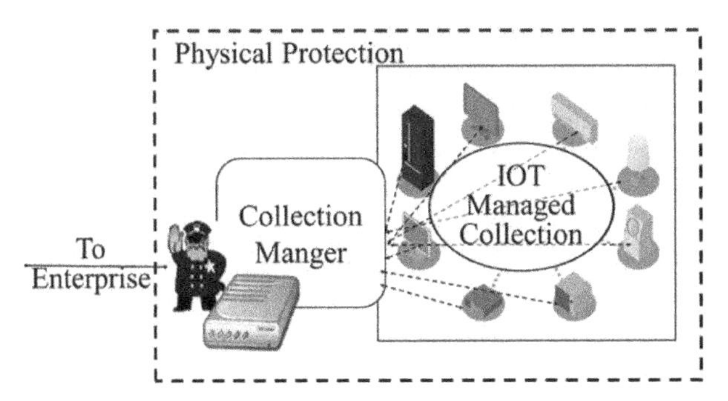

FIGURE 18.5. Managed Collection of IoT Devices

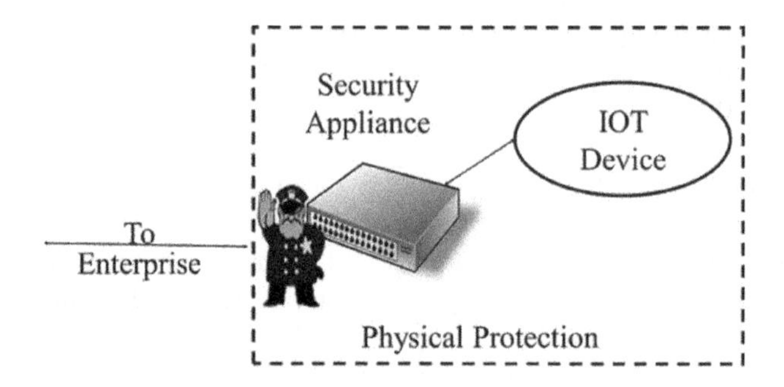

FIGURE 18.6. Security Appliance Fronted IoT Device

to a security appliance that will provide all of the ELS compliant security. The device will have only the hardwired interface active, all other ports will be shut down, including any ports designed to communicate with the manufacturer. All communications will be handled by the security appliance (the appliance may mimic device communications such as Wi-Fi, broadband, or Bluetooth), and the device plus the security appliance are treated as a single entity from an enterprise standpoint.

18.2.3 Device Endpoint Agent

The device endpoint agent is software on enterprise-approved devices that interacts with central services. It is a functional element that applies requests from the enterprise endpoint service to the local device and retrieves SKSU data from the local device for the enterprise endpoint service.

The agent is essentially a local mediation service for the SKSU and the central services. It queries the SKSU for the current state of the system, and it communicates with the central services to relay these SKSU reports and other verifiable data. When patches or updates are pushed, the agent applies them locally. Pushed packages come from the endpoint manager or, when approved by the enterprise, the application store.

18.2.3.1 Monitoring and Reporting

The agent monitors the status of the device. It periodically queries the SKSU for an attestation report. If such a report is not available or produced in error, the agent alerts the central services, which can instruct further action, such as disabling certain device functions, removing applications, or completely wiping the device's sensitive data and keys.

Under normal operations, the agent monitors connections and uses these connections to maintain a periodic heartbeat communication with the enterprise endpoint service. The agent also contacts the service upon initial connectivity and sends an attestation report with the device's status. The device status is "invalid," "current," "current awaiting update," or "not current updates needed." The agent then responds to any requests from the central services for further information or action.

18.2.3.2 Data Validation and Purging

The agent can validate SKSU signatures and data structures, but it cannot be trusted to perform a full validation of local information, because the agent itself can potentially be compromised. For this reason, the agent sends SKSU attestation reports to the central services for further validation against known good values. The central services then directs the agent whether to continue as normal or take corrective actions, such as purging data, keys, and applications from the device.

If a device is stolen and compromised, the agent functionality is compromised as well, because it is just another application on the device. Although this should not pose a serious security threat, because the SKSU and its private key(s) should still be secure, it means that a request to wipe the device can never be confirmed. The goal is not complete remote control over the device, but instead to enforce basic compliance rules before allowing users on enterprise-registered devices to connect to enterprise services. The ability of the enterprise endpoint service to revoke access to devices without valid attestation reports mitigates the device itself from becoming a new point of vulnerability.

18.2.3.3 Fulfilling Requests for Data

In addition to standard SKSU attestation, the agent can be queried for other local data available from the device itself or other local services. For example, Global Positioning System (GPS) location information could be requested or service provider information could be requested. The agent simply relays the information provided and repackages it for consumption by the central services. The agent, as a potentially compromised part of the device, cannot be trusted to relay correct information. Additional security measures, such as digital signatures, are used from the original data providers to guarantee integrity. Disabling signature or other integrity or security functions is considered nefarious behavior and subject to endpoint disabling.

The agent for fixed assets (e.g., desktops) within the enterprise reports information about the location of the devices. This can be compared against the registered location. This typically includes an address or room number that is static and configured into the machine. Because such devices are within the control of the enterprise, no dynamic location data is needed. An individual can verify the location if needed.

The agent for mobile assets provides location based on best available information (e.g., Wi-Fi access point name, mobile tower identifier, GPS coordinates, altimeter, etc.). Because such devices move frequently and connect from outside the network, dynamic information about location is important for access control or other decisions. The local device is not trusted to provide this information because it could be compromised. External sources, such as Wi-Fi connection information, GPS data, or wireless tower connection information, provide potentially valuable location data, but often do not provide security guarantees such as trusted signatures. Due to mobility, the availability of certain types of information is uncertain, so the best effort is made given the current environment and available services. The endpoint manager ascertains the veracity of the location measure using logic provided by the enterprise and may place a value of "unknown" in the dynamic file.

18.2.4 Endpoint Device Management Summary

Management of endpoint devices is required for both security and efficiency. In a high-assurance environment, maintaining tight control of both devices and users is mandatory.

ELS Extensions – Other Techniques

19 Endpoint Agent Architecture

19.1 AGENT ARCHITECTURE

Defending an enterprise and its information against external attacks has moved from the central network to the edge devices. Network monitoring provides a centralized approach where all communications can be intercepted, recorded, analyzed for malicious intent, and modified as needed. However, this is complicated by current threats and operational practices.

Widespread encrypted HTTPS traffic requires a network scanner to act as a central point of decryption. This can be accomplished by sharing server private keys with network appliances on the wire, but such an approach violates end-to-end security by breaking every secure connection within the enterprise. In addition, these network appliances provide central points of attack that enable access to all traffic and allow an attacker to impersonate any entity within the enterprise. Such a network-based approach has critical security flaws.

Moving the defense to the edge of the network offers several advantages. There is no need to break end-to-end secure connections. There is no central point of attack that can compromise all connections and impersonate any entity. The defense tools can operate at the endpoint to detect malicious behavior as it happens and directly respond instead of trying to predict it before it happens based on network traffic and then trying to respond remotely after the damage is done.

The edge defense model does have some drawbacks. The distributed nature of the defense introduces the challenge of coordination and correlation of data. End-to-end security requires new approaches to decrypt data for analysis. Also, software agents at the endpoints, which are often lightweight applications, must perform secure operations and initiate secure communication channels.

This chapter presents a method for enabling distributed endpoint-based defense while preserving end-to-end integrity, encryption, and authentication of communications across the enterprise.

19.2 RELATED WORK

Network monitoring can provide important insights into lower layer resources and communications, but it lacks access to the higher layer content due to widespread HTTPS and similar protocols. Web application firewalls (WAFs) attempt to bridge this gap by decrypting content for the server, analyzing and modifying it for security, and passing the clean content to the server. The WAF may even open files and execute code to determine if certain content presents a danger to the receiver. This approach catches many attacks that network monitoring and pattern-based detection miss, but it breaks the end-to-end security model, introduces latency in communications, and does not stop all attacks.

Endpoint agent architecture design has seen some work with varying goals. [249] describes an agent architecture that preserves battery life of mobile devices. [250] describes the potential benefits of using agents for IoT applications. [251] and [252] examine security of agents that migrate between different hosts. [253] describes a secure agent architecture for sensor networks. [254] describes a secure agent architecture for mobile agents that has similar security goals, but unlike our work, its agents operate with their own software-based private keys, and the agent code itself must be carefully protected.

There is a lot of work in the area of mobile agent computing, where agents move from device to device. However, our interest is in monitoring the device itself using agents, not doing computations that move agents across devices.

SOFTWARE AGENTS

A software agent is a goal-oriented computer program that reacts to its environment and runs without direct supervision to perform a function for an end user, the enterprise, or another entity. Some, but not all, software agents have user interfaces.

19.3 ELS AGENT METHODS

This chapter addresses the challenge of integrating endpoint device agents into the ELS architecture while adhering to and working with the existing ELS concepts, components, and protocols. This section provides an overview of integration challenges for agent-based security.

The ELS model starts with the premise that security is between endpoints. However, endpoints are one of the most vulnerable areas of any information system. As a result, ELS requires strong guarantees that the endpoints have not been compromised. For example, a stolen smart card credential compromises an individual, but such a problem is often quickly reported by the person who lost the credential. However, a compromised device can monitor user activity and act as the user surreptitiously over long periods of time with no obvious signs to the user. A systematic approach is required to monitor devices for such compromise and malicious behavior.

In addition, the ELS infrastructure includes other types of agents, such as logging and monitoring agents and endpoint device management agents.

The primary challenges for agents in a secure environment are:

- Establishing secure agent communication with external entities
- Tying agent communication to its host device

The first challenge requires that all endpoints use the same ELS methods to communicate whether they are a person, server, or other active entity in the enterprise. The agent, as the initiator of communication with a central server, gateway, or collection system, qualifies as such an active entity. It must be secured at a level comparable to a user with a hardware-based PKI credential. This is challenging because agents operate differently than normal users or other active entities.

The second challenge relates to the separate methods of authenticating endpoint requesters and the devices themselves. Users, for example, can use smart cards and servers can use HSMs to authenticate from different underlying hardware platforms or even virtual machines. However, hardware authentication must be through a different means, as it must be tied to the hardware platform itself. The challenge for agents is to tie the agent to its digital identity and then tie its digital identity to a hardware-based device identity.

19.4 ENDPOINT AGENT RESULTS

Sections 19.4.1 through 19.4.6 describe the approach for the different agents that both use ELS and expand ELS services to address enterprise needs.

19.4.1 Mobile Device Management (MDM) Agents

With the move from desktops and laptops to mobile devices like phones and tablets, the edge of the enterprise has changed. Gone are the days where employees log in from an enterprise machine in an enterprise building on an enterprise network. Current users can come from personal mobile devices in public spaces through a commercial cellular network. This motivates our first use case of endpoint device management. These endpoints include mobile devices as well as more traditional laptops, desktops, and servers. Agents for device management must have a software component for the agent code, but they must also leverage a hardware key store on the device. Unlike ELS authentication, where the keys are tied to the user or other entity using the device, agent authentication must be tied to the device hardware.

Such an agent need not have any security itself for authentication. In fact, the agent should not have any security information, because such information could be easily duplicated or extracted from a software element. The agent is similar to a web browser on a desktop. The browser does not itself authenticate to servers. It provides the means for a user to authenticate and request or provide content. The agent is similar in nature. It relies on existing device keys and certificates to authenticate and communicate securely. The source of the agent keys must be the device hardware, not a portable or external key store, because such agents speak for the device itself and not for some other entity like a person or server that can migrate from device to device.

This introduces some complications. First, the agent is a piece of software that is separate from its hardware-based keys. Hence, any agent, real or malicious, that gains access to the real agent's keys can act as a real agent. There are a number of attacks possible between a software instance and the hardware keys it uses. This is similar to the challenge of securing keys in the cloud, which has a similar key and software separation issue. The agent, and the endpoint security in general, must rely on the device to monitor itself, including the software on it, because the agent cannot be trusted by itself.

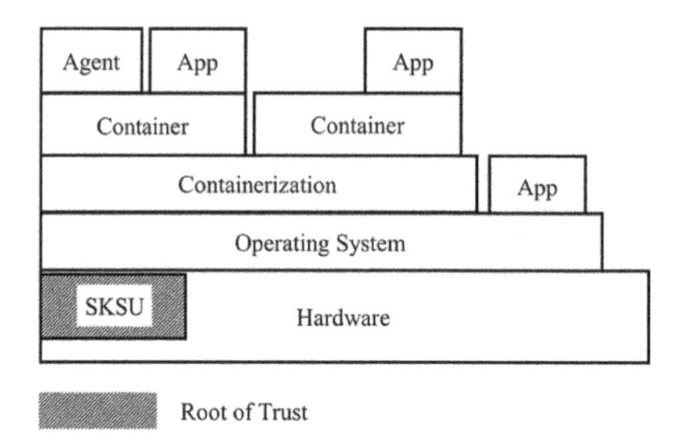

FIGURE 19.1. Using the Hardware-Based SKSU

SKSU on a device, such as a TPM, has the capability to perform attestations, and such an attestation is required to ensure that the device is running the proper agent and other software. The attestation is a report that lists the state of hardware and software on the device and provides a signature using a key associated with the particular SKSU module on the device. The SKSU hardware module serves as the root of trust for all device-based communications, as indicated in Figure 19.1. The SKSU must itself be trusted as a starting point, and from there security for the device and its software functionality can be secured using attestation reports.

The attestation report must cover the hardware, operating system, any virtualization or containerization, and the applications and agents installed on the device. For an agent to communicate securely, it must first produce an attestation report that shows that at the current time the device is running as intended with no malicious entities or configuration modifications. This is typically implemented as a white list of approved software.

The agent invokes the TPM to produce an attestation report with the required parameters. In Figure 19.2, the elements covered by the attestation report are highlighted. They include the full set of components that can affect the agent, which is running as an app in a container. The containerization and containers are trusted to isolate the apps within their containers sufficiently well that any other apps or containers are allowed to operate on the device. Other apps outside the container need not be validated, and other containers need not be validated. This might be the case for a phone with separate work and personal spaces. However, if the containerization or containers had known vulnerabilities or insufficient protections and isolation capabilities, then the attestation report would have to cover the other components as well. In general, the attestation report must cover all elements of the device and its software that could negatively affect the agent's ability to securely communicate with an external entity.

The trust starts at the bottom with hardware and works its way up the stack. The SKSU validates that the device hardware is operating correctly. It then validates that the operating system is correct. This may include checking whether the operating system is "rooted," which version is installed, and whether the software is installed

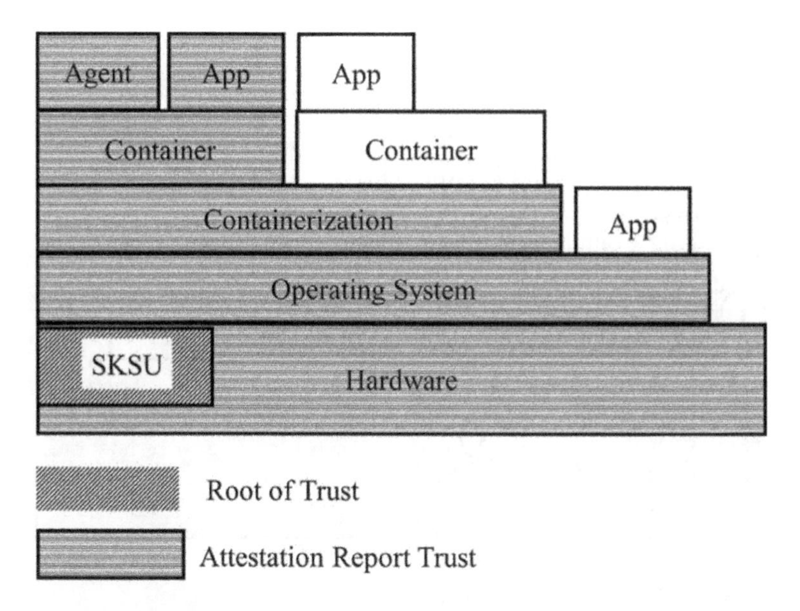

FIGURE 19.2. Extending Trust to Other Hardware and Software

properly by (for example) checking a hash of the executable against a known value. The containerization and applications, including the agent itself, can then be validated in a similar manner.

With a trusted SKSU, and a valid agent running with other valid applications in a valid container in a valid containerization method on a valid operating system on valid hardware, a high degree of trust can be established in the agent functionality. In particular, a high degree of trust can be established that a private key operation for the agent was actually initiated by the agent itself. This is required because there is no external method, such as a PIN or biometric information, to validate the agent's request at the SKSU itself. The SKSU, in combination with the full validated software stack, is required to secure the private key use by the agent. Without such validation, it may be possible for another entity to use the key, which would prevent proper authentication of the agent to the central server.

The agent, with its attestation report, communicates with the external entity, which is often an aggregation point for many device agents. After authentication, the agent may send a SAML token to the external endpoint for access, in accordance with standard ELS rules for access. A simpler alternative is to have the agent use identity-based authorization. In this case, the server maintains an ACL of the known deployed device agents. This reduces the need for a SAML token, but eliminates the efficiency that ELS provides for managing ACRs for large groups.

The external entity must be configured to expect and then validate an attestation report for an agent request. The agent's credential is stored on the TPM or other SKSU module. Such a credential alone is not sufficient for ELS authentication, because rogue software may have compromised the device and used the agent key. To secure against this attack, the attestation report validates that the proper software is installed and running at the time of the communication with the agent.

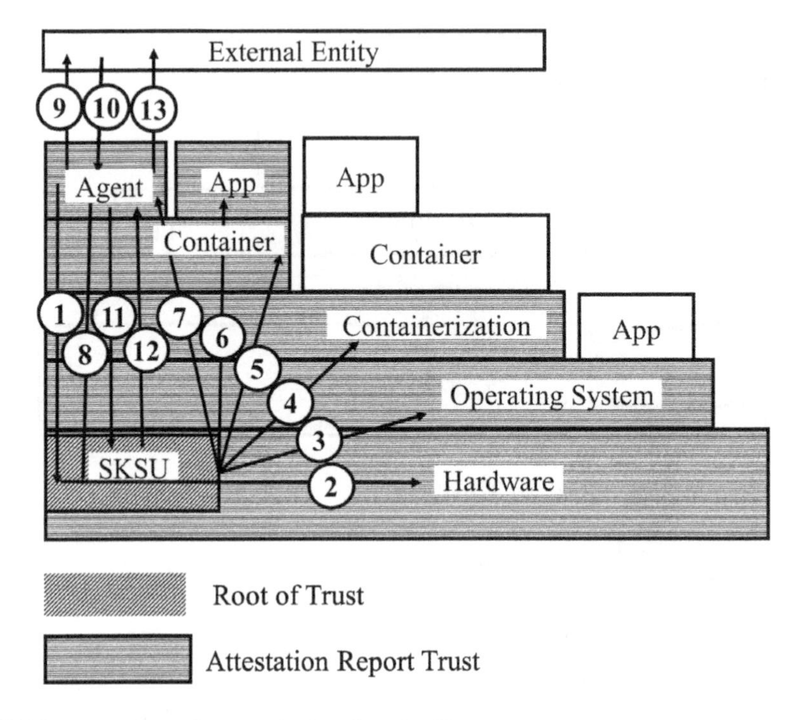

FIGURE 19.3. Agent Communication Security Flows

The SKSU module itself may be compromised, which would allow an attacker to generate valid attestation reports for a compromised device. This is addressed by choosing hardware devices that protect against such attacks. Such hardware is becoming a standard part of mobile phones, and keys generated on such devices are very difficult to extract [101, 255].

The full secure communication sequence from agent to external entity is shown in Figure 19.3. The steps are as follows:

1. The agent requests an attestation report from the SKSU module.
2. The SKSU module validates the hardware.
3. The SKSU module validates the operating system version, configuration, and hash.
4. The SKSU module validates the containerization mechanism or other isolation mechanism(s), if applicable.
5. The SKSU module validates the container or other isolation unit where the agent is located, if applicable.
6. The SKSU validates other applications in the same container as the agent.
7. The SKSU validates the agent itself.
8. The SKSU provides the attestation report to the agent.
9. The agent initiates a secure connection to the external entity and validates the external entity credentials.
10. The external entity requests authentication of the agent.

11. The agent requests a private key operation for the agent key stored in the SKSU.
12. The SKSU returns the results of the private key operation.
13. The agent uses the private key operation to authenticate to the external entity and provides the attestation report through the secure connection.

The external entity must validate that the attestation report has a valid signature from a trusted source and that the items listed for the device conform to a valid configuration of the device. At this point, the agent has successfully authenticated to the external entity using the device key in the SKSU, leveraging the SKSU and its internal key as a root of trust.

The external entity may then request an access token, or it may check the identity of the agent against an ACL for authorization. This process proceeds similarly to normal ELS SAML requests. The only difference is that authentication to the token server also uses the flows above to use the SKSU and its attestation report for authentication.

19.4.2 Monitoring Agents

In addition to device management agents, ELS requires agents for monitoring of endpoint devices. With end-to-end security, it is not possible to directly monitor the content of communication between endpoints. This information must be collected from the endpoints using agents. These agents operate on both servers and user devices. The monitoring agents watch for potentially malicious inputs and outputs, much like a network-based monitoring system does. However, the monitoring agents only process a single device's communications. This can help performance by distributing the load across all enterprise devices. However, some data must be shared with a central entity to enable cross-device correlations. The agent is responsible for communicating with the central aggregator and sending relevant data periodically or upon request. The agent also responds to configuration changes pushed from the central aggregator in response to changing monitoring needs.

The monitoring agents process security sensitive information related to device, operating system, or application anomalies and compromises, and they initiate this transmission as active entities, so they must be authenticated much like the endpoint device management agents. The monitoring agent keys are stored in the TPM and used to initiate TLS connections to central servers. The agent authenticates using its key, and this is coupled to an endpoint device management agent's attestation report that certifies the operational state of the device. Because monitoring agents and endpoint device management agents are both part of the standard ELS infrastructure, such attestation reports can be shared among the back-end servers through a common storage system.

With a TPM attestation report from the endpoint device management system, the device's state is established as "clean." Such a clean device can then be trusted to authenticate and provide proper information from all of the agents covered by the attestation report, including the monitoring agent. The monitoring agent then provides further information about potentially malicious activity on the device itself.

This information can include details of malicious operating system configuration changes, such as rooting, or malicious or anomalous application activities, such as accessing or requesting restricted resources.

19.4.3 Log Aggregation Agents

Log aggregation agents periodically assemble the relevant log content from the device, which may include monitoring logs, browser history, key usage, location history, network utilization rates, or other information as configured by the enterprise. They then send this information to an aggregator, which may further aggregate it at the enterprise level. The log information from a single device is packaged as a signed message that can be passed through multiple aggregators without loss of security properties. The intermediate aggregators are not active entities because they do not modify the data packages. They only provide performance benefits, such as load balancing or aggregation of data packets.

Log records can come from the hardware, in which case an attestation report is a natural security measure. They can also come from the operating system, which is often tightly coupled with a SKSU module, and again the attestation report is a natural choice for security. The challenge is application-layer logging, which may not be completely in control of the application that generates it. The operating system, in particular, may interfere with the log file management, make it available to other applications, or directly modify it. The operating system could also act on behalf of the application when requesting logging related activities. Again, the attestation report for the software on the device provides a method to secure against a modified or compromised operating system. The system attestation report combined with the log attestation report provides the needed security for transferring the log record to the central aggregator.

The log aggregator has a unique position. It is a passive entity with respect to the content of the log records. These are signed by the log aggregation agents on individual devices, so such content cannot be modified by the aggregator. However, the aggregator does have an important active role to play in validating the integrity of the signature. The aggregator must validate the attestation report for the device that signed the log record. A bad attestation report implies that the signature cannot be trusted, and the log aggregator is the point where this is checked. The log aggregator signs valid log records and refuses to sign invalid log records. The aggregator serves as an active entity in providing its own validation but is a passive entity with respect to the signed log records themselves.

The central aggregator need not be a central point of failure for log record security. Confidentiality is difficult to provide due to the nature of the aggregator, but integrity is often more important for log-related applications. The signatures by the device-based keys and certificates, combined with a validation of their attestation reports, provide a high level of integrity for such records. For aggregation functions, it may be necessary to strip the signatures and use the raw data for further processing. In this case, there is no direct method to validate the processed data, but because all original data is signed, it is possible to independently validate such computations.

Thus, the central aggregator is a single point of aggregation, but it is not a single point of vulnerability due to the device signatures for individual records.

19.4.4 Service Desk Agents

A self-help agent may be provided for certain devices that require complex configurations or administration. This agent can reduce the interaction with the service desk by solving many obvious configuration issues and some simple usage errors. This agent may provide remote access and capabilities for a service desk person or automated service. The service desk agent provides a higher degree of access than other agents. This is because the service desk operators often require privileged access to many functions on the device when troubleshooting an issue. The service desk agent, as a highly capable agent, introduces a potentially dangerous interface into the device and a tempting target of attack.

The security goals are slightly different for the service desk agents. For other agents, the goal is strong validation of what comes out of such agents. For the service desk agent, the goal is strong validation of what goes into the device. It is important to prevent intruders from using the service desk agent as an attack vector into the machine.

The attestation reports collected by the endpoint device management system identify devices that are out of compliance. Agents will fail to authenticate to external servers under these conditions, just as for any other agent. However, a service desk agent on an out-of-compliance device can potentially open the door for attackers, so a stronger response is required. Instead of just denying the service desk agent external access, the agent must be locked down or disabled until the device is brought into compliance.

19.4.5 Import and Mediation Agents

Import agents are used to refresh data in reference stores and mediate their content for compatibility with other information. The agents pull data through a guard for integrity and accuracy checking. Guarded and filtered inputs are aggregated. Because numerous errors and inconsistencies may exist, the guard checks for formatting errors, discrepancies between databases, incorrect or missing data, illogical data, and other undesirable conditions. Handling of discrepancies from sources depends upon the nature of the discrepancy, and corrections may be required before the data can be imported.

Import and mediation agents handle sensitive personal data that is used across the enterprise for security decisions, so they also have special responses beyond a normal agent. Any attestation report anomaly related to the import and mediation agent must lead to failure of authentication and disabling of these agents, much like the service desk agents. However, the data managed by these agents must also be rolled back to a prior known good state, because data modifications made from an import and mediation agent on a non-compliant device could have widespread lasting effects on the entire enterprise.

19.4.6 Other Agents

The preceding descriptions of agents focused on enterprise agents. These are installed on devices as part of normal enterprise operations to conform to enterprise rules for security and functionality. In addition, there may be other application-specific agents that are desired for subgroups of the enterprise or individuals within the enterprise. These may or may not have enterprise approval or support.

Such agents can operate like the monitoring or logging agents. They would ultimately rely on device hardware key storage, the operating system, and the MDM system to bootstrap the security of their communications. They would require an attestation report, a hardware-based authentication key, and possibly an access token, much like any other active entity in the enterprise.

19.5 ENDPOINT AGENT CONCLUSIONS

Moving from a centralized network-based security model to a distributed endpoint-based model provides many benefits for the current enterprise information sharing network dominated by mobile devices. However, under a high-assurance enterprise security model, the endpoint-based model requires careful planning to preserve existing security properties while adding the additional functionality.

This chapter examines the agents that must both secure the enterprise and be secured. Security relies on a hardware-based attestation of the operating state of each device. This can be provided by a software agent, but it must be tied to trusted hardware on the device. The attestation report bootstraps the software agent's actions by ensuring that they are done on a clean device. Other agents use this same bootstrapping process to secure the information they transmit about the device and applications on it. This approach ensures that the end-to-end security between all active endpoints is preserved and that existing monitoring capabilities are performed on the devices, ultimately providing a way to extend the enterprise footprint onto mobile devices outside the enterprise while maintaining security comparable to internal networks.

19.6 ENDPOINT AGENT EXTENSIONS

Other tools or applications that use agents may use the same process to provide secure device-based communication. For example, in addition to an MDM, it is possible to use a mobile application manager (MAM) from a different vendor. The MAM has a lower level of control than an MDM due to the restricted operating system interfaces. However, it would use the same basic communication methods with external servers and internal operating system components and hardware elements.

Many mobile device applications have tight ties to external servers and serve mainly as a user interface to web APIs. Such applications function much like agents because they are lightweight and communicate with a central server. As such, the architecture described in this chapter also serves as a blueprint for such applications.

20 Ports and Protocols

20.1 INTRODUCTION

Guidance and policies that govern the use, configuration, and management of the communication protocols in use by the web services and applications that are connected to the network are required for interoperability and security. Policies specify the proper use of ports and protocols to control what types of communications are allowed to cross the boundaries of the networks.

A port is an access channel to and from a specific service, and a protocol is a standardized way for computers to exchange information. Data on the network is sent and received by software that automatically organizes such data to be transferred into packets, which are made in a standardized way as defined by the protocol in use so that the destination host can recognize them as data and properly decode them. To transfer data, network clients use different ports or channels, which are given standardized numbers.

The port number and the destination IP address are included as part of the header attached to each packet in order to deliver the packet to the proper endpoint service. The policies on ports, protocols, and services (PPS) are typically enforced by network and security appliances and software such as routers, firewalls, and intrusion detection/protection devices that protect the boundary of the network or reside at the endpoints (i.e., web services or clients).

The Internet Assigned Numbers Authority (IANA) maintains the official assignments of port numbers for specific uses [256, 257]. However, many unofficial uses of both well-known and registered port numbers occur in practice. A few ports and their usage are given in Table 20.1. There are 65,536 ports available as a 16-bit unsigned integer.

Ports may be well-known, registered, and dynamic/private:

- Well-known: Port numbers 0 through 1023 are used for common, well-known services.
- Registered: Port numbers 1024 through 49151 are the registered ports used for IANA-registered services.
- Dynamic/private: Ports 49152 through 65535 are dynamic ports that are not officially designated for any specific service and may be used for any purpose. They also are used as ephemeral ports; software running on the host may randomly choose one of these ports in order to define itself. In effect, they are used as temporary ports, primarily by clients when communicating with servers. Dynamic/private ports can also be used by end user applications, but this is less common. Dynamic/private ports do not contain any meaning outside of any particular TCP connection.

TABLE 20.1.
Example Ports and Protocols

Port	Protocol	Messaging Protocol	Status
18	TCP, UDP	The Message Send Protocol (MSP) is an application layer protocol. Defined in Request for Comments (RFC) 1312 [258].	Official
80	TCP, UDP	Hypertext Transfer Protocol (HTTP). RFC 2068 [259].	Official
110	TCP	Post Office Protocol v3 (POP3) is an email retrieval protocol. RFC 1081 [260].	Official
143	TCP	Internet Message Access Protocol (IMAP) is a protocol for email retrieval and storage, as an alternative to POP. Defined in RFC 3501 [261].	Official
161	UDP	Simple Network Management Protocol (SNMP) defined in RFC 3411 [262].	Official
213	TCP, UDP	Internetwork Packet Exchange (IPX) RFC 1132 [263].	Official
443	TCP, UDP	Hypertext Transfer Protocol over TLS/SSL (HTTPS) RFC 2818. [264].	Official
587	TCP	Simple Mail Transfer Protocol (SMTP), as specified in RFC 6409 [265].	Official
1935	TCP	Adobe Systems Macromedia Flash Real Time Messaging Protocol (RTMP) "plain" protocol. Adobe proprietary [266].	Official
2195	TCP	Apple Push Notification service link. Apple proprietary [267].	Unofficial
4502	TCP, UDP	Microsoft Silverlight connectable ports under non-elevated trust [268].	Official
5672	TCP	Advanced Message Queuing Protocol (AMQP) ISO/IEC 19464 [269].	Official
8080	TCP	HTTP alternate.	Official
49342	TCP	Avanset Exam Simulator (Visual CertExam file format (VCE) Player). Avanset proprietary [270].	Unofficial

Protocol standards may be:

- Proprietary – Set by an individual developer for use with his own products or products developed by members in his consortium. This creates serious interoperability problems among different developers and is a barrier to entry to new developers who do not agree to consortium rules.
- De facto – Openly published by an individual developer, but adopted by enough developers that the protocols are widely in use. This promotes interoperability, and the open publication removes barriers to entry.
- Standards-body-based – Industry-wide protocol definitions that are not tied to a particular manufacturer. With standard protocols, you can mix and match equipment from different vendors. As long as the equipment implements the standard protocols, it should be able to coexist on the same network.

Many organizations are involved in setting standards for networking. The most important organizations for the web are:

- ISO – A federation of more than 100 standards organizations from throughout the world.
- IETF – The organization responsible for the protocols that drive the Internet. These standards are cited by reference to their Request for Comments (RFC).
- World Wide Web Consortium (W3C) – An international organization that handles the development of standards for the World Wide Web.

In this chapter, we will review the communication models for web services and the ports and assigned protocols. We will then review ELS and its basic architecture. Next, we review the threats to be considered, including how they affect server configuration and how firewalls are used for port blocking. Finally, we provide the unique factors that arise with ports and protocols with this high security environment.

20.2 COMMUNICATION MODELS

The Internet model is a group of communications protocols used for the Internet and similar networks. The Internet model is commonly known as TCP/IP, after its two most important protocols. TCP/IP provides connectivity specifying how data should be formatted, addressed, transmitted, routed, and received at the destination. This functionality has been organized into four abstraction layers:

- Application Layer – example protocols:
  - Border Gateway Protocol (BGP) [271], Domain Name System (DNS) [272], and File Transfer Protocol (FTP) [4].b),
- Transport Layer – example protocols:
  - TCP, UDP, and Datagram Congestion Control Protocol (DCCP) [273],
- Internet Layer – example Internet layer protocols:
  - IP [4].a), Electronic Communication Network (ECN) [274], and IPsec [275],
- Link Layer – example link layer protocols:
  - Ethernet [276], Digital Subscriber Line (DSL) [133], and PPP [134].

These layers are used to sort all related protocols according to the scope of the networking involved. IETF documents RFC 1122 [277] and RFC 1123 [278] describe the IP suite and model.

An alternative model, the Open System Interconnection (OSI) model [279], is often used to describe protocols. The OSI model defines protocols in seven layers. The layers are:

(1) Physical,
(2) Data link,

(3) Network,
(4) Transport,
(5) Session,
(6) Presentation, and
(7) Application.

The OSI model defines protocol implementations for its layers, and some of the specific details at each layer differ from those of the Internet model. The OSI model, while popularly referenced, has succumbed to the Internet model. Unless specified, the Internet model will be used in this document.

20.3 PORTS IN TRANSPORT PROTOCOLS

Two primary transport protocols are used in the Internet, along with a plethora of special purpose ones. In this description, we limit the discussion to TCP and UDP. The port information for both of these protocols is explicit in the header information, and it can be used by firewalls and servers to make an "accept or drop" decision.

20.3.1 The Transmission Control Protocol

TCP is one of the core protocols of the IP suite and is so common that the entire suite is often called TCP/IP. Residing at the transport layer, TCP provides end-to-end, reliable, ordered, and error-checked delivery of a stream of octets between programs running on computers connected to a local area network, an intranet, or the public Internet. Web browsers use TCP when they connect to servers on the World Wide Web, and it is used to deliver email and transfer files from one location to another. A variety of other higher-layer protocols use TCP/IP, such as HTTP, HTTPS, SMTP, POP3, IMAP, FTP, and their messages are typically encapsulated in TCP packets. TCP also provides a form of message flow control that will adapt its transmission rate to the congestion on the network. Applications that do not require the reliability of a TCP connection may instead use the connectionless UDP, which emphasizes low-overhead operation and reduced latency rather than error-checking and delivery validation.

TCP uses TCP Port Numbers to identify sending and receiving application endpoints on the hosts. Each side of a TCP connection has an associated Internet socket, defined as the host IP address and port number, reserved by the sending or receiving application. Port 0 is generally reserved and should not be used. Arriving TCP data packets are identified as belonging to a specific TCP connection by its two sockets, that is, the four-tuple from the combination of source host IP address, source port, destination host IP address, and destination port. This means that a server computer can provide several clients with services simultaneously, as long as the four-tuples differ. A single client can have concurrent requests for a service, as long as the client takes care of initiating any connections to one destination port from different source ports. Well-known applications, running as servers and passively listening for connections, typically use TCP ports. Some examples include:

- FTP (Ports 20 and 21),
- SMTP (Port 25),
- Secure Socket Layer (SSL)/TLS, HTTPS (Port 443),
- HTTP (Port 80).

20.3.2 The User Datagram Protocol

UDP is one of the core members of the IP suite (the set of network protocols used for the Internet). With UDP, computer applications can send messages, referred to here as *datagrams*, to other hosts on an IP network without prior communications to set up special transmission channels or data paths. UDP uses a simple transmission model with a minimum of protocol mechanisms and overhead. It has no handshaking dialogues and thus exposes any unreliability of the underlying network protocol to the user's program. Because this is normally IP over unreliable media, there is no guarantee of delivery, ordering, or duplicate protection. UDP provides checksums for data integrity and port numbers for addressing different functions at the source and destination of the datagram. UDP is suitable for situations when error-checking and correction either are not necessary or are performed in the application, avoiding the overhead of such processing at the network interface level. Time-sensitive applications often use UDP because dropping packets is preferable to waiting for delayed packets, which may not be an option in a real-time system. If error-correction facilities are needed at the network interface level, an application would use the TCP or Stream Control Transmission Protocol (SCTP), which are designed for this purpose.

UDP uses UDP Port Numbers to identify sending and receiving application endpoints on a host. Each side of a UDP connection may have an associated port number reserved by the sending or receiving application. However, unlike TCP, a source port is not required for UDP data packets. Packets are identified as belonging to a specific UDP connection by its combination of source host address, source port (if given), destination host address, and destination port.

Some UDP port numbers include:

- FTP (Port 20),
- Encrypted SMTP (Port 26), and
- Network Time Protocol (NTP) (Port 123).

20.4 THREATS CONSIDERED

Incoming ports are typically controlled, but outgoing ports are sometimes left uncontrolled. If some ports are not explicitly blocked for both incoming and outgoing traffic, then it may be possible for malicious code to enter through a permitted port of an allowed service and try to open or access other unused ports for malicious purposes, exfiltration of data, or reconnaissance. Restrictions should be applied to both incoming and outgoing messaging. In general, the policy should be to "deny all – permit by exception" to block all incoming and outgoing ports unless explicitly permitted. Closing of the internal ports means that the utility function ports are also blocked, and the administrators must use the same allowed communication processes as any other active entities. This essentially closes the back doors. The bilateral authentication uses PKI credentials, eliminating passwords, and the authorization is done by a SAML claims credential, eliminating the need for accounts.

At this point, the content alone does not provide enough structure to achieve this approach. Many of the common protocols and services in use have known vulnerabilities and exploits and must either be prevented from operating in ELS or conditionally allowed with mitigations implemented.

Once a list of all acceptable PPSs have been defined for an enterprise, it is necessary to correctly configure the security devices to allow only the permitted PPSs to pass through the enterprise network while blocking all others. Constant monitoring of the networks and devices is required to ensure that only the approved PPSs are allowed and that configurations have not been incorrectly modified, either by accident or by malicious intent. This is a constant issue, as the collection of permissible PPSs and their mitigations are likely to evolve over time.

20.5 ASSIGNING PORTS AND PROTOCOLS

From a technical standpoint, any port can be assigned any protocol. From a practical standpoint, that will only work if each user knows and agrees to use those combinations. For the IP suite, the IANA is responsible for the global coordination of the DNS Root, IP addressing, and other IP resources. This allows developers throughout the world to write their communication code to a standard set of ports and protocols and be reasonably assured that their communication will succeed. A list of official and unofficial port assignments for the commonly used ports from the IANA is provided in [256]. If this list appears daunting, remember that any protocol/port combination can be changed by mutual agreement and only requires that everybody reconfigure to the agreed combination. There are even lists of preferred service assignments. The importance of controlling these port assignments is universally accepted.

DoD has developed strict guidance on the control and management of PPS that can be used in national security information networks. DoD Instruction Number 8551.01 establishes policies, procedures, and responsibilities for proper use of PPS [280]. In addition to the regulations concerning PPS use, the current instruction includes requirements for continuous, real-time monitoring of configuration management as well as better mechanisms for sharing information among the user community. The main points of the policy are as follows:

- All PPS must be limited to those required for official business.
- All PPS must be assessed for vulnerabilities and recommended security mitigations.
- All PPS must be documented in a Category Assurance List (CAL).
- All PPS must be declared in a PPS Management Registry.
- All PPS must be implemented according to procedures and policy developed by a Configuration Management Board (CMB).

- All PPS must be regulated according to the ability to cause damage.
- Boundary devices such as firewalls, routers, and intrusion/protection devices must be configured to allow only approved PPS.
- PPS not implemented according to policy will be blocked with boundary devices.
- An exception process will exist.

The DoD Chief Information Officer (CIO) has overall responsibility for oversight of this instruction, and the Defense Information Systems Agency (DISA) is given the primary implementation responsibility.

In summary, all automated information systems (AIS) used on national security data networks must register the data communication modes and identify the PPS used and the network boundaries crossed. Compliance with the PPS requirements will reduce overall development time and cost, increase security, speed certification and accreditation steps, enhance AIS interoperability across the department, and speed operational deployment of all new and updated AIS.

20.6 SERVER CONFIGURATIONS

Most servers come with default ports and protocols that include most of the services available to their broad class of users. For example, the IBM WebSphere would default to all of the common ports in addition to the IBM ports and protocols for all of their services and perhaps Oracle's, etc. In the enterprise, it is not sufficient to just use the defaults provided by the vendors, because these may include banned services or may not include recommended mitigations.

A port-by-port and protocol-by-protocol examination of the traffic generated by and accepted by a vendor product must be undertaken. This can be initiated by packet captures during normal operation. The valid and necessary traffic can be identified and remaining traffic analyzed to determine if it is needed or superfluous. After assessing normal traffic, a network scan for open ports will reveal other open ports that are not being used. These should typically be closed. In addition, detailed discussions with the vendor are required to understand what other ports and protocols may be open but not utilized during normal operations, as these are potential entry points for attackers.

20.7 FIREWALLS AND PORT BLOCKING

The network boundary protection devices, such as routers, firewalls, and intrusion detection/protection devices need to be configured to block all message traffic into the enterprise (reducing external flow to externally available ports) unless it is to or from permitted services on specific ports using permitted protocols. Internally available ports may be available as discussed in the conventional methods. However, these internal ports are the same as the external ports for ELS systems.

Conventional firewalls effectively control access to and from a requested service through ports and protocols filtering. A stateful firewall is a conventional firewall that also tracks connections by the socket pairs (source IP, source port, destination IP, destination port) and uses the port number of the source IP address to protect against the use of any other egress ports to exfiltrate data. Network firewalls protect the perimeter or boundary of a portion of the network using packet header filtering. The primary concern with network firewalls is to properly configure them to block all protocols except for the ones approved and needed for the services on the trusted side (server side) of the firewall. In addition, it is imperative to make sure the configuration is current with respect to the changing ports and protocols needs and the recommendations and banned services. In addition, the firewall appliance itself must be maintained in a secure condition with current updates and bug fixes.

A network firewall can operate in transparent (or passive) mode with respect to the end-to-end communication between a service requestor and the end-service if it does not break the end-to-end encryption. In transparent mode, the firewall is not able to decrypt the contents of an encrypted packet – it is only able to filter packets based on the packet header information that is in clear text. The alternative is a proxy firewall that breaks the end-to-end connection and operates as a man-in-the-middle. The proxy looks like the service endpoint to the requestor and is able to decrypt the incoming packets and encrypt the outgoing packets. This permits the firewall to perform content filtering on the decrypted packets.

Firewalls (and other security appliances) can be operated in inline filter mode or in observer mode (also known as promiscuous mode). An *inline filter* resides in the communication path and examines all packets in real time as they traverse the firewall before passing further into the network. A firewall in observer mode is not in the direct communication path and examines a copy of the packet as it transits the firewall. The advantage of inline filters is that they can immediately block the first packet of a recognized attack (which would be passed to the destination in observer mode). The advantages of observer mode include real-time requirements being relaxed and that communication is not halted if the firewall goes down.

The firewalls should block access to and from all ports that are accessible behind (the trusted side) the firewall except those that are explicitly permitted. This is called "deny all by default, permit by exception." Firewalls that cover larger portions of the network or that front many subnets and host computers must be configured to allow any ports and protocols needed by any of the hosts on its trusted side.

Many firewall best-practices documents include details on firewall configurations (e.g., *Cisco Firewall Best Practices Guide* or the *Defense Information Systems Agency (DISA) Network Infrastructure Technology Review*). For example, tunnels require special considerations to make sure packets embedded in the tunnels do not bypass the firewall. The functionality of a network firewall can be implemented as a separate security appliance that resides either in front of the application servers or in the endpoint hosts. In the latter case, each server would implement a packet header filter to perform ports and protocols filtering in its message handling process.

20.8 APPLICATION FIREWALLS

Application Firewalls (AFWs) or application filters are designed to address specific attacks on web applications and web services that are not well addressed by other protection devices. AFWs can be specific to the particular needs of the application and protect against attacks targeted at the application layer. For example, an AFW could be used to filter damaging content or specific attachment types in incoming and outgoing email. Other types of application filters can examine the signatures on scripts (e.g., Java applets, JavaScript, ActiveX controls), the file extensions, virus scanning, blocking specific content, or use of specific commands.

In general, there are several different ways to deploy AFWs:

1) as a separate hardware or software security appliance in front of the application,
2) as part of another security device such as a network firewall or content distribution controller,
3) as a cloud service, or
4) as an agent on the application server.

The current trend is for security appliances to integrate several functions in a single device to reduce operating costs and physical space requirements. The network firewall, intrusion detection/prevention, and application content filtering are being combined in integrated security appliances. Although there are important benefits for this integration, the compromise of such a device could incapacitate all the protection functions at once.

20.9 NETWORK FIREWALLS IN ELS

In ELS, a network firewall operates in transparent mode, does not decrypt the packets, and is restricted to examining only the packet header. This is more restrictive than the capabilities being offered on many newer firewalls that offer more functionality but require the ability to decrypt the packet to examine its content. In ELS, network firewalls cannot operate as proxy firewalls or perform deep packet inspection, as TLS with mutual authentication between requestor and service is a basic ELS requirement. In Figure 20.1, a network firewall positioned in front of several servers illustrates the use of such devices for ports and protocols filtering. The firewall is shown protecting two web services implemented in two separate web servers with IP addresses IP_1 and IP_2. The firewall is configured to allow only requests to (IP address:port) combinations (IP_1:443) and (IP_2:443) and responses from them back to the requestor.

If the web service requires access to services on other ports, then that communication must be routed through a firewall that is configured to permit packets on those ports.

20.10 ENDPOINT PROTECTION IN ELS

In ELS, an agent-type model is preferred, one in which the packet header filtering and other security functions reside at the web server in the handler chain of the web service. The basic configuration of endpoint protection in ELS is shown in Figure 20.2 and provides a complete set of security functions for packet, message, and application layer security, tailored for the specific web service being protected. The new functions that are added in the server are packet header inspection, packet content inspection, message content inspection, and application protection. These functions implement the ports and protocols protection, as well as other security functions normally

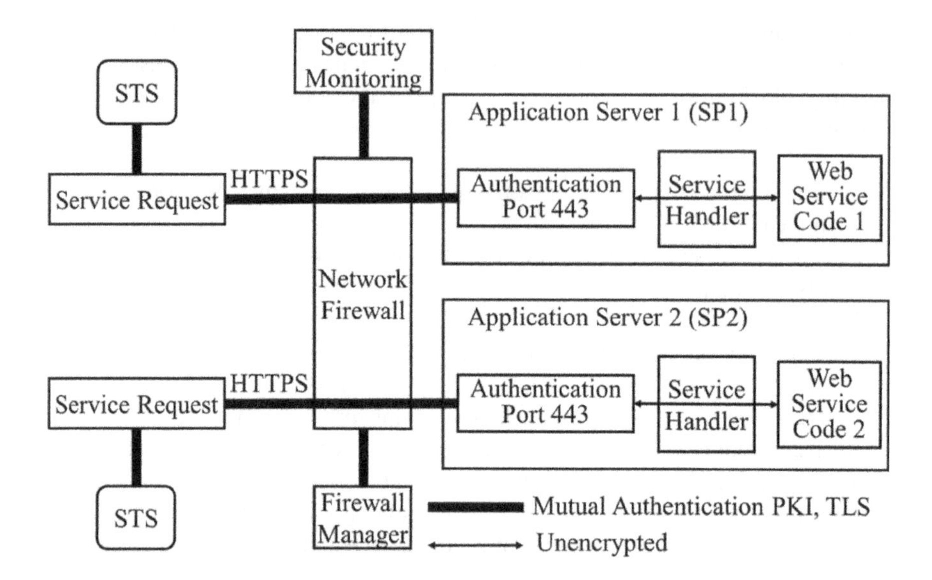

FIGURE 20.1. Network Firewall in Transparent Mode

provided by network devices such as intrusion detection/protection, packet and message content filtering, deep packet inspection, and application/web content filtering.

A service requestor uses HTTPS to establish communication with the server hosting the target web service, in line with the ELS practice. The packet is received by the destination sever, which immediately inspects the header and performs the ports and protocols blocking, source whitelist/blacklist checking, and other filtering based on only the header, including stateful tracking of client addresses and ports. Until an HTTPS session has been established, only packets addressed to the server's IP address and port 443 are allowed. Other ports may be opened when needed as part of the web service following HTTPS establishment.

On the return path, the messages follow a similar process. In effect, the packet header inspection module can perform the required network-layer filtering and can block traffic based on ports and protocols (protocol, IP address, and port).

In the ELS endpoint protection architecture, the endpoint protection modules can be configured to communicate with additional security monitoring appliances, such as a NetScout, that can compile and track statistics about the security status of the server and the web service. The security appliances should be active entities and communicate with the server via TLS with mutual authentication. If required, the server could send the decrypted message traffic to other security appliances through this interface for additional security functions.

The endpoint protection functions are configured through the server configuration management interface, which communicates with the server by TLS with mutual authentication. The ports and protocols and whitelist information and any software updates are provided through this interface.

It is recommended that the initial configuration of the packet header deny both incoming and outgoing ports and protocols (as opposed to incoming only) and that permissions be configured as they are identified.

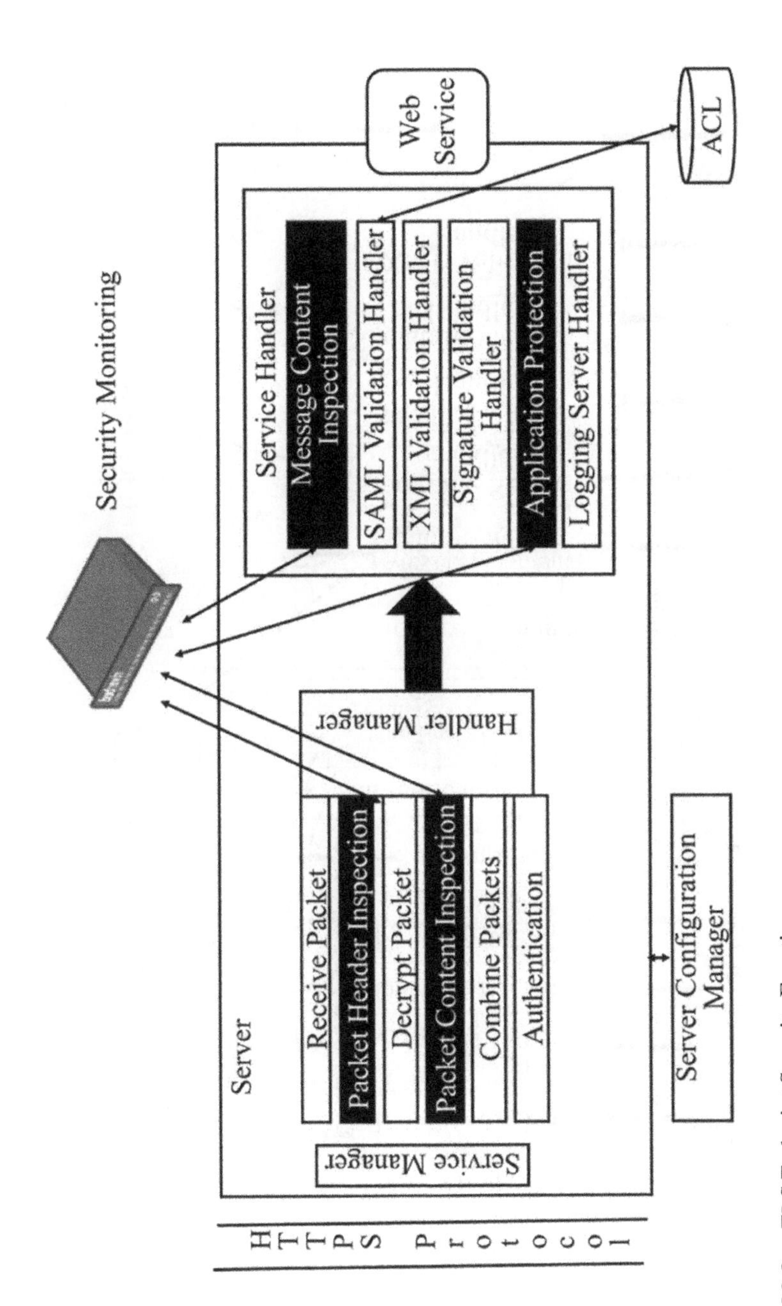

FIGURE 20.2. ELS Endpoint Security Functions

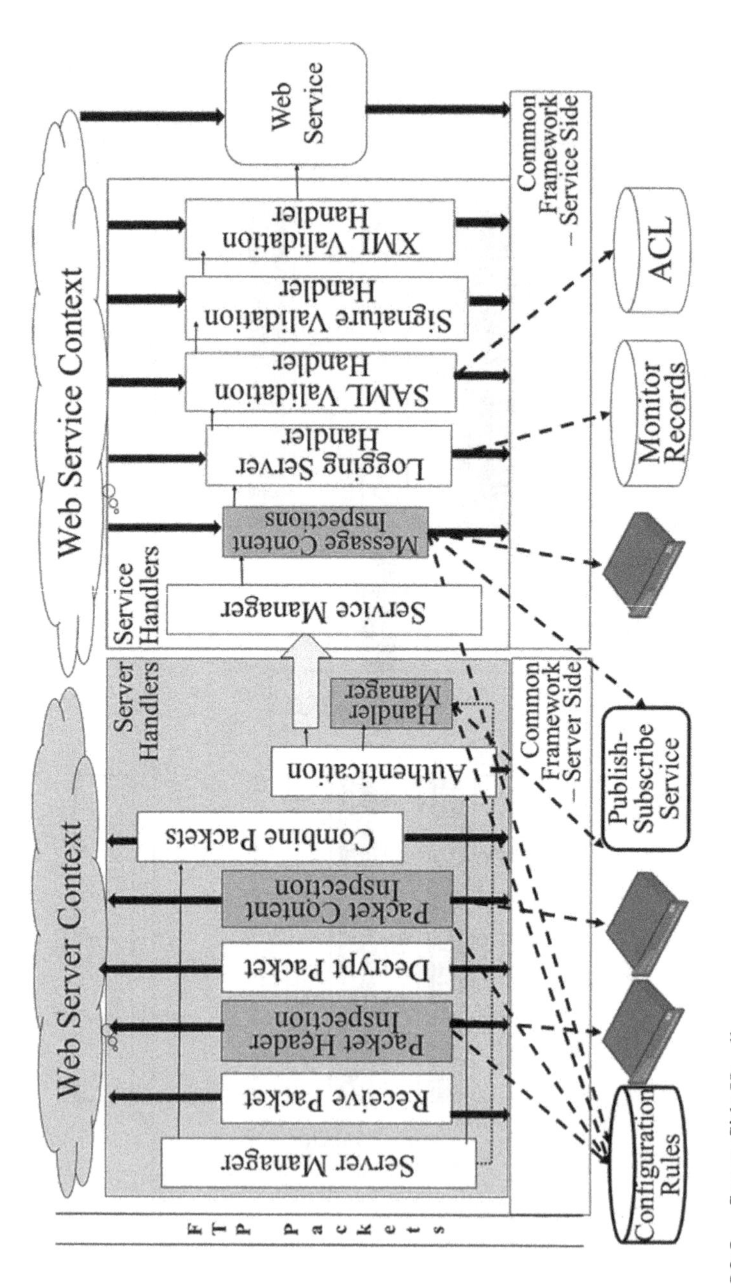

FIGURE 20.3. Server Side Handlers

20.11 HANDLING AND INSPECTION OF TRAFFIC

Handling and inspection is done in software-only modules in the server. The software functionality is embodied in handlers in the handler chain of the server as shown in Figure 20.3.

The handlers are embedded in the server handler chain at the point that the communication is prepared for their use, and the functionality has been divided along those lines as opposed to the previous functionality such as virus scan, ports and protocols, intrusion detection, or blacklist/whitelist. These are distributed to packet header inspection, packet content inspection, and message content inspection. Each of these may perform inspections related to intrusion detection or blacklist blocking, as well as other security functions. This is the preferred embodiment for enterprise applications.

This system inserts handlers within the server and service to move the inspections to the point of the application itself, where it makes most sense. The inspections that can be done without decrypting the packets may be done at the front of the web server because they are passive entities. Moving inspections of decrypted traffic inside the server not only preserves the end-to-end paradigm, but encapsulates the security and allows tailoring for the application itself. The encapsulated security with the application is virtualization ready.

20.12 ADDITIONAL SECURITY HARDENING

We assume that malicious software is present, and a request for service may come from within the enterprise, bypassing firewalls and not stating forbidden port numbers. To prevent the server software from finding a protocol resolution software set and assigning the port, all such software should be removed or not installed to begin with. The server software may come with a variety of software subsystems to satisfy a variety of customer needs, such as telnet and secure shell. If the allowable ports are known, the server software installation should not install other software (if the installation procedure permits this). If the installation procedure does not allow this, or if the allowable ports and protocols are not worked out until after server software is installed, these non-allowable protocol software sets should be actively sought out and removed.

A more difficult option that is often not possible with off-the-shelf software is code reduction. Remove all code that implements functions that are not needed or desired. With Java, for example, remove unneeded Java Archive (JAR) files or unused functions within JAR files. However, this may cause problems when updates are issued, since they revert to the "normal" set of JARs. This may require a special agreement with the vendor to support a specific configuration of their product (including testing all updates against this configuration) or manual intervention to apply updates and then remove unneeded parts and perform regression testing to ensure the updates have not changed what is or is not needed.

21 Asynchronous Messaging

21.1 WHY ASYNCHRONOUS MESSAGING?

Asynchronous messaging describes communication that takes place between one or more applications or systems in which the sender does not receive feedback from the receiver during transmission of a message. This is in contrast to synchronous communication, in which the sender of a message waits for acknowledgment or a response from the receiver before completing the transmission.

There is no assumption about which layers asynchronous and synchronous communication take place in or how these relate to each other. It is possible to implement synchronous communication using an asynchronous messaging service or an asynchronous messaging service using synchronous communication channels. In practice, asynchronous messaging often uses an underlying synchronous channel.

A common asynchronous messaging design involves one system placing a message in a message queue and continuing its processing. At the completion of message transmission, the sender does not know when or whether the receiver received it. The message queuing system is responsible for delivering the message to the recipient. Some systems use two or more queues or intermediaries.

21.1.1 Advantages of Asynchronous Communication

Asynchronous messaging solves the problem of intermittent connectivity. If the receiving equipment fails or is unavailable, the message remains in a message queue and is delivered after the failure is corrected. This is especially useful for transmission of large data files, as failures are more likely and retransmissions more costly.

An asynchronous messaging system with built-in intelligence may transform the content and/or format of the message automatically to conform to the receiving system's requirements or needed protocol but still successfully deliver the message to the recipient. This intelligence is used to provide a higher level of understanding of the content, which allows translation into other formats and protocols. Complicated transformations are better suited to asynchronous communication than synchronous communication because they may increase latency and cause connectivity problems or other underlying protocol failures for synchronous systems.

21.1.2 Disadvantages of Asynchronous Communication

The disadvantages of asynchronous messaging include the additional component of a message broker or transfer agent to ensure the message is received. This may affect both performance and reliability. Another disadvantage is the response time, which may be inconvenient and not consistent with normal dialog communication.

21.2 PRIOR WORK

A proliferation of standards for asynchronous messaging has caused interoperability problems, with each major vendor having its own implementation, interface, and management tools. Java EE systems are not interoperable, and Microsoft's MSMQ (Microsoft Message Queuing) does not support Java EE. Many of these are reviewed and compared in [281]. A few of the numerous standard protocols used for asynchronous communication as defined in the IANA protocol registries [4].m) are in Table 21.1.

21.2.1 Java Standard Messaging Protocol

Java Messaging System (JMS) is a message-oriented middleware API for communication between Java clients. It is part of the Java Platform Enterprise Edition. It supports point-to-point communication as well as a publish-subscribe model.

21.2.2 De Facto Standard Microsoft Message Queuing

Microsoft Message Queuing (MSMQ) allows applications running on separate servers/processes to communicate in a failsafe manner. A queue is a temporary storage location from which messages can be sent and received reliably as conditions permit. This enables communication across networks and between computers running Windows, which may not always be connected. By contrast, sockets and other network protocols require permanent direct connections

21.2.3 Open Source Messaging Protocols

In addition to Java and Microsoft, different open source solutions exist. RabbitMQ is an open source messaging solution that runs on multiple platforms and multiple languages. It implements Advanced Message Queuing Protocol (AMQP), in which messages are queued on a central node before being sent to clients. It is easy to deploy, but having all traffic pass through a single central node can hinder scalability.

ZeroMQ is another cross-platform, cross-language messaging solution that can use different carrier protocols to send messages. It can support publish-subscribe, push-pull, and router-dealer communication patterns. It can be more difficult to set up, but it provides more control and granularity at the lower levels to tune performance.

ActiveMQ is a compromise between the ease of use of Rabbit MQ and the performance of ZeroMQ. All three support multiple platforms and have client APIs for C++, Java, .Net, Python, and others. They also have documentation and active community support. There are many other implementations, including Sparrow, Starling, Kestrel, Beanstalkd, Amazon Simple Queue Service (SQS), Kafka, Eagle MQ, and IronMQ.

21.2.4 Emerging Standard

AMQP is an open standard application layer protocol for message-oriented middleware [2].m). It is an emerging technology addressing the standardization problem.

TABLE 21.1.
Messaging Ports

Port	TCP/UDP	Messaging Protocol and Description	Status
18	TCP and UDP	The Message Send Protocol (MSP), more precisely referred to as Message Send Protocol 2, is an application layer protocol used to send a short message between nodes on a network. Defined in RFC 1312.	Official
110	TCP	Post Office Protocol v3 (POP3) is an email retrieval protocol.	Official
119	TCP	The Network News Transfer Protocol (NNTP) is an application protocol used for transporting Usenet news articles (netnews) between news servers and for reading and posting articles by end user client applications. Defined in RFC 3977.	Official
143	TCP	IMAP is a protocol for email retrieval and storage as an alternative to POP. IMAP, unlike POP, specifically allows multiple clients to simultaneously connect to the same mailbox. Defined in RFC 3501.	Official
161	UDP	SNMP is an "Internet-standard protocol for managing devices on IP networks." Devices that typically support SNMP include routers, switches, servers, workstations, printers, modem racks, and more. Defined in RFC 3411–3418.	Official
218	TCP and UDP	Message Posting Protocol (MPP) is a network protocol used for posting messages from a computer to a mail service host.	Official
319	UDP	Event Messages for the Precision Time Protocol (PTP) is a protocol used to synchronize clocks throughout a computer network. On a local area network, it achieves clock accuracy in the sub-microsecond range, making it suitable for measurement and control systems. Defined in IEEE 1588–2008.	Official
587	TCP	Simple Mail Transfer Protocol (SMTP), as specified in RFC 6409.	
1801	TCP and UDP	Microsoft Message Queuing or MSMQ is a message queue developed by Microsoft and deployed in its Windows Server operating systems.	Official
1863	TCP	MSNP (Microsoft Notification Protocol) is used by the Microsoft Messenger service and a number of instant messaging clients.	Official
1935	TCP	Adobe Systems Macromedia Flash Real Time Messaging Protocol (RTMP) "plain" protocol.	Official
2195	TCP	Apple Push Notification service link.	Unofficial
2948	TCP and UDP	Multimedia Messaging Service (MMS) is a standard way to send messages that include multimedia content to and from mobile phones.	Official
4486	TCP and UDP	Integrated Client Message Service (ICMS). Defined in RFC 6335.	Official
5010	TCP	IBM WebSphere MQ Workflow.	Official

Implementations are interoperable. It includes flexible routing and common message paradigms like publish-subscribe, point-to-point, request-response, and fan-out.

The defining features of AMQP are message orientation, queuing, routing (including point-to-point and publish-subscribe), reliability, and security. AMQP mandates the behavior of the messaging provider and client to the extent that implementations from different vendors are truly interoperable, similar to how SMTP, HTTP, FTP, and others have created interoperable systems.

21.3 ASYNCHRONOUS MESSAGING SECURITY

Asynchronous messaging can provide authentication of the sender and receiver identities and the integrity and confidentiality of the message content if the holder of the queue is trusted. One key challenge in asynchronous messaging systems is that a third party is often involved in the transaction, which may or may not be trusted to speak for the sending or receiving entities or to view or modify content in transit. As a result, security models often require a trusted third party, which restricts deployment options. In contrast, synchronous web traffic relies on routers and other infrastructure to deliver messages, but the use of TLS provides end-to-end security without the need to trust these intermediate nodes.

21.3.1 Security for Server Brokered Invocation

Server brokered invocation uses web server middleware to manage message queues. The sender and receiver both communicate directly through secure synchronous channels to the server to send and receive messages. This model is shown in Figure 21.1. Asynchronous message security must be from sender to receiver, not just from sender to server and server to receiver. The latter fails to provide end-to-end authentication, integrity, and confidentiality, which are required for a high-assurance environment.

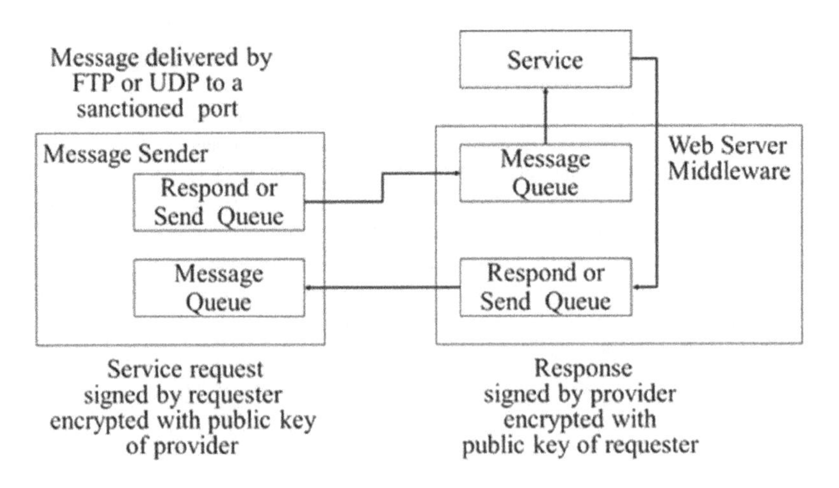

FIGURE 21.1. Server Brokered Invocation

For the parties involved in the transaction to provide accountability, integrity, and confidentiality, the service requester must authenticate itself to the receiver, encrypt the message so only the service provider can receive this message, and provide verifiable integrity checks on the full message content. The service provider must confirm that the message is from a known identity, decrypt the content with a valid key, and verify the integrity checks before that entity can take action on the message.

This is accomplished by invoking two cryptographic techniques. The first is the use of a digital signature by the sender. When the message signature is verified, the service provider knows the identity of the sender and that the content has not been altered by another entity after it was signed. The second is the encryption of the message using the public key of the service provider. This requires that the requester know the public key of the target. A response to the requester must similarly be signed and encrypted using the public key of the requester.

The use of asymmetric encryption is paired with more efficient symmetric encryption in which content is encrypted with a random symmetric key, which is itself encrypted using the receiver's public key. Additional security can be provided by message expiration deadlines within queues and central auditing of all messages sent and received.

21.3.2 Security for Publish-Subscribe Systems (PSS)

In a PSS, the queue server acts as an intermediary between sender and receiver to manage many-to-many instead of just many-to-one communications. Senders and receivers communicate with the PSS through a secure synchronous channel. The PSS collects messages and makes them available to entities based on subscriptions. This model is shown in Figure 21.2.

The PSS is an active entity and registered in the Enterprise Service Directory. Active entities act on their own behalf and are not a proxy. To preserve the end-to-end accountability chain for messages, the original publisher signs the message. However, unlike server brokered invocation, no single public key can be used for all potential receivers. One solution is to have the PSS encrypt the content to the receivers. The sender's signature remains intact, preserving integrity, but end-to-end confidentiality is not guaranteed.

A PSS may use the web server broker as shown in Figure 21.3. The web server broker is used only for notification messages, so it does not require security like

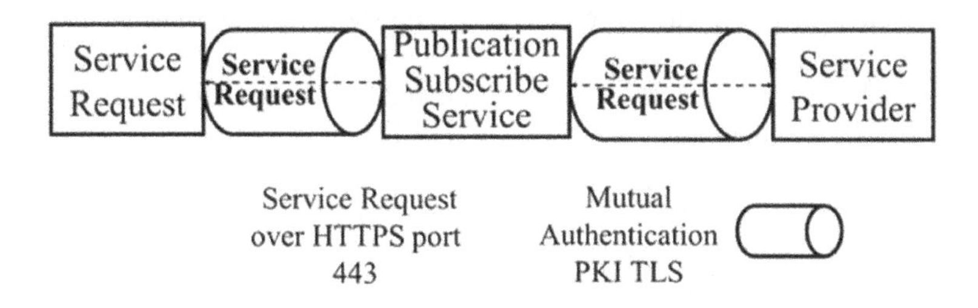

FIGURE 21.2. Publish-Subscribe Push Model

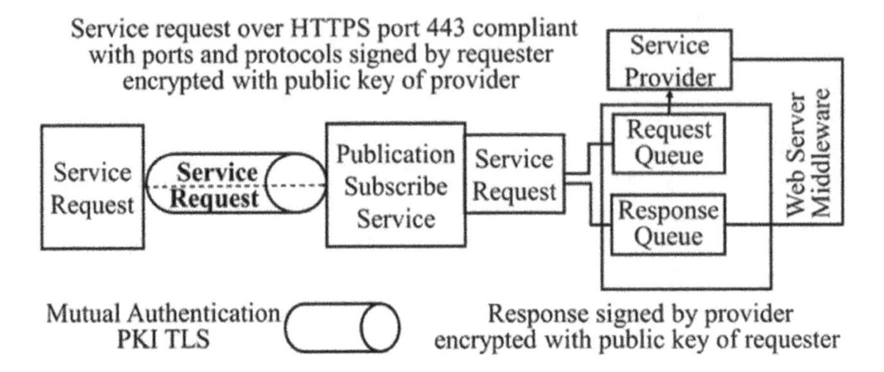

FIGURE 21.3. Publish-Subscribe Pull Model

the main channel. The transmission of the actual message is still done through the secure synchronous channel. The storage queue must be encrypted using the PSS's public key. This is piecemeal confidentiality, because the sender encrypts to the PSS, and the PSS encrypts to the receiver. This relies on trust of the PSS.

21.4 PSS ROCK AND JEWEL

The following is an approach developed to maintain high security assurances with the use of an untrusted PSS. In this formulation, the sender and receiver maintain end-to-end security because the PSS is unable to impersonate either endpoint or view or modify the content. The key concepts are the use of "rocks" and "jewels" to provide security guarantees. The "rocks" are encrypted content blocks, and the "jewels" are the decryption keys for these rocks, encrypted using public keys for the intended recipients.

21.4.1 Claims for Targeted Content (PSS)

After authentication through TLS v1.2 or later versions and authorization based on SAML claims, the sender accesses PSS services. The PSS will offer either publish or retrieve based on the values in the SAML content claim. If there are no SAML content claims, the subscriber will only receive basic services based on identity.

Publishing of content for a targeted list, as used by software publishers, is based upon registered delivery. The targeted list requires the following steps:

1. Publisher does a bilateral authentication and establishes a TLS 1.2 session with SAML authorizations for session establishment with the PSS. The PSS identifies him as a publisher. He may also be a subscriber, he may be modifying previously published content, or he may be retrieving messages, so the PSS ascertains the reason for his session.
2. Content to be published will be digitally signed by the publisher.
3. The publisher will generate an AES-256 encryption key and encrypt the content.

4. Encrypted content is placed in a queue based on an access claim and list name. The publisher will keep such lists. The PSS will assist in developing claims.
5. Access is based on a list of targets and claims. A target may be an individual subscriber or a group queue. The publisher may establish a new queue based on claims and the list for retrieval. This new queue requires an identity and a claims establishment for retrieval (see 3 above). Additional content may be published as needed.
6. Expiration time of targeted content is determined by the publisher or the messaging system.
7. The PSS will provide PKI certificates for each of the targets for the content (if the publisher needs them and they are already registered in the PSS). The publisher should check all certificates on the list for currency and revocation. If invalid certificates are discovered, the list should be pruned.
8. The publisher will prepare encrypted key sets (jewels) by wrapping the AES encryption key in each target's public key.
9. The publisher will publish the encrypted material (rocks) and the encrypted key sets (jewels) for the targets. The PSS will link these to the encrypted material and the target(s).
10. The PSS will provide notification, if desired, to the subscriber list. The PSS will assist with message selection and target details, or the publisher may script his own.
11. The publisher closes the session.

The target must be on the list and have authorization to view content. The steps are shown in Figure 21.4.

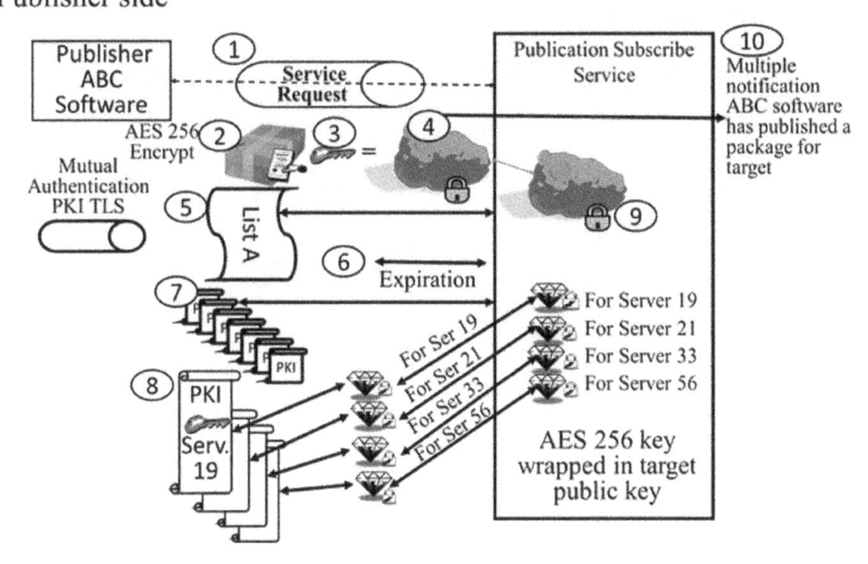

FIGURE 21.4. Publishing of Targeted Content

21.4.2 Retrieving Content for Known Claimants

Retrieval of targeted content may be achieved without the need for the targeted identities to contact the publisher. The following steps are followed:

1. Subscriber does a full bilateral authentication using TLS 1.2 with SAML authorizations for session establishment with the PSS. The claims identify him as a subscriber. He may also be a publisher, so the PSS ascertains the reason for his session.
2. The PSS offers subscriber content available for the claims in queues for which the claimant has an encrypted key available, and the subscriber chooses and retrieves the encrypted content (rock).
3. The PSS provides the encrypted key package (jewel).
4. The PSS notifies the publisher. When expiration time occurs, the server deletes the packages and notifies the publisher which packages were not delivered. The publisher may republish to that list if desired.
5. The subscriber decrypts the content encryption key (jewel) with his private key and accesses the content (rock) decryption key.
6. The subscriber decrypts the content.
7. The subscriber verifies and validates signature.
8. The subscriber closes the session or retrieves additional content.

The target must be on the list and have a content claim. The steps are shown in Figure 21.5.

21.4.3 Retrieving Content for Unknown Claimants

Unknown claimants cannot retrieve the content until registering with the content provider. The steps in that process are described below:

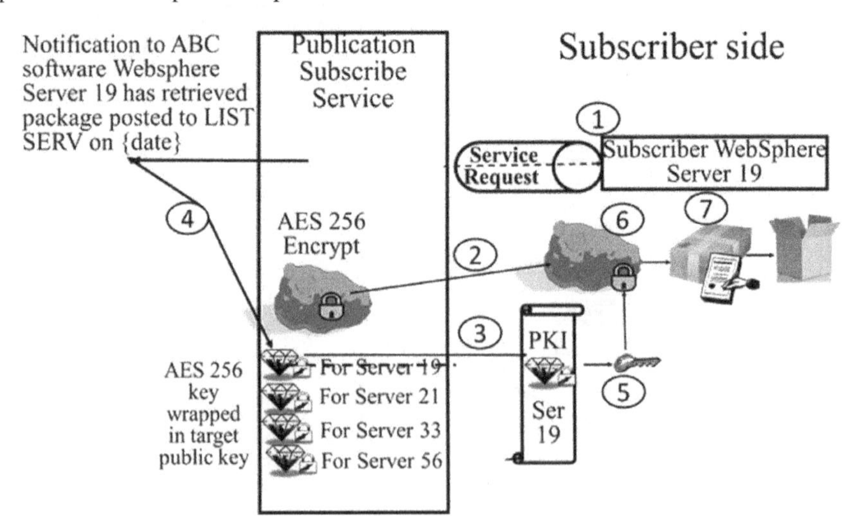

FIGURE 21.5. Subscriber Retrieval(s) from a Known Target

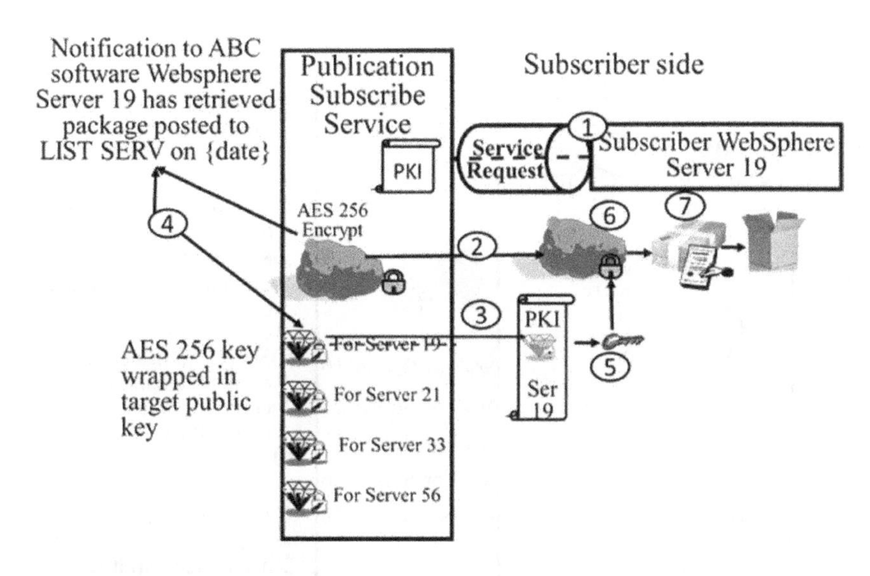

FIGURE 21.6. Subscriber Retrieval(s) from an Unknown Target

1. The subscriber does a full bilateral authentication TLS 1.2 with SAML authorizations for session establishment with the PSS. The authentication identifies him as a subscriber. He may also be a publisher, so the PSS ascertains the reason for his session.
2. The PSS checks the content claims available, and the subscriber chooses and retrieves the content for which full packages exist.
3. For the unknown list, the encrypted key package is not available. The PSS replies, "the publisher has no record of your membership. I need to contact the publisher. I will send you a notice if the publisher agrees."
4. The PSS stores a message for the publisher and notifies him that he has a message.
5. The PSS and subscriber await publisher action.
6. The subscriber closes the session or retrieves additional content.
7. The target has a content claim, but is not on the list.

The steps are shown in Figure 21.6.

21.4.4 Adjusting Publishing Targets (Untrusted PSS)

Publishers must add receivers to the distribution list before they can be provided with messages. The steps in that process are described below:

1. The publisher does a full bilateral authentication through TLS 1.2 with SAML authorizations for session establishment with the PSS. The authorization process identifies him as a publisher. He may also be a subscriber, or he may be modifying a previous publish or he may be retrieving messages, so the PSS ascertains the reason for his session.

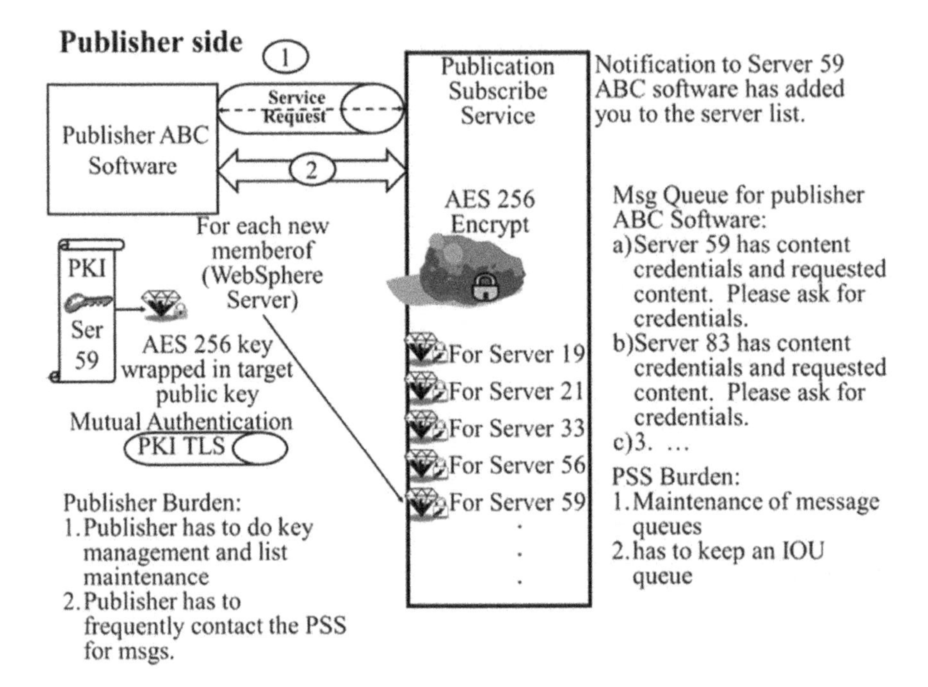

FIGURE 21.7. Publisher Message Retrieval Subsequent Actions

2. Retrieve messages. These are retrieved one by one with action taken (or not) and deletion of the message.
   - The publisher asks for credentials of previously unknown claimants he wishes to add to his lists.
     - The publisher may add claimants to the publisher's list.
     - The publisher computes jewels.
     - The publisher posts jewels.
   - The PSS notifies the subscriber that he has content available. This makes the entity a known target and Section 21.4.2 applies.
   - PSS provides messages to requester. The publisher closes the session.

The steps are shown in Figure 21.7.

21.4.5 Distribution of Burdens

Several burdens are incurred in this high security mode. The publisher is responsible for key management and list maintenance. The publisher has to frequently contact the PSS for messages for publishers. The PSS must maintain message queues for publishers. The PSS must keep a linked wrapped-key package for each target with published content. The PSS is responsible for additional notifications that are sent out. The unknown claimant may experience delays in receiving content to which he has claims.

21.5 SUMMARY

We have reviewed the basic approaches to asynchronous communication in computing environments. We have also described high-assurance approaches to the process. The proliferation of standards in this area has created a problem with high assurance. In many instances, the high-assurance elements require additional steps in the asynchronous process, but they provide a way to proceed when some intermediaries are untrusted.

22 Virtual Application Data Center

22.1 INTRODUCTION

The current configuration of network defense infrastructure is limiting our ability to move secure applications and services to a virtualized cloud environment. Appliance hardware is inserted in the network to improve performance, protect against malicious content, mitigate DoS attacks, and perform many other functions. These appliances are placed in-line between the requester and the provider, creating a fortress with strong boundaries. Figure 22.1 illustrates how these appliances are installed between the user and the application.

The numbers and types of appliances are large and include the following functional types:

- Header-based scanner/logger,
- Content-based scanner/logger,
- Header-based firewall,
- Content-based firewall – block only,
- Content-based firewall – modify content,
- Web accelerator,
- Wide Area Network (WAN) accelerator,
- Load balancer,
- Denial-of-service prevention.

Each of these appliances mitigates certain classes of threats, but each also increases the threat exposure, because none are free from vulnerabilities [287–298].

This fortress approach has many problems for enterprises moving to the cloud. In a one-size-fits-all cloud environment, custom hardware or tailored configurations are not likely to be available. Security is weakened by the many hardware appliances that are in place to serve all potential customers. The ones that are not needed for a particular application present an additional attack surface while providing no benefits. Scalability is limited by the cloud provider and their available hardware capabilities in a centralized in-line approach. Efficiency is lower because the cloud provider must allocate sufficient resources to handle the maximum request rate, but most of this sits idle in a typical scenario, so available computation resources are wasted.

The VADC approach is designed to work with the ELS architecture to mitigate the current problems. VADC extends the approach to the cloud while preserving many of the security properties that ELS provides. The following sections describe the ELS model, the VADC approach to extend ELS to the cloud, and the benefits of using VADC compared with the traditional hardware fortress model.

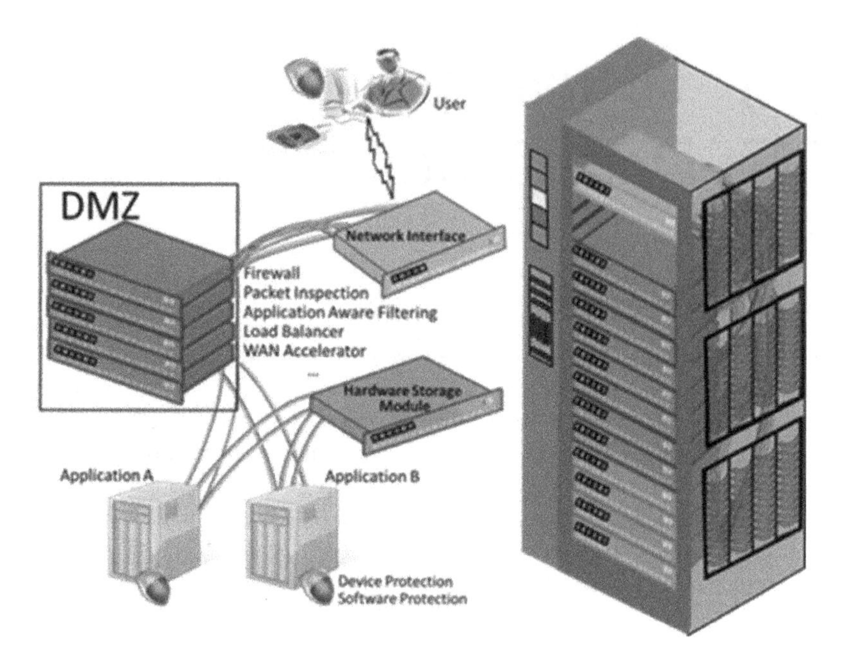

FIGURE 22.1. End Point Access

22.2 ENTERPRISE LEVEL SECURITY AND VADC CONCEPTS

The VADC is consistent with ELS and extends it for hosting in an IaaS cloud offering. It maintains much of the security of an on-premise setup while leveraging the scalability and elasticity of cloud offerings. It is based on the following key ideas:

- Capture appliance functionality in software,
- Instantiate appliance software as handlers on the servers,
- Tailor appliances to the individual servers.

An on-the-wire hardware appliance implements some function. This is encoded in the hardware, firmware, and software of the appliance, but this function can also be captured in pure software. In fact, appliance functionality is often available from vendors as software as well as the traditional hardware. Figure 22.2 shows the conversion of the particular piece of the DMZ that applies to a server into a software-only pseudo appliance.

The packets are decrypted on entry into the pseudo appliance and stay that way until they are offloaded to an external source, such as a network monitoring appliance where packets are counted and graded. This offloading will be done through an ELS-compliant communication. Although this sounds similar to the current approach, there is an important difference. The software appliance lives in the application server instead of in the network of the cloud provider. This provides the application owner, rather than the cloud provider, control over the selection and configuration of the appliances.

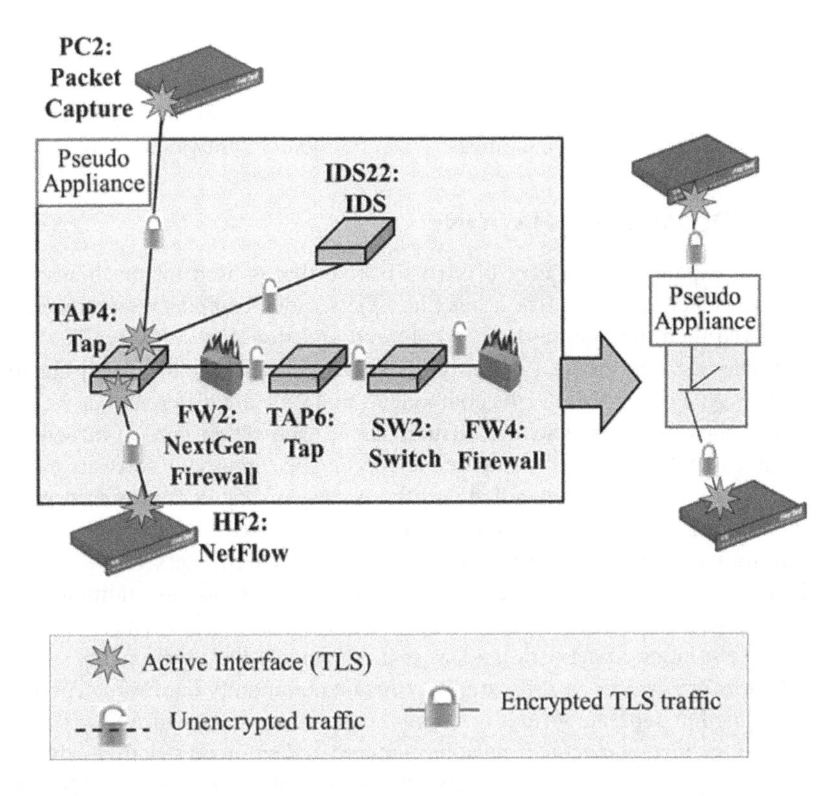

FIGURE 22.2. Creation of the Pseudo Appliance

With a pseudo appliance, we have code that we can run on the environment of our choice. For the VADC, the choice is to run this software appliance stack as handlers in the handler chain of the server, as shown in Figure 20.3. Note that the handlers are embedded in the server handler chain at the point that the communication is prepared for their use and that the functionality has been divided along those lines. These handler functions consist of packet header inspection, packet content inspection, and message content inspection. Each of these may perform inspection related to intrusion detection, blacklist blocking, or other functions.

A handler may hand off the task to an appliance through an ELS connection if development of the handler is incomplete. The configuration of handlers is tailored to the application, and these configuration files are read in at system startup. Changes to the configurations would require an update to the configuration files and a restart of the application. In cases in which frequent changes are needed, updates may be obtained through a PSS. This embedded protection process allows a true end-to-end unbroken communication path. Once the handlers are embedded in the server, the whole package is available for virtualization and can be moved between hardware platforms in an IaaS offering.

Unlike hardware appliances, for which a set of appliances is determined by the host and is the same for all servers, the VADC model allows the appliance functionality to be tailored per application and service. Instead of having a generic capability for all services, as many hardware-based appliances do, the specific set of appliances needed for a particular application or service is used with a specific configuration for that application or service. This reduces unneeded computation and enables replacement of specialized expensive hardware with commodity hardware.

22.3 VADC IMPLEMENTATION

The VADC expands the concept of virtualization that is used for machines to an entire data center. To virtualize a machine, the various components are each virtualized, and then the internal state is captured and stored in software. The result is a portable instance that can be moved from virtual machine to virtual machine using software. For the VADC, the components and state are different, but the same concept applies. As with machine virtualization, each server can be hosted on a virtual machine. External disks and file systems can be captured in software as well. Network information can be handled in different ways. Very little state information is required for a set of servers that all share a common network. However, for servers that are partitioned into different subnetworks behind routers or load balancers, it may be important to capture the network configuration as additional state information.

A simple solution to network devices is to implement the functionality of these special hardware devices in software that runs on commodity hardware. These can be instantiated as separate virtual machines in the network, in which case the connectivity of the virtual machines must be captured and enforced strictly by the hosting environment. However, this preserves these elements as high-bandwidth central bottlenecks, and often the special hardware is used specifically to provide the necessary performance to act in these roles. For this reason, this approach is not recommended for high scalability or high performance.

A more scalable solution is to implement the functionality as software on the server endpoints themselves. This is the choice for the VADC approach because it provides a more scalable solution. No additional centralized failure points are introduced, and the appliance functions are attached to the endpoint, enabling their capability to scale easily with the size of the data center. No additional high-performance hardware is needed, and no separate scalability analysis or load balancing is needed for these functions because they are built into the existing server architecture.

Moving a VADC to a new hosting environment requires moving the virtual machines, transferring the virtual disks and file systems, and capturing and recreating the virtual network architecture. The network issues are the most complicated because virtual machine movement is fairly simple and disk or file system transfer is often possible on top of existing storage options. To simplify the network architecture, a flat arrangement of servers is recommended. This preserves the distributed approach of ELS. In this setup, each server connects directly to the external network, and all servers also connect to each other. Each server uses the embedded appliance model, in which the appliance runs in software on the server itself. This eliminates the need for complicated network architectures.

In a normal in-line appliance model, private keys must be shared with the appliances to do decryption for content scans. In the VADC approach, the server allows the appliance software access to the decrypted content after the TLS driver processes it. As private keys need not be shared, they can be securely locked down in HSMs. Consistent with ELS principles, only a single instance of an application or service is allowed access to each private key. This introduces the one hardware requirement on the VADC hosting environment. The key store must be implemented in hardware. The cloud hosting environment can provide such HSMs, provided they are compatible with existing servers and applications.

The advantage of the VADC is that it facilitates moving from cloud vendor to cloud vendor. Instead of trying to understand the cloud vendor's internal network configuration, appliance architecture and functionality, and performance scalability, all that is needed is a place to put virtual machines and storage in which to put file systems. The move is primarily a transfer of data from one set of commodity components to another set of commodity components. Addressing, such as IP addressing and DNS mappings, may need to be changed, and other issues may need to be managed in the move, but otherwise the entire VADC can be moved by simple data transfer. The HSMs are the only difficulty, but because they are the core of enterprise security, it is important that they are set up in person by the enterprise and not the cloud hosting entity.

The ability to move from cloud to cloud allows diversity, ease of scale-up, and optimization of performance and cost dynamically based on different cloud vendor capability levels, locations, and pricing models.

The work of the appliances has not been eliminated, but it has been moved to a scalable commodity hardware cloud platform, which is generally easier to manage, move, and scale than a custom hardware platform. By customizing the appliance functions on a per-server basis, the total computational burden is reduced. The cost of the remaining computation is likely to be lower on commodity hardware than on custom hardware.

Figure 22.3 illustrates a simple traditional hardware appliance stack. A group of N requesters sends requests in a certain period of time. The requests are indicated by

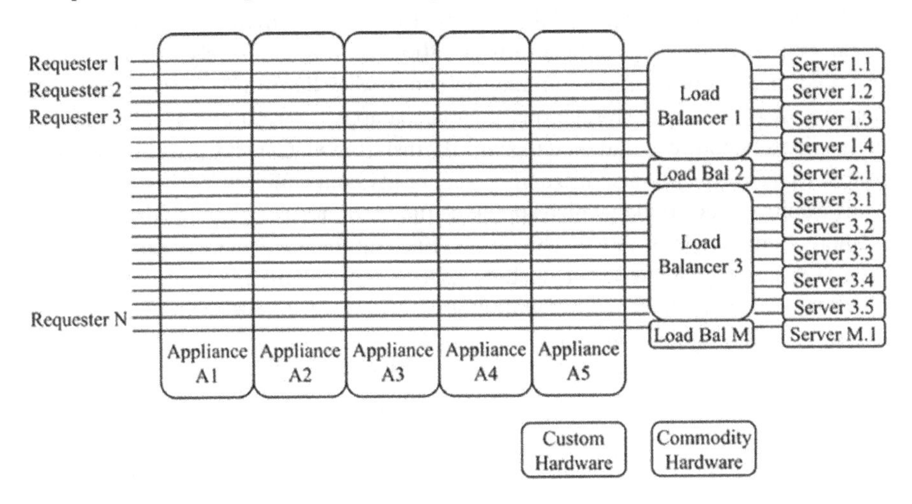

FIGURE 22.3. Hardware Appliance Architecture

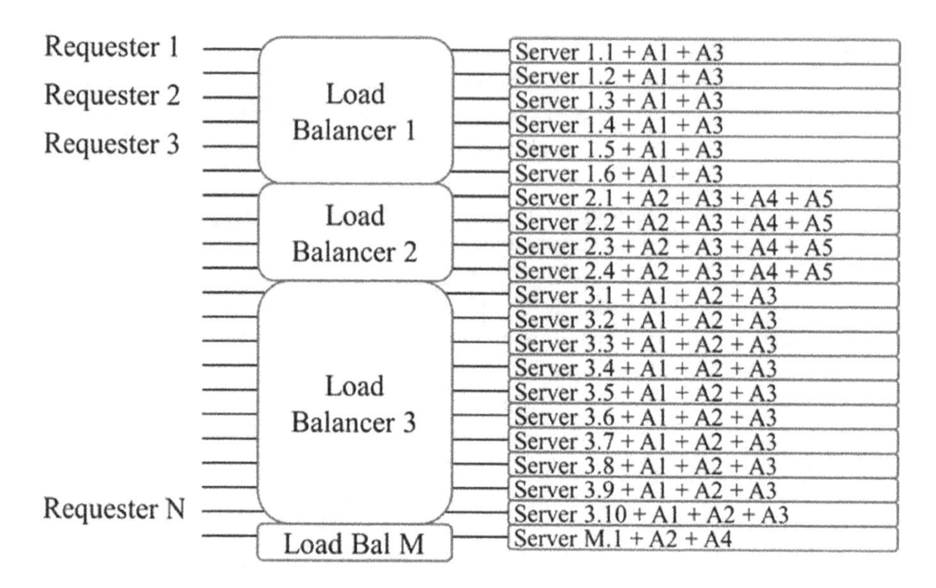

FIGURE 22.4. Software Appliance Architecture

the horizontal lines. These pass through each of the appliances, arrive at the appropriate load balancer, and are divided among the available server instances. Some applications require only a single server, such as the one hosted on Server 2.1. Others require more, such as Servers 3.1 through 3.5.

Figure 22.4 illustrates the same setup using the VADC concept. Requesters connect directly to load balancers, and appliance functionality is moved into the server instances. In this case, the servers use different appliance functions, and more instances of each are needed to support this additional computation. Server 1 adds two software appliances and increases from four to six instances. Server 2 adds four software appliances and increases from one to four instances.

By adopting the VADC model, movement to a cloud environment and between cloud environments is simplified. Functionality is captured entirely in software and installed on virtual machines running on commodity hardware. Storage uses local machine storage, cloud storage, or separate databases on other virtual machines. Network architecture is flattened to simplify installation. Centralized appliances are moved to the edges for customizability, scalability, and simplicity.

The ability to customize which appliance functions are associated with each server is another advantage of the VADC model. Each appliance provides some enhancement or capability to the server, such as performance optimization or security functionality. Each appliance has its own set of security vulnerabilities and increases the end-to-end communication attack surface. With the hardware approach, the appliance is often provided with the private key of the server, so an attack on the appliance can be as devastating as an attack on the server itself. If the appliances are not monitored as closely as the server, an attack could become more severe by remaining undetected longer. These appliances are hidden from view because they do not present their own operational endpoints like a server, and the interfaces for management are often custom software and formats, so security shortcuts, like default passwords, are more likely on such devices.

Integrating the appliances into the server eliminates many of these problems. Only the appliances that are actually used are integrated for a particular server, reducing the attack surface. The appliance code can be minimized to eliminate unnecessary interfaces and modules that might introduce vulnerabilities. The appliance software is monitored as part of the server for which it is functioning, so maintenance and policy are applied uniformly to both the server and the additional appliance functions. The code can be analyzed more easily, if desired, in software form than on hardware, and vulnerabilities can be addressed through established software patch procedures.

22.4 RESOURCE UTILIZATION

The VADC model provides more efficient resource utilization by reducing the total work that the appliances must perform and tailoring the amount of resources used to this level of work. This section provides a detailed look at where efficiencies can be gained.

Consider an enterprise with some number of servers, $N = 4$. In most cases, this number will be much higher, but for this example, a small number is considered. For these servers, the number of appliances is $M = 5$. Again, this may be much larger for large enterprises. Table 22.1 shows information about the servers and their performance. The second column lists each server's request rate, and the third column lists how much compute time each request requires of the server hardware. By multiplying these, we obtain the last column, which lists how many server machines are required to handle the incoming requests. We assume a fairly uniform request rate and a standard cloud-based hardware platform through an IaaS offering.

Table 22.2 shows information about the appliances. The low, medium, and high columns indicate options for different hardware appliance throughputs, where the numbers represent the request rate they can handle per millisecond. The "Server N uses?" columns, $N = 1, 2, 3, 4$, have a 1 when the appliance is to be used for server N. The next column lists the number of requests per millisecond that the appliance must handle, based on which servers use it and their request rates from Table 22.1. Based on the best available hardware option among low, medium, and high values, the next

TABLE 22.1.
Server Statistics

Server #	# requests/millisecond	milliseconds/request	# servers
1	2	38	76
2	3	28	84
3	5	19	95
4	1	4	4
Total	11		259

TABLE 22.2.
Appliance Data

Appliance #	HW Low option	HW Med option	HW High option	Server 1 uses?	Server 2 uses?	Server 3 uses?	Server 4 uses?	# requests/ milliseconds	Wasted capacity	milliseconds/ request	# servers needed
1	5	10	20	1		1		7	3	2	14
2	8	16	32		1	1	1	9	7	1	9
3	8	16	32	1	1	1		10	6	5	50
4	5	10	20		1		1	4	1	8	32
5	6	12	24		1			3	3	3	9
Total											114

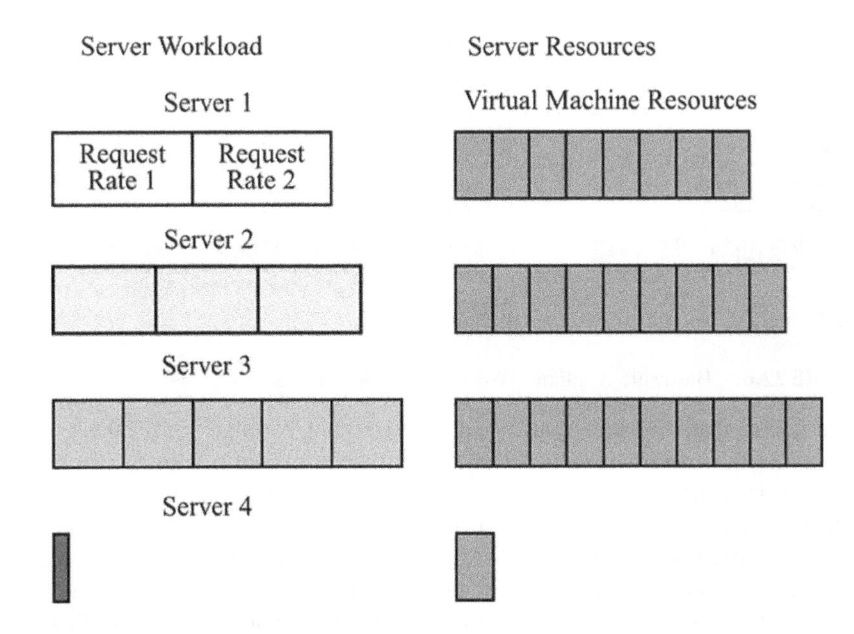

FIGURE 22.5. Server Workload and Resources

column indicates the wasted resources, measured in requests per millisecond that are available but not used. The next column lists the time to process each request by the appliances using commodity hardware. The final column lists the number of servers required to host the appliance functionality on commodity hardware. Note that the hardware options under the low, medium, and high options are typically not run on commodity hardware, and the last two columns represent a software-based implementation run on the same cloud IaaS platform as the servers.

Based on the numbers above, we can compute some of the efficiencies gained through the VADC approach. First, we look at the workload on each server in Figure 22.5. Each block on the left represents one incoming request per millisecond, and the length of the block represents the amount of processing required in milliseconds to satisfy the request.

On the right, we see the required server resources, assuming servers are allocated in groups of 10. The resources allocated roughly match the workload, with a remainder that is less than one server allocation unit per server. Thus, the wasted resource amount is on average about $N/2$ server allocation units, or 2 out of a total of 28 in this example. For large-scale, multi-server applications and services, this is a small price, and it becomes smaller as application resource requirements increase.

The hardware appliance workload is shown on the left in Figure 22.6. Each box represents the compute time associated with one request, where the resources required are indicated by the size of the box. In this case, all 11 requests per millisecond must be processed by each appliance.

On the right, the hardware option that best fits the workload is chosen, and the associated computing power is indicated by the size of each box. In this case, the hardware may be very different from the commodity servers, so the measure is based

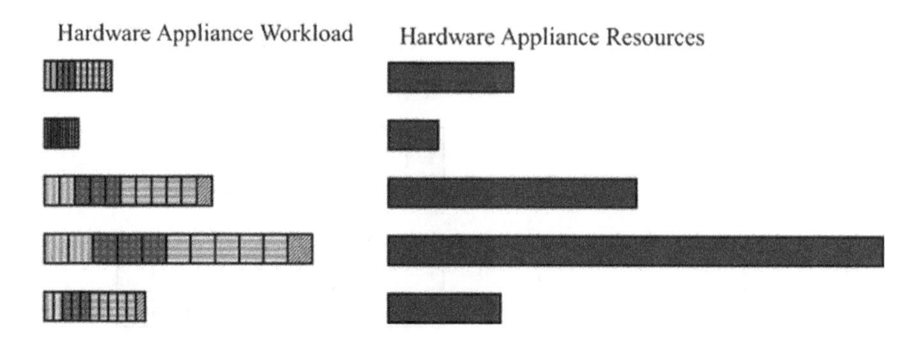

FIGURE 22.6. Hardware Appliance Workload and Resources

on the commodity hardware requirements as a common baseline. Unlike the servers, the appliance hardware does not always match the workload as closely. The availability of fixed increments of capability, often exponential instead of linear, creates large mismatches that result in wasted capacity.

We now examine the VADC approach using software appliances. The top of Figure 22.7 shows the combined workload associated with each appliance based on the number of servers that actually install it at the endpoint. This is lower than the across-the-board 11 requests that the hardware must handle in Figure 22.6. For the last two appliances, the workload is significantly reduced because only one or two servers use these appliances.

The resulting resources required from an IaaS offering are shown on the bottom. Again, these match the workload, much like the server resources.

In Figure 22.8, the full workload and resource requirements are shown for the servers and hardware appliances on the top and for the VADC model on the bottom. For hardware, a request flows through each of the appliances and then is directed to the appropriate server cluster.

For the VADC model using software appliances, the requests go directly to the endpoint, which includes appliance functionality.

The expected wasted resources for hardware are $M/2 \cdot$ (total server request rate), while for software it is just $N/2 \cdot$ (server allocation block size). In general, we may assume that the total server request rate goes up roughly proportionally to the number of servers, N, and hardware waste scales with $N \cdot M/2$, while VADC waste scales with $N/2$. So, the more appliances required, the more efficient the VADC model becomes compared to hardware.

Cost generally follows resource usage, so although this calculation focuses only on resources, it is expected that the VADC model will save money as well. The advantages of the VADC model include:

- Specialized hardware is more expensive to build and maintain than commodity IaaS servers.
- For very large scale, appliances may increase in price rapidly, whereas extra IaaS instances scale linearly.
- Adding capacity requires hardware changes that may have additional costs and delays, whereas software takes advantage of cloud elasticity.

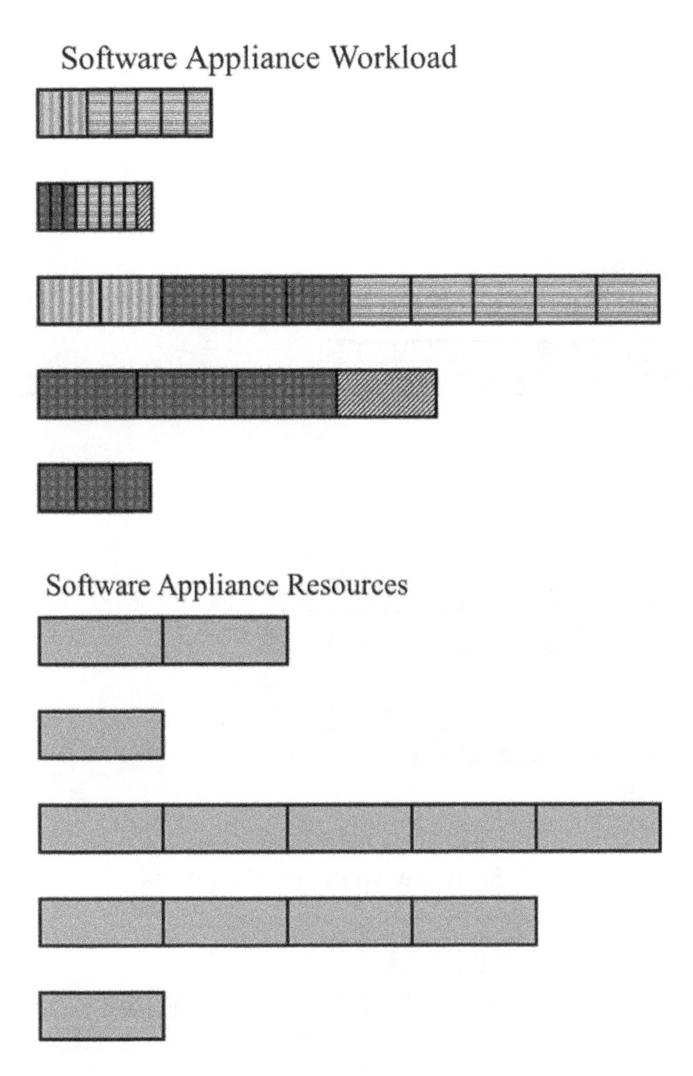

FIGURE 22.7. Software Appliance Workload and Resources

Some reasons that the VADC model may not perform as well as indicated include:

- Hardware appliance costs may scale better than linearly for the performance range actually used.
- Hardware may be configurable to process only the desired traffic and efficiently skip the rest.
- Hardware may offer finer-grained performance to better match workloads.

22.5 DISTRIBUTED BENEFITS AND CHALLENGES

The VADC approach enables a distributed approach to security, in which individual applications and services can compare the benefits of adding another appliance

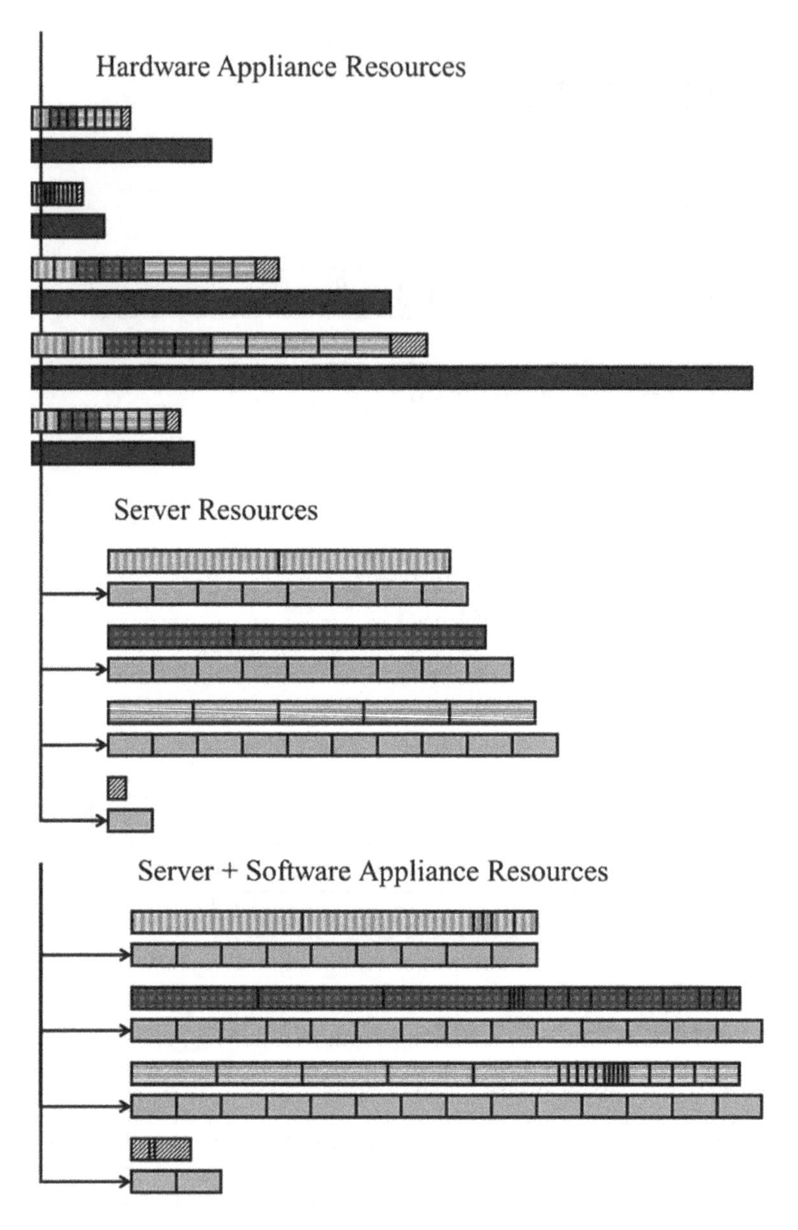

FIGURE 22.8. Total Resources VADC Software Appliances

function and the costs of adding it, including both the resource requirements for the function and the security vulnerabilities it introduces. Providing this on a per-application basis allows finer-grained control over functionality and security to the application owner instead of having the data center owner making these tradeoffs for all applications. This provides better tailoring of the applications and appliance functions and better visibility into which appliances are actually desired and used versus which are installed and in use but not needed or desired. This also provides more choices for where to host, as the requirements on the host do not include any supporting hardware infrastructure.

One challenge associated with this approach is managing the appliance software stack. Instead of a single point of management and control, each server instance is now responsible for providing its own appliance functionality for capability and protection. Also, appliances that rely on aggregated data across all servers may need to be redesigned. Instead of putting the appliance in the network where it has direct access to traffic, servers instead capture the traffic and send it to a central aggregator.

The method of providing data to the software appliance depends on the appliance function. Some appliances need to see only the lower-layer packet headers. Others need encrypted application layer content. The encrypted content can be provided decrypted after the server TLS driver is invoked. This can be integrated into the server handler chain of a standard web server.

For raw packet data, a different approach is used. The web server often receives data from a TCP stream or other higher-level communication channel that obscures the IP and MAC headers. By instead installing each server on its own virtual machine, which contains standard packet capture tools, this lower-layer data can be captured at the virtual machine boundary and sent to an aggregator. This will increase network traffic (in comparison with a central in-line appliance), but many appliances simply work within a given application, and it will be only local traffic that increases, which has higher bandwidth than external requests.

22.6 VIRTUAL APPLICATION DATA CENTER CONCLUSIONS

The VADC approach eliminates the standard hardware appliance stack used in a one-size-fits-all approach to provide security to a data center. This hardware stack often includes unused or undesired functionality, difficult scalability involving insertion of new hardware, and a mismatch between what the data center offers and what applications and services actually want. Moving this stack to software gives the application or service owner control over which functions are provided and how they are configured. No keys need to be shared, which improves security. Resource utilization better matches computational needs, potentially saving costs. The result of moving to the VADC model is improved scalability, flexibility, and security in the cloud.

23 Managing System Changes

23.1 SYSTEM CHANGE

Information systems are complex. They are built using products with configurations, settings, and best practices that can be difficult to understand and implement. The products use protocols, which are instantiated in implementations that themselves have engineering trade-offs and configurations. These implementations build on underlying networking infrastructure, protocols, and configurations which rely on algorithms, mathematics, and physics to work. Just the simple act of loading a web page has a vast array of built-in technologies, configurations, settings, and other considerations developed over many years by thousands of individuals, companies, and other entities and refined by billions of users and trillions of interactions. This situation is only becoming more complex as new protocols, mathematics and physics research, products, and operational guidance are developed.

The first challenge for an enterprise is not just how to build an information-sharing system, but how to even define the goals in such a changing landscape. The goals must be set at the appropriate level. Too high, and they fail to guide real-world choices. Too low, and they become too rigid when new technologies emerge. After determining the right goals, the second challenge is to understand the past, present, and future. The past comprises all the systems already purchased and operating. The present is the set of systems being put into place now. The future is the vision for upcoming systems, and the direction in which to move current systems. With this understanding of past, present, and future, the final challenge is to integrate and manage these in a cohesive way. As time progresses, the future becomes the present, the present becomes the past, and the past is retired. This cycle should be continuous to preserve a functioning system rather than lurch between shiny, new systems with great promise that quickly become frustrating old systems that no longer function.

23.2 CURRENT APPROACHES

Some current approaches to information system management include the following:

- The expert
- The bureaucracy
- The vendor

23.2.1 The Expert

With the expert approach, a single expert or small group owns the problem and the solution to all information system issues. They plan, coordinate, and direct computer-related activities in an organization, help determine the information technology goals of an organization, and are responsible for implementing computer systems to meet those goals [282]. Their competence enables the enterprise to rely on them for all its needs, and the expert is rarely questioned. This is partly because their competence allows them to make good choices, keep the systems running, and respond quickly to requests, but also because no one else in the enterprise is qualified to ask the right questions to challenge them.

This approach has the benefits of efficiency, consistency, and good alignment with enterprise goals. However, the expert (whether a single person or a small group) may have their own hidden agenda or biases that drive their decisions. This would be difficult to stop or even discover. Also, an individual or small group may retire, take another job, or otherwise leave the enterprise scrambling for a replacement. A system maintained by a single person may have idiosyncrasies that this person created and kept up with, but others coming into the job would not understand. Thus, changing experts requires a complete system overhaul, where a lot of the accumulated knowledge about the system, its users, and best practices is lost. Relying on these experts can be beneficial in the short term, but they may limit the growth and continuous improvement of the organization [283].

23.2.2 The Bureaucracy

A bureaucracy can address some of the failings of the expert. It is a system for controlling or managing an organization that is operated by a large number of officials employed to follow rules carefully [284]. Instead of a largely unaccountable single person or group, a bureaucracy documents all of its procedures, processes, and decisions in detail. It often has oversight and periodic reviews as well. This allows the function of the bureaucracy to continue even as the people within it are constantly changing.

However, bureaucracies can often diverge from their original intent as they survive through funding variances and changing political pressures. Also, bureaucracies are inefficient and slow to change, and they often make decisions based on those who complain loudest or who have the most influence instead of those who have the best ideas. They lack the accountability of a single person or small group [285]. Where the expert can exercise good judgment on a case-by-case basis, bureaucracies are constrained by their own operating procedures, which do not always fit well with future problems that arise.

23.2.3 The Vendor

Vendors ultimately provide the products that are used to build information-sharing systems. They are current with technology, products, and best practices. They anticipate future needs and work to meet them in their products. As a result, vendors are often more knowledgeable than a bureaucracy about building systems. Also, many vendors work as integrators to provide cohesive solutions for a related set of information-sharing problems.

It is often tempting to go to vendors looking for solutions. However, the vendor goal is profit. Profit can be aligned with providing a good solution, but often, in the long term, it is not. In particular, vendors often strive to lock customers into their solutions by providing functionality that works well as part of their overall solution but does not integrate with other solutions [286]. When an organization is locked in, the vendor can increase prices until they are close to the significant cost to switch vendors. Comparing vendors or choosing a different vendor is not the solution, because the problem is inherent in the vendors' goals and the structure of the relationship.

23.3 THE VISION

A new approach is needed to address current problems. Our vision includes the following components:

- Describe design principles and goals
- Document the past, present, and future
- Trickle down from future to present to past
- Dedicate teams to continuously review and update documentation

The first part, where design principles and goals are described, forms the foundation for all later work. Current work on the ELS security model starts with a set of tenets, as shown in Figure 1.2. These are basic design principles that are used to build the ELS architecture.

Examples include simplicity, assuming malicious entities cannot be kept out of our system, extensibility, and accountability. These basic ideas and goals shape all detailed decisions for the system. Tied to these tenets are a set of key concepts for our system. These include important protocol decisions, the need to name all entities, and the need to authenticate all entities. Unlike the tenets, which could be applied to many different types of systems, the key concepts are related specifically to our information system. Tied to these concepts is a list of requirements. These include specific naming requirements, the requirement for unique identities, and the restriction against anonymity in communications. The requirements are still not particular to any product or service, but they apply generally across many products. These are high-level requirements for the entire information-sharing system. This basic security model is described in more detail in [11].

Beyond these tenets, principles, and goals is a set of documents that discuss specific technologies. These document the past, present, and future. The future is closely tied to the design principles and goals. This is the "Target Baseline," which consists of documents that describe the goal for the near future for different technologies. The first set of these documents consists of "Scenarios," which describe different mission enterprise needs and the questions they raise about how to use technology. The second part consists of "Technical Profiles," which describe how to use different technologies. These include authentication, access control, and other basic security functions. They also include MDM, databases, and operating systems, which rely on the basic security documentation and requirements. Scenarios are written as mission enterprise needs are identified. Technical profiles are written as the scenarios raise technology questions.

The Scenarios and Technical Profiles describe the goal for the ideal future state. These documents seek to apply the design principles and goals to particular technology problems by proposing technical solutions that are consistent with the design goals.

The present-looking documents are the "Implementation Baseline," which describe current products. Each document provides an assessment of how a currently available product compares against relevant Technical Profile requirements. "Capability Profile" documents bridge the gap between the Target Baseline and Implementation Baseline. These describe the capability a product implements and the relevant target baseline document requirements that apply.

A product with an Implementation Baseline document is not an approved product. It is simply a product that has been analyzed with respect to the goals for the security model and information sharing. With this analysis, it is possible to make informed decisions for risk management. The document identifies shortcomings in security and capability. It quantifies the security risks and provides forms of mitigation that may reduce risk.

The Implementation Baseline documents also include information about product vendor plans for the future, such as whether or when they plan to release an updated version that meets certain requirements or mitigates risks. For example, when setting up an encrypted communication path, a product may use several standard approaches. For many reasons, including vulnerabilities and compromises, the more current standards may be required as part of the baseline. The current release of a product may have implemented TLS version 1.0. This may not meet the baseline requirement of TLS 1.2 or subsequent. However, the developer may plan to provide TLS 1.2 in its next release. This future-looking assessment can be used to decide whether a product is more or less likely to meet future enterprise needs by comparing their plans to the future goals as stated in the Target Baseline. In some cases, the product will not be recommended if it is not on a path to satisfy the baseline.

The final set of documents is the "Operational Baseline," which looks to the past and describes the currently fielded products and their operational rules, configurations, and best practices. Like the implementation baseline, this operational baseline identifies shortcomings in security and capability. It quantifies the security risks and provides forms of mitigation that may reduce that risk. It can also provide an upgrade approach through the implementation baseline for current software that will bring it more in line with the target baseline. The operational baseline can be used to set budgets and provide support for vulnerability mitigation work. It is understood that these products probably do not meet the future goals, so the focus is on how these products are being used to best conform to the goals as described in the future-looking documents.

Figure 23.1 describes the overall vision. It starts at its core with the tenets, which are represented by solid rocks that are difficult to move or change. These are surrounded by concepts, which are represented by wood, which is still solid but more

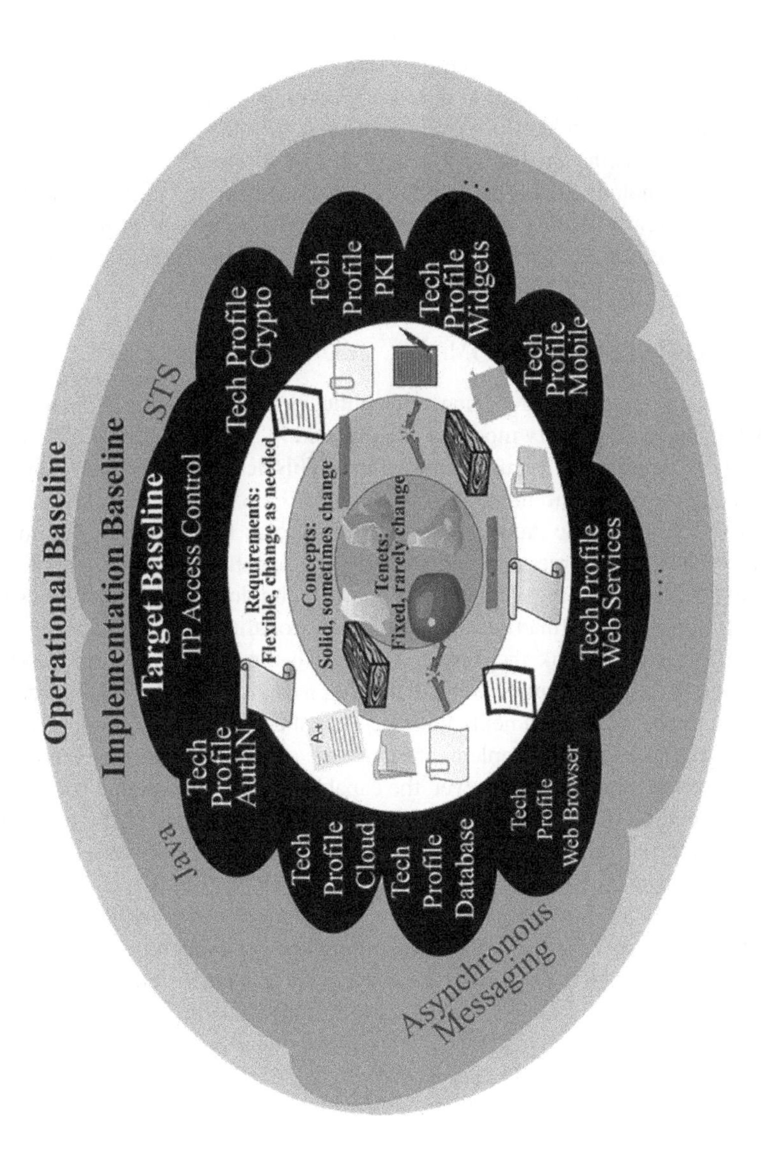

FIGURE 23.1. The Vision, from Tenets to Operational Baseline

flexible than the tenets. The requirements are represented by formal documents, which can be changed easily but still have significant weight attached to them.

Underpinning these central ideas are the three layers of documentation, the Target Baseline, the Implementation Baseline, and the Operational Baseline. Each layer is primarily related to and affected by the neighboring layers. The Target Baseline is directly driven by the requirements, which are a practical expression of the higher-level concepts and ultimately the tenets. The Implementation Baseline products are evaluated directly against the Target Baseline's Technical Profile document requirements. In addition, as products are evaluated, there is a feedback process that can adjust the Target Baseline and the Technical Profile requirements to better align them with current technology. The Operational Baseline relates to the Implementation Baseline for currently fielded products that were not previously evaluated in the Implementation Baseline. These product configurations and operational practices are documented in the Operational Baseline.

23.4 REALIZING THE VISION

Scenarios include many different questions about how to perform different enterprise goals. The basic security model is documented in a special "Design Technical Profile" called "Application Security Guidelines." This describes the tenets, key concepts, and high-level requirements for building an ELS system. "Building Block Technical Profiles" include Authentication, PKI, Access Control, and Monitoring. These apply across a large number of different capabilities and technologies. "Capability Technical Profiles" include the many technologies and capabilities that build on the core security functions to provide functionality for the enterprise.

"Capability Profiles" link the Target Baseline to the Implementation Baseline. These documents must determine what constitutes a capability versus a requirement. The capabilities in these documents must be described at a high enough level that they do not restrict a vendor's implementation. This allows for vendor creativity and inclusion of new technologies. However, the capabilities must be defined specifically enough that vendors cannot simply bypass key security requirements by using new and different approaches that are not proven or secure. Table 23.1 shows a sample list of Scenarios, Technical Profiles, and Capability Profiles.

The Implementation Baseline contains several documents. A potential set of these documents is listed in Table 23.2. It can be difficult to get enough information from vendors to assess their products against the fairly detailed security requirements in the Target Baseline Technical Profiles. It is tempting to simply ask the vendors if they meet all the requirements and happily accept a "Yes" answer to all such questions. However, the purpose of these documents is to provide reliable information about products, and vendors do not always provide such information freely, especially the information about requirements their products do not meet. To improve the overall evolution, the groups producing Target Baseline and Implementation Baseline documentation are provided assistance. The groups writing the Target Baseline are given feedback about the requirements they write. The group writing the implementation baseline is educated about current Target Baseline requirements and the motivation behind them.

TABLE 23.1.
Target Baseline Documentation

#	Technical Profiles	#	Scenarios
1	Application Security Guidelines	1	Access Management
2	Configure IDPS	2	Application Hosting
3	Manage Info – Provide Digital Policy with QoS	3	Application Performance Management
4	Provide Access Control	4	Data Management and Info. Exchange
5	Provide Access Control Annexes	5	Data on Human User
6	Provide Authentication	6	Edge Information Management
7	Provide Automated Info Capture Services	7	Elasticity
8	Provide Cloud Services	8	Enterprise Info. Management
9	Provide Consolidated Storage Services	9	Ground Segment Telem. and Command
10	Provide Cryptographic Services	10	Incident Response
11	Provide Data Mining Services	11	Infrastructure and Application Defense
12	Provide Data/Info/Protocol Mediation Services	12	IT Service Management
13	Provide Database Services	13	Key Management
14	Provide Domain Name Services	14	Leverage Digital Signature
15	Provide Load Balancing	15	Leverage Infrastructure Services
16	Provide Messaging Services	16	Mobile Enterprise
17	Provide Metadata Tagging and Discovery Services	17	Mobile Enterprise Annex 1 AIDC
18	Provide Mobile Ad Hoc Network Services	18	Mobile Enterprise Annex 2 Loc. Services
19	Provide Monitoring Services	19	Mobile Enterprise Annex 3 Wireless
20	Provide Network and Application Defense	20	Mobile Enterprise Annex 4 Device Mgt
21	Provide Operating System Services	21	Mobile Enterprise Annex 5 loT
22	Provide Public Key Infrastructure Services	22	Network and Precision Timing
23	Provide Presentation Services	23	Resiliency
24	Provide Service Desk Management Services		
25	Provide Streaming Media Services		
26	Provide Virtualization Services		
27	Provide Web Browsing		
28	Provide Web Hosting		
29	Provide Web Services	#	Capability Profiles
30	Provide Widget Services	1	Endpoint Management Service (CP)
31	Provide Ports and Protocol Policy		
32	Provide Satellite Communications		
33	Establish Space Time Information Correlation		
34	Provide Collaboration Services		
35	Provide Endpoint Device Management		

TABLE 23.2.
Implementation Baseline Documentation

#	Implementation Baseline Document
1	Managed Platforms .NET Baseline
2	Application Services
3	Managed Platforms Database Server Baseline
4	ELS Capability
5	Managed Platforms ERP Systems
6	Managed Platforms Java Baseline

The process to perform full assessments is still under development. The need for full-time trained professionals in this field is great.

The first step for the final component, the Operational Baseline, is to identify all current products in use. This is a considerable effort for a large enterprise, and results are often incomplete. Currently assigned personnel at the operational level do not have time to organize this aspect; additional staffing may be needed for this function. Essential feedback to both the target baseline and implementation baseline will improve the overall continuous improvement of the enterprise IT. It is expected that these documents will have very limited distribution.

Figure 23.2 shows the relationships between the different types of documentation. The Target Baseline also describes some of its internal structure.

The dashed lines indicate paths of influence between the document types. For example, mission needs identified in the Scenarios shape the Capability Technical Profiles, the products analyzed for the Implementation Baseline, and the assessment of vendors' future product plans. There is mutual feedback between the capability assessments of the Implementation Baseline and Operational Baseline. Upgrades for the Operational Baseline are influenced by, and can also influence, the core security requirements in the Building Block Technical Profiles. Many other interactions are possible. These help to keep all the documents more cohesive and relevant to each other and to current technology trends and products.

In addition to the influence between documents, the periodic discussions that follow these dashed lines help to inform owners of each document type about the other documents that are relevant. This helps to accomplish the following:

- Finding Target Baseline shortfalls in the Implementation Baseline and properly assessing associated risks.
- Finding, understanding, and assessing shortfalls, risks, and mitigations to the Operational Baseline.
- Adding necessary upgrades to the Operational Baseline, or replacing products if upgrades are not available or insufficient.
- Updating the Target Baseline to better align with current products and practices and avoid significant divergence from the commercial state-of-the-art.

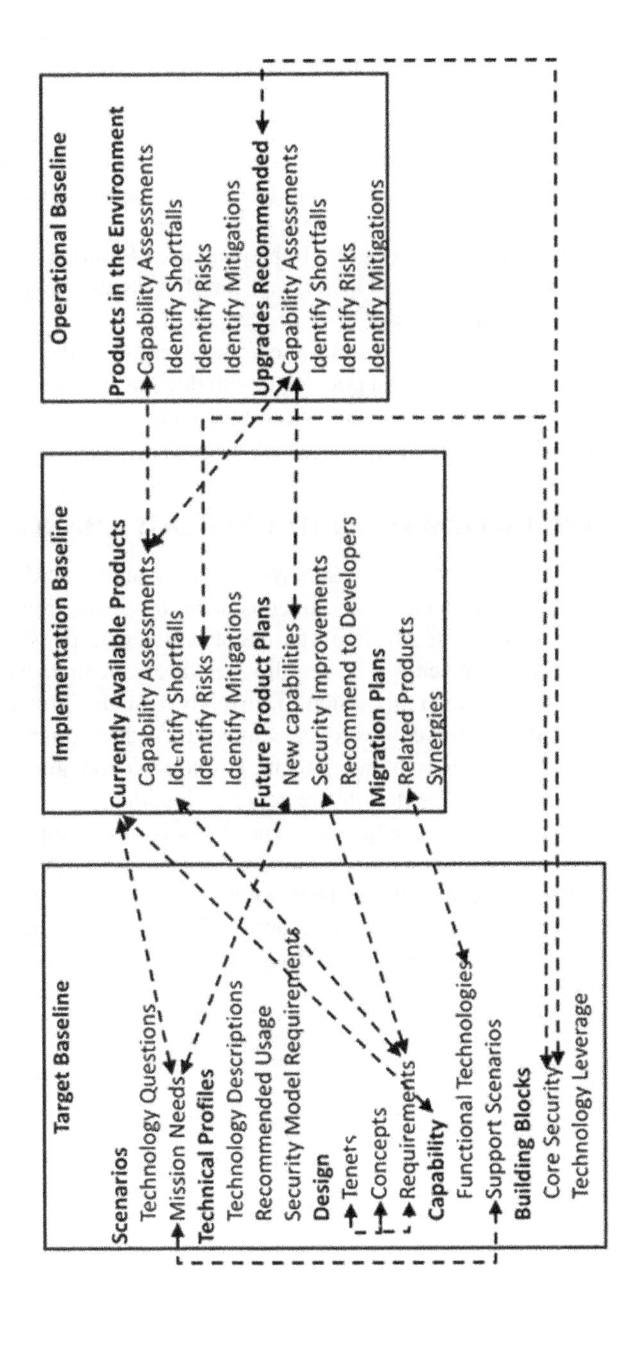

FIGURE 23.2. Documentation Hierarchy

23.5 MOVING INTO THE FUTURE

Moving forward, we expect to see more products meeting the old requirements. The Implementation Baseline documents will be updated to reflect the current status of products with respect to the original Target Baseline. They will also be assessed against the updated Target Baseline as it evolves. For example, an Implementation Baseline document for a product may contain a history of relevant Target Baseline requirements and when they were first met. This provides information about a vendor's follow-through when promises are made to upgrade and become compliant with Target Baseline requirements.

As new products are purchased using the Implementation Baseline as guidance, these products will evolve toward the Operational Baseline as their configuration, use, and best practices are established.

Thus, with time, the Implementation Baseline, and eventually the Operational Baseline, will become more mature and populated with documentation. The process to track technology goals, products, and how we use them reduces the need for a full assessment from scratch.

23.6 MANAGING INFORMATION TECHNOLOGY CHANGES

The ability to maintain a secure information system is a daunting task. We have developed a systematic way to identify and document future goals, translate these to current actions, and track these over the lifetime of products in the system until they no longer meet operational needs. This requires a dedicated team to work on the future vision, another team to map this vision to currently available products, and a third to document operational procedures for current products. By maintaining these teams and fostering communication between them, it is possible to maintain the collective knowledge of an expert. The periodic review and documentation provides the stability of a bureaucracy. The mapping to current products in the Implementation Baseline and Operational Baseline ensures that these ideas track with current best practices of vendors. This approach has been implemented and is evolving and maturing as more enterprise needs are raised, more technologies are analyzed, and more products are reviewed, and as the maturing operational procedures for these products are documented.

24 Concluding Remarks

If you read through all the chapters, congratulations! Ideally, you have gleaned a few techniques that may help you in setting up your enterprise. It has taken the authors 16 years to arrive at this point, and as you can see, there is considerably more to do. But you should understand that you may have missed the most important part of this body of work. Many of the techniques do not work alone and the complete architecture is needed. A small deviation may result in multiple headaches.

Although this book has "Advanced Techniques" in its title, the topics covered may look familiar as common capabilities enterprises are deploying. What is advanced is not the techniques, but the approach to provide capabilities for that topic in accordance with a consistent security model based on sound principles. Too many solutions for the topics presented in this book are based on capabilities with little or no underlying security.

24.1 STAYING SECURE IN AN UNCERTAIN WORLD

Security requires constant attention and maintenance. A system that is secure today must adapt to new threats, increasing computational power, technology changes, and improved theoretical results that may compromise core security functions. Security always requires "moving forward to stand still." The problem we attempt to address in this book is how to design a system that can be managed with a slow jog instead of a constant, frenzied sprint.

The current approaches in production are based on sprinting. Today's products set up proxies and open communication ports at will. In many instances, they expect you to share private keys and subscribe to SSO ways of doing business. It takes a lot of add-on security tools to secure these design choices. These require constant maintenance, vigilance, and expense.

ELS focuses on a solid design that reduces the noise in the system and allows anomalies to stand out. The work is done up front in the design, making operation and maintenance more efficient. Sprints may be needed from time to time, but it is easier to ramp up from a slow jog to a sprint for a short time than to wear yourself out by sprinting all the time.

24.2 THE MODEL IS IMPORTANT

Holding the line on the model is vitally important. The current approach finds a fix for all the vulnerabilities that compromises in security make, and sells you a solution for each. The entire IT ecosystem is connected in ways that make every exploit an entrance to the enterprise.

ZERO TRUST

Zero Trust was designed to address lateral threat movement within the network. Zero Trust embraces the principle of never trust, always verify.

There are no low-security elements in the enterprise. The "bad guys" are innovative, and they are among us. Defense needs to counter everything, while offense requires a single exploit, and we are unable to even enumerate the flaws, much less test for them. There is bad news daily on the cyber front. IT systems are invaded, and simply reusing the invaders' tactics does not ensure security. The current approaches are not working, and many of our IT professionals are doubling down by investing more and more in what has not worked in the past.

The complexity of the problem precludes a design by formal methods with formal proofs, but it does not preclude a methodical analysis and a set of experiments to validate conclusions. The processes in our first book on ELS and in this book were developed and continue to be developed on a set of principles we labeled "tenets" that are covered in the first chapter of both books as they continue to evolve.

24.3 ZERO TRUST ARCHITECTURE

Because it is assumed that covertly controlled code is present in the system, we put our emphasis on positive identification of all entities in every transaction. The transactions must be executed with confidentiality and integrity. Further, we expect that identity alone is insufficient evidence to provide access and privilege and require an additional credential for that purpose. These factors are provided by the STS using a strong back office determined separately from identification.

Items in the current system that would interrupt that model are obstacles to be worked around or through. This includes proxies and portals and "friendly" man-in-the-middle instantiations, as well as nefarious masquerades and impersonations. Automated systems are preferred over manual administrator functions, although we recognize that some things need an administrator to provide capabilities despite our best efforts at anticipating all contingencies. One goal is to use every case of intervention as a learning experience to reduce the need for future intervention. Administrators often overcome shortcomings of the automated systems and in some instances, such as delegation (see Chapter 10), solutions are provided.

We recognize that the techniques herein are not familiar to those already involved in IT architectures and security issues. Current systems make use of identity-based access control, and this implies that the services must have accounts maintained by administrators. The enterprise described in this book has no passwords and no accounts. Integrity and accountability are given a high priority. It relies on credentials that can be verified and validated. The first rule is to trust no entities or processes if it is at all possible to treat them as untrusted. The last point is especially true of legacy systems that have not had the benefit of this security model.

24.4 COMPUTING EFFICIENCIES

24.4.1 Need for Speed

Speed is more than just a desirable attribute in computing systems. It is the primary driving force for development over the course of computer history. Doing the same thing faster enables us to do more in the same amount of time, and over time, this has elevated computers from interesting hobbies to the primary means of communication, storage, and computation.

Security requires and is enabled by these advances in speed. For example, public key cryptography requires a certain amount of computational capability to be practical. The fact that security uses compute cycles, storage, and communication bandwidth means that it is in competition for these resources with business-related activities.

The common wisdom is that security hurts performance. The less common "wisdom" is that the proper type of security enhances performance. The resolution of this apparent contradiction lies in the baseline assumptions.

Those who claim security hurts performance refer to the low-level performance of simple, individual tasks in isolation. Their implicit baseline is a system that is completely secure from attack with a focus on computation within that framework. They see additional security measures as a computational burden on their externally secured system.

Those who claim security enhances performance consider the system in the real world. A system with no security provides no functionality, because it is quickly compromised and subverted by an attacker. The implicit baseline here is a system with no security and hence a system about which no guarantees can be made. Without these assurances, no functionality can be provided, because such functionality relies on proper execution by the right people on the right data. Security moves from this completely non-functional system to one in which certain operations can be performed with some certainty.

The right answer lies somewhere in the middle. All systems have some security built in, and no systems are completely secure. Adding security does hurt the lowest level of performance, but done properly, it enables operations that were previously unreliable or operations that required constant maintenance, scanning, and fixing to run largely on their own.

At the enterprise level, the emphasis should shift more toward security than efficiency. There is too much to lose and there are too many attackers to rely on partial security. For example, the Chinese Remainder Theorem (CRT) [299] is a shortcut used to reduce computational costs in the TLS setup using RSA keys. This mathematical optimization can cut the raw computation time roughly in half [300]. However, it may open up a vulnerability that reveals the server's private key. [89]. The CRT actually breaks up the computation of large exponents into smaller pieces. Tripping a fault in that computation produces a result that reveals the private key. A reliable server would seldom make an error in this computation, but in an age of cloud computing where personnel are less vetted, an insider may tamper with the environment, such as temperature, radiation, or supply voltage, to cause the error. This unforeseen consequence arises from the saving of a few milliseconds in the session setup.

Often, such vulnerabilities are not widely known or they are viewed as unlikely. Combating these one at a time is not a viable solution. A fundamentally secure design like ELS provides a structured way to implement security, so any such vulnerability can be placed within this framework and assessed in context. The goal is to design a system that resists entire classes of vulnerabilities by default. ELS does not address individual vulnerabilities at the highest level, so it must rely on implementation rules and purchasing decisions, such as refusing to purchase HSMs that use CRT or disabling CRT on those that do.

24.4.2 Security Protocols and Algorithms

Protocols and algorithms are crafted to achieve security properties and any changes should be very carefully tested. In the rework of TLS 1.2 to TLS 1.3, several steps in the handshake exchange were combined to save time. This led to a number of discovered vulnerabilities [301–303], leading to remediation attempts that may well cost more compute cycles than the original changes saved. With the advent of 5G and fog computing, savings as small as 1 millisecond are vigorously pursued. There is a concern that the algorithmic and programmatic shortcuts will be pursued without significant due diligence.

24.4.3 Evaluation of Security Products

The U.S. DoD has mandated a requirement for common criteria evaluation in defense products [304]. Current evaluation processes under common criteria only include security functionality, and they should be required to undergo vulnerability analysis and have strong flaw remediation processes. If the common criteria do not add these assurance requirements, they should be specified over and above the security evaluation requirements.

24.5 CURRENT FULL ELS SYSTEM

The current full system instantiation of the ELS system includes most of the advanced areas discussed in this book with the exception of those that are yet to be implemented (Mobile Ad Hoc Networking (Chapter 17) and PHE (Chapter 14), for example). The full instantiation continues to grow in sophistication and complexity. This current full instantiation is presented in Figure 24.1. However, only the needed parts should be added to the minimal instantiation shown in Figure 3.6.

24.6 FUTURE DIRECTIONS

The fact that the original book on ELS has a sequel suggests that this work is ongoing. Even as we finish writing this book, we see many new challenges and opportunities on the horizon.

Quantum computing threatens to disrupt cryptography, which is the foundation of many security protocols that we use today. If optimistic estimates prevail, this will happen long before we are ready for it. Even if we can use encryption methods that are "quantum safe," all of our currently encrypted data is vulnerable to decryption by a quantum method. The question is no longer how long it takes to decrypt the data using classical methods, but how long until quantum methods are available.

Homomorphic encryption and computation are seeing rapid growth. Although FHE is very slow, many approaches integrating different forms of PHE are finding

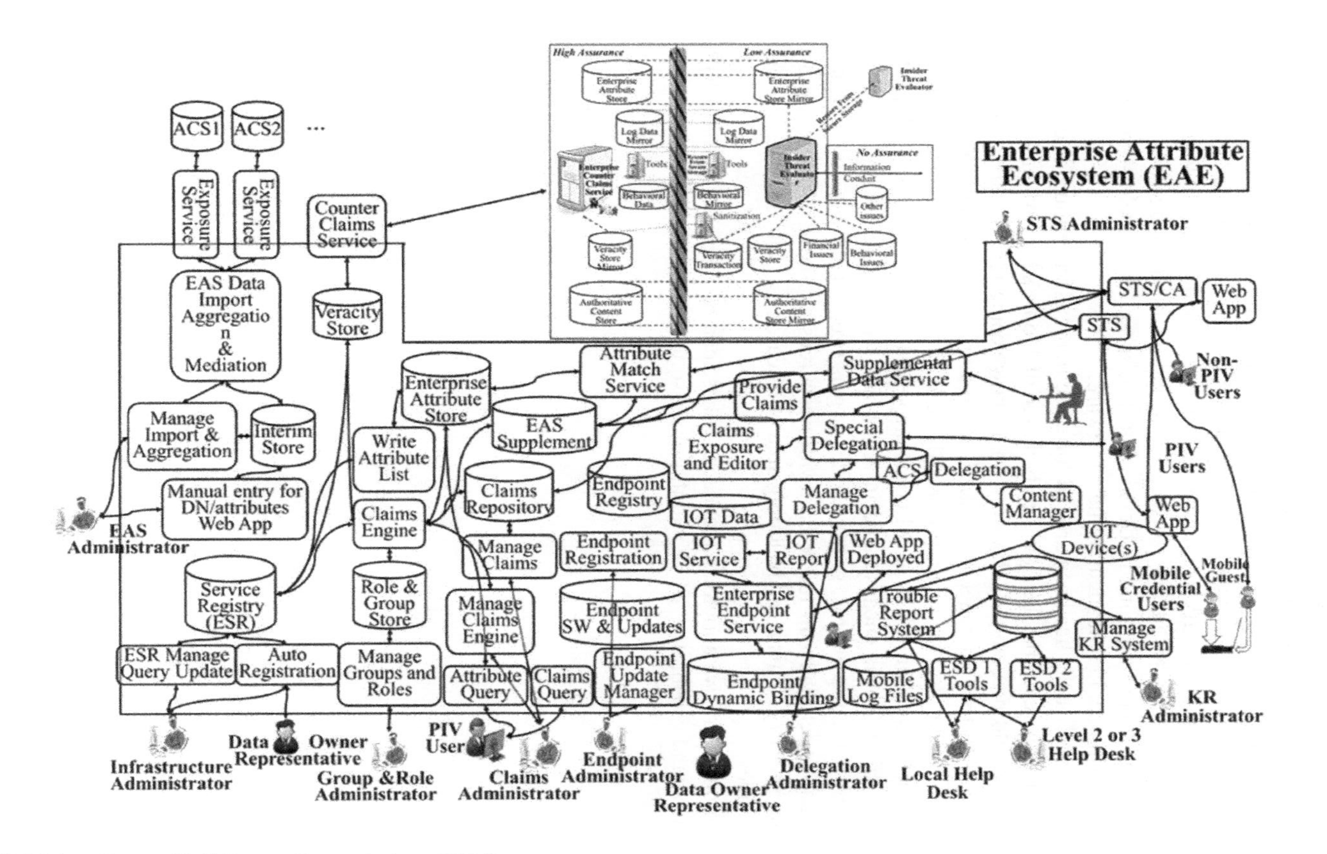

FIGURE 24.1. Current Full System Instantiation of ELS

their way to the market. The current offerings often solve very narrowly defined problems, but improvements and innovations in this area are likely to change the nature of cryptography, much like public/private key cryptography did years ago. The question is whether or when this will become commonplace.

5G and IoT together will change what the Internet means. It is no longer people talking to servers or other people. It is machines talking en masse to each other. Just as it is now uncommon to talk to a human on a phone, it will be rare to find a person on the Internet. What this means for security is that we must change our notion of identity and the security around it. Devices must be more like people – unique and uniquely identifiable, independent of their software.

Artificial intelligence has been around for more than half a century, and its slow steady march may resemble the slow steady march of Moore's Law when the transistor numbers could be counted. However, we're now seeing real-world capabilities, such as speech-to-text, language translation, self-driving cars, and the ability to play and win "Go," and they are coming in rapid succession. Major technology companies are positioning themselves as AI companies. Instead of competing to hire the best talent, this talent is encapsulated in AI, which won't leave for higher pay or better benefits. It never retires, grows senile, or gets tired, and it can be duplicated instantly and indefinitely up to the hardware resources available. How do we use new AI for security? This is a developing area of research on both the offensive and defensive sides.

With proper care, we anticipate that each of these can be integrated into the ELS design to expand capabilities while maintaining a solid security foundation.

References

[1] OASIS Open Set of Standards

a) N. Ragouzis et al., Security Assertion Markup Language (SAML) V2.0 Technical Overview. OASIS Committee Draft, March 2008.
b) P. Madsen et al., SAML V2.0 Executive Overview. OASIS Committee Draft, April 2005.
c) P. Mishra et al., Conformance Requirements for the OASIS Security Assertion Markup Language (SAML) V2.0. OASIS Standard, March 2005.
d) S. Cantor et al., Bindings for the OASIS Security Assertion Markup Language (SAML) V2.0. OASIS Standard, March 2005.
e) S. Cantor et al., Profiles for the OASIS Security Assertion Markup Language (SAML) V2.0. OASIS Standard, March 2005.
f) S. Cantor et al., Assertions and Protocols for the OASIS Security Assertion Markup Language (SAML) V2.0. OASIS Standard, March 2005.
g) S. Cantor et al., Metadata for the OASIS Security Assertion Markup Language (SAML) V2.0. OASIS Standard, March 2005.
h) F. Hirsch et al., Security and Privacy Considerations for the OASIS Security Assertion Markup Language (SAML) V2.0. OASIS Standard, March 2005.
i) J. Hodges et al., Glossary for the OASIS Security Assertion Markup Language (SAML) V2.0. OASIS Standard, March 2005.
j) "WS-Trust Specification 1.4." http://docs.oasis-open.org/ws-sx/ws-trust/200802, OASIS, February 2009.
k) "WS-ReliableMessaging Specification 1.2." http://docs.oasis-open.org/ws-rx/wsrm/200702, OASIS, 2 February 2009.
l) "WS-SecureConversation Specification 1.4." http://docs.oasis-open.org/ws-sx/ws-secureconversation/200512, OASIS, February 2009.
m) "WS-Security Specification 1.1." OASIS, November 2006, UDDI Version 3.0.2.
n) UDDI Spec Technical Committee Draft, Dated 20041019, Document identifier: uddi_v3. Latest version: http://uddi.org/pubs/uddi_v3.htm.

[2] National Institute of Standards, Gaithersburg, MD:

a) NIST Special Publication 800-38, Recommendation for Block Cipher Modes of Operation: 38A, Methods and Techniques, December 2001; 38B, The RMAC Authentication Mode, November 5 2002 Draft; 38C, The CCM Mode for Authentication and Confidentiality, May 2004.
b) Recommendation for Block Cipher Modes of Operation: 38A, Methods and Techniques, December 2001; 38B, The RMAC Authentication Mode, November 5 2002 Draft; 38C, The CCM Mode for Authentication and Confidentiality, July 2007.
c) NIST Special Publication 800-53, Recommended Security Controls for Federal Information Systems and Organizations, Revision 3, August 2009.
d) NIST Special Publication 800-67, Version 1.2, Recommendation for the Triple Data Encryption Algorithm (TDEA) Block Cipher, Revised January 2012.
e) NIST Special Publication 800-95, Guide to Secure Web Services. http://csrc.nist.gov/publications/nistpubs/800-95/SP800-95.pdf, accessed on 19 February 2011, Federal Information Processing Standards Publication 140, Security Requirements for Cryptographic Modules, 25 May 2001.

f) NIST Special Publication 800-144, Guidelines on Security and Privacy in Public Cloud Computing, Wayne Jansen, Timothy Grance, December 2011.
g) NIST Special Publication 800-145, Cloud Computing, Computer Security Division, Information Technology Laboratory, National Institute of Standards and Technology, Gaithersburg, MD, Peter Mell, Timothy Grance, January 2011. https://www.nist.gov/news-events/news/2011/10/final-version-nist-cloud-computing-definition-published, September 2011, last accessed on 19 May 2020.
h) Federal Information Processing Standards Publication 140, Security Requirements for Cryptographic Modules, 25 May 2001.
i) Federal Information Processing Standards Publication 180-3, Secure Hash Standard, August 2002.
j) Federal Information Processing Standards Publication 186-3, Digital Signature Standard, June 2009.
k) Federal Information Processing Standards Publication 196, Entity Authentication Using Public Key Cryptography, 18 February 1997.
l) Federal Information Processing Standards Publication 197, Advanced Encryption Standard (AES), November 2001.
m) Federal Information Processing Standards Publication 188, 1994 September 6, Standard Security Label for Information Transfer. Withdrawn 15 October 2019.

[3] Common Criteria for Information Technology Security Evaluation:
a) Version 3.1, Revision 3, July 2009. Part 1: Introduction and General Model.
b) Version 3.1, Revision 3, July 2009. Part 2: Functional Security Components.
c) Version 3.1, Revision 3, July 2009. Part 3: Assurance Security Components.
d) Common Methodology for Information Technology Security Evaluation, Version 3.1, Revision 3, July 2009.

[4] Internet Engineering Task Force (IETF) Standards:
a) STD 5 (RFC0791) Internet Protocol, J. Postel, September 1981, and Subsequent RFCs 791/950/919/922/792/1112.
b) STD 9 (RFC0959) File Transfer Protocol, J. Postel, J. Reynolds, October 1985.
c) STD 66 (RFC3986) Uniform Resource Identifier (URI): Generic Syntax, T. Berners-Lee, R. Fielding, L. Masinter, January 2005.
d) RFC 1321, The MD5 Message-Digest Algorithm, April 1992.
e) RFC 2104, HMAC: Keyed-Hashing for Message Authentication, February 1997; STD 9 (RFC0959), File Transfer Protocol, J. Postel, J. Reynolds, October 1985.
f) RFC 2406, IP Encapsulating Security Payload, November 1998.
g) RFC 2459, Internet X.509 Public Key Infrastructure Certificate and CRL Profile, January 1999.
h) RFC 2560, X.509 Internet Public Key Infrastructure Online Certificate Status Protocol – OCSP, June 1999.
i) RFC 2829, Authentication Methods for LDAP, M. Wahl, H. Alvestrand, J. Hodges, R. L. Morgan, May 2000.
j) RFC 3305, Report from the Joint W3C/IETF URI Planning Interest Group: Uniform Resource Identifiers (URIs), URLs, and Uniform Resource Names (URNs): Clarifications and Recommendations, August 2002.
k) RFC 4120, The Kerberos Network Authentication Service V5, updated by RFC 4537 and 5021.
l) RFC 4510, Lightweight Directory Access Protocol (LDAP): Technical Specification Road Map, June 2006.
m) RFC 5246, The Transport Layer Security (TLS) Protocol Version 1.2, August 2008.
n) RFC 5751, Secure/Multipurpose Internet Mail Extensions (S/MIME) Version 3.2 Message Specification, July 2010.

o) RFC 6151, Updated Security Considerations for the MD5 Message-Digest and the HMAC-MD5 Algorithms, March 2011.
p) Web Services Architecture, W3C Working Group Note, 11 February 2004, Latest version: http://www.w3.org/TR/ws-arch/.

[5] World Wide Web Consortium (W3C):
a) XML Encryption Syntax and Processing, 10 December 2002.
b) XML Signature Syntax and Processing, 10 June 2008.
c) XML Canonical XML Version 1, Mar 2001.
d) XML-Exclusive Canonicalization Version 1, July 2002.
e) W3C XML Schema Definition Language (XSD) 1.1 Part 2: Datatypes, W3C Recommendation, 5 April 2012, Latest version: http://www.w3.org/TR/xmlschema11-2/, last accessed on 19 May 2020.
f) W3C XML Schema Definition Language (XSD) 1.1 Part 1: Structures, W3C Recommendation, 5 April 2012, Latest version: http://www.w3.org/TR/xmlschema11-1/, last accessed on 19 May 2020.
g) SOAP Version 1.2 Part 1: Messaging Framework (Second Edition), 27 April 2007.
h) Web Services Description Language (WSDL) Version 2.0 Part 0: Primer, W3C Recommendation, 26 June 2007.
i) Web Services Description Language (WSDL) Version 2.0 Part 1: Core Language, W3C Recommendation, 26 June 2007, Latest version: http://www.w3.org/TR/wsdl20, last accessed on 19 May 2020.
j) Web Services Description Language (WSDL) Version 2.0 Part 2: Adjuncts, W3C Recommendation, 26 June 2007.
k) Semantic Annotations for WSDL and XML Schema, W3C Recommendation, 28 August 2007.
l) Web Services Architecture Requirements, W3C Working Group Note, 11 February 2004.
m) HTML 4.01 Specification, W3C Recommendation, 24 December 1999.
n) XHTML™ 1.1 - Module-Based XHTML - Second Edition, W3C Recommendation, 23 November 2010.

[6] Gemalto Blog – Conversations Around Digital Security, "Three-Factor Authentication: Something You Know, Something You Have, Something You Are," 16 May 2018. https://blog.gemalto.com/security/2011/09/05/three-factor-authentication-something-you-know-something-you-have-something-you-are/, last accessed on 23 August 2019.

[7] William R. Simpson, *Enterprise Level Security – Securing Information Systems in an Uncertain World*, Boca Raton, FL, CRC Press, by Auerbach Publications, May 2016, ISBN 9781498764452.

[8] William R. Simpson and Kevin E. Foltz, Lecture Notes in Engineering and Computer Science, "Mobile Ad Hoc for Enterprise Level Security," *Proceedings World Congress on Engineering and Computer Science (WCECS) 2018*, Volume 1, pp. 172–177, Berkeley, CA, October 2018, ISBN: 978-988-14048-1-7, ISSN: 2078-0958.

[9] Kevin E. Foltz and William R. Simpson, "Enterprise Level Security with Homomorphic Encryption," *Proceedings of the 19th International Conference on Enterprise Information Systems (ICEIS 2017)*, Volume 1, pp. 177–184, Porto, Portugal, SCITEPRESS – Science and Technology Publications, 25–30 April, 2017, ISBN: 978-989-758-247-9. doi: 10.5220/0006245901770184.

[10] Coimbatore Chandersekaran, William R. Simpson, and Andrew Trice, "A Persona-Based Framework for Flexible Delegation and Least Privilege," *Electronic Digest of the 2008 System and Software Technology Conference*, Las Vegas, NV, May 2008.

[11] Kevin E. Foltz and William R. Simpson, "Enterprise Level Security – Basic Security Model," *7th International Multi-Conference on Complexity, Informatics, and Cybernetics: IMCIC 2016*, Orlando, FL, March 2016.

[12] Coimbatore Chandersekaran, William R. Simpson, and Andrew Trice, "Cross-Domain Solutions in an Era of Information Sharing," *The 1st International Multi-Conference on Engineering and Technological Innovation: IMETI 2008*, Volume I, pp. 313–318, Orlando, FL, June 2008.

[13] Coimbatore Chandersekaran and William R. Simpson, "The Case for Bi-lateral End-to-End Strong Authentication," *World Wide Web Consortium (W3C) Workshop on Security Models for Device APIs*, 4 pp., London, England, December 2008.

[14] Coimbatore Chandersekaran and William R. Simpson, "Federated Trust Policy Enforcement by Delegated SAML Assertion Pruning," *World Wide Web Consortium (W3C) Workshop on Security Models for Device APIs*, 4 pp., London, England, December 2008.

[15] Coimbatore Chandersekaran and William R. Simpson, "A SAML Framework for Delegation, Attribution, and Least Privilege," *3rd International Multi-Conference on Engineering and Technological Innovation (IMETI 2010)*, Volume 2, pp. 303–308, Orlando, FL, July 2010.

[16] William R. Simpson and Coimbatore Chandersekaran, "Information Sharing and Federation," *The 2nd International Multi-Conference on Engineering and Technological Innovation: IMETI 2009*, Volume I, pp. 300–305, Orlando, FL, July 2009.

[17] Coimbatore Chandersekaran and William R. Simpson, "A Persona Framework for Delegation, Attribution and Least Privilege," *The International Conference on Complexity, Informatics and Cybernetics: CCCT2010*, Volume II, pp. 84–89, Orlando, FL, April 2010.

[18] Ebrima Ceesay, Coimbatore Chandersekaran, and William R. Simpson, "An Authentication Model for Delegation, Attribution and Least Privilege," *The 3rd International Conference on Pervasive Technologies Related to Assistive Environments: PETRA'10*, Samos, Greece, June 2010.

[19] Coimbatore Chandersekaran, Kevin Foltz, and William R. Simpson, "Assessing SOA Performance," *The 15th International Command and Control Research and Technology Symposium: ICCRTS2010*, Santa Monica, CA, June 2010.

[20] Coimbatore Chandersekaran and William R. Simpson, "Use Case Based Access Control," *The 3rd International Multi-Conference on Engineering and Technological Innovation: IMETI 2010*, Volume 2, pp. 297–302, Orlando, FL, July 2010.

[21] Coimbatore Chandersekaran and William R. Simpson, Lecture Notes in Computer Science, "A Model for Delegation Based on Authentication and Authorization," *Proceedings of the First International Conference on Computer Science and Information Technology (CCSIT-2011)*, Springer Verlag, Berlin-Heidelberg, 20 pp., CCSIT 2011, Part III, CCIS 133, pp. 217–236, Bangalore, India, 4 January 2011, *Advanced Computing, Communications in Computer and Information Science*. doi: 10.1007/978-3-642-17881-8_22.

[22] Coimbatore Chandersekaran and William R. Simpson, "Using SAML for Attribution, Delegation and Least Privilege," *The Journal on Systemics, Cybernetics and Informatics (JSCI)*, Volume 9, Number 1, pp. 1–7, January 2011.

[23] Coimbatore Chandersekaran and William R. Simpson, "Enterprise Delegation for Service Based Systems," *International Journal of Network Security & Its Applications (IJNSA)*, Volume 3, Number 3, pp. 138–161, May 2011.

[24] William R. Simpson and Coimbatore Chandersekaran, "An Agent Based Monitoring System for Web Services," *The 16th International Command and Control Research and Technology Symposium: ICCRTS2011*, Volume II, pp. 84–89, Orlando, FL, April 2011.

[25] Coimbatore Chandersekaran and William R. Simpson, "A Multi-Tiered Approach to Enterprise Support Services," *1st International Conference on Design, User Experience, and Usability, part of the 14th International Conference on Human-Computer Interaction (HCII 2011)*, 10pp, Orlando, FL, July 2011. Also published in: A. Marcus (Ed.), *Design, User Experience, and Usability*, Pt I, HCII 2011, LNCS 6769, pp. 388–397, 2011. © Springer-Verlag, Berlin Heidelberg, 2011.

[26] Coimbatore Chandersekaran and William R. Simpson, "Personal Delegation by Persona Creation," *International Journal of Computer Technology and Application (IJCTA)*, Volume 2, Number 6, pp. 413–423, June 2011.

[27] Elizabeth A. McDaniel, William R. Simpson, Coimbatore Chandersekaran, and Kevin Foltz, "Transitioning to Secure Web-Based Standards and Protocols," *IDA Research Notes, Challenges in Cyberspace*, Volume 2, pp. 8–10, Summer 2011.

[28] William R. Simpson and Coimbatore Chandersekaran, "An Agent-Based Web-Services Monitoring System," *International Journal of Computer Technology and Application (IJCTA)*, Volume 2, Number 9, pp. 675–685, September 2011.

[29] William R. Simpson, Coimbatore Chandersekaran, and Ryan Wagner, Lecture Notes in Engineering and Computer Science, "High Assurance Challenges for Cloud Computing," *Proceedings World Congress on Engineering and Computer Science 2011*, Volume I, pp. 61–66, Berkeley, CA, October 2011.

[30] Coimbatore Chandersekaran and William R. Simpson, "A Web Service Monitoring System for the Enterprise," *The Journal on Systemics, Cybernetics and Informatics (JSCI)*, Volume 10, Number 2, pp. 40–51, 2012.

[31] Coimbatore Chandersekaran and William R. Simpson, Lecture Notes in Engineering and Computer Science, "Claims-Based Enterprise-Wide Access Control," *Proceedings World Congress on Engineering 2012, The 2012 International Conference of Information Security and Internet Engineering*, Volume I, pp. 524–529, Imperial College, London, July 2012.

[32] Coimbatore Chandersekaran and William R. Simpson, Lecture Notes in Engineering and Computer Science, "Assured Content Delivery in the Enterprise," *Proceedings World Congress on Engineering 2012, The 2012 International Conference of Information Security and Internet Engineering*, Volume I, pp. 555–560, Imperial College, London, July 2012.

[33] William R. Simpson and Coimbatore Chandersekaran, Lecture Notes in Electrical Engineering 170, "Co-Existence of High Assurance and Cloud-Based Computing," in Haeng Kon Kim, Sio-long Ao, and Burghard B. Rieger (eds.), *IAENG Transactions on Engineering Technologies - Special Edition of the World Congress on Engineering and Computer Science 2011*, pp. 201–214, May 2012. doi: 10.1007/978-94-007-4786-9_16, ISBN: 978-94-007-4785-2, Chapter 16, Co-authored by Coimbatore Chandersekaran.

[34] Coimbatore Chandersekaran and William R. Simpson, Lecture Notes in Engineering and Computer Science, "Enterprise High Assurance Scale-up," *Proceedings World Congress on Engineering and Computer Science 2012*, Volume 1, pp. 54–59, Berkeley, CA, October 2012, Co-authored by Coimbatore Chandersekaran.

[35] Coimbatore Chandersekaran and William R. Simpson, "A Uniform Claims-Based Access Control for the Enterprise," *International Journal of Scientific Computing*, Volume 6, Number 2, pp. 1–23, December 2012, ISSN: 0973-578X, Co-authored by Coimbatore Chandersekaran.

[36] Coimbatore Chandersekaran, William R. Simpson, and Ryan Wagner, "Secure Cloud Based Computing," *IDA Research Notes, Best Publications in the Open Literature*, pp. 21–27, Winter 2012–2013.

[37] Coimbatore Chandersekaran and William R. Simpson, Lecture Notes in Engineering and Computer Science, "Claims-Based Authentication for a Web-Based Enterprise," *Proceedings World Congress on Engineering 2013, the 2013 International Conference of Information Security and Internet Engineering*, Volume I, pp. 524–529, Imperial College, London, July 2013.

[38] William R. Simpson and Coimbatore Chandersekaran, authors, H. K. Kim et al. (eds.), Lecture Notes in Electrical Engineering 247, "High Assurance Enterprise Scaling Issues," *IAENG Transactions on Engineering Technologies*, Chapter 23, pp. 317–331, Springer Science+Business Media, Dordrecht, 12 September 2013.

[39] Coimbatore Chandersekaran and William R. Simpson, Lecture Notes in Engineering and Computer Science, "Cryptography for a High-Assurance Web-Based Enterprise," *Proceedings World Congress on Engineering and Computer Science* 2013, Volume 1, pp. 23–28, Berkeley, CA, October 2013, Co-authored by Coimbatore Chandersekaran. Award: *Certificate of Merit for International Conference on Computer Science and Applications*, 2013.

[40] William R. Simpson and Coimbatore Chandersekaran, authors, S. Hammoudi, L. Maciaszek, and J. Cordeiro (eds.), "Vulnerability and Remediation for a High-assurance Web-based Enterprise," *Proceedings of the 16th International Conference on Enterprise Information Systems*, Volume 2, pp. 119–128, Lisbon, Portugal, pp. 27–30, SCITEPRESS – Science and Technology Publications, April 2014, ISBN: 978-989-758-028-4.

[41] William R. Simpson and Coimbatore Chandersekaran, Lecture Notes in Engineering and Computer Science, "Cloud Based Forensics Issues," *Proceedings World Congress on Engineering 2014*, Volume 1, pp. 475–480, Imperial College, London, July 2014.

[42] Coimbatore Chandersekaran, Kevin Foltz, and William R. Simpson, Lecture Notes in Engineering and Computer Science, "Distributed Versus Centralized Protection Schema for the Enterprise," *Proceedings World Congress on Engineering and Computer Science 2014*, Volume 1, pp. 228–234, Berkeley, CA, October 2014.

[43] Kevin Foltz and William R. Simpson, Lecture Notes in Engineering and Computer Science, "Wide Area Network Acceleration in a High Assurance Enterprise," *Proceedings World Congress on Engineering 2015*, Volume 1, pp. 502–507, Imperial College, London, July 2015.

[44] Kevin E. Foltz and William R. Simpson, "Building a Secure Enterprise," Post *Proceedings of The 20th World Multi-Conference on Systemics, Cybernetics and Informatics: WMSCI*, Conference Version, electronic only, *WMSCI 2016*, Orlando, FL, 8–11 March 2016.

[45] William R. Simpson and Kevin E. Foltz, "Security Issues in Content Modification Processes," in H. K. Kim et al. (eds.), *Transactions on Engineering Technologies, Special Issue of the World Congress on Engineering and Computer Science 2015*, Chapter 31, pp. 429–441, Springer, Dordrecht, July 2016.

[46] William R. Simpson and Kevin E. Foltz, "Access and Privilege in Secure Big Data Analysis," Wessex Institute, *Proceedings of the International Conference on Big Data, BIG DATA 2016*, pp. 193–205, Alicante, Spain, 3–5 May 2016.

[47] Kevin E. Foltz and William R. Simpson, Lecture Notes in Engineering and Computer Science, "Simplified Key Management for Digital Access Control of Information Objects," *Proceedings of the World Congress on Engineering (WCE) 2016*, pp. 413–418, Imperial College, London, June 2016.

[48] William R. Simpson and Kevin E. Foltz, "Federation for a Secure Enterprise," *Proceedings of the 21ST International Command and Control Research and Technology Symposium (ICCRTS)*, London, England, September 2016. http://www.dodccrp-test.org/s/paper_2.pdf.

[49] Kevin Foltz and William R. Simpson, Lecture Notes in Engineering and Computer Science, "Enterprise Considerations for Ports and Protocols," *Proceedings World Congress on Engineering and Computer Science (WCECS) 2016*, Volume 1, pp. 124–129, Berkeley, CA, October 2016.

[50] Eric D. Trias, William R. Simpson, Kevin E. Foltz, and Frank P. Konieczny, "Enterprise Level Security," *Proceedings of the 35th MILCOM Conference*, pp. 31–36, MILCOM 2016 Track 3 - Cyber Security and Trusted Computing, Baltimore, MD, November 2016. http://ieeexplore.ieee.org/document/7795297/.

[51] William R. Simpson and Kevin E. Foltz, "The Virtual Application Data Center," *Proceedings of the Information Security Solutions Europe (ISSE) 2016*, pp. 43–59, Paris, France, November 2016, ISBN: 9781541211445. https://www.amazon.com/isse2016-3-Information-Security-Solutions-Europe/dp/1541211448.

[52] William R. Simpson and Kevin E. Foltz, "Digital Key Management for Access Control of Electronic Records," *IAENG International Journal of Computer Science*, Volume 43, Number 4, pp. 411–426, December 2016.

[53] William R. Simpson and Kevin E. Foltz, "High Assurance Asynchronous Messaging Methods," in Haeng Kon Kim and Mahyar A. Amouzegar (eds.), *Transactions on Engineering Technologies, Special Issue of the World Congress on Engineering 2015*, Chapter 15, pp. 205–220, Springer, Dordrecht, 2017. doi: 10.1007/978-981-10-2717-8.

[54] William R. Simpson and Kevin E. Foltz, "Ports and Protocols Extended Control for Security," *IAENG International Journal of Computer Science*, Volume 44, Number 2, pp. 227–240, June 2017, ISSN: 1819-656X.

[55] William R. Simpson and Kevin E. Foltz, Lecture Notes in Engineering and Computer Science, "Assured Identity for Enterprise Level Security," *Proceedings of the World Congress on Engineering (WCE) 2017*, pp. 440–445, Imperial College, London, July 2017, IBSN: 978-988-14047-4-9.

[56] Kevin E. Foltz and William R. Simpson, "Data Mediation with Enterprise Level Security," *Proceedings of the 21th World Multi-Conference on Systemics, Cybernetics and Informatics: WMSCI, WMSCI 2017*, Orlando, FL, 8–11 July 2017.

[57] William R. Simpson and Kevin E. Foltz, "Escalation of Access and Privilege with Enterprise Level Security," *Proceedings of the 22nd International Command and Control Research and Technology Symposium (ICCRTS)*, Los Angeles, CA, September 2017, ISBN: 978-0-9997246-0-6.

[58] William R. Simpson and Kevin E. Foltz, Lecture Notes in Engineering and Computer Science, "Enterprise Level Security: Insider Threat Counter-Claims," *Proceedings World Congress on Engineering and Computer Science (WCECS) 2017*, Volume 1, pp. 112–117, Berkeley, CA, October 2017.

[59] William R. Simpson and Kevin E. Foltz, "Ports and Protocols for Enterprise Level Security," in Sio-Long Ao, et al. (eds.), *IAENG Transactions on Engineering Sciences, Special Issue of the Association of Engineers Conferences 2016*, Volume II, pp. 447–460, World Scientific Publishing, Singapore, 2018, ISBN 978-981-3230-76-7.

[60] William R. Simpson and Kevin E. Foltz, "Electronic Record Key Management for Digital Rights Management," in Sio-Long Ao, et al. (eds.), *IAENG Transactions on Engineering Sciences, Special Issue of the Association of Engineers Conferences 2016*, Volume II, pp. 475–488, World Scientific Publishing, Singapore, 2018, ISBN 978-981-3230-76-7.

[61] William R. Simpson and Kevin E. Foltz, "Secure Identity for Enterprises," *IAENG International Journal of Computer Science*, Volume 45, Number 1, pp. 142–152, February 2018, ISSN: 1819-656X.

[62] Kevin E. Foltz and William R. Simpson, "Extending CryptDB to Operate an ERP System on Encrypted Data," *Proceedings of the 20th International Conference on Enterprise Information Systems (ICEIS* 2018), Volume 1, pp. 103–110, SCITEPRESS – Science and Technology Publications, March 2018, ISBN: 978-989-758-298-1. doi: 10.5220/0006661701030110.

[63] William R. Simpson and Kevin E. Foltz, Lecture Notes in Engineering and Computer Science, "Enterprise End-Point Device Management," *Proceedings of the World Congress on Engineering (WCE) 2018*, pp. 331–336, Imperial College, London, 4–6 July 2018, IBSN: 978-988-14047-9-4, ISSN: 2078-0958.

[64] Kevin E. Foltz and William R. Simpson, "Delegation of Digital Access and Privilege in a Secure Enterprise," *Proceedings of the 22th World Multi-Conference on Systemics, Cybernetics and Informatics: WMSCI, WMSCI 2018*, Volume 1, pp. 125–132, Orlando, FL, 8–11 July 2018.

[65] William R. Simpson and Kevin E. Foltz, "Cloud Security Impact on Scalability," *Proceedings of the 8th International Conference on Electronics, Communications and Networks (CECNet 2018), Volume 1*, p. 27, Bangkok, Thailand, November 2018.

[66] William R. Simpson and Kevin E. Foltz, "Insider Threat Metrics in Enterprise Level Security," *IAENG International Journal of Computer Science*, Volume 45, Number 4, pp. 610–622, December 2018, ISSN: 1819-656X.

[67] William R. Simpson and Kevin E. Foltz, "Insider Threat Veracity Issues," in Sio-Long Ao, et al. (eds.), *Transactions on Engineering Technologies, Special Issue of the World Congress on Engineering 2017*, Chapter 21, pp. 303–315, Springer Nature Singapore Pte Ltd, 2019. doi: 10.1007/978-981-13-2191-7.

[68] William R. Simpson and Kevin E. Foltz, "Message in a Bottle - Content Object Uniqueness for Attribution," *Proceedings of the Digital Image & Signal Processing (DISP'19)*, Oxford, UK, April 2019.

[69] William R. Simpson and Kevin E. Foltz, "Managing Enterprise End-Point Devices," in Sio-Long Ao, et al. (eds.), *IAENG Transactions on Engineering Sciences, Special Issue of the International Association of Engineers World Congress of Engineering (WCE) 2018*, Chapter 15, pp. 262–276, Springer, Dordrecht, 2019. doi: 10.1007/978-981-10-2717-8.

[70] William R. Simpson and Kevin E. Foltz "Enterprise Mobile Ad-Hoc Implementation," in Sio-Long Ao, et al. (eds.), *IAENG Transactions on Engineering Sciences, Special Issue of the World Congress of Engineering and Computer Science 2018*, p. 22, 15 pp., Springer, Dordrecht, 2019.

[71] William R. Simpson and Kevin E. Foltz, "Secure Enterprise Mobile Ad-Hoc Networks," *IAENG International Journal of Computer Science*, Volume 46, Number 2, pp. 243–256, June 2019, ISSN: 1819-656X.

[72] Kevin E. Foltz and William R. Simpson, Lecture Notes in Engineering and Computer Science, "Maintaining High Assurance in Asynchronous Messaging," *Proceedings World Congress on Engineering and Computer Science 2015*, Volume 1, pp. 178–183, Berkeley, CA, October 2015.

[73] William R. Simpson, and Kevin E. Foltz, Lecture Notes in Engineering and Computer Science, "Mobile Ad-Hoc for Enterprise Level Security," *Proceedings of the World Congress on Engineering and Computer Science 2018*, pp. 172–177, San Francisco, CA, 23–25 October 2018.

[74] X.509 Standards
  a) DoDI 8520.2, Public Key Infrastructure (PKI) and Public Key (PK) Enabling, 24 May 2011.

b) JTF-GNO CTO 06-02, Tasks for Phase I of PKI Implementation, 17 January 2006.
c) X.509, Certificate Policy for the United States Department of Defense, Version 9.0, 9 February 2005.
d) FPKI-Prof Federal PKI X.509, Certificate and CRL Extensions Profile, Version 6, 12 October 2005.
e) RFC Internet X.509, Public Key Infrastructure: Certification Path Building, 2005.
f) Public Key Cryptography Standard, PKCS #1 v2.2: RSA Cryptography Standard, RSA Laboratories, 27 October 2012.
g) PKCS#12 format PKCS #12 v1.0: Personal Information Exchange Syntax Standard, RSA Laboratories, June 1999, http://www.rsa.com/rsalabs/node.asp?id =2138; PKCS 12 Technical Corrigendum 1, RSA Laboratories, February 2000.

[75] TLS Family Internet Engineering Task Force (IETF) Standards
a) RFC 2830, Lightweight Directory Access Protocol (v3): Extension for Transport Layer Security, May 2000.
b) RFC 3749, Transport Layer Security Protocol Compression Methods, May 2004.
c) RFC 4279, Pre-Shared Key Ciphersuites for Transport Layer Security (TLS), December 2005.
d) RFC 5246, The Transport Layer Security (TLS) Protocol Version 1.2, August 2008.
e) RFC 5289, TLS Elliptic Curve Cipher Suites with SHA-256/384 and AES Galois Counter Mode (GCM), August 2008.
f) RFC 5929, Channel Bindings for TLS, July 2010.
g) RFC6358, Additional Master Secret Inputs TLS, January 2012.
h) RFC 7251, AES-CCM Elliptic Curve Cryptography (ECC) Cipher Suites for TLS, June 2014.
i) RFC 7301, Transport Layer Security (TLS) Application-Layer Protocol Negotiation Extension, July 2014.
j) RFC 7457, Summarizing Known Attacks on Transport Layer Security (TLS) and Datagram TLS (DTLS), February 2015.

[76] Organization for the Advancement of Structured Information Standards (OASIS) Open Set of Standards
a) N. Ragouzis et al., Security Assertion Markup Language (SAML) V2.0 Technical Overview. OASIS Committee Draft, March 2008.
b) P. Mishra et al., Conformance Requirements for the OASIS Security Assertion Markup Language (SAML) V2.0. OASIS Standard, March 2005.
c) S. Cantor et al., Assertions and Protocols for the OASIS Security Assertion Markup Language (SAML) V2.0. OASIS Standard, March 2005.

[77] William List and Rob Melville, IFIP Working Group 11.5, Integrity in Information, Computers and Security, Volume 13, Number 4, pp. 295–301, Elsevier, 1994. doi: 10.1016/0167-4048(94)90018-3.

[78] J. W. Butts, R. F. Mills, and R. O. Baldwin, Lecture Notes in Computer Science, "Developing an Insider Threat Model Using Functional Decomposition," in V. Gorodetsky, I. Kotenko, and V. Skormin, (eds.), *Computer Network Security*, Volume 3685, pp. 412–417, Springer, Berlin/Heidelberg, 2005. doi: 10.1007/1156032632.

[79] R. Chinchani, A. Iyer, H. Q. Ngo, and S. Upadhyaya, "Towards a Theory of Insider Threat Assessment," *Proceedings of the* 2005 *International Conference on Dependable Systems and Networks (DSN'05)*, pp. 108–117, Yokohama, Japan, IEEE, June–July 2005.

[80] ITU-T Recommendation X.509: Information Technology – Open Systems Interconnection - The Directory: Public-Key and Attribute Certificate Frameworks. http://www.itu.int/rec/T-REC-X.509/en.

[81] CNSSI 1300, Public Key Infrastructure X.509 Certificate Policy Under CNSS Policy No. 25, 19 December 2014.

[82] CNSSP 25, National Policy for Public Key Infrastructure in National Security Systems, 1 March 2009.

[83] DoDI 8520.02, Public Key Infrastructure (PKI) and Public Key (PK) Enabling. https://www.esd.whs.mil/Portals/54/Documents/DD/issuances/dodi/852002p.pdf, May 2011.

[84] Merriam Webster online dictionary for identity. http://www.learnersdictionary.com/definition/identity.

[85] Lily May Newman, "Massive Bug May Have Leaked User Data from Millions of Sites. So…Change Your Passwords," *Wired*, February 24, 2017.

[86] Nate Lord, "What Is Cloud Account Hijacking?" *The Guardian*, September 28, 2015.

[87] Imperva, "Man in the Cloud (MITC) Attacks," *Hacker Intelligence Initiative*, 2015.

[88] A. J. Duncan, S. Creese, and M. Goldsmith, "Insider Attacks in Cloud Computing," *IEEE 11th International Conference on Trust, Security and Privacy in Computing and Communications*, pp. 857–862, Liverpool, 2012. doi: 10.1109/TrustCom.2012.188.

[89] Marco Ortisi, "Recover a RSA Private Key from a TLS Session with Perfect Forward Secrecy," *Black Hat USA 2016*, Las Vegas, August 2016.

[90] "CVE-2015-5464." Common Vulnerabilities and Exposures (CVE), 2015, Web, The MITRE Corporation, 23 May 2017.

[91] Brendan Dolan-Gavitt, T. Leek, J. Hodosh, and W. Lee, "Tappan Zee (North) Bridge: Mining Memory Accesses for Introspection," *Proceedings of the ACM Conference on Computer and Communications Security (CCS)*, Berlin, Germany, 4–8 November 2013.

[92] Craig Gentry, "A Fully Homomorphic Encryption Scheme." Doctoral thesis. Stanford, CA, Stanford University, 2009.

[93] Andrew Chi-Chih Yao, "How to Generate and Exchange Secrets (Extended Abstract)," *27th IEEE Symposium on Foundations of Computer Science (FOCS)*, Toronto, ON, pp. 162–167, IEEE Computer Society Press, October 1986.

[94] Amazon Web Services (AWS), "AWS CloudHSM." https://aws.amazon.com/cloudhsm/.

[95] Microsoft Inc., "Azure Dedicated HSM." https://azure.microsoft.com/en-us/services/azure-dedicated-hsm/.

[96] Google Inc., "Cloud Key Management Service." https://cloud.google.com/kms/.

[97] Virgil Gligor and Maverick Woo, "Establishing Software Root of Trust Unconditionally," *Network and Distributed Systems Security (NDSS) Symposium* 2019, San Diego, CA, 24–27 February 2019. doi: 10.14722/ndss.2019.23170.

[98] Personal Discussions with Representative of Thales, *ISSE Conference*, Brussels, Belgium, 6–7 November, 2018.

[99] Personal Discussions with Representatives of Major HSM Providers, *RSA Conference*, San Francisco, CA, 4–8 March 2019.

[100] Personal Discussions with Representatives of Major HSM Providers, *BlackHat*, Las Vegas, NV, 7–8 August 2019.

[101] Apple Inc., "iOS Security, iOS 12.3." May 2019. https://www.apple.com/business/docs/site/iOS_Security_Guide.pdf.

[102] Microsoft Inc., "Trusted Platform Module Technology Overview." 29 November 2018, https://docs.microsoft.com/en-us/windows/security/information-protection/tpm/trusted-platform-module-overview.

[103] Nathan Ingraham, "Senator Confirms FBI Paid $900,000 to Unlock San Bernardino iPhone," Engadget, May 8, 2017. https://www.engadget.com/2017/05/08/fbi-paid-900000-to-unlock-san-bernardino-iphone/.

[104] Virgil D. Gligor, "Homomorphic Computations in Secure System Design," *Final Report*. Pittsburgh, PA: Carnegie Mellon University, 2014.

[105] Virgil D. Gligor and Pompiliu Donescu, "Design Services for Encrypted Database Systems," *Final Report*, Pittsburgh, PA: Carnegie Mellon University, 2017.

[106] Richard Chirgwin, "IBM's Homomorphic Encryption Accelerated to Run 75 Times Faster," *The Register*, March 8, 2018. https://www.theregister.co.uk/2018/03/08/ibm_faster_homomorphic_encryption/.

[107] Alireza Pirayesh Sabzevar and Angelos Stavrou, "Universal Multi-Factor Authentication Using Graphical Passwords," *IEEE International Conference on Signal Image Technology and Internet Based Systems, 2008. SITIS '08*, Bali, Indonesia, IEEE, 2008.

[108] Gordon, Whitson, "Two-Factor Authentication: The Big List of Everywhere You Should Enable It Right Now," *LifeHacker*, Australia, 3 September 2012. Retrieved 1 November 2012.

[109] Leslie Lamport, "Password Authentication with Insecure Communication," *Communications of the ACM*, Volume 24, Number 11, pp. 770–772, 1981.

[110] Dena Terry Bauckman, Nigel Paul Johnson, and David Joseph Robertson, "Multi-Factor Authentication," U.S. Patent No. 20, 130, 055, 368, 28 February 2013.

[111] Bhargav-Spantzel, Abhilasha, et al., "Privacy Preserving Multifactor Authentication with Biometrics," *Journal of Computer Security*, Volume 15, Number 5, pp. 529–560, 2007.

[112] Fadi Aloul, Syed Zahidi, and Wassim El-Hajj, "Two Factor Authentication Using Mobile Phones," *IEEE/ACS International Conference on Computer Systems and Applications, 2009*, AICCSA 2009, IEEE, 2009.

[113] Bruce Schneier, "The Failure of Two-Factor Authentication," March 2005. https://www.schneier.com/blog/archives/2012/ 02/the_failure_of_2.html.

[114] Mohammed Alzomai, Bander AlFayyadh, and A. Josang, "Display Security for Online Transactions: SMS-Based Authentication Scheme," *2010 International Conference for Internet Technology and Secured Transactions (ICITST)*, London, UK, 8–10 November2010.

[115] "ISO/IEC 11889-1:2009 – Information Technology – Trusted Platform Module – Part 1: Overview," ISO.org. International Organization for Standardization, May 2009.

[116] Bill Gertz, "The Cyber Threat: Snowden—Ultimate Insider Threat Missed by NSA Security," *The Washington Free Beacon*, 20 September 2016. http://freebeacon.com/national-security/cyber-threat-snowden-insider-threat-at-nsa/, accessed on 17 April 2017.

[117] Steve Fishman, "Bradley Manning's Army of One," *New York Magazine*, 3 July 2011. http://nymag.com/news/features/bradley-manning-2011-7/, accessed on 17 April 2017.

[118] Ryan Francis, "9 Employee Insiders Who Breached Security," *CSO Online*, 6 October 2014. http://www.csoonline.com/article/2692072/data-protection/data-protection-165097-disgruntled-employees-lash-out.html, accessed on 17 April 2017.

[119] Wikipedia, "Insider Threat", October 2016. https://en.wikipedia.org/wiki/Insider_threat.

[120] Barack Obama, "Executive Order 13587 – Structural Reforms to Improve the Security of Classified Networks and the Responsible Sharing and Safeguarding of Classified Information," The White House, Office of the Press Secretary, October 7, 2011.

[121] Ann Margaret Strosaker and Michael Thomas Strosaker, "Determining Veracity of Data in a Repository Using a Semantic Network," US 8108410 B2, International Business Machines Corporation, 31 January 2012. https://www.google.com/patents/US8108410, accessed on 17 April 2017.

[122] Geoffrey Lee, "Candidate-Initiated Background Check and Verification," US 20050055231 A1, published March 10, 2005. http://www.google.com/patents/US20050055231, last accessed on 19 May 2020.

[123] Eileen Shapiro and Steven Mintz, "System and Method for Providing Access to Verified Personal Background Data," US 20040168080 A1, 26 August 2004. http://www.google.com/patents/US20040168080.

[124] Yu Zhao and Jianqiang Li, "Hierarchy Extraction from the Websites," US 20090327338 A1, Nec (China) Co., Limited, 31 December 2009. https://www.google.com/patents/US20090327338.

[125] J. Hunker and C. W. Probst, "Insiders and Insider Threats – An Overview of Definitions and Mitigation Techniques," *Journal of Wireless Mobile Networks, Ubiquitous Computing, and Dependable Applications (JoWUA)*, Volume 2, pp. 4–27, 2011.

[126] Wikipedia, "Integrity." https://en.wikipedia.org/wiki/Integrity, last edited 4 May 2020, last accessed on 19 May 2020.

[127] Dictionary.com, "Reputation." http://www.dictionary.com/browse/reputation, accessed on November 2016.

[128] Gerrit J. van der Geest and Carmen de Ruijter Korver, Microsoft, "Managing Identity Trust for Access Control," The Architecture Journal, pp. 12–17, July 2008. https://blogs.msdn.microsoft.com/nickmac/2009/05/21/the-architecture-journal/.

[129] Merriam-Webster, "Veracity," http://www.merriam-webster.com/dictionary/veracity, accessed on November 2016.

[130] The Channel Co., CRN Staff, "How to Avoid the Five Biggest BYOD Mistakes," *CRN Magazine*. https://www.crn.com/blogs-op-ed/channel-voices/240006736/how-to-avoid-the-five-biggest-byod-mistakes.htm, accessed on 26 June 2018.

[131] William Long, "BYOD: Data Protection and Information Security Issues," *Computer Weekly*. https://www.computerweekly.com/opinion/BYOD-data-protection-and-information-security-issues, accessed on 26 June 2018.

[132] South Carolina Enterprise Information System (SCEIS), "SCEIS Data Cleansing General Guidelines." http://sceis.sc.gov/documents/data_cleansing_guidelines_v2.doc, accessed on 26 June 2018.

[133] Wikipedia, "Digital Subscriber Line." https://en.wikipedia.org/wiki/Digital_subscriber_line, accessed on 9/1/2015.

[134] RFC 2516, A Method for Transmitting PPP Over Ethernet (PPPoE), February 1999. http://tools.ietf.org/html/rfc2516.

[135] Liu, Ranganathan, and Riabov, "Specifying and Enforcing High-Level Semantic Obligation Policies," *Eighth IEEE International Workshop on Policies for Distributed Systems and Networks (POLICY'07)*, Bologna, Italy, pp. 119–128, 2007.

[136] Walt Yao, Lecture Notes in Computer Science, "*Fidelis*: A Policy-Driven Trust Management Framework," *First International Conference on Trust Management, iTrust*, Volume 2692, pp. 301–317, Heraklion, Crete, Greece, Springer, 2003.

[137] He Wang and Sylvia L. Osborn, "Delegation in the Role Graph Model," *Proceedings of the Eleventh ACM Symposium on Access Control Models and Technologies*, Lake Tahoe, CA, 07–09 June 2006.

[138] Longhua Zhang, Gail-Joon Ahn, and Bei-Tseng Chu, "A Rule-Based Framework for Role-Based Delegation and Revocation," *ACM Transactions on Information and System Security (TISSEC)*, Volume 6, Number 3, pp. 404–441, August 2003.

[139] James B. D. Joshi and Elisa Bertino, "Fine-Grained Role-Based Delegation in Presence of the Hybrid Role Hierarchy," *Proceedings of the Eleventh ACM Symposium on Access Control Models and Technologies*, Lake Tahoe, CA, 07–09 June 2006.

[140] Jacques Wainer and Akhil Kumar, "A Fine-Grained, Controllable, User-to-User Delegation Method in RBAC," *Proceedings of the Tenth ACM Symposium on Access Control Models and Technologies*, Stockholm, Sweden, 01–03 June 2005.

[141] Roberto Tamassia, Danfeng Yao, and William H. Winsborough, "Role-Based Cascaded Delegation," *Proceedings of the Ninth ACM Symposium on Access Control Models and Technologies*, Yorktown Heights, NY, 02–04 June 2004.

[142] Xinwen Zhang, Sejong Oh, and Ravi Sandhu, "PBDM: A Flexible Delegation Model in RBAC," *Proceedings of the Eighth ACM Symposium on Access Control Models and Technologies*, Como, Italy, 02–03 June 2003.

[143] JongSoon Park, YoungLok Lee, HyungHyo Lee, and BongNam Noh, "A Role-Based Delegation Model Using Role Hierarchy Supporting Restricted Permission Inheritance," *Proceedings of the International Conference on Security and Management, SAM '03*, pp. 294–302, CSREA Press, 2003.

[144] Jean Bacon, Ken Moody, and Walt Yao, "A Model of OASIS Role-Based Access Control and Its Support for Active Security," *ACM Transactions on Information and System Security (TISSEC)*, Volume 5, Number 4, pp. 492–540, November 2002.

[145] E. Barka and R. Sandhu, "Framework for Role-Based Delegation Models," *Proceedings of the 16th Annual*; Ezedin S. Barka and Ravi Sandhu, "A Role-Based Delegation Model and Some Extensions." *23rd National Information Systems Security Conference*, October 2000. http://csrc.nist.gov/nissc/2000/proceedings/papers/021.pdf.

[146] Ravi Sandhu and Qamar Munawer, "The ARBAC99 Model for Administration of Roles," *Proceedings of the 15th Annual Computer Security Applications Conference*, Los Alamitos, CA, p. 229, 06–10 December 1999.

[147] Cheh Goh and Adrian Baldwin, "Towards a More Complete Model of Role," *Proceedings of the Third ACM Workshop on Role-Based Access Control*, pp. 55–62, Fairfax, VA, 22–23 October 1998.

[148] Ravi S. Sandhu, Edward J. Coyne, Hal L. Feinstein, and Charles E. Youman, "Role-Based Access Control Models," *Computer*, Volume 29, Number 2, pp. 38–47, February 1996.

[149] Jacques Wainer, Paulo Barthelmess, and Akhil Kumar, "WRBAC - A Workflow Security Model Incorporating Controlled Overriding of Constraints," *International Journal of Cooperative Information Systems*, Volume 12, Number 4, pp. 455–486, 2003.

[150] Jacques Wainer, Akhil Kumar, and Paulo Barthelmess, "DW-RBAC: A Formal Security Model of Delegation and Revocation in Workflow Systems," *Information Systems*, Volume 32, Number 3, pp. 365–384, May 2007.

[151] Chun Ruan and Vijay Varadharajan, "Resolving Conflicts in Authorization Delegations," *Proceedings of the 7th Australian Conference on Information Security and Privacy*, Wollongong, NSW, Australia, pp. 271–285, 03–05 July 2002.

[152] Vijayalakshmi Atluri and Avigdor Gal, "An Authorization Model for Temporal and Derived Data: Securing Information Portals," *ACM Transactions on Information and System Security (TISSEC)*, Volume 5, Number 1, pp. 62–94, February 2002.

[153] Åsa Hagström, Sushil Jajodia, Francesco Parisi-Presicce, and Duminda Wijesekera, "Revocations-A Classification," *Proceedings of the 14th IEEE Workshop on Computer Security Foundations*, Cape Breton, NS, Canada, p. 44, 11–13 June 2001.

[154] Evgeny Dantsin, Thomas Eiter, Georg Gottlob, and Andrei Voronkov, "Complexity and Expressive Power of Logic Programming," *ACM Computing Surveys (CSUR)*, Volume 33, Number 3, pp. 374–425, September 2001, *Computer Security Applications Conference*, p. 168, 11–15 December 2000.

[155] Ronald Fagin, "On an Authorization Mechanism," *ACM Transactions on Database Systems (TODS)*, Volume 3, Number 3, pp. 310–319, September 1978.

[156] Patricia P. Griffiths and Bradford W. Wade, "An Authorization Mechanism for a Relational Database System," *ACM Transactions on Database Systems (TODS)*, Volume 1, Number 3, pp. 242–255, September 1976.

[157] A. S. M. Kayes, Jun Han, Wenny Rahayu, Md. Saiful Islan, and Alan Colman, "Context-Aware Access Control to Information Resources," 7 March 2017. https://arxiv.org/pdf/1703.02162.pdf.

[158] Antonio Corradi, Rebecca Montanari, and Daniela Tibaldi, "Context-Based Access Control for Ubiquitous Service Provisioning," *Proceedings of the 28th Annual International Computer Software and Applications Conference (COMPSAC '04)*, Hong Kong, 28–30 September 2004.

[159] Michael J. Covington, Wende Long, Srividhya Srinivasan, Anind K. Dey, Mustaque Ahamad, and Gregory D. Abowd, "Securing Context-Aware Applications Using Environment Roles," *Proceedings of the Sixth ACM Symposium on Access Control Models and Technologies (SACMAT'01)*, Chantilly, VA, 3–4 May 2001.

[160] Gustaf Neumann and Mark Strembeck, "An Approach to Engineer and Enforce Context Constraints in an RBAC Environment," *Proceedings of the Eighth ACM Symposium on Access Control Models and Technologies (SACMAT'03)*, Como, Italy, 2–3 June 2003.

[161] Geetanjali Sampemane, Prasad Naldurg, and Roy H. Campbell, "Access Control for Active Spaces," *ACSAC'02*, Las Vegas, NV, 9–13 December 2002.

[162] Devdatta Kulkarni and Anand Tripathi, "Context-Aware Role-Based Access Control in Pervasive Computing Systems," *Proceedings of the Thirteenth ACM Symposium on Access Control Models and Technologies (SACMAT'08)*, 11–13 June 2008, Estes Park, CO.

[163] Sigrid Schefer-Wenzl and Mark Strembeck, "Modelling Context-Aware RBAC Models for Mobile Business Processes," *International Journal of Wireless and Mobile Computing*, Volume 6, Number. 5, pp. 448–462, 2013.

[164] Elisa Bertino, Piero Andrea Bonatti, and Elena Ferrari, "TRBAC: A Temporal Role-Based Access Control Model," *ACM Transactions on Information and System Security*, Volume 4, Number 3, pp. 191–223, August 2001.

[165] J. B. D. Joshi, E. Bertino, U. Latif, and A. Ghafoor, "A Generalized Temporal Role-Based Access Control Model," *IEEE Transactions on Knowledge and Data Engineering*, Volume 17, Number 1, pp. 4–23, January 17 2005.

[166] Elisa Bertino, Barbara Catania, Maria Luisa Damiani, and Paolo Perlasca, "GEO-RBAC: A Spatially Aware RBAC," *Proceedings of the Tenth ACM Symposium on Access Control Models and Technologies (SACMAT'05)*, pp. 29–37, Stockholm, Sweden, 1–3 June 2005.

[167] Suroop Mohan Chandran and J. B. D. Joshi, "LoT-RBAC: A Location and Time-Based RBAC Model," *Proceedings of the 6th International Conference on Web Information Systems Engineering (WISE'05)*, pp. 361–375, New York, NY, 20–22 November 2005.

[168] James B. D. Joshi, Elisa Bertino, Usman Latif, and Arif Ghafoor, "A Generalized Temporal Role-Based Access Control Model," *IEEE Transactions on Knowledge and Data Engineering*, Volume 17, Number 1, pp. 4–23, January 2005.

[169] Shohreh Hosseinzadeh, Seppo Virtanen, Natalia Diaz-Rodriguez, and Johan Lilius, "A Semantic Security Framework and Context-Aware Role-Based Access Control Ontology for Smart Spaces," *Proceedings of the International Workshop on Semantic Big Data (SBD'16)*, San Francisco, CA, 26 June–1 July 2016.

[170] Michal Trnka and Tomas Cerny, "On Security Level Usage in Context-Aware Role-Based Access Control," *Proceedings of the 31st Annual ACM Symposium on Applied Computing (SAC'16)*, pp. 1192–5, Pisa, Italy, 4–8 April 2016.

[171] J. Bacon, K. Moody, and W. Yao, "A Model of OASIS Role-Based Access Control and Its Support for Active Security," *ACM Transactions on Information and System Security (TISSEC)*, Volume 5, Number 4, pp. 492–540, 2002.

[172] "Break Glass Procedure: Granting Emergency Access to Critical ePHI Systems," Yale University. http://hipaa.yale.edu/security/break-glass-procedure-granting-emergency-access-critical-ephi-systems.

[173] "Emergency Access Procedures," University of Iowa College of Public Health, 18 December 2013. https://www.public-health.uiowa.edu/emergency-access-procedures/.

[174] J. F. Ebert, L. Huibers, F. K. Lippert, B. Christensen, and M. B. Christensen, "Development and Evaluation of an 'Emergency Access Button' in Danish Out-of-Hours Primary Case: A Study Protocol of a Randomized Controlled Trial," *BMC Health Service Research*, Volume 17, pp. 379, 31 May 2017. doi:10.1186/s12913-017-2308-y.

[175] "Security Standards: Technical Safeguards," *HIPAA Security Series*, Volume 2, Paper 4, Health and Human Services, Health Insurance Portability and Accountability Act, May 2005. https://www.hhs.gov/sites/default/files/ocr/privacy/hipaa/administrative/securityrule/techsafeguards.pdf.

[176] Guowei Wu, Dongze Lu, and Lin Yao, "A Fault-Tolerant Emergency-Aware Access Control Scheme for Cyber-Physical Systems," *Information Technology and Control*, Volume 40, Number 1, pp. 29–40, 2011.

[177] Aimee Goodsall, LINNWORKS, 2018. What are Product Identifiers & GTIN'S? LINNWORKS BLOG. http://blog.linnworks.com/what-are-product-identifiers, accessed on 14 September 2018.

[178] U.S. Department of Health and Human Services, Food and Drug Administration, "Product Identifier Requirements Under the Drug Supply Chain Security Act – Compliance Policy Guidance for Industry," *Draft Guidance*, 2017. https://www.fda.gov/downloads/Drugs/GuidanceComplianceRegulatoryInformation/Guidances/UCM565272.pdf, accessed on 14 September 2018.

[179] Sarah Fister Gale, "Innovations in Traceability Systems and Product ID Tools," *Food Safety Magazine*, Tech Trends, January 2006. https://www.foodsafetymagazine.com/magazine-archivel/december-2005january-2006/innovations-in-traceability-systems-and-product-id-tools/, accessed on 14 September 2018.

[180] BBC News, Technology, "Suspects Behind Expendables 3 Leak Arrested in UK," November 2014. https://www.bbc.com/news/technology-30192568, accessed on 14 September 2018.

[181] R. Gennaro, C. Gentry, and B. Parno, "Non-Interactive Verifiable Computing: Outsourcing Computation to Untrusted Workers," *Proceedings of the 30th Annual Conference on Advances in Cryptology*, Santa Barbara, CA, 2010.

[182] C. Gentry, S. Halevi, and N. Smart, "Homomorphic Evaluation of the AES Circuit," *Advances in Cryptology - CRYPTO 2012*, Santa Barbara, CA, 19–23 August 2012, pp. 850–8, Springer, 2012.

[183] J. H. Cheon, J. Coron, J. Kim, M. S. Lee, T. Lepoint, M. Tibouchi, and A. Yun, "Batch Fully Homomorphic Encryption Over the Integers," in T. P. Johansson and Q. Nguyen (eds.), *EUROCRYPT 2013. LNCS*, pp. 315–335, Volume 7881, Springer, Heidelberg, 2013.

[184] Y. Doroz, Y. Hu, and B. Sunar, "Homomorphic AES Evaluation Using NTRU," *Cryptology ePrint Archive*, Report 2014/039, 2014.

[185] K. Lauter, M. Naehrig, and V. Vaikuntanathan, "Can Homomorphic Encryption Be Practical?" in C. Cachin and T. Ristenpart (eds.), *CCSW '11*, Chicago, IL, October, 2011, pp. 113–124, ACM, 2011.

[186] W. Joppe, K. Lauter, J. Loftus, and M. Naehrig, Lecture Notes in Computer Science, "Improved Security for a Ring-Based Fully Homomorphic Encryption Scheme," *Fifth International Conference on Post-Quantum Cryptography*, Limoges, France, last update 24 June 2013, *PQCrypto*, pp. 45–64, Springer, 2013.

[187] A. Acar, H. Aksu, A. S. Uluagac, and M. A. Conti, "Survey on Homomorphic Encryption Schemes: Theory and Implementation," *arXiv preprint arXiv:1704.03578v1*, 12 April 2017.

[188] R. A. Popa, C. M. S. Redfield, N. Zeldovich, and H. Balakrishnan, "CryptDB: Processing Queries on an Encrypted Database," *Communications of the ACM*, Volume 55, Number 9, September 2012 (also *Proc. of 23rd ACM SoSP*, September 2011).

[189] I. H. Akin and S. Berk, "On the Difficulty of Securing Web Applications Using CryptDB," *International Association for Cryptologic Research*, 2015. https://eprint.iacr.org/2015/082.

[190] Z. N. Dayıoğlu, "Secure Database in Cloud Computing: CryptDB Revisited," *International Journal of Information Security Science*, Volume 3, Number 1, pp. 129–147, 2015.

[191] M. Naveed, S. Kamara, and C. V. Wright, "Inference Attacks on Property-Preserving Encrypted Databases." *CCS'15, Proceedings of the 22nd ACM SIGSAC Conference on Computer and Communications Security*, Denver, CO, October 2015, pp. 644–655, https://doi.org/10.1145/2810103.2813651.

[192] S. Wang, D. Agrawal, and A. E. Abbadi, "Is Homomorphic Encryption the Holy Grail for Database Queries on Encrypted Data?" *Technical Report*, Department of Computer Science, University of California Santa Barbara, 2012.

[193] S. Tu, M. F. Kaashoek, S. Madden, and N. Zeldovich, "Processing Analytical Queries Over Encrypted Data," *Proceedings of the 39th International Conference on Very Large Data Bases (PVLDB'13), VLDB Endowment, Part I*, Michael Böhlen and Christoph Koch (Eds.), Santa Barbara, CA, 18–22 August 2013, pp. 289–300.

[194] J. Li, Z. Liu, X. Chen, F. Xhafa, X. Tan, and D. S. Wong, "L-encdb: A Lightweight Framework for Privacy-Preserving Data Queries in Cloud Computing," *Knowledge-Based Systems*, Volume 79, pp. 18–26, 2015.

[195] E. Pattuk, M. Kantarcioglu, V. Khadilkar, H. Ulusoy, and S. Mehrotra, "Bigsecret: A Secure Data Management Framework for Key-Value Stores," *International Conference on Cloud Computing*, Bristol, UK, December 2013.

[196] R. Macedo, et al., "A Practical Framework for Privacy-Preserving NoSQL Databases," *2017 IEEE 36th Symposium on Reliable Distributed Systems (SRDS)*, pp. 11–20, Hong Kong, 2017.

[197] R. A. Popa, et al., *CryptDB: Protecting Confidentiality with Encrypted Query Processing*, ACM Press, 2011, 85. doi: 10.1145/2043556.2043566.

[198] M. Varia, S. Yakoubov, and Y. Yang, "HEtest: A Homomorphic Encryption Testing Framework," *Paper Presented at 3rd Workshop on Encrypted Computing and Applied Homomorphic Cryptography*, San Juan, Puerto Rico, 30 January 2015.

[199] R. A. Al-Shibib, "Performance Analysis for Fully and Partially Homomorphic Encryption Techniques," Master's thesis, Middle East University, Amman, Jordan, May 2016.

[200] NIST, NIST Big Data Interoperability Framework (seven volumes), NIST Special Publication 1500-1, NIST Big Data Public Working Group (NBD-PWG) Definitions and Taxonomies Subgroup, Information Technology Laboratory, 2015.

[201] R. Magoulas and B. Lorica, "Introduction to Big Data," Release 2.0, O'Reilly Media, Sebastopol, CA, 2009.

[202] G. Siwach and A. Esmailpour, "Encrypted Search & Cluster Formation in Big Data," *ASEE 2014 Zone I Conference*, University of Bridgeport, Bridgeport, CT, March 2014.

[203] J. Ullman, *First Course in Database Systems*, New Delhi, Prentice–Hall Inc., Simon & Schuster, 1997.

[204] W. Hershey and C. Easthope, "A Set Theoretic Data Structure and Retrieval Language," *Spring Joint Computer Conference, May* 1972 *in ACM SIGIR Forum*, Volume 7, Number 4, pp. 45–55, 1972.

[205] Oracle, "My SQL Stored Programs and Views." http://docs.oracle.com/cd/E19078-01/mysql/mysql-refman-5.0/stored-programs-views.html#stored-routines-syntax, accessed on October 2014.

[206] Purdue, "Using Stored Procedures to Set Views." https://www.cs.purdue.edu/homes/ninghui/projects/Topics/DB_FineGrained.html, accessed on October 2014.

[207] "The OSI Model's Seven Layers Defined and Functions Explained." https://support.microsoft.com/en-us/kb/103884.

[208] "WEP vs WPA Encryption," NETGear Support, http://kb.netgear.com/app/answers/detail/a_id/20043/~/wep-vs-wpa-encryption?cid=wmt_netgear_organic.

[209] Understanding Voice and Data Link Networking, "Northrop Grumman's Guide to Secure Tactical Data Links," http://www.northropgrumman.com/Capabilities/DataLinkProcessingAndManagement/Documents/Understanding_Voice+Data_Link_Networking.pdf.

[210] MANET Definition, http://techterms.com/definition/manet.

[211] S. Ghemawat, H. Gobioff, and S.-T. Leung. The Google filesystem. In SOSP, 2003.

[212] G. Graefe, "Query Evaluation Techniques for Large Databases." *ACM Computer Survey*, Volume 25, Number 2, pp. 73–169, 1993.

[213] J. Hammerbacher, "Managing a Large Hadoop Cluster. Presentation," Facebook Inc., May 2008.

[214] P. Mishra and M. H. Eich, "Join Processing in Relational Databases," *ACM Computer Survey*, Volume 24, Number 1, pp. 63–113, 1992.

[215] C. Olston, B. Reed, U. Srivastava, R. Kumar, and A. Tomkins, "Pig Latin: A Not-So-Foreign Language for Data Processing," *SIGMOD*, Vancouver, Canada, June 2008, pp. 1099–1110, 2008.

[216] Common Access Card (CAC). http://www.cac.mil/common-access-card/.

[217] Trusted Platform Module (TPM) Summary. http://www.trustedcomputinggroup.org/trusted-platform-module-tpm-summary/.

[218] D. A. Schneider and D. J. DeWitt, "A Performance Evaluation of Four Parallel Join Algorithms in a Shared-Nothing Multiprocessor Environment," *SIGMOD*, Portland, OR, June 1989.

[219] IBM Corporation, "Mobile Device Management (MDM)." https://www.ibm.com/security/mobile/maas360/mobile-device-management, last accessed on 18 November, 2017.

[220] AT&T Business, "CYBERSECURITY SOLUTIONS: Mobile Security." https://www.business.att.com/solutions/Family/cybersecurity/mobile-security/, last accessed on 18 November, 2017.

[221] PC Magazine, "The Best Mobile Device Management (MDM) Solutions of 2017." https://www.pcmag.com/article/342695/the-best-mobile-device-management-mdm-software, last accessed on 18 November, 2017.

[222] MindWireless – Strategic Telecom Management, "Enterprise Mobility Management." https://mindwireless.com/services/enterprise-mobility-management, last accessed on 18 November, 2017.

[223] Technical Profiles for the Consolidated Enterprise IT Baseline, release 4.0. Not available to all, https://intelshare.intelink.gov/sites/afceit/TB.

[224] Peter Mell and Timothy Grance, "NIST SP 800-145 Draft: Cloud Computing," Computer Security Division, Information Technology Laboratory, National Institute of Standards and Technology, Gaithersburg, MD, January 2011. http://csrc.nist.gov/publications/drafts/800-145/Draft-SP-800-145_cloud-definition.pdf.

[225] Wayne Jansen and Timothy Grance, "NIST SP 800-144 Draft: Guidelines on Security and Privacy in Public Cloud Computing," Security Division, Information Technology Laboratory, National Institute of Standards and Technology, Gaithersburg, MD, January 2011. http://csrc.nist.gov/publications/drafts/800-144/Draft-SP-800-144_cloud-computing.pdf.

[226] Daniele Catteddu and Giles Hogben, "European Network Information Security Agency (ENISA), Cloud Computing Risk Assessment," November 2009, http://www.enisa.europa.eu/act/rm/files/deliverables/cloud-computing-risk-assessment.

[227] Cloud Security Alliance, Security Guidance for Critical Areas of Focus in Cloud Computing V2.1, December 2009. https://cloudsecurityalliance.org/csaguide.pdf.

[228] Frank Konieczny, Eric Trias, and Nevin Taylor, "SEADE: Countering the Futility of Network Security," *Air and Space Power Journal*, Volume 29, Number 5, p. 4, 2015.
[229] Raymond R. Burke, "Technology and the Customer Interface: What Consumers Want in the Physical and Virtual Store," *Journal of the Academy of Marketing Science*, Volume 30, Number 4, pp. 411–432, 1 September 2002.
[230] Bill Williams, "The Role of Customer Interface in Customer Experience Management," blog 23 May 2013. http://usan.com/omnichannel/the-role-of-customer-interface-in-customer-experience-management/ accessed on 18 June 2018.
[231] TPM Main Specification Version 1.2, Revision 116, 1 March 201, TCG Published. https://trustedcomputinggroup.org/wp-content/uploads/TPM-Main-Part-1-Design-Principles_v1.2_rev116 _01032011.pdf.
[232] H. Ferraiolo, et al., NIST Special Publication 800-157, "Guidelines for Derived Personal Identity Verification (PIV) Credentials," December 2014. doi: 10.6028/NIST.SP.800-157.
[233] IBM Corporation, IBM Security, "Ten Rules for Bring Your Own Device (BYOD) - How to Protect Corporate Data on Personal Devices Used for Work." https://www.slideshare.net/ibmmobile/ten-rules-for-bring-your-own-device-byod, January 2018, accessed on 26 June 2018.
[234] ESET Corporation, "7 Tips to Tighten Mobile Security." https://business.eset.com/bring-your-own-device-security, accessed on 26 June 2018.
[235] Tzur-David, Shimrit, Secret Double Octopus, "Making BYOD Work in the Era of GDPR," 24 April 2018. https://doubleoctopus.com/blog/making-byod-work-in-the-era-of-gdpr/, accessed on 26 June 2018.
[236] "Top POS Systems." https://www.top10bestpossystems.com/, accessed on 26 June 2018.
[237] Software Advice, "What Is a Point of Sale System?" https://www.softwareadvice.com/resources/what-is-a-point-of-sale-system/, accessed on 26 June 2018.
[238] Doug Drinkwater, EMEA content director at IDG, CSO from IDG, "10 Steps for a Successful Incident Response Plan," June 26, 2017. https://www.csoonline.com/article/3203705/security/10-steps-for-a-successful-incident-response-plan.html, accessed on 26 June 2018.
[239] Nate Lord, Digital Guardian, "What Is Incident Response," 28 September 2015. https://digitalguardian.com/blog/what-incident-response, accessed on 26 June 2018.
[240] STOPit, "STOPit Insurance Solutions." http://www.stopitsolutions.com/stopit-solutions-insurance, accessed on 26 June 2018.
[241] Neal McCarthy, Secureworks, "Integrate Cyber-Insurance into Your Cybersecurity Incident Response Plans." https://www.secureworks.com/blog/integrate-cyber-insurance-cybersecurity-incident-response-plans, 16 January 2017, accessed on 26 June 2018.
[242] PC Magazine, Encyclopedia, "Definition of Heartbeat." https://www.pcmag.com/encyclopedia/term/44190/heartbeat, last accessed on 15 November 2017.
[243] James W. Hong, et al., "Enterprise Network Traffic Monitoring, Analysis, and Reporting Using Web Technology," *Journal of Network and Systems Management*, Volume 9, Number 1, 2001.
[244] W. Stallings, *SNMP, SNMPv2, SNMPv3, and RMON 1 and 2*, Third Edition, California, Addison-Wesley, 1999.
[245] Hiroshi Tohjo, Tetsuya Yamamura, and Tetsuaki Goto. "ITU-T Recommendation X. 711| ISO/IEC 9596-1: 1991 (E), Information Technology-Open Systems Interconnection-Common Management Inf ITU-T Recommendation X. 711| ISO/IEC 9596-1: 1991 (E), Information Technology-Open Systems Interconnection-Common Management Inf, 1992," *IEICE Transactions on Communications*, Volume 80, Number 10, pp. 1421–1428, 1997.

[246] Techopedia Home Dictionary Tags, "Bricking-Definition and Explanation." https://www.techopedia.com/definition/24221/bricking, last accessed on 15 November 2017.

[247] TechTarget Search Mobile Computing, "Remote Wipe." http://searchmobilecomputing.techtarget.com/definition/remote-wipe, last accessed on 15 November 2017.

[248] Mathew J. Schwartz, "Attacks Targeting IoT Devices and Windows SMB Surge," Bank Info Security. https://www.bankinfosecurity.com/attacks-targeting-iot-devices-windows-smb-surge-a-13082, last accessed on 10 October 2019.

[249] Alf Inge Wang, Carl-Fredrik Sørensen, and Eva Indal, "A Mobile Agent Architecture for Heterogeneous Devices," Dept. of Computer and Information Science, Norwegian University of Science and Technology, N-7491 Trondheim, Norway, 2003. https://pdfs.semanticscholar.org/874b/20fbd73f5c598c8032db0c6c9e5708bc7cec.pdf, last accessed on 10 October 2019.

[250] Alexander Assink, "The Potential of Agent Architectures," 2016. https://dzone.com/articles/the-potential-of-agent-architectures.

[251] S. Berkovits, J. D. Guttman and V. Swarup, "Authentication for Mobile Agents," in G. Vigna (eds.), *Mobile Agents and Security*, Lecture Notes in Computer Science, Volume 1419, Springer, Berlin/Heidelberg, 1998.

[252] V. Varadharajan and David Foster, "A Security Architecture for Mobile Agent Based Applications." *World Wide Web*, Volume 6, pp. 93–122, 2003. doi: 10.1023/A:1022360516731.

[253] Z. Liu, and Y. Wang, "A Secure Agent Architecture for Sensor Networks," *Proceedings of the International Conference on Artificial Intelligence, IC-AI '03*, 23–26 June, Las Vegas, NV, 2003.

[254] Branislav Šimo, Zoltán Balogh, Ondrej Habala, Ivana Budinská, and Ladislav Hluchý, "Architecture of the Secure Agent Infrastructure for Management of Crisis Situations," Institute of Informatics, Slovak Academy of Sciences, Dúbravská cesta 9, 845 07 Bratislava, Slovakia, 2009. http://www.secricom.eu/images/articles/UISAV_simo_final.pdf.

[255] Trusted Computing Group, "TPM 2.0 Library Specification," 29 September 2016. https://trustedcomputinggroup.org/resource/tpm-library-specification/.

[256] M. Cotton, L. Eggert, J. Touch, M. Westerlund, and S. Cheshire, "Internet Assigned Numbers Authority (IANA) Procedures for the Management of the Service Name and Transport Protocol Port Number Registry," *RFC*, Volume 6335, pp. 1–33, 2011.

[257] Michelle Cotton, Lars Eggert, et al., Internet Assigned Numbers Authority (IANA) Procedures for the Management of the Service Name and Transport Protocol Port Number Registry. IETF. BCP 165. RFC 6335, August 2011. http://tools.ietf.org/html/rfc6335.

[258] RFC 1312, Message Send Protocol, 2 April 1992. http://tools.ietf.org/html/rfc1312.

[259] RFC 2068, Hypertext Transfer Protocol HTTP/1.1, January 1997. http://tools.ietf.org/html/rfc2068.

[260] RFC 1081, Post Office Protocol – Version 3, November 1988. http://tools.ietf.org/html/rfc1081.

[261] RFC 3501, Internet Message Access Protocol – Version 4 rev1, March 2003. http://tools.ietf.org/html/rfc3501.

[262] RFC 3411, An Architecture for Describing Simple Network Management Protocol (SNMP) Management Frameworks, December 2002. http://tools.ietf.org/html/rfc3411.

[263] RFC 1132, A Standard for the Transmission of 802.2 Packets Over IPX Networks, November 1989. http://tools.ietf.org/html/rfc1132.

[264] RFC 2818, HTTP Over TLS, May 2000. http://tools.ietf.org/html/rfc2818.

[265] RFC 6409, Message Submission for Mail, November 2011. http://tools.ietf.org/html/rfc6409.

[266] Adobe Proprietary, H. Parmar and M. Thornburgh (eds.), *Adobe's Real Time Messaging Protocol*, Adobe, 21 December 2012. http://www.adobe.com/content/dam/Adobe/en/devnet/rtmp/pdf/rtmp_specification_1.0.pdf.

[267] Apple Proprietary. https://en.wikipedia.org/wiki/ Apple_Push_Notification_Service.

[268] Microsoft Silverlight. https://en.wikipedia.org/wiki/Microsoft_Silverlight, accessed on 1 September 2015.

[269] ISO/IEC 19464:2014, Information Technology – Advanced Message Queuing Protocol (AMQP) v1.0 Specification. http://www.iso.org/iso/home/store/catalogue_tc/catalogue_detail.htm?csnumber=64955.

[270] Avanset proprietary. http://www.avanset.com/purchase/vce-exam-simulator.html.

[271] RFC 4271, Border Gateway Protocol 4 (BGP-4), January 2006. http://tools.ietf.org/html/rfc4271.

[272] RFC 1035, Domain Names – Implementation and Specification, November 1987. http://tools.ietf.org/html/rfc1035.

[273] RFC 4340, Datagram Congestion Control Protocol (DCCP), March 2006. http://tools.ietf.org/html/rfc4340.

[274] RFC 3540, Explicit Congestion Notification (ECN) - An Extension to the Internet Protocol. [20] Robust Explicit Congestion Notification (ECN) Signaling with Nonces, June 2003. http://tools.ietf.org/html/rfc3540.

[275] RFC 4945, The Internet IP Security PKI Profile of IKEv1/ISAKMP, IKEv2, and PKIX, August 2007. http://tools.ietf.org/html/rfc4945.

[276] IEEE 802.3, Ethernet Working Group. http://www.ieee802.org/3/, accessed on 9/1/2015.

[277] RFC 1122, Requirements for Internet Hosts – Communication Layers, October 1989. http://tools.ietf.org/html/rfc1122.

[278] RFC 1123, Requirements for Internet Hosts – Application and Support, October 1989. http://tools.ietf.org/html/rfc1123.

[279] Margaret Rouse, OSI Reference Model (Open Systems Interconnection) Definition. http://searchnetworking.techtarget.com/definition/OSI, accessed on 9/1/2015.

[280] Department of Defense Instruction Number 8551.0, Ports, Protocols, and Services Management (PPSM), 28 May 2014.

[281] Message Broker Comparison. http://lifecorporatedev.blogspot.com/2012/07/recently-i-have-been-given-task-to-find.html.

[282] United States Labor Department, "Bureau of Vital Statistics, Occupational Outlook Handbook, Computer and Information Systems Managers," April 2018. https://www.bls.gov/.ooh/management/computer-and-information-systems-managers.htm, accessed on 11 October 2018.

[283] Francesca Gino and Bradley Staats, "Why Organizations Don't Learn," *Harvard Business Review*, November 2015. https://hbr.org/2015/11/why-organizations-dont-learn.

[284] Cambridge University Press, Cambridge Dictionary. https://dictionary.cambridge.org/dictionary/english/bureaucracy, accessed on 11 October 2018.

[285] Ronald N. Johnson and Gary D. Libecap, *The Federal Civil Service System and The Problem of Bureaucracy*, University of Chicago Press, January 1994. http://www.nber.org/chapters/c8632.pdf.

[286] Opara-Martins et al., "Critical Analysis of Vendor Lock-In and Its Impact on Cloud Computing Migration: A Business Perspective," *Journal of Cloud Computing: Advances, Systems and Applications*, Volume 5, Number 4, 2016. doi: 10.1186/s13677-016-0054-z.

[287] Rolf Oppliger, "Internet Security: FIREWALLS and BEYOND," *Communications of the ACM*, Volume 40, Number 5, p. 94, May 1997.

[288] Kenneth Ingham and Stephanie Forrest, "A History and Survey of Network Firewalls", University of New Mexico, Technical Report, January 2002.

[289] Rocky Chang, "Defending Against Flooding-Based Distributed Denial-of-Service Attacks: A Tutorial." *IEEE Communications Magazine*, Volume 40, Number 10, pp. 42–43, October 2002.

[290] Virgílio Almeida, Azer Bestavros, Mark Crovella, and Adriana de Oliveira, "Characterizing Reference Locality in the WWW," *Proceedings of the Fourth International Conference on Parallel and Distributed Information Systems*, pp. 92–107, Miami Beach, FL, 18–20 December 1996.

[291] Mehmet Altinel, Christof Bornhövd, Sailesh Krishnamurthy, C. Mohan, Hamid Pirahesh, and Berthold Reinwald, "Cache Tables: Paving the Way for an Adaptive Database Cache," *Proceedings of the 29th International Conference on Very Large Data Bases*, pp. 718–729, Berlin, Germany, 09–12 September 2003.

[292] K. Amiri, R. Tewari, S. Park, and S. Padmanabhan, "On Space Management in a Dynamic Edge Cache," *Proceedings of the Fifth International Workshop on the Web and Databases (WebDB 2002)*, 37–42, Madison, WI, ACM, New York, 2002.

[293] Jesse Anton, Lawrence Jacobs, Xiang Liu, Jordan Parker, Zheng Zeng, and Tie Zhong, "Web Caching for Database Applications with Oracle Web Cache," *Proceedings of the* 2002 *ACM SIGMOD International Conference on Management of Data*, Madison, WI, 03–06 June 2002. doi: 10.1145/564691.564762.

[294] Li Wen-Syan, K. Selçuk Candan, Wang-Pin Hsiung, Oliver Po, Divyakant Agrawal, Qiong Luo, Wei-Kuang Waine Huang, Yusuf Akca, and Cemal Yilmaz, *"Cache Portal: Technology for Accelerating Database-Driven E-commerce Web Sites," VLDB*, pp. 699–700, 2001.

[295] B. Cain, O. Spatscheck, M. May, and A. Barbir, "Requestrouting Requirements for Content Internetworking," 2001. http://www.ietf.org/internet-drafts/draft-cain-request-routing-req03.txt.

[296] K. Selçuk Candan, Wen-Syan Li, Qiong Luo, Wang-Pin Hsiung, and Divyakant Agrawal, "Enabling Dynamic Content Caching for Database Driven Web Sites," *Proceedings of the* 2001 *ACM SIGMOD International Conference on Management of Data*, pp. 532–543, Santa Barbara, CA, 21–24 May 2001. doi: 10.1145/375663.375736.

[297] J. Challenger, P. Dantzig, and A. Iyengar, "A Scalable System for Consistently Caching Dynamic Web Data," *Proceedings of the 18th Annual Joint Conference of the IEEE Computer and Communications Societies (INFOCOM)*, New York, NY, IEEE Computer Society Press, Los Alamitos, CA, 294–303, 1999.

[298] Carlos Cunha, Azer Bestavros, and Mark Crovella, *Characteristics of WWW Client-Based Traces*, Boston University, Boston, MA, 1995.

[299] Ireland David, DI Management Services, "The Chinese Remainder Theorem, Gauss's Algorithm." http://www.di-mgt.com.au/crt.html#chineseremaindertheorem.

[300] Ireland David, DI Management Services, "Using the CRT with RSA." http://www.di-mgt.com.au/crt_rsa.html.

[301] Hacker News, "Downgrade Attack on TLS 1.3 and Vulnerabilities in Major TLS Libraries." https://news.ycombinator.com/item?id=19111707, last accessed on 7 October 2019.

[302] Natasha Mathur, Cybersecurity, "Security Researchers Discloses Vulnerabilities in TLS Libraries and the Downgrade Attack on TLS 1.3." https://securityboulevard.com/2019/02/security-researchers-discloses-vulnerabilities-in-tls-libraries-and-the-downgrade-attack-on-tls-1-3/, last accessed on 7 October 2019.

[303] Catalin Cimpanu, Zero Day, "New TLS Encryption-Busting Attack Also Impacts the Newer TLS 1.3." https://www.zdnet.com/article/new-tls-encryption-busting-attack-also-impacts-the-newer-tls-1-3/, last accessed on 7 October 2019.

[304] Committee on National Security Systems, CNSS Policy No. 11, "National Policy Governing the Acquisition of Information Assurance (IA) and IA-Enabled Information Technology Products," 10 June 2013.

Acronyms

5G	Fifth Generation Wireless
ACL	Access Control List
ACM	Association for Computing Machinery
ACR	Access Control Rules
ACS	Authoritative Content Store
AES	Advanced Encryption Standard
AFW	Application Firewall
AIS	Automated Information Systems
API	Application Programming Interface
AUTHN	Authentication
BGP	Border Gateway Protocol
BYOD	Bring Your Own Device
CA	Certificate Authority
CAC	Common Access Card
CAL	Category Assurance List
CM	Configuration Management
CMB	Configuration Management Board
CMIP	Common Management Information Protocol
CPU	Central Processing Unit
CRL	Certificate Revocation List
CRT	Chinese Remainder Theorem
DB	Database
DCCP	Datagram Congestion Control Protocol
DIL	Disconnected, Intermittent, and Limited Bandwidth
DMZ	Demilitarized Zone
DN	Distinguished Name
DNS	Domain Name System
DoD	Department of Defense
DoS	Denial of Service
EAE	Enterprise Attribute Ecosystem
EAS	Enterprise Attribute Store
EE	Enterprise Edition
ELS	Enterprise Level Security
ERP	Enterprise Resource Planning
ESD	Enterprise Support Desk
ESR	Enterprise Service Registry
FHE	Full Homomorphic Encryption
FTP	File Transfer Protocol
GB	Giga-Byte
GEO	Geographic Location
GHz	Giga Hertz

GPS	Global Positioning System
HOK	Holder of Key
HR	Human Resources
HSM	Hardware Security Modules
HTML	Hypertext Markup Language
HTTP	Hypertext Transfer Protocol
HTTPS	Hypertext Transfer Protocol Secure
HW	Hardware
IaaS	Infrastructure as a service
IANA	Internet Assigned Numbers Authority
IBM	International Business Machines
ICS	Industrial Control Systems
ICMS	Integrated Client Message Service
ID	Identity
IDA	Institute for Defense Analyses
IEC	International Electrotechnical Commission
IEEE	Institute of Electrical and Electronics Engineers
IETF	Internet Engineering Task Force
IMAP	Internet Message Access Protocol
IoT	Internet of Things
IP	Internet Protocol
IPsec	Internet Protocol Security
IPv4	Internet Protocol version 4
IPv6	Internet Protocol version 6
ISO	International Organization for Standardization
IT	Information Technology
JAR	Java Archive
JMS	Java Messaging Service
JPG	Joint Photographic Experts Group
KB	Kilobyte
LLC	Logical Link Control
MAC	(1) Message Authentication Code
	(2) Media Access Control
MAM	Mobile Application Manager
MB	Megabyte
MDM	Mobile Device Management
MFA	Multi-factor Authentication
MHz	Megahertz
MITM	Man in the Middle
MMS	Multimedia Messaging Service
MPP	Message Posting Protocol
MQ	Message Queue
MSP	Message Send Protocol
NAT	Network Address Translation
NIST	National Institute of Standards and Technology
NNTP	News Network Transfer Protocol

NPE	Non-Person Entity
NTP	Network Time Protocol
NoSQL	Not only SQL
OASIS	Organization for the Advancement of Structured Information Standards
OCSP	Online Certificate Status Protocol
OOB	Out Of Band
OS	Operating System
OSI	Open System Interconnection
PDF	Portable Document Format
PII	Personally Identifiable Information
PIN	Personal Identification Number
PIV	Personal Identity Verification
PHE	Partial Homomorphic Encryption
PKI	Public Key Infrastructure
PNG	Portable Network Graphics
POP	Post Office Protocol
POP3	Post Office Protocol Version 3
POS	Point of Sale
PPP	Point-to-Point Protocol
PPS	Ports, Protocols, and Services
PSS	Publish-Subscribe System
PTP	Precision Time Protocol
RA	Registration Authority
RC4	Rivest cipher 4
RFC	Request for Comment
RSA	Rivest, Shamir, Adleman (encryption algorithm)
RTMP	Real Time Messaging Protocol
SAML	Security Assertion Markup Language
SKSU	Secure Key Storage and Use
SLA	Service Level Agreement
SMTP	Simple Mail Transfer Protocol
SNMP	Simple Network Management Protocol
SOAP	Simple Object Access Protocol
SQL	Structured Query Language
SSID	Service Set Identifier
SSL	Secure Socket Layer
SSO	Single Sign-On
STS	(1) Security Token Service (2) Security Token Server
STS/CA	STS with Certificate Authority
TCP	Transmission Control Protocol
TCP/IP	Transmission Control Protocol over Internet Protocol
TLS	Transport Layer Security
TPM	Trusted Platform Module
UDP	User Datagram Protocol
UID	Unique Identifier

URL	Uniform Resource Locator
USB	Universal Serial Bus
W3C	World Wide Web Consortium
WAN	Wide Area Network
WEP	Wired Equivalent Privacy
WPA	Wi-Fi Protected Access
Wi-Fi	IEEE 802.11
XML	Extensible Markup Language

Index